Collector's Dictionary of Clocks and Watches

Collector's Dictionary of Clocks and Watches

ERIC BRUTON
F.B.H.I.

NAG Press
an imprint of Robert Hale · London

© *Eric Bruton 1999*
First published in Great Britain 1999

ISBN 0 7198 0300 4

Robert Hale Limited
Clerkenwell House
Clerkenwell Green
London EC1R 0HT

2 4 6 8 10 9 7 5 3 1

Typeset by
Derek Doyle and Associates, Liverpool.
Printed through
Bookbuilders, Hong Kong

Introduction

Many years ago I was asked by a British publisher to write a basic horological dictionary. I was asked because at that time one of my several occupations was editing the *Horological Journal*, probably the oldest continuously published technical journal with the first edition published in September 1858, so was used to answering a wide selection of readers' questions. This initial effort comprised only 200 small pages of entries, but to my surprise (and I suspect, the publishers') it not only sold well in the UK but had a successful American edition. Later there was a pirated edition in America produced by another publisher!

That initial success encouraged me to start collecting potential entries for the present work some years later, but during that time, collectors' items that had been within many people's budgets moved out of reach and others that had once been despised suddenly became desirable. They included later English watches, French marble clocks, novelty and Black Forest clocks, electric and industrial clocks, and smaller tower clocks. Some even chase after Roscopf watches.

The spread is therefore quite wide, covering terms, people who made important contributions over the 600 years of mechanical horology, parts and their functions, but most of all the vast numbers of different types and styles of clocks and watches produced over these years, with special attention to collectable ones.

Pictures are vital for the obvious reason that they often transcend description. To include such a wide variety, of clocks in particular, would have been impossible without the willing co-operation of Christie's and Sotheby's, as well as other auction houses, private collectors, and museums, in supplying prints.

As well as identifying descriptions and dates of different types of watch and clock, there are brief definitions of terms. As current collectors know, clock and watch enthusiasts use a special language. Just as 'rope' meaning 'sheet' can receive a cold look from a yachtsman, so 'cog' instead of 'wheel' or 'pinion' sends shudders down the back of a true horological convert, even a dealer, although he may not show it. There are plenty of terms without equivalents, such as all-or-nothing piece, fusee, jumper, spring click, and surprise piece.

A dictionary cannot be absolutely impersonal because the selection and rejection of items is personal and at times idiosyncratic. For example a certain clock or watch may be mentioned in preference to another because the author had a chance to examine it. Fashions also have some influence. For many years to call a balance spring a 'hairspring' caused pain to the purists, who also took a long time and a Swiss decree to make them accept the description 'chronometer' applied to a watch as well as the original ship's chronometer with a different kind of escapement. One term that still bothers horologists is the layman's use of the word 'face', referring to a dial.

Inevitably some personal choice is involved; for example only a few famous makers are mentioned for one reason or another, plus some of the more obscure ones who have made important but less well-known contributions. The logic of this is that a very able maker may be 'famous' because a large number of his clocks is still available today, yet he may have contributed little or nothing to horological progress. Again someone who has made a contribution, however small, may be included although he or it is little known, because his contribution is of interest.

I have very many people to thank for the knowledge they have passed on to me over many years, too many to list and many unfortunately no longer with us. There are probably even more to thank for correcting my false notions, most of all Beresford Hutchinson, who originally set out to be a biologist but came under the influence of a lecturer at university whose hobby was horology. That converted Mr Hutchinson, who went on to be the British Museum's specialist on their magnificent collection, and later Keeper of the National Maritime Museum. He kindly undertook the tricky task of checking my manuscript and correcting it where I had gone astray or been careless and to him I am very indebted.

A

A, R Letters at the end of the INDEX of some continental mechanical watches meaning *Avance* and *Retard* (fast and slow).

Abbess watch Swiss watch with the ROCK CRYSTAL case in the form of a cross. Made about the mid-16th c and worn round the neck.

Accumulator watch Swiss electric watch made in the 1960s, driven by a rechargeable cell in the back of the case. Using a special adapter, an ordinary torch battery would recharge it in a few hours.

Abrasive Clock and watchmakers use emery for coarse and oilstone dust for finer preliminary surfacing, each being mixed with clock oil. For finishing, DIAMANTINE or RED STUFF is mixed into a paste with watch oil, traditionally on a zinc block. American factories once used Vienna lime (a chalk) mixed with spirits of wine (alcohol distilled from wine), which was believed to be the quickest way of polishing. For taking out deeper scratches before using an abrasive paste, a slip made of carborundum or finer synthetic material is used for steel, and WATER OF AYR STONE for softer materials such as brass, silver and gold.

Acanthus decoration Stylised leaves of the Mediterranean acanthus plant, used especially in the capitals of Corinthian columns, which were reproduced in clock case pillars at various times, particularly on longcase and bracket clocks in England from 1660 to 1700. Also used for friezes, SPANDRELS and engraved BACK PLATES.

Accuracy in timekeeping Has different meanings in different contexts. A mechanical alarm that is within a minute of correct time at the end of six weeks would be considered good enough for average domestic usage, but one that was five minutes slow would probably not. Yet the first may vary from day to day because of POSITIONAL or TEMPERATURE ERRORS and the second may not vary in its losing and therefore have perfect RATE for navigational and scientific use. Accuracy is sometimes shown as a percentage. As there are 86,400 seconds in a day, one second a day fast or slow is 99.9988% accurate and one minute a year is 99.9981% accurate.

Accuracy of clocks Timekeeping of mechanical clocks with VERGE ESCAPEMENTS made from about 1300 varied by +/– half an hour or more a day. Spring-driven clocks were even more inaccurate until the hog's BRISTLE REGULATOR improved them after 1550. The CROSS-BEAT ESCAPEMENT improved accuracy of special clocks to as close as +/-30 sec/day. The bracket clock after 1675 with spring and FUSEE drive, verge escapement and short pendulum could keep time to about +/-30 sec/day over short periods. A SECONDS PENDULUM clock with PIN-WHEEL ESCAPEMENT should behave about as well, and one with ANCHOR ESCAPEMENT to +/-10 sec/day. A DEAD BEAT or a PIN-WHEEL ESCAPEMENT is much better at +/-10 sec/week. An electric MASTER CLOCK will maintain +/-0.5 sec/week, and a MARINE CHRONOMETER about 0.3 sec/day. A FREE PENDULUM observatory clock is accurate to within 1 sec/year, and a good modern domestic quartz clock should not be too far from that. An observatory quartz clock will keep time to within one second in 30 years; an ATOMIC CLOCK is accurate to the equivalent of one second in 3,000 years but the pulsar PSR 0437-4715 could be 100 times more accurate than that. In

1997 it was discovered at the National Physical Laboratory how to control with lasers a single atom of the rare earth element ytterbium which 'ticks' every decade to give an accuracy of one second in 5,000 million years.

Accuracy of watches Mechanical watches are inherently less accurate than clocks because they are moved about, which causes POSITIONAL ERRORS. This is also true of ELECTRIC WATCHES and to a much lesser extent of TUNING FORK WATCHES. Position has little effect on quartz watches. A cheap mechanical watch should keep time to within 1 min/day, a good one within 1 min/week, a tuning fork watch to within 1 min/month, and a good quartz watch to within 1 min/year.

Accutron The first watch using a tuning fork as its oscillator, made by Bulova Watch Co. in the U.S.A. from 1960 until superseded by the quartz watch. It was the second to incorporate a transistor (the French Lip electric was first) and the first to have guaranteed timekeeping, to 1 min/month, because POSITIONAL ERRORS were small and consistent, to about +/-5 sec/day. The inventor was a Swiss, Max Hetzel. The tuning fork, about 205cm (1in) long, is kept vibrating at 360 cycles a second by electromagnetic coils of 16,000 turns of wire driven from a power cell. A miniature spring pawl on the tuning fork drives a ratchet wheel of about 2.5mm (under $1/10$in) diameter with 300 teeth, which turns the hands without jerks. There is no tick but a faint hum. Power consumption is about 8 millionths of a watt.

Acorn A clock case decoration or FINIAL of metal or wood in the shape of an oak acorn in its cup.

Acorn watch One with an acorn-shaped case made in Germany from the early 17th c.

Acorn clock Rare American SHELF CLOCK with the outline of an acorn, designed by J.C. Brown and manufactured between 1847 and 1850. It is spring-driven unlike almost every other shelf clock, and about 65cm (25in) high with a wooden FUSEE in the base. Later models have the fusees mounted below the brass movement. Some later models are nearly 1m (39in) high.

Act of Parliament clock In 1797, William Pitt put a tax on 'every Clock or Timekeeper ... placed in or upon any dwelling house or any office or building ... whether public or private'. Large TAVERN CLOCKS that attracted custom from people wanting to know the time, later became known as and are still called 'Act of Parliament clocks'. The Act was repealed in the following year. The clock is hung on the wall. The wooden dial is very large, about 60cm (2ft) across and round or polygonal (sometimes with curved edges), with no glass and, usually, brass SPADE style hands. The trunk below the dial is long enough to enclose a SECONDS PENDULUM. The movement has tapered plates and, as it does not strike, there is a single weight, usually rectangular in shape. The case is often black and sometimes green with gold dial markings and decoration.

An **Act of Parliament clock** c1797 by Dickerson, Framlingham. The dial is 0.76m (2ft 6in) wide (*Biggs of Maidenhead*)

Action The movement of the BALANCE or oscillator; hence a watch has a 'good action' (see BALANCE ARC) or 'poor action'. The word is not normally used of a pendulum.

Activate When an animal or vegetable product, such as neat's foot oil, olive oil, porpoise oil or stearic acid, is incorporated in a lubricating oil or grease, it is said to be 'activated'.

Adam and Eve automata An animated scene of the Bible's first man and woman alternately reaching for an apple in a tree was a favourite subject for watch and clockmakers of the 19th c. It could easily be operated by a wire from the ANCHOR ESCAPEMENT and was located in the dial arch. See AUTOMATON.

Adam and Eve watch The Swiss made some watches c1840–50 that were rather crude for the time, having a small dial with hour and minute hand and a circular framed coloured picture of Adam and Eve above it. The watch, wound through the dial, was for a low-priced market like the FARMER'S WATCH.

Adam-style clock The architect Robert Adam encouraged a revival of classical Roman style in the second half of the 18th c. Some clock cases followed this neo-classical style.

Adjusted Corrected for timekeeping to a particular standard, usually in relation to POSITIONAL ERROR (of a watch) and/or TEMPERATURE ERROR. Some mechanical watches were marked 'adjusted' on the movement to indicate that they had been checked at the factory only in two positions. A mechanical CHRONOMETER watch is adjusted in five positions and at two temperatures.

Adjuster Highly skilled craftsman who can regulate mechanical watches to a high degree of precision by manipulation of the escapement and balance and spring.

Adjusting rod Tool for measuring the TORQUE of a clock or watch spring, used mainly for SETTING UP a FUSEE and MAINSPRING. It comprises a 25cm (10in) steel measuring rod with a clamp at one end to fix it at right angles to the fusee SQUARE. Two weights can be slid along the rod and clamped, to balance the spring torque.

Admiralty time trials Between 1822 and 1835, the British Admiralty gave annual prizes for the best performances of individual chronometers during trials conducted at Greenwich Observatory. Many performed very well, e.g. a Frodsham chronometer in 1830 had a rate error of 0.57 seconds after a year.

Affix Auxiliary TEMPERATURE ERROR compensating device consisting of a small bimetallic blade, one end of which is fixed to the rim of a balance. Two affixes attached to a chronometer balance help to correct MIDDLE TEMPERATURE ERROR. See AUXILIARY TEMPERATURE COMPENSATION.

Agate watch Agate was sometimes used for a watch case after about 1600, around the same period as the ROCK CRYSTAL case. Pallets of some clocks with DEAD BEAT ESCAPEMENTS were made of agate.

Age of moon dial See MOON DIAL.

Ageing Physical change that alters the rate of vibration of a quartz crystal as used in a timekeeper. A usual ageing rate is from two to five parts in a million a year, equal to about those numbers of seconds a year in a timepiece with a frequency of 32kHz, i.e. 32,000 cycles a second. If a quartz timekeeper is stopped, as when changing a power cell, the quartz crystal starts a new ageing cycle. When the hands or DIGITAL DISPLAY are stopped for, say, resetting, the oscillator does not stop.

Ahaz, dial of Chapter 20, verse 11, of the second Book of Kings in the Old Testament of the Bible refers to a public shadow clock comprising a wall and a flight of steps. The shadow on the wall falling on a particular step indicated the time. Excavations have shown that such timekeepers existed.

Ainsworth, George   See SIGNATURES.

Air clock   Clock of the mid-17th c in which air escaping from a bellows into which it has been pumped controls the fall of the weight, thus replacing the FOLIOT or BALANCE.

Air resistance   See BAROMETRIC ERROR.

Air-tight case   Rusting of steel parts is a considerable danger to precision time-keepers, particularly marine chronometers exposed to salt-laden air. In 1714, Jeremy Thacker invented the VACUUM CASE (actually kept at a lower pressure than atmospheric). Then followed many air-tight cases for marine chronometers over a century later, such as that patented by E. Dent in 1840.

Airy's bar   It is difficult to shift the weights on a COMPENSATION BALANCE of a marine chronometer by a very small amount. In 1871, Sir George Airy, Astronomer Royal, invented a friction-tight cross-bar with a much smaller weight at each end. Very small adjustments of the small weight had the same effect as the usual larger ones.

Alarm   Timepiece that can be set to provide an audible warning at a pre-selected time. Alarums were the oldest form of monastic, public and domestic mechanical time-teller. They struck one blow at the hour and could be set to ring a bell at pre-set times. They may have been designed to alert a sexton, whose task it was in the 13th c to sound a bell in a tower to summon monks to prayer or their duties. Earliest alarms still extant are WATCHMAN'S CLOCKS and MONASTERY CLOCKS dating from about 1400. An early alarm has a wheel with a series of holes around it that revolves once in 12 or 24 hours. A pin is placed in the hole marked with the hour at which the alarm is needed and this trips the alarm mechanism when that time is reached. The principle of the later mechanical alarm is the same, except that a slip ring is turned to the appropriate position on the turning wheel by means of a button. Many turn on or flash a light,

play a tune or turn on the radio, and also repeat the alarm after an interval. More exotic versions nudge a sleeper or draw aside curtains and an early one operated a trip that tipped the sleeper out of bed. An anonymous poem says it all:

> All through the silent hours of night
> I wait the early morning light,
> And when I judge the moment right,
> At last release my pent-up spite,
> And exercise, without compunction,
> My useful, irritating, function.

Alarm-and-candle clock   A clock made about the mid-18th c that lit a candle at a pre-set time. When set, the candle lies flat and is lit from tinder touching the wick. The tinder is ignited by a flintlock released by the clock. When lit, the candle springs upright. See FLINTLOCK ALARM.

Alarm and tea-maker   SYNCHRONOUS electric alarm clock with an attachment that makes a pot of tea before the alarm sounds and also, in some models, switches on a light.

Alarm attachment   For early DRUM CLOCKS, which had a hand on the top and were made in the 16th and 17th c, an alarm attachment was sometimes provided. This is an alarm movement in a separate drum with a bell on top, supported on three legs, which clips over the dial of the table clock, the hour hand of which trips the alarm at the pre-set time. Similar attachments were made in the 19th c for converting pocket watches into alarms overnight.

Alarm pocket watch   Alarms were sometimes incorporated in pocket watches, which came into use c1670.

Alarm ring   Finger ring containing a small watch with an alarm comprising a steel pin that pricks the finger. A 19th c version was made by Meylan of Geneva.

Alarm wrist watch   One with an alarm mechanism. The first was Swiss, the Eterna of 1912–14. Later there were models with elapsed time dials to show the time remaining before the alarm sounds, useful when car parking and skin-diving.

Alarum An earlier word for what is now called an ALARM. However, the term *horologia excitatoria* (awakening clocks) appears in old monastic records.

Albert In 1845, Albert, the Prince Consort, was presented by the jewellers of Birmingham with a gold watch chain, seal and watch key, and these became known as 'Alberts'. A bar for fastening to a waist-coat button is attached to the middle of the chain, one end of which is latched to the BOW of a watch in one waistcoat pocket, and the other to the key and seal in the opposite pocket. See FOB CHAIN.

Alfred's candle According to Asser, Alfred the Great, when a fugitive in his own country, vowed to devote eight hours daily to religion and ordered 72 pennyweights of candle wax to be made daily into six candles each 6in long and marked every inch to represent an hour of burning.

Algerian water clock SINKING BOWL timer used in Algeria to apportion water for irrigation.

Alidade See ASTROLABE.

All-or-nothing piece If the lever or push piece of a simple REPEATER is not fully pressed, only some of the hours may be repeated. Incorporation of an all-or-nothing piece ensures that only full depression of the lever or push piece will release the striking.

Almanac clock Another name for a calendar clock.

Almanus manuscript Extremely valuable source of information about 15th c clocks, discovered in 1939 by Prof. E. Zinner. A translation of the manuscript appeared in English in 1971 by J.H. Leopold of the Gröninger Museum, Holland. Eight of the 30 clocks described were spring-driven. Almanus was a German friar working as a clockmaker in Rome from about 1475.
See FUSEE.

Alpha clock A STRUT CLOCK in the general shape of a capital A.

Altar clock Wooden clock, usually Italian, sometimes German and very occasionally English, of the later 17th and early 18th c, shaped like an altar of the time. The MALTESE CLOCK was based on this design, usually being ebonised and about 60cm (2ft) high.

Altitude dial Portable sundial which measures the time by the altitude or height of the sun in the sky, e.g. by the length of a shadow. Some Roman ones still exist and large numbers were in use in the 16th and 17th c. One common form was a small cylinder with a horizontal GNOMON, hung from a cord, also called a 'shepherd's dial'. Curved lines on the cylinder show the hours and vertical ones indicate which part to use for each month. Another type, introduced about 1400, was like a napkin ring with a hole in one side. When suspended from a cord with the hole towards the sun, a spot of light fell on a scale of hours on the opposite inner surface. The other form of portable sundial was the COMPASS SUNDIAL. See UNIVERSAL SUNDIAL.

Amber watch Watch with a case carved from a solid block of amber in the Garnier collection in the Louvre, Paris. It is unsigned, probably German, dated early 17th c and the only amber watch known.

American Horologe Co. Company formed in the early 1850s by Aaron DENNISON and Edward Howard with the financial backing of Samuel Curtis of Boston, to mass-produce watches. By 1853 when the first watches were produced, in the English full plate style, the name was changed to the Warren Manufacturing Co (after the hero of the Battle of Bunker Hill in 1775). The firm eventually became the Boston Watch Co, then Dennison, Howard and Davis, of Waltham. See WALTHAM WATCH CO.

American horological industry The earliest clockmakers in North America were European immigrants during the 17th c, mainly from Britain, Germany, Holland and Sweden. Two main clockmaking communities emerged, one based in Philadelphia, and the other in Boston. Those from Philadelphia spread up the Delaware valley to New York and into Virginia and Carolina. Those from Boston scattered over New England, eventually the states of Connecticut, Maine, Massachusetts, New Hampshire, Rhode Island and Vermont. Dials, in particular, were commonly imported from England, even after the Revolution. Napoleon's blockade of England caused severe metal shortage and the wooden clock movement was developed, mainly by Eli TERRY, who introduced mass-production methods. Terry's patents were not enforceable and many large and small businesses sprung up after c1830. Distinctive American clock styles emerged, such as the BANJO, GIRANDOLE, SHELF CLOCK, STEEPLE, etc. Companies like ANSONIA reproduced designs from the German, French and other industries at very low prices. Eventually American production and export was so huge, it almost ruined the then dominant BLACK FOREST HOROLOGICAL INDUSTRY, until Gerhart JUNGHANS adopted American methods. The Americans were the first to mass-produce watches successfully in c1850 after many false starts. Many millions were made, and after c1875 there were many inexpensive models, some selling for under a dollar. Exports severely damaged the Swiss industry, which was forced to adopt similar methods. American electronic firms pioneered mass production and marketing of quartz watches in the 1960s and 1970s, but fell behind the Swiss and Japanese, having no well-known brand names. See also ACCUTRON, AMERICAN HOROLOGE CO, AUBURNDALE ROTARY WATCH, BRIGGS ROTARY CLOCK, COLUMBUS CLOCK, DENNISON Aaron, DOLLAR WATCH, DUEBER-HAMPDEN, ELECTRIC WATCH, ELGIN WATCH, FRANKLIN CLOCK, GROANER, HOADLEY, INGERSOLL, INGOLD, INGRAHAM, IVES, JEROME, MASSACHUSETTS SHELF CLOCK, QUAKER CLOCK, REGULATOR American, RITTENHOUSE, ROXBURY WATCH CO, SHAKER CLOCKS, SHARP GOTHIC CLOCK, SMEATON-FRANKLIN DIAL, STEEPLE CLOCK, THOMAS Seth, TIFFANY CLOCK, TIMEX QUARTZ WATCH, WAGGON SPRING CLOCK, WALTHAM WATCH CO, WARREN MOTOR, WATERBURY LONG-WIND WATCH, WATERBURY ROTARY WATCH, WELCH ROTARY CLOCK, WILLARD BROTHERS, WOODEN CLOCK.

American screw   Early American watch factories made their own screws, which were not interchangeable with those of other factories.

American Watchmakers Institute Organisation of all watchmakers in the U.S.A. formed in 1960 by the amalgamation of the Horological Institute of America and the United Horological Association of America. Address: 3700 Harrison Avenue, Cincinatti, Ohio 45211.

Amplitude   The extent of swing of a balance or pendulum, measured in degrees. Also called 'action'. See ARC.

Analemmatic sundial   A sundial that indicates the time only when the sun is on or near its MERIDIAN. Some such dials are recognised by the figure-of-eight scale with a line through its length on a south facing wall. The horizontal STYLE throwing the shadow usually has a pierced disc at the end to project a bright sunspot. It gives noon by APPARENT SOLAR TIME on the straight line and by MEAN SOLAR TIME on the curved line. The dial therefore indicates the EQUATION OF TIME. Also called a 'meridian dial'. An analemma is a NOON MARK. It was sometimes combined with a horizontal sundial because when the combined instrument was turned so that both showed the same time, that was the correct time. This avoided the need for a compass to set the horizontal dial.

Analogue display   After the introduction of the quartz crystal electronic watch with DIGITAL DISPLAY, electronics manufacturers introduced the jargon 'analogue display' for a dial with hands. This is strictly correct because the hands are analogous to the passage of the sun or rotation of the Earth.

Anchor escapement Most widely used and successful mechanical escapement for pendulum clocks. Also called the 'recoil' escapement because the escape wheel (and seconds hand if fitted to this wheel as with most grandfather clocks) recoils slightly after every tick. It has two parts, an escape wheel and an anchor, on the ends of which are the curved PALLETS. The pendulum is connected to the anchor by a CRUTCH so that the anchor rocks as the pendulum swings. The escape wheel is driven by the weight or mainspring and train of gears. A tooth of the wheel is held up by a pallet. The tooth presses on the pallet, moving it aside and swinging (IMPULS-ING) the pendulum. The tooth is suddenly released by the swinging pallet and the escape wheel jumps forward until another tooth is inter-cepted by the other pallet, which has now descended as the pendulum swings in the opposite direction. Because of its inertia, the pendulum does not then stop dead at the end of each swing, but continues until the pressure of the tooth on the pallet stops it. This causes the escape wheel to recoil. The action is then repeated, with first one and then the other pallet holding up the escape wheel. The DROP, or jump of a tooth and its sudden halting by the pallet, causes the noise of a TICK as the metal MOVE-MENT resonates. Recoil helps to compensate for CIRCULAR ERROR. The anchor replaced the VERGE and crown wheel escapement. It is like a two-dimensional version of the three-dimensional verge and is equally robust. English clocks usually have 30 escape wheel teeth because the wheel will rotate once a minute with a SECONDS PENDULUM and twice with half-seconds pendulum which changes the count of the train (the number of teeth in the wheels). Some French makers decided on the length of the pendulum the clock case would allow, then cut the number of escape wheel teeth to suit, leaving the rest of the move-ment more or less standard. Thirty-six and 40 were the most common numbers of teeth. French pallets also span fewer than 7½ teeth, which is usual with English clocks, but no fewer than 5½. In both countries the pallets were of filed and polished steel. From the late 18th c, the Germans and Americans began to use strip steel for the escapements of mass-produced clocks, which was copied, particularly for cheap alarms, in other countries. The anchor was invented c1670 and represented a big step in the accuracy of mechanical clocks. Its inventor was long thought to be Robert HOOKE, then to be William Clement, a London clockmaker, who in c1671 made a turret clock with a form of anchor that has hardly changed through the years. Joseph KNIBB is another possible inventor. Before this date he was experimenting with an escape wheel like that of the anchor, but with separate pallets. A wrought iron BIRD-CAGE CLOCK by him in Burley Church, Rutland, dated 1678, has an anchor with an unusual form of crutch.

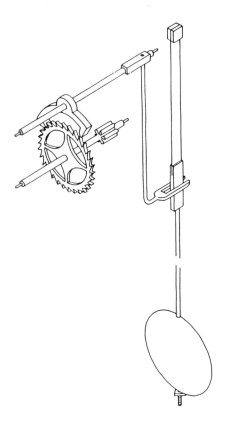

The **anchor escapement** used with a crutch and long pendulum with spring suspension.

Android AUTOMATON that imitates the actions of a human being. A clockwork android was made to play a harpsichord, and another to write a letter of about 50 words by JACQUET-DROZ. Vaucanson made one play a flute by breathing, moving the lips and tongue, and fingering. Others play a small organ and a zither. In some cases the figures move their whole bodies and seem to breathe. There is a woman android who plays a mandolin in the National Museum for the Conservation of Arts and Crafts, Paris. The many automata that go through the motions of playing, with the music coming from a hidden mechanism, are not androids. An android hitting a bell is called a JACK.

Angle clock A clock showing on its dial 360 degrees, 60 minutes of a degree, and 60 seconds of a minute, instead of 24 hours, 60 minutes and 60 seconds. It is regulated to SIDEREAL TIME and shows the position of the heavens instead of the time, i.e. the angle through which Earth has turned in a given time, because 1 degree of arc equals 4 minutes of time. The earliest known was designed by John FLAMSTEED, and made by Thomas Tompion, dated 1691, and is now in the Octagon Room at the Old Royal Observatory, Greenwich.

Angle meter Tool with two protractors on centres that can be moved apart by a vernier gauge. Used to measure the angles of the pallets of a LEVER ESCAPEMENT.

Animated clock Clocks operating models, AUTOMATA and JACKS, have been made since the earliest days of the clock. The earliest was probably the model of a man striking a bell and replacing a real man (probably the earliest redundancy caused by automation!) as in Montpellier, France, in 1410, when it was decided to replace the clock-keeper with a new clock with a jack from Dijon. Animated figures were often man-sized. Domestic clocks with small animated figures, human and animal, were made in Renaissance Europe for the rich of Europe and the East. Some merely blinked their eyes; others were immensely complicated table pieces intended perhaps to perform at banquets, like the NEF or ship clock probably made about 1580 in Prague, and now in the British Museum. It shows activities on the decks, in the crow's nests and with the guns, while the enthroned emperor on the poop deck is greeted by trumpeters (there is an organ in the clock). The small silver and enamel dial is at the foot of the main mast, which is about 1m (40in) high. In the Bowes Museum, Yorkshire, is a triumphal car about 50cm (20in) high with a fat figure in it accompanied by a cherub, and others and drawn by two smaller elephants with mahouts. The whole is animated and moves on wheels. It was made in AUGSBURG c1600. Many clocks with animated scenes in the arch above the dial were made in the BLACK FOREST of Germany, in the Netherlands and in England in the 17th and 18th c, the most popular subjects being rocking ships, Adam and Eve picking an apple, scenes with windmills, figures sawing wood and Father Time scything. Another area of animation was in the PICTURE CLOCK. A favourite with some French clockmakers was water running from a pump, simulated by a rotating rod of twisted glass. In the later 19th and 20th c, American factories revived interest in animated clocks by producing figures with MOVING EYES and a clock dial in the belly. There was also a vogue for animated advertising clocks. Not all animated clocks were for amusement; the earliest were for the serious purpose of demonstrating the movement of the planets, as in the ASTRONOMICAL CLOCK, GLOBE CLOCK, and ORRERY. See also BIRD BOX, CHESS CLOCK, GUINNESS CLOCK, JACQUET-DROZ, SINGING BIRD, STRASBOURG CATHEDRAL CLOCK. Mass-production in America introduced a new era of animated clock dials, mainly alarms, from the 1870s until the early 20th c. Large numbers were made in the U.S.A., Germany and the U.K. There were many variations: paddle-wheel steamers, watermills, windmills, rocking horses, bull fighters, banjo players, nursing mothers, dancing girls, gymnasts, trapeze artists, clowns, cobblers, cowboys, feeding birds, drinkers, girls with fans, fishermen, soccer players, cowboys, washerwomen, kissing couples, Mickey Mouse, and many more. See DAVID AND GOLIATH, and picture on p. 78.

Animated watch Tiny moving figures (AUTOMATA) were incorporated on the dials or backs, or under a cover, in some pocket watches from c1550 to 1630 in France and elsewhere. The fashion was revived from c1775 to 1830, in Geneva in particular. Earlier cases were often repoussé and later ones often enamelled. The most common display showed one or more figures appearing to strike a bell or bells, the sound actually coming from a gong around the movement. Other popular themes were FATHER TIME swinging a scythe, a knife grinder, a spinner, a windmill, a woman pumping water, and very occasionally Moses striking a rock for water. Sometimes a twisted glass rod rotates to imitate flowing water (more common in clocks). A rare theme is a BARKING DOG WATCH. Automata were popular in the Louis XVI period, as were lovers' watches with, for example, the lover dressed as a blacksmith or page forging a Cupid's arrow on a forge and sharpening it, and PORNOGRAPHIC

Two figures appear to strike bells on this **animated watch** when the pendant at the top is pressed.

WATCHES. MUSICAL WATCHES sometimes included automata playing instruments such as harps, lyres, mandolins, guitars, violins, cellos, hurdy-gurdies, triangles, cymbals, etc. Some had a child on a swing (SWING CLOCK), an acrobat, or dancers performing to the musicians. Automata were sometimes included with watches in snuff boxes, work boxes, embroidery cases, scent bottles and, rarely, finger rings. Some animated watches were also FORM CLOCKS OR WATCHES, in the shape of a mandolin, heart, etc.

Anne Boleyn clock Ornamental metal bracket clock believed to have been given to Anne by Henry VIII of England on their wedding in 1532, now in the library at Windsor Castle.

Anniversary clock Another name for a year clock or FOUR HUNDRED DAY CLOCK popular in the U.S.A. because it is usually wound on a particular anniversary.

Annular balance Wheel BALANCE or balance wheel.

Ansonia Clock Co. American company, famous for its novelty clocks and huge production, originating in 1850 from a copper rolling mill near Derby in Connecticut, at a place named Ansonia. French ORMOLU cases of many patterns with figures were imitated in cast iron and so were French marble mantel clocks, in marble, cast iron, and black-enamelled wood. Among alarms called 'Ansonia Bees' was one wound by turning the bell on top. A novelty RACK CLOCK sold for $3.50 in 1926. Novelties included one like the front of a locomotive; the PLATO ticket clock; an alarm with a model tree on one side and a doll moving on a swing; and another version in which a doll on a swing bobbed up and down, patented in 1886. See SWING CLOCK. Ansonia had a chequered history. In 1878 it was reformed and moved to Brooklyn, New York. It exported to 25 countries, with a sales office in London and agents in Australia, China, India, Japan and New Zealand. Before the First World War, non-jewelled watches were added to the company's lines. In 1929 it went out of business. The Ansonia trade mark is a capital A inside a diamond inside a circle. The movements have pierced PLATES stamped out of rolled brass.

Anti-friction wheel See FRICTION ROLLERS.

Anti-magnetic Any part of a timepiece, particularly balance, balance spring and escapement, that has become magnetised will affect timekeeping, so makers sought material which will resist being magnetised. Gold was the earliest for balance springs, employed by John ARNOLD in MARINE CHRONOMETERS. Palladium was introduced c1880 by C. Paillard and glass springs by BREGUET and others (see BALANCE SPRING, HELICAL). ELINVAR solved many problems, and later GLUCYDUR solved most of the rest. Additional protection is provided by enclosing the movement in a mu-metal screen. Today's hazards are the high magnetic fields in TV sets, etc. The Earth's field or the magnetised hull of a ship is not strong enough to affect rate. See MAGNETISM. Repairers use DEMAGNETISERS. There are various national standards of anti-magnetic protection. Quartz watches are not particularly affected.

Antiquarian Horological Society An active organisation formed in 1953 to stimulate original research and preserve records and fine examples of clock and watchmaking and DIALLING. The A.H.S. publishes *Antiquarian Horology* quarterly and holds regular meetings and visits to places of horological interest. Address: New House, High Street, Ticehurst, Wadhurst, Sussex, TN5 7AL, England.

Anvil See BEAK IRON.

Apparent solar time Time shown by the position of the sun in the sky, or by a sundial. Apparent solar days vary in length, so mean solar days and hours (equal hours) as kept by clocks are more practical in living. A chronometer will show noon sometimes before the sun crosses the MERIDIAN and sometimes

after. See EQUATION OF TIME. When sundials were the main timekeepers TEMPORAL HOURS were in use.

Appointments clock Late 19th c wooden-cased clock that, at the set time, delivers, into a small tray on the front of the clock, an ivory slip on which details of an appointment had previously been written. An electric bell rings until the slip is removed. Slips are placed into the appropriate slots of a revolving drum on top of the clock. A 20th c appointments clock has a pointer moving down a pad, marked with times, on which appointments are written.

Apprentice First clock and watchmakers were blacksmiths, locksmiths, and gun founders who became organised into trade GUILDS in the 16th and 17th c, introducing apprenticeship (from French *apprendre*, to learn) schemes surprisingly similar in the different centres of Augsburg, Nuremberg, Blois, Paris, Rouen, Geneva, London, etc. The apprentice was indentured to a MASTER clock and watchmaker for six to eight years and lived in his household. Numbers were strictly controlled and special privileges allowed to the sons of masters. Faithful apprentices were admitted to the Freedom of the Guild, then for two more years would 'serve his Master, or some other of the same Fellowship', living out as a journeyman, during which time he would prepare his masterpiece for submission to the Court of the Guild. If this were accepted, he could set up as a workmaster and take an apprentice of his own. The Worshipful Company of Clockmakers in London allowed a second apprentice to be taken only after the first had served for five years, a regulation that riled workmasters and was frequently broken. At each of his steps, an apprentice had to pay a fine. That for becoming a Master in Paris in the 17th c was so high that few could afford to pay it. London seems to have been the only Guild to admit women apprentices, in c1715, but it was very reluctant to make master clockmakers of them. The Paris and Blois Guilds allowed widows of masters to take male apprentices only. An apprentice learned his trade from verbal and practical instruction. Rare textbooks appeared in the late 17th c. The 'art and mystery' (skill and labour) of all crafts were trade secrets. The apprentice first learned the basic skills of filing metals, sawing them, flattening and hardening brass plates with a planishing hammer and scraping them, drilling with a bow drill, burnishing, annealing, soldering and brazing, wire drawing, using the rolls, tapping, forging, and so on, then moved on to the use of TURNS and THROWS, DEPTHING TOOLS, SECTORS, WHEEL CUTTING ENGINES, etc and the vital task of marking-out. The CLOCKMAKERS COMPANY sometimes admitted clockmakers belonging to other Guilds as 'brothers'.

Apron   Ornamental 'fringe', usually of wood, under a dial or plinth, which hangs like an apron. Also called a 'label'. Some early bracket clock movements had a decorative brass cover over the pallet bridge also called an 'apron'.

The **apron piece** on the bottom of a mahogany long-case clock by Edmund Prideau, London. (*Christie's*)

Arabesque   Intertwining scrolling and foliage in elaborate and fanciful patterns used in particular for late MARQUETRY cases. The origin may be Saracen.

Arabic numerals   Arabic as well as Roman numerals have been used on clock and watch dials from at least the early 16th c. Early German dials showed two hour systems, I to XII repeated (the

DOUBLE-TWELVE system) and 1 to 24. During the Renaissance, Roman numerals were usual for the hours and Arabic for the minutes. In the 20th c Arabic became more common for hours until mainly displaced by batons (bars) or dots in about the 1930s.

Arbor   Axle or shaft of a wheel or PINION such as centre wheel arbor and barrel arbor. Two arbors have a different name, the BALANCE STAFF and the PALLET STAFF. Also short shafts between which work is mounted for turning, each having a pointed end. See THROW and TURNS. Precision arbors with hollow ends for this purpose are known as 'mandrels'.

Arc   Abbreviation of 'circular arc', the total angle through which a pendulum or balance swings. Half of it, from the centre line, is the semi-arc. Changes in pendulum arc through escapement design and variations of air pressure cause ESCAPEMENT ERROR and BAROMETRIC ERROR. The same applies to a balance because its spring is not ISOCHRONOUS. Pendulum arcs may be as small as 2° or 3° on a precision clock and as much as 45° or so in a novelty clock. Balance arcs may be as low as 45° in an old watch and over 300° at times in a modern one.

Arch dial   Dial or dial aperture with an arched top, is a very common style in many countries. Probably introduced c1700, but popular later. A plain arch is where the curved top springs straight from the sides, and a BREAK ARCH where the arched portion is less than the full width of the top.

Arched minute ring   Instead of the minute ring being plainly circular, there are 'humps' between every five minutes. Favoured occasionally in the 18th c, perhaps more in Dutch clocks.

Architectural case   Case, usually of wood in England but often of metal or mineral elsewhere, with the lines of classical Greek architecture, based on the colonnade or covered passageway, often taking the form of a triangular top with two or four columns. First popular after c1660 in England and revived a number of times, such as during the French Regency period, and later the English Regency, when side columns were often omitted. Particularly popular during the French Empire period (1800–30), was the colonnaded or triumphal arch with four pillars, the clock dial and pendulum being suspended under the architrave. The ubiquitous French marble mantel clocks of the early 20th c were copied in cast iron, wood and other materials by other European clock industries, and eventually by the then new water- and steam-driven clock factories of America and Germany.

The **architectural case** of a striking bracket clock c1665–70 by Edward East with a phase and age of moon dial. The metal capital is missing from the left pillar.

Arkansas stone   Very fine-grained silicon stone found in Arkansas, U.S.A. and used for honing steel cutting edges. It is either white or black; the latter is said to be more effective.

Armillary sphere   Globe made up of a number of bands, used for demonstrating aspects of Ptolemaic astronomy according to the theory of the spheres. In the centre is a small ball representing the Earth. Around it, bands show the CELESTIAL EQUATOR, tropics, and arctic and antarctic circles. An oblique band represents the ECLIPTIC, marked with the signs of the zodiac, and the FIRST POINT OF ARIES and of Libra, indicating the spring and autumn equinoxes where the celestial equator intersects the ecliptic. Other rings, through the north and south poles, illustrate MERIDIANS. Armillary spheres were being made from at least the 11th c in China (see SU SUNG'S CLOCK), and were still being made in the late 18th c. Most were of metal and wood, but papier maché export versions were made in France from c1760, usually in pairs as toys to show the difference between the Ptolemaic and Copernican systems. Sometimes incorporated in ASTRONOMICAL CLOCKS. Some were operated by clockwork, one of the most important being one in Rosenborg Castle Museum, Copenhagen, made by Isaac HABRECHT in 1594. Clockwork drives the heavens around a central Earth and a dial at the north pole shows SIDEREAL TIME and phases of the Moon. Other dials are mounted in the base. Emblem of the BRITISH HOROLOGICAL INSTITUTE.

Armorial case   Pocket watch with a coat of arms depicted on the case.

Arnold, John   (1736–99) One of the most famous English makers whose inventions developed the MARINE CHRONOMETER.   See   ANTI-MAGNETIC, COMPENSATION   CURB,   RING WATCH.

Arrow clock   17th c clock comprising a round mirror with 12 ornaments round the frame and an arrow-shaped hand moving round the edge.

Arrow head hands   Earliest clock and watch hands were often like simple arrow heads, usually with a long tail so that finger and thumb could be used for turning them. The tail was sometimes an alarm indicator as well.

Art deco   Fashionable modernist style from c1918 to 1939, which superseded ART NOUVEAU. The name, however, was derived later in 1925 during the Paris Exposition International des Arts Decoratifs, when René Lalique was a prime exponent, mainly in glass. Designs and decorations were geometrical, often with brash colours, and reflected the machine age. Cartier made some elegant art deco clocks, including MYSTERY CLOCKS.

Art nouveau Decorative style that began in the 1880s and ended with the First World War, having peaked c1900. Named after a dealer's Paris shop, Maison l'Art Nouveau and typified by flower and leaf motifs with limply curving lines, often in symmetrical designs, and also by similarly flowing female figures with long hair. Clocks in the style came from Liberty's in London, the Bauhaus in Germany, and Tiffany's of New York. Watches were also made with cases in art nouveau style.

'Artificial Clockmaker, The' The title of the most famous early book on clock- and watchmaking, written by William Derham, F.R.S., published in London in 1696. A mechanical clock was called 'artificial' to distinguish it from a natural clock such as a sundial.

Ashley escape wheel E. Ashley, c1800, invented a CYLINDER ESCAPEMENT wheel with the teeth at different heights to work on different parts of the cylinder and thus reduce wear.

Ashmolean Museum This museum in Oxford has some interesting timepieces including a MUSK BALL WATCH of c1550.

Assortiments Swiss and French name for parts of escapements.

Aster automatic watch SELF-WINDING WRIST WATCH made from c1928 to 1930 by La Champagne S.A., Bienne, Switzerland, using the same principle as the SELF-WINDING POCKET WATCH.

Asthmometer Special CHRONOGRAPH for timing 15 respirations (20 or 25 with some versions) which then shows at a glance the number per minute.

Astrolabe One of the most important astronomical, navigational, and timekeeping instruments of the ancient world, named 'astrolabium' by Ptolemy. Further developed by the Arabs after the sacking of Alexandria in 389AD and again in 641. Instruments of the 10th c still survive. In use in Europe from before 1200 to 1700. The body of the astrolabe (the mater) has, pivoted in the centre of the front, a bar with sights (the alidade). By holding a ring on the top of the instrument, the sun or another star can be sighted with the alidade and its height above the horizon measured on a scale. From this, the time in TEMPORAL or EQUAL HOURS and the latitude can be calculated graphically. The back plate is engraved with a circular map of the stars seen from a CELESTIAL POLE. Over it is a fretwork plate (the rete) to indicate the position of the sun in the zodiac and the positions of the stars in relationship to each other. Some astrolabes had interchangeable star plates. The Arabs made many of the finest. Sources included Persia, India, Italy, Flanders, France and England. See ASTROLABIC CLOCK, NOCTURNAL.

Astrolabic clock Clocks of various styles were made in the 16th and 17th c with an ASTROLABE incorporated in the dial centre, the alidade acting as an hour hand. An early DRUM CLOCK sometimes had a dial like the back plate of an ASTROLABE, on which a hand took the place of the alidade, showing the altitude of the sun, and thus the time.

Astrolabic watch Small portable version of an ASTROLABIC CLOCK.

Astrological clock Astrology had great influence in ancient regimes. Astrologers more skilled in observation and more logical in deductions separated from the occult aspects became astronomers. Famous astronomers like Tycho Brahe and Johannes Kepler in the 16th c were officially court astrologers. Astrologers believe that a person's life is ruled by the positions of the planets in the ZODIAC at the time of his birth and that events influencing him depend upon the position of his 'star'. To astrologers the 'stars' are the planets, the sun, and the moon, because they still work from a Ptolemaic Earth-centred universe. Star positions are identified according to which of the 12 signs of the zodiac and also which of the 12 celestial houses they are in. A house is like the blade of a 12-bladed fan with its pivot where the MERIDIAN meets the horizon. A spring-driven painted iron clock of the Danube school dated 1545 in the Kunsthistorisches Museum, Vienna, Austria, shows the positions of sun and moon in the zodiac and time of day on the main dial. Other dials show the position of the sun in the heavens and the day of the week. An astrological dial on the back shows the ruling planet for the current hour. Other dials show time on a 24-hour dial, phases of the moon, days of the week, and age of the Moon. Some hands are driven by cords and pulleys. Also in Vienna, in the Technisches Museum, is a BELFRY CLOCK about 1m (40in) high with Moorish decoration signed 'Philip Imbser, Tuebingen, 1555'. As well as astronomical indications and automata, circles on a globe show astrological houses. Clocks with 'astrological hours' engraved on a dial, and a hand showing the hourly influence of the 'stars', are very rare. A series of rings of engraved numbers is needed because the sequence of 'stars' is different every day of the week. Some early clocks have 'iatro-mathematical' dials, which provide pseudo-medical advice such as when to carry out bleeding and the best days for cutting toe nails!

Astronaut's clock Special QUARTZ CLOCKS have been developed for use in space that are relatively unaffected by varying gravitational and centifugal forces. Examples are satellite timers, used for switching circuits on and off, and Earth path indicators for indicating the position of the Earth underneath the space capsule. Ground control uses quartz clocks controlled by ATOMIC CLOCKS.

Astronomer Royal The first Astronomer Royal was John FLAM-STEED, appointed in 1674 at the age of 28 by King Charles II and provided with a home, now Flamsteed House, in the

Royal Park at Greenwich. From 1971 the two appointments of Astronomer Royal and Director of the Royal Greenwich Observatory were made separately.

Astronomer Royal for Ireland A chair of astronomy endowed in Trinity College, Dublin, in 1783 became defunct in 1921 after the declaration of a Republic in 1919, but there is still a Royal Astronomer in Armagh, Northern Ireland.

Astronomer Royal for Scotland Appointment created by royal warrant in 1834, to provide a director for the Royal Observatory in Edinburgh.

Astronomer's pendulum Before c1675, astronomers used a weight hanging from a cord and counted the swings when timing astronomical events. Several of them tried to make the counting automatic, i.e. to invent a pendulum clock. Two succeeded, HUYGENS and GALILEO.

Astronomical clock One that has indications of one or more astronomical events, excluding the simple calendar dial, phase and age of moon dial, TIDAL DIAL and EQUATION DIAL. Included are clocks showing the position of the sun in the zodiac; complex information about the moon, such as an indication of the NODES, SIDEREAL TIME, rising and setting of the sun and moon; complex calendar information such as SOLAR and LUNAR CYCLES and the dates of movable feasts; and movements of the planets and their satellites shown by ASTROLABE, GLOBE CLOCK, ORRERY, PLANISPHERE, etc. An ASTROLOGI-CAL CLOCK is a form of astronomical clock. In the past, quite complex astro-nomical WATER CLOCKS were made. Even an inaccurate timekeeper can oper-ate astronomical work with relative accuracy if adjusted over periods from years to centuries, but important ones were eventually scrapped because subse-quently no-one knew how to adjust them. See DONDI'S CLOCK, STRASBOURG CATHEDRAL CLOCK, TURLER COSMIC CLOCK, WELLS CATHEDRAL CLOCK.

side of the pendulum rod only, used with a DEADBEAT ESCAPEMENT on some REGULATORS.

Atala and Chactas clock   French Empire clock depicting an American Indian squaw freeing a negro tied to a palm tree, based on a story.

French **Atala and Chactas** clock in ormolu and in the Empire style. (*Christie's*)

Father Philip Hahn of Echterdingen made this **astronomical clock** in 1781. On top is a celestial sphere showing motions of the sun, moon and Venus. (*H. Bertele Coll*)

Astronomical Ephemeris Tables of figures, including the EQUATION OF TIME, essential to astronomers and navigators, published jointly since 1960 by the Royal Greenwich Observatory and the United States Naval Observatory. Superseded the *NAUTICAL ALMANAC*.

Astronomical watch Similar to an ASTRONOMICAL CLOCK, usually giving a limited amount of information. The earliest were of the 16th and 17th c. Today some are quartz wrist watches.

Asymmetrical crutch A one-sided CRUTCH which appears to impulse one

Atelier Name sometimes applied to a workshop in the watch and clock and allied trades, especially to the 18th c ones in Swiss homes.

Atmos clock Self-winding clock operated by changes in atmospheric temperature or pressure, invented in 1913 by J.E. Reuther of Paris, which was similar to AUTOMATIC WINDING invented in 1765 by James COX of London, but employing an aneroid bellows instead of a Fortin barometer. Not developed at the time owing to lack of suitable metals, but later put into production by the Swiss firm of Jaeger-Le Coultre. Aneroid bellows containing ethyl chloride, which is sensitive to temperature changes, operate a high ratio gear train to rewind the mainspring. A TORSION PENDULUM takes so little power that a change of only 1°C will keep the clock going for 24 hours. When fully wound, the reserve is 100 days.

This **Atmos clock** is one of the Jubilé limited edition sold by subscription only in 1979 by Jaeger-Le Coultre.

A.T.O. clock See KUNDO CLOCK.

Atomic clock An atomic clock uses the vibrations of an atom as its time standard instead of those of a piece of quartz as in a quartz clock or a pendulum. Made possible by the invention of the maser, which also spawned the laser. One of the first developed by the National Bureau of Standards in the U.S.A. in 1948, it depended upon the vibrations of the nitrogen atoms in ammonia gas. The caesium atomic clock was invented by Louis Essen and J.L.V. Parry at the National Physical Laboratory (N.P.L.), Teddington, England, the first version being installed in 1955. A later version showed that the Earth's rate of rotation was slowing down by about a second a year. See ATOMIC TIME. Early clocks were large but portable versions were soon made, e.g. for the calibration of navigational systems such as Loran C and Decca. The clock has an accuracy equivalent to 1 second in 3,000 years. In 1997, a clock based on an atom of ytterbium was developed by Paul Taylor and Mat

Roberts of the N.P.L, which gives time to one second in 5,000 years.

Atomic time The caesium ATOMIC CLOCK proved to be much more accurate than any other method of measuring time. It is twice as accurate as astronomical measurement over three years. On 1 January 1958, astronomers abandoned the Christian system of using the birth of Christ as a datum point for astronomical time and started a new era of 0 hours, 0 minutes and 0 seconds from the beginning of that year, defining the passage of time in atomic seconds. International Atomic Time (T.I.A.) was adopted on 1 January 1965, at the 12th General Conference for Weights and Measures, based on the second defined by the caesium atom. On 1 January 1972, co-ordinated UNIVERSAL TIME (U.T.C.) was introduced to replace Greenwich Mean Time. The Earth's rotation is slowly slowing down by about a second a year and ten countries, including the U.K., U.S.A. and Switzerland, adopted T.I.A. and the introduction of leap seconds to be applied when agreed, to compensate for the running down of the Earth. The first was deducted in October 1972.

Attachment, point of Inner pinning point of a balance spring, fastening it to the collet on the BALANCE STAFF. Loosely referred to as the 'point of attach'. The spring cannot be pinned on the exact axis of the balance staff, so the centre of gravity is eccentric and moves as the balance swings, affecting the RATE. In precision watches, the point of attach is manipulated by ADJUSTERS. For factory production, the geometry of the inner coil of the spring is altered. See BALANCE SPRING.

Auburndale rotary watch Watch where the movement revolves **in the** case in order to reduce POSITIONAL ERRORS, patented in the U.S.A. by Jason R. Hopkins (1815–1902) of Washington, DC, which he believed could be sold for only about 50 cents. The entire movement revolved in about 2fi hours. The watches were put into production by W.B. Fowle of Auburndale, Massachusetts, in 1877. No more than about 1,000 were made because the cheaper WATERBURY ROTARY WATCH was about to be launched.

Audemars Piguet Jules Audemars (24) and Edward Piguet (22) founded this company in Le Brassus in 1875, specialising in COMPLICATED WATCHES of the highest quality. See KEYLESS WINDING. They were making a gold HUNTER watch with MINUTE REPEATER, PERPETUAL CALENDAR, phases of the MOON DIAL, SPLIT SECONDS chronograph, and POWER RESERVE INDICATOR before the turn of the century.

Augsburg Southern German town that was one of the earliest centres of clockmaking, gradually taking over from NUREMBERG in the second half of the 16th c, and remaining the centre of production of fine clocks, instruments, and silversmiths' wares for about two centuries. Metal cased spring-driven TABLE CLOCKS and BELFRY CLOCKS were produced in quantity and, from about 1570, large numbers of animated clocks in which the clock was part of a case with a human or animal figure (or part of one) which had moving eyes or limbs. Some makers continued to construct elaborate GLOBE and ASTRONOMICAL CLOCKS. In the 17th c, Augsburg was producing ALTAR and MONSTRANCE clocks, mostly with metal but some with wooden cases, and it remained a centre for these and figure clocks with models of elephants, lions, dogs, cows, etc, as well as humans in gilt metal or silver on wooden (ebony) bases. From about 1720 to 1775, makers produced many TELLEUHREN and ZAPPLER clocks, but before the end of the period, France and England had taken the lead and the industry in Augsburg died. The town had a large export trade, including making fine and specialist clocks for the Far East. The most famous Augsburg makes were Johann Reinhold, George Roll, and the Buschmann family. A clock in the Kunsthistorisches Museum, Vienna, by Hans Buschmann dated 1624 has a small rock crystal dome on top which contains a carved ivory skeleton that turns – another kind of skeleton clock! See

ELEPHANT CLOCK for picture. Such clocks still come up at auction. Some watches were also made in Augsburg and Matthaus Buschmann may have done so before the mid-16th c.

A typical early **Augsburg** clock showing a lion with blinking or moving eyes.

Austrian horological industry Austria shared in the development of clockmaking in southern Germany in the early 17th c but, by the end of the century, both were in decline with the increasing dominance of the English and the French. During 1789–90, the government organised the immigration of 150 watchmakers and small ancillary craftsmen from

Switzerland. Clockmaking revived later, reaching its peak artistically and technically from c1800 to c1850, producing a variety of table and bracket clocks, ZAPPLERS, and particularly VIENNA REGULATORS. They also made BIEDERMEIER CLOCKS. Centres were Vienna, Graz, Innsbruck, Linz, Radkersburg, Salzburg and Styria.

Auto-restart unit Unit for a synchronous electric public clock, made by Smiths of Derby, to restart it automatically at the correct time of day after a power cut or any other stoppage. A 'black box' containing a battery-operated quartz clock turns the power on again in 24 hours, minus the time for which the clock has been stopped.

Automatic watch Swiss name for the SELF-WINDING WRIST WATCH.

Automatic winding Attempts to wind timepieces automatically by using natural energy date from early times. In 1636, Daniel Schwenter of Nuremberg referred to a French idea for connecting a watch to the wearer's belt, to wind it by the movement of breathing. In 1664 Gaspar Schott proposed a clock wound by a fan in a chimney, and in 1678 Jean de Hautefeuille designed a 2m (6ft) bar made from several pieces of pine, cut across the grain, that lengthened and shortened with humidity changes, to wind a clock through a rack. A clock by James Cox with BAROMETRIC WINDING still exists. A similar principle is used in the ATMOS CLOCK, except that temperature changes cause the movement of an aneroid bellows. John Harwood, inventor of a SELF-WINDING WRIST WATCH, also devised an automobile clock wound by the motion of the vehicle. Automatic winding used to be confused with PERPETUAL MOTION CLOCKS. See SELF-WINDING CLOCK, SELF-WINDING POCKET WATCH, AUTOMATIC WINDING FOR TURRET CLOCKS.

Automatic winding for turret clocks The 17th c ENDLESS ROPE OR CHAIN system of Huygens is still common today, electrified with a chain, for large public clocks, because hand winding is no longer economic. It is incorporated in new clocks and many old ones have been converted. Historic clocks need not be damaged by conversion and a long weight fall is unnecessary. When it has dropped 1m (3ft) or so, the weight trips a mercury switch, which activates an electric motor to rewind it. At the top of its travel, it trips another switch that stops the motor. The motor can double as the weight ('monkey up a rope'). An epicyclic or differential gear can replace the endless rope.

Automaton Animated figures (automata) have been made for at least 2,300 years, the earliest known having been made in Alexandria and operated by water in ancient Egypt. Ctesibius made water clocks on which a moving figure indicated the hour. His pupil, Hero of Alexandria, invented many, some operated by steam-reaction turbines. In Byzantine times the Arabs, in particular, and also the Persians developed the art. The Emperor Charlemagne was presented, in 807AD, with an Arabic water clock which sounded the hours by dropping the appropriate number of small brass balls into a brass basin. At noon, 12 horsemen came out of 12 windows that closed behind them. There is still part of a similar public clock made by Abou Inane, at Fez, Morocco. The mechanical clock gave a new impetus to the making of automata. See ANIMATED CLOCK, ANIMATED WATCH, JACK (for picture), PEACOCK CLOCK, SINGING BIRD and STRASBOURG CATHEDRAL CLOCK.

Automobile clock One on the dashboard of a motor car, perhaps introduced by Rolls-Royce. Normally spring-wound before electric ones, but see AUTOMATIC WINDING. Also an INDUSTRIAL CLOCK set in a model of an automobile – the wheels of the car turn when separately wound.

Autowrist Form of SELF-WINDING wrist watch invented by John HARWOOD, made for a few years in the late 1920s by the A. Schild ÉBAUCHES factory and sold by Fortis S.A.,

A French **automobile clock**. The wheels revolve; they are not driven by the mainspring but by another spring.

Switzerland. The watch case is rectangular, and one strap lug is hinged and sprung. Movement of the owner's wrist causes the lug to move backwards and forwards to wind the mainspring. Because the stroke is short but strong, a toothless ratchet is employed. The system works quite well, but the case is not dust-proof.

Auxiliary temperature compensation A CUT BALANCE used with a hairspring only compensates timekeeping at two different temperatures. Between them, the timepiece gains (MIDDLE TEMPERATURE ERROR). So forms of auxiliary compensations were devised in the 19th c. Many famous makers tried to solve the problem.

Auxiliary dial   See SUBSIDIARY DIAL.

B

B.T-H. electric clock   See CLINKER
ELECTRIC MAINS CLOCK.

Babylonian hours   TEMPORAL HOURS
used for centuries BC by the Babylonians
and numbered from 1 to 24, starting each
day at sunrise. See HOUR. Shown on
some early special clocks.

Bacchus clock   Clock bearing a model of
the Greek god of wine. Wine vendors are
said first to have associated the figure
with their sundials. AUGSBURG makers
animated the figure. At the hours Bacchus
raises the flask to his lips and opens his
mouth. His eyes swing with the ticking.
In the early 19th c, the Wellington Inn,
Belfast, Northern Ireland, had a clock
over the door which operated an arm of
Bacchus beckoning in customers.
Temperance Association members were
blamed for smashing it.

Back cock   COCK on the back plate of a
clock in which there is a bearing hole for
the pallet arbor. It often also acts as the
suspension point for the pendulum.

Back plate   Brass plate of a clock or
early watch furthest from the dial, except
in most English clocks, and normally the
one that can be removed to release the
barrels and train of wheels, etc. Attached
by the ends of pillars passing through
holes in the plate and held by taper pins,
or for special earlier clocks, by latches.
Nuts were used in later ones. Back plates
in early clocks were often decorated with
engraved borders, foliage (usually
ACANTHUS leaves), tulips by makers of
Dutch origin, and cartouches or plain
panels with the maker's name and loca-
tion. Cases for such clocks usually had
glazed back doors.

The **back plate** of a Daniel Quare bracket clock with
elaborate acanthus engraving. Note the bob pendulum
held by a latch, used when moving the clock.
(*Sotheby's*)

Back stop   Spring-loaded lever or
JUMPER that prevents a ratchet wheel
from moving backwards when the PAWL
that moves it forwards is being withdrawn, as when winding up a
MAINSPRING. If backward movement is
needed, as when setting an IMPULSE
DIAL, it is not made strong enough to
prevent this. See RATCHET DRIVE.

Back wind   With the KEY or WINDING
SQUARE at the back. Most early clocks
and watches were wound from the front,
through the dial. Introduced in the late
19th c on the Continent, but earlier in
England for clocks as they became
smaller and more portable. Factory-
produced mechanical alarms often have
fixed back-wind keys. Weight-driven
clocks are always wound from the front
because of the difficulty of disturbing

them, as the back usually faces a wall. Some very small watches had back wind.

Bain clock One made by the electric clock pioneer Alexander Bain (1810–77). Some have SECONDS PENDULUMS and are in long cases; others are large mantel clocks. The pendulum moves a sliding switch. This connects impulsing coils forming the pendulum BOB (or fixed coils with a magnetic bob) to a battery. In 1842, Bain invented the earth battery, which lasts indefinitely. Coke and zinc or iron in separate pits in the ground, kept damp, form the poles. Only two of his mantel clocks are currently known. One c1847 shown at a Science Museum, London, exhibition in 1976–7, was a skeleton clock. A PAWL and RATCHET WHEEL turns the hands. The clock operates contacts every two hours for a purpose unknown.

Balance Oscillator that is not dependent directly on gravity, like the pendulum, for its timekeeping. The earliest practical balance was the FOLIOT, used in the form of a BAR BALANCE for watches, and the circular balance for clocks and watches. See BALANCE WHEEL.

Balance arc The number of degrees through which a balance swings.

Balance bridge BRIDGE that holds the balance pivot bearing in the TOP PLATE (farthest from dial) of a French watch of the 17th–18th c, like the BALANCE COCK in an English watch. Often oval and elaborately engraved and pierced in earlier versions. From c 1735, it carried a steel end plate, called a COQUERET, for the balance pivot, until JEWELS and END STONES were introduced.

Balance cock COCK that holds the bearing of the balance pivot bearing on the TOP PLATE of a watch movement. The earliest type of the 16th c was S-shaped with a BAR BALANCE. Gradually it became bigger and round, to cover the BALANCE WHEEL. Decoration was usually elaborate and is a guide to the age of the watch. The finest cocks were made from the second quarter of the 17th to the early 18th c. From

the early 18th c, more and more English watch cocks had ruby or diamond END STONES mounted in them. Cocks were becoming wedge-shaped at the end of the 18th c. After the first quarter of the 19th c, with the introduction of three-quarters and half instead of whole top plate (at the back) movements, and the later BAR MOVEMENTS, the cock was moved to the inside of the bottom plate, which reduced the thickness of the movement. The decoration quickly disappeared. The Germans and Swiss made watches with balance cocks similar to the English, but the Dutch and French favoured a BALANCE BRIDGE. Continental cocks and bridges were not jewelled until the beginning of the 19th c, with the exception of watches by BREGUET, who had an English jeweller working for him. The balance cock in a factory-made watch is still used to allow the balance and spring to be removed separately, but also carries the SHOCK ABSORBER jewelled bearing, the STUD, the INDEX, and, in some, a BEAT ADJUSTER. Balance cocks are also employed in clocks with balance and spring, often on a PLATFORM ESCAPEMENT.

A large **balance clock** on a full-plate watch movement signed Thos. Earnshaw.

Balance lathe Special Lancashire late 18th c lathe for turning and polishing the rims of BALANCE WHEELS; used with a BOW.

Balance screws Small screws round a BALANCE rim. The two at the ends of the CROSSING and the two equidistant between them adjust MEAN TIME. The others adjust for temperature changes.

Balance spring The fine spirally-coiled spring used in conjunction with a BALANCE WHEEL in a watch. The wheel is a substitute for the pendulum in a clock and the spring a substitute for the force of gravity. In earlier watches the spring was under the balance wheel (under-sprung). Now all are over it. Confusingly called a 'pendulum spring' in the past, after the inventor HUYGENS devised his 'geared pirouette' in 1675 for the navigation of sailing ships, to substitute for a pendulum. HOOKE and others contested the invention. Some balance springs have terminal curves or OVER-COILS to improve isochronism (see ISOCHRONOUS). Other shapes used, particularly in marine chronometers, include the CYLINDRICAL BALANCE SPRING, helical, conical, OVERCOIL, double overcoil, and even straight line and spherical springs. See HAIRSPRING.

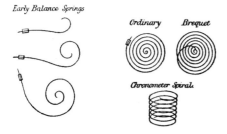

Early Balance Springs

Ordinary *Breguet*

Chronometer Spiral

Balance springs of the late 17th and early 19th c.

Balance staff The steel axle of a BALANCE. Normally a BALANCE WHEEL is riveted on to it. The COLLET, to which the inner end of the BALANCE SPRING is attached, may be integral with it or a separate tightly fitting brass collar.

Balance turns Tool for making watch BALANCES. See TURNS.

Balance wheel The common oscillator for watches and clocks. Early versions had no BALANCE SPRINGS. The first circular balances for watches were introduced before the mid-16th c, the STAFF being a VERGE, which was oscillated by

a CROWN WHEEL, in the same way as in a clock. They had only one spoke to allow the amplitude to be limited by hog's BRISTLE REGULATOR (see for picture). The spiral balance spring, introduced after 1675, improved timekeeping immensely. In 1761, Pierre Le Roy invented the bi-metallic CUT BALANCE, the principles of which were incorporated into most good quality watches from the early 19th c. In the rim are TIMING SCREWS with large heads used for setting to time and POISING. Temperature errors were tackled by a COMPENSATION BALANCE and a COMPENSATION CURB, acting on the balance spring. These errors were largely eliminated by the invention of ELINVAR and GLUCYDUR, but manufacturers continued to use balances with screws in the rims until about 1958 because they were symbols of quality. In most cheap watches, plain balances were used, but even some of these had the rims milled to imitate screws. The abandonment of screws allowed for larger balances with less weight for the same moment of iner tia and reduced air disturbances. Later better quality balances were poised by milling under the rim. Most balances have two crossings (arms), but earlier steel balances sometimes had three. The timekeeping of a balance and spring is determined by the moment of inertia of the balance and the bending moment of the balance spring. The term once meant the crown wheel of a verge escapement i.e. the ESCAPE WHEEL.

Balance wheel engine Tool of the late 18th c and onwards for cutting VERGE escape wheels, the rims of which are bands with teeth along one edge. A cutter is revolved using a BOW. The trade of cutting balance wheels (i.e. ESCAPE WHEELS) was often combined with FUSEE cutting. The tool for making watch balances was called the BALANCE TURNS.

Ball-and-tape clock A form of FALLING-BALL CLOCK that shows the time on a tape that is gradually drawn out of it as it descends.

Ball clock There are four meanings. (1)

Clock, usually French, shaped like a ball. Some have curved hands moving over a spherical dial and others a moving band round the circumference showing the hours. One of the moving band type, reproduced in quantity from about 1875 to 1925, had a sphere on the head of a bust of a female Atlas, with a cherub on each side. (2) FALLING-BALL CLOCK. (3) ROLLING BALL CLOCK, where a ball bearing running along a track is the time-keeper. See CAMPANUS CLOCK, CONGREVE CLOCK, TOWER OF BABEL CLOCK and SANDSTROM CLOCK. (4) Clock in which the driving power is provided by heavy steel balls. See BALL DRIVE CLOCK and GROL-LIER.

Ball-driven clock   One powered by steel balls falling in succession into cups on the edge of a driving wheel or equivalent. The earliest version, by Padre Francesco Eschinardi in 1670, employed a flexible band with cups turning the CROWN WHEEL arbor. On reaching the bottom, the ball is returned to the top by a motor drive which releases the next ball and also operates the time indicator. The ball is therefore also the timekeeping element. A recent version is 'The Juggler', comprising a 1.8m (6ft) high, quite slen-der hollow tree trunk with a trap by the bottom which throws each ball high in the air so that it falls into the top of the trunk to percolate down past a series of holes and release the trap to fire the next ball. It is mains-driven and time is shown on a small dial. Some ball drives are illu-sory, like the Wishing Fish Clock in the Regent shopping arcade in Cheltenham. Seemingly golden eggs are laid in a stream by a huge duck 12m (40ft) high and descend in cups; seemingly empty cups ascend. This and other AUTOMATA there are driven by electrics and pneu-matics. See SANDSTROM CLOCK.

Ball watch   Swiss ball-shaped watch on a chain made in large numbers in the second half of the 19th c. Wound by turn-ing the upper part of the case.

Balloon clock   Style first introduced in France c1715. It has a waist and was stood on a wall bracket, the case and bracket being elaborately decorated with ORMOLU and often, except in later versions, being in BOULLE work. Popular in France during the Regency and often made as a CARTEL CLOCK, i.e. a wall clock with a built-in false bracket. Copied in other countries, it became so popular in Switzerland that it was adopted by Neuchâtel makers and is now known as a 'Neuchâteloise clock'. Favoured in England during the Regency period and later, in a much plainer case. Smaller mantel versions were produced in quantity in Europe in the first part of the 20th c with solid mahogany veneered cases and drum movements with cylin-der escapements. The outline was associated with early hot air balloons first launched by the Montgolfier brothers in Paris in 1783, many years after the clock style was introduced.

A Joseph Thompson mantel clock of c1820 with a **balloon case**, which has had periods of popularity.

Band   Another name for a watch strap or bracelet.

Band dial   Revolving horizontal band marked with the hours, I to XII or with DOUBLE-TWELVE HOURS, showing time against a fixed pointer. Popular in France in the 18th c on BALL or GLOBE

CLOCKS, and vase or URN CLOCKS. The moving band is much earlier, appearing on FALLING BALL CLOCKS of the mid-17th c.

Banding   Narrow border of contrasting inlaid wood often used as decoration of clock cases. When the grain lies along the band, it is 'straight banding', when across, 'cross banding', and when at an angle 'feather banding'. Very narrow banding is called 'stringing'.

Banjo clock   Popular name for a wall clock design introduced into the U.S.A. by Simon Willard in 1802, and called his 'Patent Timekeeper'. He patented the shape as well as the simplified eight-day movement without striking, and a pendulum positioned in front of the driving weight. The bottom of the case has a glass with EGLISOME PAINTING, usually of geometric pattern. Railway companies adopted the clocks as station waiting room attractions. It remained popular during the 1830s. Other makers were Lemuel Curtis, Curtis and Dunning, Reuben Tower and David Williams. See LYRE CLOCK.

Banking   Action of a moving part, especially of an escapement, coming up against a stop. One of the earliest was a pin on top of a LANTERN CLOCK that limited the swing of the circular BALANCE. One side or the other of the single spoke would bank on the pin if the driving weight were too heavy. With a VERGE ESCAPEMENT, a BANKING PIN on the balance swung against two stops on the BALANCE COCK. The same system was used with the CYLINDER ESCAPEMENT. In a LEVER ESCAPEMENT, the lever is limited in movement by solid banking (part of the plate or PALLET COCK), or by two banking pins. A pocket chronometer has two pins in the crossings (spokes) of the balance, to limit the action of the BALANCE SPRING, not the balance itself. See OVER BANKING and RUN TO BANKING. Electro-mechanical watches have magnetic banking.

Banking pin   Pin to prevent excessive motion of a BALANCE, PALLET lever or other moving part. See BANKING.

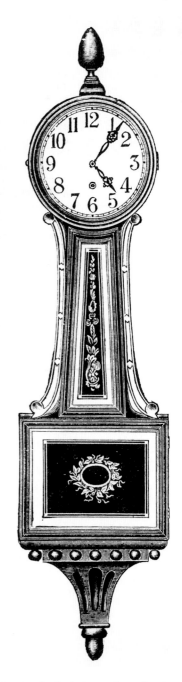

An American **banjo clock,** one of a number shown in a Simon Willard catalogue.

Banking screw   Adjustable screw in a chronometer ESCAPEMENT, the head of which forms a stop for the DETENT so that the amount of LOCKING can be regulated.

Bar Generic term for a BRIDGE or COCK (half a bridge), which is used, particularly in watches, to hold the bearings of PIVOTS, so that parts may be removed without dismantling the whole movement. Usually identified by the part it holds, e.g. barrel bar, centre wheel bar, and held by a screw and STEADY PINS.

Bar, spring To avoid having to sew the halves of a strap onto bars between wrist watch case lugs, bars that were sprung into holes in the lugs were generally introduced in mid-20th c. The normal type has a solid pin at one end and a spring-loaded one at the other. Less common is one with two holes in the bar and a pin on each lug. If the lug holes are blind, a special tool is used to remove a bar.

Bar balance Oscillating horizontal bar used as a controller in the earliest portable clocks and watches. A FOLIOT is a form of bar balance, but with hanging weights on the ends for adjustment. Some bar balances have threaded nuts instead, but most were plain with rounded ends, called 'dumbbell balances'. A vertical bar is not a bar balance but a COMPOUND PENDULUM.

Bar movement For centuries, watches had frames made of two plates, like clocks. In the late 18th c, the top plate (at the back) was reduced to three-quarter and then to half size, then abolished in the LEPINE CALIBRE. Bars (BRIDGES) were used on the front plate, which reduced the thickness and allowed parts to be removed without disturbing others.

Barber's clock American wall clock made in the late 19th c by the Waterbury Clock Co. for barbers' shops. The hour numerals are laterally inverted so that the customer can read the clock behind him in the mirror in front of him.

Barking dog clock One of many types of AUTOMATON clock produced in the 17th c in South Germany. The figure of a dog has constantly moving glass eyes

(operated by the pendulum) and moves its jaws as if barking as the hours are struck. Some were made of wood, others metal.

Barking dog watch A Swiss ANIMATED WATCH showing a dog barking at a swan. The REPEATER sounds as 'barks' instead of on bells or gongs. There is one in the museum in Geneva and another was sold by Christie's in 1978.

Barlow, Edward (1636–1716) Invented the very important RACK STRIKING for clocks c1676 and REPEATING WORK for watches in 1686, but see QUARE. Another of his inventions was a form of CYLINDER ESCAPEMENT in 1695.

Barleycorn One of the small projections on case or dial in the pattern caused by engraved lines crossing each other produced by ENGINE TURNING.

Barograph clock One that turns a drum once in a week (usually). A paper chart marked in hours and days and in millibars is attached to the drum and a pen on an arm attached to aneroid bellows draws a graph of the atmospheric pressure. Robert HOOKE invented the system. In one made in 1765 by Alexander Cumming for King George III, a column of mercury works a marker recording on a paper ring moving round the dial of a longcase clock.

Barometric error Changes in RATE caused by changes in air pressure which affect a pendulum in at least three ways. Ignoring consequential errors such as those caused by changes in ARC, the density of the air affects the apparent weight of the BOB, but not its mass, so the clock will lose when the barometer is high. This is called the 'flotation effect' and is equivalent to a change in gravitation. A SECONDS PENDULUM with a brass bob will lose about $\frac{1}{5}$ second a day for every 2.5cm (1in) rise of mercury. The second effect is frictional. The denser the air, the more friction between it and the pendulum and bob, but skin friction has a negligible effect on rate. The third effect is air disturbance as the pendulum bob swings, pushing the air in opposite directions. The inertia of the moving air abstracts energy from the pendulum. Its effect is very difficult to calculate. The total barometric influence on an accurate pendulum clock is up to about +/-1 sec a day per inch of mercury. Compensators operated by mercury or by aneroid barometers have been invented, but the most satisfactory method is to eliminate the air by using a VACUUM CASE. To reduce the error in free air, the pendulum bob should be a cylinder, as wide as it is high, of the densest possible material, according to Colin Frye (1956). On the other hand, RIEFLER published results in 1907 of tests carried out at different air pressures in an air-tight case in which an approximately lens-shaped bob (two flat cones base to base) gave the best result. A spherical bob, also of brass and the same weight, was worse, and a similar cylindrical one worse still. Nevertheless, Riefler used cylindrical bobs in airtight cases because of the width of the flat bob. Marine chronometers and watches are affected by barometric error, but very much less, so that it is generally ignored, although low-pressure cased chronometers and watches have been introduced. See AIR-TIGHT CASE.

Barometric winding Winding automatically by changes in atmospheric pressure. The most famous clock is a large one in the Victoria and Albert Museum, London, made by James COX, the 18th c London automata clock maker. It employs a Fortin barometer comprising two glass vessels. The upper one, with a long neck, is the barometer and holds 68kg (150lb) of mercury. It is up-ended in the other vessel. Both are suspended and as the atmospheric pressure changes, they move apart or together to wind the clock via a ratchet mechanism.

Baroque style Very exuberant style of decoration originating in Italy near the beginning of the 17th c. It spread first to Holland, being especially favoured by silversmiths. In France, it became the LOUIS XIV style and in England was seen during the Restoration and Queen Anne periods. Clock design was most influenced in France.

Barrel Drum (wooden or metal) on which the rope, gut line, or wire of a weight-driven clock is wound. Also the drum-shaped box containing the MAINSPRING which is the 'power-pack' of the mechanical timepiece. The spring is enclosed in it by a disc-shaped snap-in cover. Its outer end is fastened to the barrel by a brace and the inner end hooks on to an ARBOR (axle) in bearings in the barrel and its lid. Both bearings normally have raised bosses to widen them and make them last longer. See FUSEE, GOING BARREL, HANGING BARREL, MUSICAL BARREL, REMOVABLE BARREL, RESTING BARREL, STANDING BARREL, TANDEM DRIVE BARREL and SETTING UP.

Barrel arbor The axle in a mainspring BARREL round which the spring is coiled. It has a hook to engage a hole in the spring.

Barrel contractor If a barrel becomes bell-shaped so that the cover will not snap in, it can be restored more or less to its original diameter using a special steel plate with a series of tapered holes, into one of which the open side of the barrel is tapped, using a mallet.

Barrel cover Lid of the MAINSPRING BARREL, which has a bevelled edge so that it can be snapped into a corresponding groove in the open end of the barrel.

Barrel engine Form of lathe for cutting grooves in a longcase clock barrel, to guide the gut on which the weight is hung. A tool held in a slide rest is moved across the barrel to give one spiral groove of about 16 turns. Similar to a FUSEE ENGINE.

Barrel hook Fixed or detachable projection on the inside of a spring BARREL over which a hole in the outer end of the MAINSPRING is hooked.

Barrel ratchet When a MAINSPRING is wound by a KEY or KEYLESS WINDING, it is prevented from unwinding by a ratchet wheel on the barrel ARBOR and a fixed PAWL, called a 'click', on the plate. To avoid coil binding, the click is normally designed to recoil so that, when fully wound, the spring is let down very slightly by an elongated hole or a jamming cam. See STOP WORK.

Barring-off wheel Wheel with 24 teeth which controls striking and chiming. Normally one tooth is released before every hour, which allows normal sound. At, say, night, the wheel can be set not to turn, which locks the chiming or striking train and silences the clock.

Barrow, Nathaniel Famous early maker, active from 1660 to c1700. He made watches with BALANCE SPRINGS after their invention in 1675.

Barrow regulator Early REGULATOR for watches named after Nathaniel BARROW, for whom the invention has been claimed. A screw across the back of the movement with a squared end to take a KEY will move a nut left or right. Two CURB PINS on the nut embrace the straight outer end of the BALANCE SPRING and to alter timekeeping. Now very rare.

Bascine case Pocket watch case with smooth rounded sides and no beading. Also spelt 'bassine'.

Basket top Style of decorated top to a BRACKET CLOCK used from c1680. It is bell-shaped in profile and made of cast and pierced brass, or rarely silver, to match similar work on the door frame and sides of the case. The handle is mounted on top. A more elaborate version is the double-basket top, with two tiers of basket work, popular from c1770.

Basle hours Before HOUR RECKONING was standardised, Basle, in Switzerland, measured the hours from midday, counting this as one o'clock.

Basse taille Enamelling method invented in France in the early 14th c. A translucent coloured enamel is laid over engraved gold (or silver). The colour is

A bracket clock with a **basket top** and three-train movement with ringed winding holes. The dial has cherub spandrels.

strongest where the engraving is deepest. Very rarely used on early watch cases over small pieces of gold or silver and combined with CHAMPLEVE or CLOISONNEE engraving. Sometimes used over ENGINE TURNING in the 18th c.

Bassine See BASCINE CASE.

Bath Tompion One of TOMPION'S most famous clocks, which he presented to the Pump Room, in Bath, Somerset, in 1709, after treatment there. It goes for a month and has an EQUATION OF TIME dial in the BREAK-ARCH dial and HOOD. The case has a pillar-like front.

Battersea enamel Enamelled watch cases were made by the Battersea Enamel factory from c1750 to 1756. They were also made elswhere including BILSTON.

Battery An electric battery comprises two or more cells linked in series or parallel and is used in some clocks, such as

MASTER CLOCKS. Almost every domestic clock and watch that needs electric energy has a single POWER CELL.

Battery clock   Any clock drive by battery or power cell, such as an A.T.O. CLOCK, BAIN CLOCK, BULLE CLOCK, CORDLESS CLOCK, ELECTRIC CLOCK, EUREKA CLOCK, TUNING FORK CLOCK.

Battleship clock   French INDUSTRIAL CLOCK in this shape with a clock in the side.

A well-armed **battleship clock**, one of the many industrial clocks, which were mainly French.

Baume and Mercier   The Baume family was making watch parts in the Swiss Jura from 1542 and descendants registered a company to make complete watches in 1834. Paul Mercier joined in 1918, but their record was not notable. In the mid-1950s, the old-established PIAGET took a majority holding and soon produced an AUTOMATIC WATCH. They also produced one of the first TUNING FORK watches. In 1988, they and PIAGET were acquired by CARTIER International.

Beak iron   A very small anvil, held in a vice, on which metal is hammered into shape.

Beam engine clock   Popular novelty clock made in several forms during the French Industrial Revolution, but usually after 1870. Many are quite elaborate, but in one, the beam is part of the pendulum and the 'piston rods' merely dangle in the 'cylinders'. In many, the engine is operated only at the hour by a separate mechanism. See INDUSTRIAL CLOCKS.

Bearing   The earliest clocks had iron pivots running in iron holes, lubricated by animal fat, e.g. goose grease. Parts and bearings of the same metals tend to 'pick up', i.e. create tiny local welds if tight. It was found that steel pivots running in brass gave the longest wear with least friction over long periods of time. Wooden pivots in wooden plates were used in early BLACK FOREST clocks and some early wooden mass-produced American clocks for minute wheel ARBORS and pipes. Later, steel pivots ran in holes in wooden plates and in the wooden rollers of some LANTERN PINIONS. Brass bushes are common in cast iron and steel frames of TURRET CLOCKS and in the wooden, and more unusual, zinc or duralumin plates of smaller clocks. The use of JEWELS reduces friction by running steel in or on gem minerals. Plastics are also used for clock and watch bearings. See FRICTION and WEAR.

Beat   Horological name for the alternate motion of a balance or pendulum. Ticks and tocks indicate the beat. A beat is 0.5 hertz (Hz), so a pendulum beating seconds has a frequency of half a cycle a second. The beat of a watch is often indicated by the number of beats or vibrations an hour. Thus one with an 18,000 train ticks that number of times an hour. See BEAT ADJUSTER, FAST BEAT, IN BEAT, OSCILLATOR.

Beat adjuster   Precision timepieces are often provided with a means of putting them IN BEAT, i.e. making the ticks evenly spaced, without having to bend the CRUTCH of a pendulum clock or move the balance spring collet of a balance and spring. In a clock, the crutch has two adjusting thumbscrews, one each side of the crutch, to alter its position in relation to the pendulum. In watches, a device rotates the outer pinning point and the inner POINT OF ATTACHMENT of the balance spring. Modern pendulum clocks sometimes have automatic beat adjustment. The crutch has a friction joint so that if the clock is not level, the escapement will bank (see BANKING) and the pendulum, as it continues to swing, will move the crutch to a new position, to bring the escapement more or less into beat.

Beat plate A plate behind the pointed end of a pendulum showing the angle of swing and useful in adjusting the BEAT.

Bedpost frame Although early TURRET CLOCKS had rectangular POSTED FRAMES made of wrought iron with more substantial corner posts (called at the time 'birdcage frames'), some were made of wood like bedposts. There are examples at Croxton, Cambridgeshire (1682); Coddenham Church, Suffolk; Edith Weston Church, Leicestershire; and elsewhere. As cast iron came into use in Victorian times, iron bedpost frames continued into the 18th and 19th c.

Beehive case Name given to an American SHELF CLOCK of GOTHIC arch shape. That with rounded beading is called 'rounded beehive'.

Beetle hand Early hour hand with two 'wings' vaguely resembling a beetle, but more like spectacles. Used with a POKER minute hand – a plain pointer.

Belfry clock Early large metal domestic clock of TOWER CLOCK form that can be viewed from any side and is spring-driven. They were made from about 1540 in Nuremberg, then in many sizes in Augsburg. Some French and German 19th c clocks had doors at the bottom of the tower that opened on the hour to show the figure of a monk pulling a cord to sound the hours. See TABERNACLE CLOCK, WATCHMAN'S CLOCK.

Bell The first clocks had no dial or hand, the hour being indicated by a single blow on a bell. Some gave an alarm on a bell. Early bells were of traditional shape with concave sides and were shaken by the clock, as that described in the Almanus Manuscript (1474–85), where a barrel wound with a weighted cord turned a cranked ARBOR that jerked a wire attached to a hand bell. Cowbells

were also used as seen in a 14th c WATCHMAN'S CLOCK in the Mainfrankisches Museum, Würzburg, Germany. One of the earliest illustrations of a fixed bell with a moving hammer is in the Hausbuch of the Prince of Waldburg-Wolfegg-Waldsee, c1480. A bell at the top of a clock became standard practice in miniature BELFRY CLOCKS and in Gothic iron clocks, and continued for most clocks through the centuries until it was replaced by the GONG. Early bells were deep with steep sides, called PORK PIE BELLS. They became more shallow over the years. (KNIBB continued the old style.) Bells were used in 'nests' (fitting one into the next) in MUSICAL CLOCKS and WATCHES. Earlier clockmakers cast their own in an alloy of copper and tin or pewter. Large bells were, and are, cast by specialist bell founders. The largest clock bell in the UK is Great Tom, the hour bell of the St Paul's Cathedral clock, which weighs 16.8 tonnes and was cast by the Taylor Bell Foundry at Loughborough. BIG BEN was cast by the Whitechapel Bell Foundry. Gillet and Bland, of Croydon, TURRET CLOCK makers, used to cast their own bells until the Second World War. A 'maiden' is a large bell that has been calculated and cast so accurately in diameter and thickness that it does not require tuning. A maiden peal of bells is very rare. One of the best proportions of

The watch with the large **bell** in the case on which to strike hours is by Thomas Tompion and dated 1675. Note the toothed wheel (dark coloured) and endless screw for setting up the mainspring. The watch movement at bottom left also has a striking movement and is by Tompion. Edward East made that at top left in 1635. All are in the Ilbert Collection in the British Museum.

copper to tin for large bells is said to be 13 to 4 by weight. Some bells have been cast in steel in Germany and the U.K., but Lord GRIMTHORPE, designer of Big Ben, remarked, 'All that can be said of them is that they make the greatest noise for the least money.' See ALARM, musical BARREL, and CARILLON.

Bell basket top Another name for BASKET TOP, although it is used sometimes to refer to a more exaggerated form, popular for a time at the end of the 17th c.

Bell punch Centre punch (one with a pointed end) which slides in a bell-shaped holder. It is used to mark accurately the centre of the ends of a rod for mounting in a lathe or drilling.

Bell standard Post holding the bell in a clock or watch.

Bell top Top of a clock case that has a convex top with concave sides. See DOUBLE-BASKET TOP, INVERTED BELL TOP.

The **bell top** of a Josiah Emery bracket clock of c1780 with a subsidiary dial for adjusting the rate by the pendulum length at top left and strike/silent dial at top right.

Belmont/Lord Harris Collection Near Faversham, Kent. The finest private collection of clocks and watches by TOMPION, EAST, KNIBB, QUARE, Delander, LEPAUTE, BREGUET, etc.

Belt buckle watch The earliest watches were attached to a belt or hung around the neck. Centuries later belt buckle watches enjoyed a short revival as an impractical novelty.

Bench key Several different sizes of clock or watch keys in one, usually mounted radially. See BIRCH KEY.

Benzine Effective degreasing agent, distilled from petroleum and used for cleaning watch and clock parts. It is considered too dangerously inflammable for general use. Benzene is similar.

Berthoud, Ferdinand (1727–1807) Eminent French maker and horological inventor who probably devised the DETENT ESCAPEMENT independently of FARNSHAW. He wrote a number of books on horology. The British Museum has a Berthoud DUMB REPEATER of c1760 which goes for a month.

Besançon Centre of French watch manufacturing in Franch-Comté on the Daubs river which runs west of the Jura Mountains. Former French centres were Beaucourt and Badeval, locations of the JAPY factories, which became by far the biggest in France. The present watch industry is organised like that of the Swiss. LIP is a prominent maker. See FRENCH HOROLOGICAL INDUSTRY.

Bevel gear To drive a shaft through a right angle, a CONTRATE WHEEL is normally used in clocks and watches, but a bevel gear, which will also drive at other angles, was employed in the SU SUNG CLOCK of c1090, and Leonardo da Vinci sketched one in 1488–9. In recent times the bevel gear is found in earlier KEYLESS WINDING and in the LEADING-OFF WORK of TURRET CLOCKS driving the hands.

Bezel The rim, normally of metal, that retains the glass of a clock or watch.

Bi-metallic balance See CUT BAL-ANCE.

Biedermeier clock Wall or mantel clock in the French Empire style by BLACK FOREST and AUSTRIAN HOROLOGI-CAL INDUSTRY makers from c1860 to 1880, following an earlier style for furniture from 1825 to 1848. A fictional character, Biedermeier, typified the stolid German bourgeoisie.

Big Ben The hour bell of the Palace of Westminster clock, part of the Houses of Parliament, jokingly named after Sir Benjamin Hall, a large man who was Minister of Works, and who made a speech calling for a dignified name for the bell. The name follows a tradition, however, e.g. GREAT TOM. Lord GRIMTHORPE, designer of the clock, drew up a specification for a 14 ton hour bell, the largest ever to be cast in the U.K., but the shape was modified as the architect had not allowed for hauling a large bell up the tower. The first casting, by Warners of Cripplegate, London, in a borrowed foundry at Stockton-on-Tees in 1856, produced a bell that was 2 tons overweight and half a note out, but it was accepted and taken to London by sea. Hung from a frame in Westminster Yard, it gave insufficient sound until a very heavy hammer was used, and that cracked it. About two years later, the Whitechapel foundry in London recast it to a modified shape and the present 13.8 tonne bell resulted. Hour striking began in July 1859, two months after the clock was started, and the quarter bells followed in September. After a few months, the new hour bell cracked and was silenced for three years, during which time hours were sounded on the largest quarter bell. Grimthorpe wanted it recast, but it was given a one-eighth turn and a lighter hammer, and has continued to be struck ever since. If it is ever out of action, Great Tom stands in. The name 'Big Ben' is commonly used for the clock itself today. See WESTMINSTER PALACE CLOCK.

Billodes Name used on Zenith watches specially made for the Turkish market between 1900 and 1914.

Bilston enamel As well as watch cases, hand-painted and fired enamel boxes in the shapes of watches were made from 1760 to 1830 in Bilston, south Staffordshire, England, following the style of the earlier Battersea enamels. Some were real watch cases, without movements but with glasses, hands and false winding mechanisms, and could only be differentiated by examination. Others had painted hands and glass and some were very simple boxes with rings and chain. A fashion for wearing a real watch with a FALSE WATCH continued well past the mid-19th c.

Bim-bam strike Two different notes sounded consecutively at the hour instead of one, or two together. Not to be confused with TING-TANG. Used in some German clocks for the Continental market for some years before the Second World War.

Binnacle clock A clock for ships to show and strike the eight-hour watches. The 'hour' hand circuits the dial in eight hours and the 'minute' hand in 30 minutes. The binnacle is correctly the container for the compass. See SHIP'S BELL CLOCK.

Biological clock Formerly called 'animal clock'. All living things have one or more forms of clock mechanism controlling their behaviour. Man relied on his biological clock long before a mechanical one. About 200BC, the Roman poet, Plautus, wrote, 'In my youth there was only one timekeeper, your belly, which was the truest of all . . . Ever since the city has been filled with sundials, people go famished and thin.' The basic rhythm is circadian (about a day) depending upon the 24-hour cycle of the sun, but every plant and animal has a circadian rhythm exclusive to itself, usually between 23 and 25 hours, which adjusts to the length of the day. In continuous darkness, it will revert to its own rhythm. Flower opening times can make a FLOWERING CLOCK. See also CHEMICAL CLOCK.

Birch key Universal watch KEY with spring-loaded jaws which will grip winding SQUARES of different sizes.

Bird, singing The oldest mechanical singing bird extant is probably the cockerel of c1350 on the first STRASBOURG CATHEDRAL CLOCK, which used to crow (if that is singing). Hero of Alexandria and others made bird songs by steam or compressed air in the 2nd or 3rd c BC. In 1599 Thomas DALLAM took one he made to the Sultan of Turkey. Early in the 18th c, clockwork and musical pin BARRELS were used to operate rows of pipes. In 1750, Pierre JAQUET-DROZ made a bird move its wings, head and beak while singing. Simplified mechanisms later made the bird's song and movements very realistic. Clockwork operates a small pair of bellows and turns profile cams, one of which moves a plunger up and down in the pipe to make the tune. Other cams cause the bird's movements by wires in tubes. Some mechanisms were made small enough to go in snuff boxes, occasionally with a watch as well. Robert Houdin made some mantel clocks with figures and singing birds. See BIRDCAGE CLOCK. Some big cages contain many life-sized birds that sang the correct songs intermittently over a period of about five hours. Very occasionally earlier birds were made with the mechanisms in the bodies. Singing birds are still made in Switzerland. Makers from the 18th c included: Benoit, Geneva; Bontems, Paris; Brugier, Geneva; Fournier, Paris; Frisard, Bienne; Frisard, London; Golay, LeChenit; Gradjean, Le Locle; Griesbaum, Triburg; Humbert Frères, Geneva; INGOLD, Paris and London; Jaquet-Droz P., La Chaux-de-Fonds; Jaquet-Droz, Geneva and Paris; Lami, Geneva; Lemaire, Paris; Leschot, Geneva; Maillardet, Fontaines and London; Metert, Geneva; PINCHBECK, London; Robin, Paris; Rochat, Brassus and Geneva; Schlingoff, Hanau, Slajoulet, Paris; Stauffer, Geneva; Vaucanson, Grenoble and Paris; and Virgneur, Geneva.

Bird box Snuff box, work box or similar, often in precious metal with enamel, having a model bird, or birds, that pop up as the lid is opened. Some birds sing and some are animated, too. See SINGING BIRD.

Bird watch A FORM WATCH first seen in the early 17th c. The DIAL is under the bird's silver body.

Birdcage clock Birdcage with a SINGING BIRD in it and a dial on the bottom, so that the cage had to be hung high. Another version had the cage on top of the clock. Introduced by the Swiss c1780.

Birdcage frame An earlier name for a POSTED FRAME.

Bissextile French for leap year, seen on French PERPETUAL CALENDAR clocks when the four year wheel that allows a February of 29 days is often marked: 1e anné, 2e anné, 3e anné, *bissextile*.

Black Forest clocks Clocks have been made from after the mid-17th c in the once isolated Black Forest (Schwarzwald) area of Baden and Württemberg, in south west Germany, when farmers who carved wooden articles to sell to tourists began making wooden timepieces. The area, almost parallel to the Rhine, became well-established in clockmaking. The first wooden clocks were like iron WATCHMAN'S CLOCKS, with a VERGE and FOLIOT, single hand and stone weight. Crown wheels comprised wooden discs with steel pins near one edge, parallel to the ARBOR (axle). From 1720 to 1730 Christian Wehrle introduced a short pendulum, swinging in front of the dial, called the COW TAIL (*Kuhschwanz*). Glass making being a local industry, glass was used for the bells when hour striking was introduced. They were like wine glasses with ball feet, hung upside down. Metal bells replaced them gradually through the later 18th c. Wire gongs appeared c1830, but were not popular then. The movement was of wooden POSTED FRAME construction, the rear compartment housing either the ALARM or striking mechanism. By c1830, the pendulum was normally suspended inside the case. WHEELS, DIALS, and HANDS were wooden but LANTERN PINIONS had steel pins and the pendulum was hung from a wire loop, not a strip of spring. About 1740, the ANCHOR ESCAPEMENT and LONG PENDULUM came into use, with brass ESCAPE WHEEL from NUREMBERG and elsewhere. From about the mid-18th c, brass escape wheels were cast in the Forest, then bronze bells, and eventually, c1790, wheels. Arbors remained of wood with the brass wheels and steel pivots working in brass bushes in wooden plates. They persisted until c1870, and beech wood plates even longer. The FOLIOT persisted to c1760, although the anchor was introduced c1740 and was common from c1750. The first dials were wooden, and then enamel from c1800. Wood persisted for hands until c1740–50 when brass and pewter superseded it. Striking was controlled by COUNT WHEEL, although occasionally by a local system, WHIZZING WORK (*Surrerwerk*). Rack striking appeared in the later 19th c. After c1760, musical clocks with organ pipes, BELLS or strings, some complicated, became a speciality and were made in large numbers. Some early clocks had AUTOMATA. One of the earliest was Death, swinging a scythe; most common were little men striking the hours and half-hours on bells in an arch above the dial. There were CUCKOO CLOCKS and CUCKOO-QUAIL CLOCKS (see for picture), clocks with models of humans or animals with moving eyes operated by the pendulum and sometimes jaws that dropped in time with the striking. A late example is the TRUMPETER CLOCK. See JOCKELE CLOCK, PICTURE FRAME CLOCK, POSTMAN'S ALARM (picture), SCHOT-TENUHR, SCHILD CLOCK, a very popular export, and SORGUHR CLOCK (picture). Black Forest clocks were sold by the clockmakers themselves, and later by salesmen, wearing traditional knee breeches, white stockings, silk waistcoats and full coats, with packs of clocks on their backs and umbrellas and bundles of pendulums in their hands. Novelty clocks were made representing them and copies were made again after the Second World War. In the past, Black Forest clocks were often wrongly called 'Dutch clocks', because the salesmen called them 'Deutsch'.

A typical **Black Forest** wall clock with a painted dial and pull wind (pull-up weights).

Black Forest horological industry

After 1842, clockmakers were threatened by competition from American factory-made clocks. That and domestic events almost destroyed the industry. Many clockmakers emigrated to America, so the Baden government set up clockmaking schools. Hand methods were abandoned and the first factory was probably that of Eduard Hauser, in Lenzkirch, which in 1856 began making good quality versions of the VIENNA REGULATOR (made elsewhere in Germany from 1854). Erhart JUNGHANS was responsible for the introduction of the American system in Schramberg from about 1864, producing spring-driven 'marine' and MANTEL CLOCKS with BALANCES, as well as weight-driven pendulum clocks. After his death, a son-in-law started the Hamburg Amerikanische Uhrenfabrik (H.A.U.) in 1892, known in the U.K. as H.A.C., with crossed arrows as a trade mark. The Black Forest turned out many cheap reproductions of small and large American SHELF CLOCKS and other styles in the 1880s, French-style mantel clocks and English DIAL CLOCKS, as well as German styles. Frederick Mauthe established a factory in 1870, Thomas Haller one in 1883, and Schlenker and Kienzle theirs in 1883, all in Schwenningen. By the end of the 19th c, only four firms – Junghans and Thomas Haller (who had amalgamated, but later split), H.A.C., Mauthe, and Schlenken and Kienzle – produced half of the Forest's 8.2 million clock output, mainly in American styles. After the First World War, larger groups were formed, the biggest being Junghans, H.A.C., a group of factories in Freiburg–Schlesien, and another of Kienzle and Haller. Mauthe stayed independent. During the Second World War, the entire industry was engaged in fuse and armament making and afterwards brass was so short that zinc plates with brass bushes were used. The making of striking and chiming clocks was restricted to Junghans, Kienzle, and Mauthe. Large numbers of American-style OGEE CLOCKS were made from 1865, but spring- not weight-driven, with a pendulum in front of the movement. A great variety of mantel clocks followed. Black Forest makers competed with the American and French on the British market, where the home industry had refused to modernise, and copied French styles that the British favoured. They also supplied their versions of the VIENNA REGULATOR in large numbers, some now collectors' items, until c1914, when a smaller wall pendulum clock in an oak case supplanted it. From c1920 to 1930, the most popular wooden case was in the shape of Napoleon's hat. The JOKELE CLOCK reappeared, but with spring drive and false weights, as well as many earlier novelty clocks, such as the cuckoo clock, now with brass plates and quarter-hour notes. The 400-DAY CLOCK, was an early factory product. The KITCHEN

PLATE CLOCK and other new designs followed the Second World War with old favourites, but today often having electric or electronic modules.

Black polish Using traditional methods, watch- and clockmakers can produce a polish on steel so high that it looks black. They used a hard steel flat polisher charged with oilstone dust and oil to remove graining, then a similar polisher charged with DIAMANTINE and oil for the final polish.

Blackamoor clock Once popular name for a clock with a case incorporating a black figure but now, of course, an unacceptable name.

Blancpain Jehan Jacques Blancpain made his first complete watch in 1735 and nearly a century later his great-grandson founded a small watch factory and the business passed from father to son for 13 generations. The firm made the prototype of John HARWOOD's first SELF-WINDING WRIST WATCH, then in 1953 a wrist watch waterproofed to 200m down that Jacques Cousteau wore. Problems caused the firm to be taken over twice. Since 1991 it has been producing fine COMPLICATED WATCHES and no QUARTZ WATCHES.

Blind man's clock One by which the time can be read in the dark. Many clocks of the 16th, 17th and even 18th c had TOUCH KNOBS (see for picture) or feeling knobs marking the hours around their open dials.

Blind man's watch One with TOUCH KNOBS at the hours. Later pocket and wrist watches had robust hands, even dials with Braille numbers. Early ones were meant mainly for finding the time in the dark. REPEATERS served the same purpose. See TACT WATCH.

Blinking eyes clock Form of MOVING EYES CLOCK in which the eyes open and close instead of swinging from side to side. The earliest were probably made in AUGSBURG (see picture). Many were made in America from c1856, the earliest being Sambo, which was 41cm (16in)

high, a black figure with a banjo and eyes that moved up and down. Those that followed were Topsy, David Crockett, Owl, and Lion. Several firms made them. They were discontinued in c1875.

Blois enamel The early French watch-making town of Blois had five watchmakers before 1550 and 63 in 1610. The diarist Evelyn visited it in 1644 and wrote, 'The people are so ingenious that, for goldsmiths' work and watches, no place in France afford the like.' The industry became famous for its school of enamellers on gold watch cases from c1630 but declined rapidly from 1660 to 1680. Opaque and transparent enamels were used at a time when the circular case was replacing the oval shape. Enamelled cases were exported to watch-makers in other countries. There is an English watch by Edward EAST in a Blois case in the ASHMOLEAN MUSEUM, Oxford. Favourite themes were flowers, buds and foliage, and religious scenes in delicate colours, sometimes inside and outside the case. Blois cases are now very rare. See TOUTIN.

Bluing Old method of colouring steel to reduce corrosion and improve the appearance of HANDS, CLICKS, RATCHET WHEELS, screw heads, some levers, etc. The part is highly polished, thoroughly degreased and placed in a bluing pan or small trough in some fine dry sand or metal filings and heated slowly over a flame until the desired colour appears on the surface of the steel. Items like screws have to be partly buried in the sand.

Bluestone See MONTGOMERIE STONE and WATER-OF-AYR STONE.

Board of Longitude See BOUNTY TIMEKEEPER.

Bob Weight at the end of a pendulum, usually of lenticular shape in domestic clocks, and cylindrical in regulators and master clocks.

Bob pendulum One with a small pear-shaped bob, used in early pendulum

clocks with VERGE or TIC-TAC escape-ments. To avoid having to cut internal threads, the earliest versions had a core of wood drilled for the threaded pendulum rod to be screwed into it. See ACAN-THUS ENGRAVING for picture.

Body heat watch Early in the 1980s, the Bulova Watch Co. announced a quartz wrist watch powered by heat from the wearer's wrist, the average temperature of which is 37°C (98.6°F), which operated a miniature thermogenerator delivering 8–12 micro watts. The watch consumed 2mw; the rest was stored.

Bolt and joint Until the late 19th c only the front of the watch case could be opened. The movement was hinged in the case by a joint at the pendant side and held by a latch (the bolt) opposite, so that it could be swung out for inspection.

Bolt and shutter Form of MAINTAIN-ING POWER used mainly on quality weight-driven LONGCASE CLOCKS from c1660 to c1760. The winding hole of the GOING TRAIN is covered by a shut-ter. Pulling a cord uncovers the hole and presses a spring-loaded chamfered bolt against a wheel tooth to keep the clock running while being wound.

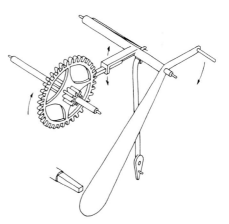

A **bolt and shutter** maintaining power for a longcase clock, which keeps the clock going while being wound.

Bolt spring Curved spring operating the bolt which secures a watch movement in its case.

Bomb clock INDUSTRIAL CLOCK shaped like a bomb stood vertically with a clock in the side.

Bone ash Better alternative to chalk for cleaning watch and clock plates using a soft brush. Made by burning a mutton or lamb bone in a fire until it is white and powdery when cold. Good for gilded surfaces.

Book clock Early table clock of the 16th c with a case of gilt brass and occasionally leather-bound to look like a book. Some were small enough to be regarded as watches. The best known maker was the Bavarian, Hans Kiening.

Book pallets Verge pallets that were a fairly common alternative to simple plates, being of shallow box section with one wide side removed.

Boot A watch regulator has two curb pins to limit the sideways movement of the BALANCE SPRING. Sometimes in Swiss watches, there is a projecting piece at right-angles on the end of one curb pin to prevent the spring from coming out. This is called a 'boot', 'buckle' or 'key'.

Borgel watch case Swiss dustproof pocket watch case manufactured by François Borgel (1856–1912). The movement screwed into the case.

Bornholm clock Danish LONGCASE CLOCK made in the English style from c1750, after a ship load of English longcase clocks on the way to Russia was wrecked on the island of Bornholm. Early cases were painted to imitate lacquer. An EMPIRE STYLE followed and the late ones had arched case tops.

Bottom plate The plate of a watch frame nearest the dial. It was the PILLAR PLATE in old watches. Also called 'dial plate' or 'main plate'. The term is not used for clocks although 'front-plate' is.

Bouchon A brass or bronze bush in a plate acting as a bearing for a PIVOT. Bouchons pressed in clock plates are used to replace worn holes.

Boudoir clock Fashionable name given to any small fancy alarm in the first half of the 20th c.

Boulle marquetry A Frenchman, Charles-André Boulle (1642–1732), developed a form of Italian marquetry to a fine art. Tortoiseshell was inlaid with brass or copper (and vice versa) on flat, curved and even toroidal surfaces. Leaves of shell and brass were glued together and a design cut out with a very fine piercing saw. The parts were unglued and separated into two versions of the original design, one with the metal on a tortoiseshell ground (the 'first part') and the other with a metal ground (the 'counter-

Boulle marquetry in brass and brown tortoiseshell decorates the case of this Louis XIV bracket clock signed Boucheret, Paris. Cleopatra is killing herself on top of the cartouche-shaped case. (*Christie's*)

part'). They were glued on paper and transferred to the prepared clock case carcase. The glue was set with the aid of presses and heat. Finally, the surface was finely sanded and cleaned with lime before final polishing, a laborious task because of the different hardnesses of the materials. Jean Berain (1649–1711) made a number of the intricate scrolling and geometric designs favoured. Very popular in France in the Louis XIV period and throughout the 18th c in France and England. Parts of cases, and particularly furniture, not covered by Boulle were veneered with ebony. Followers of Boulle sometimes coloured or foiled the back of the tortoise-shell and added inlays of mother-of-pearl or horn stained with bright colours.

Boulton, Matthew (1728–1809) Pioneer of the Industrial Revolution, collaborator with James Watt in inventing the steam engine, and founder of the famous ORMOLU, silverware, and Sheffield plate factory in Soho, Birmingham. He also designed and made clocks. Best known was a SIDEREAL CLOCK, the ormolu case illustrating the laws of Nature, which he tried unsuccessfully to sell to Catherine the Great, Empress of Russia, then at a Sotheby's auction in 1772. The clock was in St Petersburg for 11 years, returned to Soho, then disappeared for 200 years until saved for the nation in 1987 by order of Boulton's descendants. See SIGNATURES.

Bounty timekeeper The second time-keeper (K2) made by Larcum Kendall for the Board of Longitude and completed in 1772. It was a simplified and cheaper version of HARRISON'S marine timekeepers and was issued to Captain Bligh of *Bounty*. After the mutiny Bligh was cast adrift with a quadrant and compass, while the chief mutineer, Fletcher Christian, kept the ship's charts and K2. The mutineers returned to Tahiti for their women, then disappeared. In 1808, the American whaler Topaz put into the Pitcairn Islands and found Christian gone. The only survivor was seaman John Adams with about 34 Tahitian women and children. The captain bought K2 from Adams but it was stolen from him. It turned up next in Concepcion, Chile, where a Spanish muleteer acquired it.

When he died it was sold for $50 to a ship's captain who eventually presented it to the United Services Museum. Today it is in the National Maritime Museum, Greenwich.

Bow Cane strung with gut like a bow for arrows, but used with a twist of the gut around the work to be rotated in TURNS, JACOT TOOL, etc. Also made with whalebone or steel with a waxed thread, horsehair or, today, nylon thread. A pole lathe is worked in a similar fashion, but by treadle not by hand.

Bow, watch The ring on a pocket watch for attachment to a latch on a strap, ribbon, chain, ALBERT, etc. The earliest, in the 15th c was soldered to the DRUM WATCH case. In the 16th c the soldered ring was turned through a right angle and a loose ring threaded through it. The loose ring was across the case to take a ribbon hung round the neck. By the mid-17th c, most rings were in the same plane as the dial. Bow-shaped rings were common in the 18th c, but in the 19th they became round again, looped through the pendant knob. With the introduction of a stem in the pendant for KEYLESS WINDING, the bow was pivoted into the pendant.

Bowell, George Bennet (1875–1942) Formed the Silent Electric Clock Co. in London and made the first English electric clocks employing the continental HIPP TOGGLE. They were mainly MASTER CLOCKS with SLAVE DIALS for hospital and other non-domestic uses.

Bowl sundial One shaped as a full bowl. See HEMICYCLIUM.

Box chronometer Marine chronometer in a box, normally with GYMBALS so that it always remains level. Similar chronometers in boxes without gymbals are used for surveying.

Boxing-in Name for the separate trade of fitting a pocket watch into its case (including mounting the keyless work) when watchmaking was a cottage industry.

Boxwood A strip of this, charged with abrasive powder, is used as a hand tool, and a charged disc of it as a lathe tool, e.g. with diamond powder for polishing watch jewels. Parts cleaned with cleaning fluids are often dried in boxwood dust, which does not leave rings.

Brace Addition to the outer end of a MAINSPRING to anchor it to the BARREL. Also called a T-piece because of its shape.

Bracelet, watch Strictly, a metal band for a wrist watch. The first were of precious metal set with gems and many still are. With its popularity, the bracelet became cheaper, being mass-produced of base metals, such as stainless steel and gold plated or rolled gold on gilding metal. Two types are EXPANDING and FLEXIBLE.

Bracket clock Strictly, a clock that stands on a bracket on the wall, but used in the U.K. for a certain style of wooden-cased PENDULUM CLOCK introduced c1660, some of which were supplied with brackets. To start a stopped bracket clock, gently lift and lower one side.

Bras-en-l'air watch Novelty made in Geneva in the first half of the 18th c. Some are repeaters. A female AUTOMATON on the dial raises her arms to point to the hours and minutes each side of her on semi-circular scales. Each arm jumps back on reaching 12 hours or 60 minutes.

A **bras-en-l'air** watch of c1800, the arms showing the time. When they reach the bottom, they jump back. It is a remontoire. (*Die Uhr, Germany*)

A **bracket clock** by Mudge and Dutton on its original bracket, c1770. It is a repeater (see cord on left) and has a break-arch dial and top.

Brass Alloy of copper and zinc intro-duced into clockmaking on the continent in the 16th c and in England c 1600. First used for cases and DIALS, its use was extended to PLATES, then, in the early 17th c, to WHEELS. ARBORS, PINIONS and levers continued to be made of steel. The clockmaker cast his own brass and hardened it by hammering, until rolled brass from the factories was introduced in the first half of the 19th c for factory-made clocks. Factory firms sometimes 'prink' thinner plates with rows of tiny dents to flatten them.

Break arch Shape of square dial with the top broken by an arch, introduced for LONGCASE CLOCKS c1695 by Thomas TOMPION, and c1710 for bracket clocks. Most common from c1725. See BRACKET CLOCK for picture.

Breguet, Abraham-Louis (1747–1823) The most famous watchmaker of all time, born in Neuchâtel, Switzerland, and apprenticed in Versailles, France, at 15. Later worked for F. BERTHOUD and probably visited London, where Louis Recordon later became his agent, and John ARNOLD his friend. Set up in business in Paris c1775, introduced JEWELLING (then an English monopoly) in 1780, developed the SELF-WINDING WATCH (*perpetuelle*) and made it in quantity. During the French Revolution, he returned to Switzerland to work in Neuchâtel and Le Locle, where he invented the TOURBILLON, a perpetual calendar, the RUBY CYLINDER escapement, and some CONSTANT FORCE ESCAPEMENTS, as well as the TACT WATCH (see for picture). In 1795, he returned to Paris where he introduced his relatively low-priced SOUSCRIPTION WATCH (see for picture), and also a SECRET SIGNATURE to identify his works from forgeries. His pieces are superb in both conception and execution. Invented shock resistant bearings with his 'parachute system', and developed the LEVER ESCAPEMENT to the point where little more needed to be done before its universal acceptance. His thinner watch cases changed the entire concept of the pocket watch (see MOON DIAL for picture). He also excelled at making clocks, inventing the remarkable PENDULE SYMPATHIQUE (see for picture), and a few marine chronometers. His firm began as Breguet at the Quai d'Horloge, Paris. In 1870, it was acquired by Edward Brown, an Englishman who had been the foreman, and on Brown's death, passed to his son, then his grandson, Henri Brown. It was later acquired by the fine jewellers, Maison Chaumet. The Breguet brand is still in production in L'Abbaye, Vallée de Joux, making some Breguet type watches.

A **Breguet** watch of typically elegant style. Attached is the Breguet tipsy key. (*Sotheby's*)

Breguet hands The name by which the MOON HANDS that BREGUET used for most of his watches became known.

Breguet key KEY with a RATCHET between the handle and the winding end, permitting it to wind in one direction only. Used for watches, but by other makers mainly for chronometers, where more damage might be done by winding backwards. Also called a 'tipsy key'.

Breguet spring BALANCE SPRING devised by BREGUET with the outer end raised and curved back towards the centre, to make the spring 'breathe' more evenly and improve isochronism. See ISOCHRONOUS and OVERCOIL.

Breguet style A number of makers followed BREGUET'S inspiration and distinctive type, among them Louis Audemars, Henri Robert, Louis-Frederick Perrelet, Charles Mugnier (who copied SOUSCRIPTION WATCHES), Rabi (a pupil of Breguet's), Jean-Aime Jacob, Joseph Winnerl, Adolph-Ferdinand Lange, Charles and Joseph Oudin, Louis Tavernier (who worked for Breguet), Heinrich Kessels, Urban Jurgensen, Achille Benoit, Pierre-Frederic Ingold,

James Ferguson Cole (the 'English Breguet'), and today George Daniels of London.

Bretteluhr Cheap 18th c Austrian 'board clock', with the spring- or weight-driven movement and pendulum in a small box with a long back board that hangs on the wall. Rather like a Dutch STAARTKLOK.

Brevet Seen on French and Swiss watches, means 'patented'.

Brickwork case Longcase with a brickwork pattern on the edges of the plinth, developed in the Liverpool area of Lancashire about the mid-18th c.

Bridge BAR with a support at each end.

Bridge, balance BRIDGE, usually engraved, on the top plate of 18th and 19th c French and some other Continental watches, which holds the balance PIVOT. English watches had BALANCE COCKS.

Briggs rotary clock John C. Briggs of Concord, New Hampshire, invented a ROTARY PENDULUM CLOCK. The Welch Manufacturing Co. made most of them.

Brillié pendulette French electric clock of the early 20th c made by Brillié Frères for domestic use in a FOUR-GLASS CLOCK case. It is based on the electric pendulum clock of Prof. Charles Fèry of 1908, with a specially shaped horseshoe magnet for the pendulum BOB, which enters an electromagnetic coil to drive the clock. A spherical bob above the magnet is merely decorative. Variable contact resistance was minimised by using a special silver chloride cell. Accurate enough to warrant a centre seconds hand. Like the BULLE CLOCK, it has to be level to operate and has levelling feet.

Bristle regulator Forerunner of the BALANCE SPRING. In early watches, oscillation of the BAR BALANCE was limited by a short and stiff pig's bristle, mounted upright on a pivoted arm to act like a spring. Moving the arm altered the permitted arc of the balance to provide

rough timekeeping adjustment. In another form, a longer bristle was mounted horizontally over the balance, which had two vertical pins fixed to it. The pins bounced on the bristle, the effective length of which could be altered to provide crude regulation. When the circular balance was introduced about the mid-16th c, an elbow-shaped lever holding a short upright bristle was mounted within the rim so that the single spoke banked on it. A pointer moving over a rough scale shifted the bristle in- or outwards to adjust timekeeping. Also called 'hog's bristle regulation'. See STACKFREED for picture.

A **bristle regulator**, stiff hog's bristles standing up each side of the single spoke of the balance wheel of early lantern clocks (see right of hammer). This clock is by Nicolas Coxeter, London, (d.1679). Note the single hand with no minute divisions on the dial. If there *are* minute divisions, suspect a fake and if two hands, a conversion.

British and Irish Magnetic Co. Private company for sending telegraphs and time signals. In 1862, together with the District Telegraph Company, it transmitted time signals by a special wire along the South

Eastern Railway from the master clock at the Greenwich Observatory to various places, including the council room of the British Horological Institute in Clerkenwell, London. The receiving instrument was a galvanometer with a needle that was deflected at the hours of 2 and 8 pm, when one of the staff checked the Institute's Reid and Auld regulator.

British horological industry The industry began by the making of large clocks for public display such as the SALISBURY CATHEDRAL CLOCK of 1386 and the HAMPTON COURT CLOCK of 1540. Domestic clockmaking began in England in c1600 with brass LANTERN CLOCKS. Before then most clocks were Continental. See ROYAL CLOCKMAKER. Watchmaking started about the same time. The industry grew rapidly in the 17th c until it dominated those in other countries in the 18th, particularly after the introduction of the PENDULUM. The earliest centre was London, in the Fleet Street area and around, and the trade was controlled by the CLOCKMAKERS COMPANY. It was the first to use watch JEWELS. After London lost its dominance, almost every town in the U.K. eventually had its clockmaker and sometimes watchmaker. These gradually became assemblers, and then retailers with the growth of EMBRYO FACTORIES (see THWAITES AND REED). In the later 18th and early 19th c, CLERKENWELL became the centre for making ENGLISH LEVER watches (see BRITISH HOROLOGICAL INSTITUTE). After Swiss competition in the 1850s virtually eliminated the Clerkenwell trade, which would not change from the FUSEE, centres for batch production of GOING BARREL watches, like the Swiss, were established in LIVERPOOL, PRESCOT and COVENTRY (see ROSKELL and ROTHERHAM AND SONS). Between the two world wars, the German government successfully dumped clocks on the French and U.K. markets to destroy potential fuse-making industries. After the Second World War, the British government re-established the British industry by grants and the provision of factories. SMITHS CLOCKS AND WATCHES became very successful as watch and clock producers, particularly

of alarms. They and several smaller firms had been producing domestic clocks. The last such firm was F.W. Elliott, which moved to Hastings, Sussex. In 1947 a consortium of Smiths Clocks and Watches, INGERSOLL, and the armaments firm, Vickers, set up a factory in Ystradgynlais, Wales, mass-producing low-priced watches. Smiths also developed a jewelled LEVER WATCH of their own design at Cheltenham. There was large production of alarm clocks elsewhere. These enterprises were eventually closed down because of excessive trade union demands, increased competition, and the government policy switch towards electronics.

British Horological Institute Formed in 1858 to develop the science of horology and encourage high craftsmanship. Today it conducts examinations for Fellowship and other diplomas, runs correspondence courses and classes in technical horology, registers qualified repairers, organises exhibitions and advises on national matters. Headquarters are at Upton Hall, Upton, Newark, Nottinghamshire, NG23 5TE, which also houses the ILBERT LIBRARY and a museum. Its monthly *Horological Journal* has been published since September 1858.

British Museum collection In Great Russell Street, London. Received the Fellowes collection of 17th c watches in 1866 and that by C. Octavius Morgan in 1888 which comprised late 16th to 18th c watches, fine European Renaissance clocks, and the monumental Strasbourg clock of 1598 by Habrecht. Before that it had acquired a gilt NEF c1580 attributed to Hans Schlotheim. The collection was greatly augmented by the purchase, through generous donations, of the Courtney A. ILBERT COLLECTION, which was due to be auctioned in 1958. The Museum's horological collections were housed in a purpose-built gallery in 1975 and the reserve collections in the Horological Students' Room, accessible by appointment. The students' specimens duplicate those on permanent display and there is a great range of reference material including clock and watch movements, tools, a comprehensive reference library and relevant journals and ephemera that can be viewed at relatively short notice.

Brocot calendar Popular PERPETUAL CALENDAR, invented by the French maker Achille Brocot, which is a separate mechanism from the clock. Appeared in several versions, one showing the month, day and date, and EQUATION OF TIME by hands, with a phase of the MOON DIAL on one. The whole is operated by one projecting lever, which is moved about midnight by a pin on a 24-hour wheel in the clock. The day of the month wheel has 31 ratchet teeth and is moved one tooth daily by the lever. The same lever advances the seven toothed day of the week wheel. Both wheels are attached to hands to show day and date. JUMPERS make them flick over accurately. The month wheel is geared at 12 to 1 to another hand which turns in a year. Attached to this is a kidney-shaped cam, the edge of which moves a geared sector to turn a hand backwards or forwards and show whether the sundial is fast or slow compared with the clock. The phase of the moon dial is a disc with three blue circles painted on it. As one passes behind a circular aperture of the same size in the dial, the white background represents the phase of the moon. The arrangement is much more accurate than the usual moon dial period of 29½ days. At the end of a month, the day of the month disc is advanced by two teeth in months of 30 days, three in February, and four in leap years. This is effected by a wheel turning once in four years. In the edge are 20 notches representing the number of short months in that period. The depth of the slot determines how far a lever pushing a pin on the date of the month wheel will advance it. The calendar is set by looking at a diary or almanac to find the day of a new or a full moon. The day of the week hand is turned by a knob at the back until the moon is correct, then turned backwards to show the correct day of the week. Then the day of the month is set on that dial, which also sets the month hand. Now the whole calendar can be advanced to the current date by the operating lever.

Brocot escapement PIN-PALLET ANCHOR ESCAPEMENT for clocks invented by Achille Brocot (1817–78). In French clocks, it is usually in front of the dial, a visible escapement. The pallet pins are of D-section and made of steel or cornelian. Often seen on marble mantel clocks (see SUNRISE AND SUNSET DIAL for picture.)

Brocot suspension Suspension for a short PENDULUM devised by Achille Brocot (1817-78). A KEY will lower or raise two CHOPS through which the suspension spring passes and thus adjust the timekeeping. On French clocks, the SQUARE for regulation, by a small key, is normally in the dial above XII.

Broken arch   See BREAK ARCH.

Bronze case Bronze is an alloy of copper and tin that is better than brass for casting and soldering. The more brass-like alloy devised by the brothers Keller, of 90 parts copper, 7 zinc, 2 tin and 1 lead, was also employed in France, where bronze ornaments were introduced on furniture at the end of the 17th c and to clocks in Louis XIV's reign, then for complete cases in the Louis XV period (1723–74). See ORMOLU. Bronze cases were cast in sand from models and finished by sanding, hammering, and engraving, and finally MERCURIC GILDING, all over or partly, the finish being known as ORMOLU. The use of gold for ornamentation was forbidden in France in 1687 and bronzes were finished in gold-coloured varnish. Some bronze cases from 1745, when a tax was applied to works of copper, carry a stamp of a crown over the letter C. In the 19th c many copies of French bronze cases were made in SPELTER, and later by ELECTROTYPE.

Bronze looking-glass clock American SHELF CLOCK made in Connecticut that came into fashion after the PILLAR AND SCROLL CLOCK. Revised by Darrow and Darrow, it had a mirror in the door and stencilled design in a bronze colour along the top of the case. Movement and dial were wooden. Sold from 1828 to c1845.

Brooch watch   See NURSE'S WATCH.

Buchon   A tubular piece of brass used to replace a worn hole in a clock PLATE by BUSHING.

Bulkhead clock   A spring-driven, PLATFORM ESCAPEMENT clock with a bold dial and spade hands, fitted in a strong drum-shaped brass case with a flange at the back to attach to a ship's bulkhead by screws. See SHIP'S BELL CLOCK.

Bulle clock   French electric clock invented by Maurice Favre-Bulle and Prof. Marcel Moulin in 1920 and sold in some thousands. The British Horo-Electric Ltd, were British agents for the Paris makers. In the earliest, made from 1921, a thick column holds the single LECLANCHÉ CELL. The PENDULUM BOB, is a metal bobbin with high resis-

A **Bulle clock** of the 1920s, powered by an electric LeClanché cell in the brass cylinder at the back of the case.

tance winding which passes round a curved bar magnet with consequent poles, i.e. one in the middle and the other at both ends. Near the top of the PENDU-LUM ROD is a silver pin contact, which rocks a pivoted fork to and fro. One side of the fork is also a silver contact, allowing current to flow through the bob. Pendulum amplitude is limited by back e.m.f. (opposing current) which also reduces current consumption. The metal bobbin is split along its length to reduce eddy currents. Very unusual in that the system provides a self-starting pendulum clock. Hands are driven by a PECKING PAWL acting on a CROWN WHEEL. A later version was reduced in height by making the bar magnet U-shaped. Later a cheap version was sold under the brand name of Tempex.

Bullseye glass   Old crown glass was made by blowing a bulb, cutting off the top, and spinning the rest to form a sheet, which was cut into small window panes. The thick centres were sometimes mounted as LENTILLES in the doors of early LONGCASE CLOCK cases.

Bun feet   Feet of bun, i.e. squashed globe, shape, made of wood or metal, used on some BRACKET and MANTEL CLOCKS and on some early LONGCASE CLOCKS of all countries.

Bun finials   Ornaments of flat bun shape on the top of a clock.

Burmann calendar   Mechanism for showing the day of the week and date in the month on concentric rings round the DIAL.

Burnish   To polish metal with a burnisher, a highly polished steel tool.

Bush   A tube used to replace a worn PIVOT hole.

Bushing   Replacing a worn PIVOT hole in a clock or watch PLATE by reaming it out larger and inserting a piece of rod with the correctly sized pivot hole in it (the bush). The bush was once rivetted after first making a chamfer round the hole. Earlier in the century the friction tight bushing tool, a small screw press, was introduced, with a set of reamers and accessories for different sizes of BOUCHON, a friction tight bush.

Butterfly escapement   The HIPP TOGGLE on an electric clock sometimes has attached to it a wire with a paper or mica vane (called a 'butterfly'). The air resistance makes it lag behind the pendulum.

Buttress post   Corner post of an ancient four-post wrought iron POSTED FRAME, such as those formerly known as BIRD-CAGE or BEDPOST clock frames. The post has a profile like the buttress of a Gothic style church, set at 45° to the side frames. On the Continent, architectural features were copied in more detail.

C

Cabinetmaker Early clockmakers learned about metal case making during apprenticeships; when wooden cases became popular after c1600, they were not equipped to make them, so employed cabinetmakers. Many early cases were excellent specimens of furniture. Lesser ones were made by joiners and cheap ones in country districts by carpenters. In the 18th c some cabinetmakers specialised in clock cases, but few names are recorded.

Cabinotier A home workshop, of which there were many in Switzerland in the 19th c where watches were assembled and adjusted.

Cadrature The mechanism immediately beneath a DIAL that makes a REPEATER WATCH or clock sound the time on BELLS or rod GONGS.

Caesium clock See ATOMIC CLOCK.

Calendar The calendar is intimately involved with timekeeping because it fixes the lengths of a month and a year. Before 4200BC, the Egyptians used a year of 12 lunations, then a solar year of 365 days divided into 12 months of 30 days, plus five separate days. Astrologers noted that the point where the star Sirius rose on the horizon moved slowly through the seasons. From this, they calculated a year of 365¼ days. Priests who controlled the lunar calendar resisted reform until c238BC, when Ptolemy III decreed the introduction of a leap year of one extra day every four years, but it was not generally adopted. After the METONIC CYCLE was discovered, the correction became more scientific. The Julian calendar is the basis of the present-day calendar. The arbitrary division of time into weeks, with no natural cycle, is of religious, probably Semitic origin, and was grafted on to the Roman calendar by the Christians in the 4th c. It was adopted by the Christian Council of Nicaea in 325AD. (The notation AD, *Anno Domini*, starting from the birth of Christ in 1AD, was introduced by the Abbot Dionysius in Rome about 497AD. The use of BC came much later.) The seven-day week complicated the fixing of moveable feasts such as EASTER, and GOLDEN NUMBERS and DOMINICAL LETTERS were introduced to aid such calculations. There was still a drift in the calendar and Pope Gregory XIII decreed that in 1582 the ten days between 5 and 14 October were to be omitted. To keep the new calendar from drifting, centennial years (those ending in 00, e.g. 1700) would not be leap years except every 400 years (e.g. 1600, 2000, 2400). Roman Catholic countries adopted the Gregorian calendar, but it was three centuries before the rest of Europe came into line. Its introduction in Britain was in 1752, when September was reduced to 19 days, starting on Tuesday 1st, and so on. There were only 355 days in that year, a leap year. Tales of riots over the 'lost eleven days' are apparently untrue. Russia did not adopt the Gregorian calendar until 1923. Astronomers now use 1 January 1972, not the birth of Christ, as a starting point for their calendar. See ATOMIC TIME, CALENDAR REFORM, DECIMAL TIME.

Calendar aperture The opening in a DIAL, usually square or round, through which the date is shown on a disc marked from 1 to 31 which is stepped forward around midnight.

Calendar clock One showing the date, sometimes the month, and even the day

The clocks left and centre are American **calendar clocks** with the large lower dials indicating the date. (*Hagans Clock Manor Museum, U.S.A.*)

of the week. Most have to be corrected at the end of months of less than 31 days. Self-correcting versions are called ANNUAL and PERPETUAL CALENDARS. A pin on a wheel turning once in 24 hours operates the mechanism around midnight. SHELF CLOCKS with a separate large calendar dial below the main one became popular in the U.S.A. until about 1900, after a patent was filed c1860.

Calendar dial Subsidiary dial showing the date. Some also name the month, and a few the day of the week. Occasionally an 18th c Dutch clock is found indicating the day of the week through a fan-shaped aperture, a few with an engraving of the mythological deity concerned.

Calendar reform The present calendar wastes time and money because of the varying lengths of months, different accounting periods and different days on which festivals occur. The League of Nations proposed a reform and so has the United Nations (UN). Neither has been accepted. The UN World Calendar gives 26 working days in each month and 91 in each quarter. Days of months would always fall on the same dates. This leaves an odd day at the end of the year without a number to be called World Day (or New Year's Day). Leap Year's Day would fall similarly between 30 June and 1 July, and be unnumbered.

Calendar watch Wrist or pocket watch showing the date through an aperture in

the dial. On earlier versions the date is reset by moving the minute hand back and forth across 12 o'clock (midnight). On the earliest, the hands have to be

A lacquered quarter-striking 19th c bracket clock by Ralph Gout with a large unusual **calendar dial** inside the chapter ring and acorn finials on top. The dial plate is painted with flowers. A strike/silent dial is in the arch. (*Christie's*)

twirled through 24 hours to move each date. A separate button is used to move the date on some earlier watches. Mechanical watches are now reset by an intermediate position of the winding button turned one way or the other.

Calendar work   Mechanism operating a CALENDAR; normally a disc with numbers 1 to 31 is advanced by a pin on a wheel turning once in 24 hours. The disc has 31 teeth and is moved one tooth before midnight. Corrections at the end of the months are made by hand. In ANNUAL CALENDARS a wheel turning once a year has the correct number of teeth for the days of each month. The date is shown on a dial covering the whole year. PERPETUAL CALENDARS have a further wheel at the February position which turns every four years to gather an extra tooth in leap years. See BROCOT CALENDAR.

Calibre   (Also spelled 'caliber'). Size and type of a watch movement. Henry SULLY first used the term in c1715. Swiss watch manufacturers divide calibres into general groups: round, shaped, LEPINE, open face, and HUNTER. One calibre has the transmission and RATCHET WHEELS on top of the MOVEMENT, which the French call *calibre-à-vue*.

Calotte   Travelling alarm that folds into a purse or leather case. A *calotte de protection* is the thin metal box used by factories to protect a movement before it is cased up.

Camel clock   Models of camels were a feature of some French EMPIRE CLOCKS after Napoleon's unsuccessful expedition to Egypt (1798–9).

Camera timer   Special QUARTZ (formerly mechanical) CLOCK combined with a special camera used for timing certain sporting events such as horse racing, sprinting, and bicycle racing. The camera has no shutter, but a vertical slit only 0.1mm wide that remains open. The film moves continuously behind the slit at a speed appropriate to the contestants. The camera is trained on the finishing line from a vertical angle of 30° and

Viennese **camel clock** with a verge watch movement that is quarter-repeating on two gongs. (*Christie's*)

photographs everything passing over the line, and only that. A runner's hand in front of him would be photographed before his body and his rear leg. Legs and arms are often distorted because the film speed is regulated according to the speed of the runners' bodies and not the varying speeds of their limbs. The quartz timer is coupled to an optical system in the camera and prints hundredths of a second on the bottom of the film. The time is set off by a starting gate opening, e.g. by competitors breaking a light ray. Quick development enables negatives to be examined in 30 seconds.

Campanus clock   Members of the Campani family such as Petrius Thomas and Joseph are usually associated with NIGHT CLOCKS, but Giuseppe Campanus of Rome (c1650–1715) invented and made a BALL CLOCK. Time was kept by three balls running in turn down inclined grooves in 30 seconds in front of a mirror, powered by three GOING BARRELS with three trains of wheels. It was partially destroyed in 1943 during the bombing of Kassel.

Candle clock   Form of FIRE CLOCK that is also a source of light. A candle has bands marked on it to indicate passing time. Said to have been invented by King Alfred and also by King Alphonso of Castille. Some were used in the Roman Church for timing prayers. Sometimes metal pins were stuck in the grease at hour marks to fall into a bowl and make a noise at each hour. See OIL LAMP CLOCK, INCENSE CLOCK.

Candlestick clock   American mid-19th c style with the clock in a glass dome on top of an imitation candlestick.

Canister case   See DRUM CLOCK.

Cannon clock   See TIME GUN.

Cannon pinion   Tube with a toothed end that carries the minute hand. It is fitted friction tight on the centre wheel, which revolves once an hour. The toothed part drives the MOTION WORK with the hour hand. Pins or cams on the cannon pinion release the striking or chiming trains.

Cannon wheel   Attached to the CANNON PINION.

Canonical hours   Seven periods known as Matins, Prime, Tierce, Sext, Nones, Vespers and Compline, into which early monasteries divided the day to control working and prayer times. Froissart, in his 'Chronicles', refers to canonical hours before 1377 and a.m. and p.m. after that date.

Canopy   Separate hood over a clock, usually one standing on a bracket, as in the case of a Dutch FRIESLAND clock.

Cap   Separate dustproof cover inside a watch case to cover the MOVEMENT, common from about 1750. Superseded by the Borgel screwed-up case and others which were more dustproof, to today's WATER-RESISTANT case. Held in place by a curved steel latch, slid to one side by a knob to release the cap.

Cap jewel   A flat jewel bearing used over a JEWEL hole to avoid dust entering the bearing and/or to act as an END STONE or bearing.

Capstan wind   Hand winding system where four spokes are provided on the weight barrel. See DOVER CASTLE CLOCK for picture. Found on very early iron CHAMBER CLOCKS, and on many TOWER CLOCKS. It was followed by winding with a crank or a winding jack until AUTOMATIC WINDING FOR TURRET CLOCKS was devised.

A **capstan wind** (the four arms on the bottom wheel) on a very early verge clock. Note the primitive bell. Capstan wind was commonly used on old turret clocks.

Captain Scott's watch   A DECK WATCH made by S. SMITH & SONS, recovered from the body of Captain Scott in the Antarctic and used by Dr Fuchs on the trans-Antarctic expedition of 1961. It was stolen at London Airport in 1961.

Capucine clock Distinct form of French LANTERN CLOCK of the late 18th and early 19th c, the name suggesting a hooded monk. Intended for travellers, it is about 30cm (12in) high in brass, and kept in a leather-bound travelling case. At the top is a bell with a handle above it. Successor to the PENDULE D'OFFICIER. Made at first with short pendulum and VERGE and later with BALANCE WHEEL and CYLINDER ESCAPEMENT. Some had ALARMS, striking work and REPEATING WORK. Most ran for eight days, some for 15. See PENDULE DE VOYAGE.

Carcase The bare case of a clock before any mouldings etc have been applied.

Card clock Digital quartz alarm clock the size of a credit card produced by Casio in the late 1980s.

Carillon Tuned set of BELLS hung dead (fixed in position) in a frame. A chime with more than two octaves is a carillon. Normally controlled by a PIN BARREL which operates levers. Some TURRET CLOCKS also have provision for playing by keyboard.

A **carillon clock** by Nicholas Vallin of 1598, which plays different chimes on thirteen bells. It is in the Ilbert Collection in the British Museum.

Carillon barrel MUSICAL BARREL with pins like one for chiming or playing tunes.

Carillon clock Clock incorporating a CARILLON of bells operated by a BARREL pegged to play on the carillon.

A brass **capucine clock** of c1820 with an alarm and an hour and half-hour repeater. (*Galerie Genevoise*)

The International Horological Museum in La Chaux de Fonds has a very unusual one in which the steel tubes of the carillon move in rhythm with the tunes.

Carriage clock In orthodox form, a small rectangular brass clock with bevelled glass panels in the four sides and the top, where there is a handle. The spring-driven MOVEMENT has a horizontal PLATFORM ESCAPEMENT at the top. Some have ALARMS, some strike, including half hours and GRAND SONNERIE, some are REPEATERS. Descendant of the PENDULE D'OF-FICIER although BREGUET produced the first of the orthodox style c1775. First quantity makers were in Saint-Nicholas-d'Aliermont near Dieppe and the Jura region of the Franche-Comté near the Swiss border. Both supplied raw movements to Paris makers and also complete clocks. The biggest was JAPY FRERES in the Jura. The Americans mass-produced them with PIN-PALLET ESCAPEMENTS from c1880 to c1914, the main makers being Ansonia; Seth Thomas, Waterbury

and E.N. Welch. The German BLACK FOREST industry also produced many, one style being the JOKER MUSICAL ALARM. British makers concentrated on higher quality and smaller numbers. The main period was from 1830 to 1930, but they are still made and popular today. See CAPUCINE CLOCK, CHAISE WATCH and SEDAN CLOCK.

Carriage watch Travelling or CHAISE WATCH. Later versions were probably made more for house use. Charles K. Aked has suggested that, since so many coaches were robbed and carriage watches still survive, earlier ones were rarely taken on journeys and later versions were probably made more for house use. The miniature wooden cased bracket clock was a competitor in the early 18th c, then the TRAVELLING CLOCK.

A **carriage watch** by Staples, London, c1790, showing the time, day, date and difference between north and south moon times. It strikes and repeats hours and quarters and plays tunes on bells. Behind 'curtains' at the back is an animated pornographic display. (*Galerie d'Horlogerie Ancienne, Geneva*)

A French-style porcelain sided **carriage clock** by Barwise, London, which strikes and repeats. (*Christie's*)

Cartel clock Variety of wall clock with a round dial and half second pendulum produced by French makers in ornate rococo cases, often asymmetrical and including false brackets. Later ones were neo-classical of lyre and other shapes. Most cases were of gilded wood but the best were ORMOLU. Most early movements were plated with a BROKEN ARCH shape at the bottom where the BARREL was positioned. From the early 19th c DRUM CLOCK movements became more popular.

Cartier Louis-François Cartier took over a Paris workshop in 1847 and became a famous French jeweller who, after 1904, also produced some elegant watches, using AUDEMARS PIGUET, VACHERON CONSTANTIN and JAEGER LE-COULTRE movements. By 1965 all family connections had been severed and in 1981 a Swiss businessman formed Cartier International, later acquiring BAUME AND MERCIER and PIAGET.

Cartouche Tablet or scrolled plate attached to or engraved on a DIAL. Used for the makers' name, etc, and on some French clocks for the hour numerals. Also used on the backs of watch cases by EMBOSSING, CHASING or ENGRAVING.

Carved column clock Misleading name for a form of American SHELF CLOCK made in some numbers in Bristol, Connecticut, in the 1830s, mainly by Ingrahams. The column each side and top were carved by immigrant German carvers.

Carved wooden case Style fashionable from time to time. The Dutch favoured it for many WALL CLOCKS, like the STOELKLOK. Yorkshire and Lancashire makers supplied LONGCASE CLOCKS with carved oak cases from about 1780 to 1810, following the vogue for carved 'Jacobean' furniture. CHIPPENDALE designed some. In the later 18th and 19th c many clock movements imported into Australia from the U.K. were fitted into locally carved long cases.

Caryatid Formal female figure used as a column, as in the Parthenon in Athens. Employed by some clock case makers in

An extraordinary **carved wooden case** of a grandfather clock. (*Major Heathcote Coll.*)

the Louis XIV period and English makers in bracket clocks towards the end of the 18th c.

Case clock The earliest clocks known had no cases, but soon metal panels were used between vertical corner posts to keep out dust, as in the LANTERN CLOCK. Even today TURRET CLOCKS rarely have protective cases. Decorative cases go back four centuries when elaborate engraving, REPOUSSÉ carving on brass or precious metals, and ROCK CRYSTAL were employed. Almost every material available has since been used, from reinforced concrete to cardboard, even paper. The most common materials are wood, brass, ceramics and plastics for domestic clocks. The makers of MOVEMENTS and cases were usually different people in different trades. Case-makers of English clocks were very rarely recorded, but French clock case-makers sometimes signed them and later were obliged by law to do so.

Case, watch The earliest watch cases were ball-shaped (NUREMBERG EGG) and made of gilded brass. Gilded bronze was common in the 16th c. The ball was rapidly superseded by the DRUM shape which became rounded at the edges after about 1575, when octagonal shapes also appeared. Oval shapes were introduced just before 1600. See PURITAN WATCH. There were no glasses and the single hand was read through the pierced decoration of the cover, although ROCK CRYSTAL was sometimes used as a 'glass'. The movement was hinged in the bottom of the case. Many earlier watches were made in triangular, octagonal, star, cross and other shapes. The PAIR CASE increased in popularity after the mid-17th c. See CAP. Considerable decoration was applied from this time, of rock crystal, enamel, chasing, chiselling and REPOUSSÉ. Gold, silver, brass, and PINCHBECK were used and outer pair cases were sometimes of leather. See PINWORK, SHAGREEN or PIQUE. Enamelled watch cases were common over a long period. See ENAMEL, BLOIS, and LIMOGES ENAMEL. Modern wrist watch cases are of gold alloy, stainless steel or (for cheap ones) aluminium alloy and plastics. They are machined from a solid shaped bar, or formed from sheet by press tools by specialist manufacturers. The fine finish on gold is obtained by diamond tools. Such cases are three-piece, two-piece, or one-piece ('opened' by removing the UNBREAKABLE GLASS). See WATERPROOF CASE. Makers of precious metal cases in England and some other countries must have them HALL-MARKED. See COIN WATCH.

Case on case The case of an American Massachusetts SHELF CLOCK looks like a small case standing on a larger one.

Cassiobury clock Four post, iron-framed TURRET CLOCK of c1620 with its original FOLIOT and VERGE ESCAPEMENT formerly at Cassiobury Park, Hertfordshire, and now in the BRITISH MUSEUM.

Castle wheel Special wheel on the winding shaft of a keyless watch with ratchet teeth and one end and ordinary ones at the other.

Cathedral clock Traditionally a special clock in a cathedral such as the STRASBOURG CATHEDRAL CLOCK and the SALISBURY CATHEDRAL CLOCK. Also a clock with a case made in the shape of a cathedral building or the MOVEMENT itself, as with many SKELETON CLOCKS. See GONG also. Other public buildings were also used for inspiration.

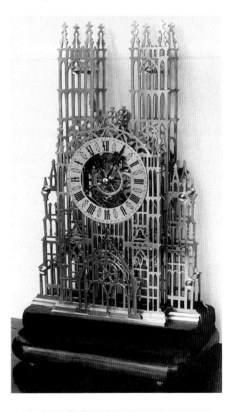

York Minster **cathedral clock** of the 19th c made in a skeleton clock version by J. Smith and Sons, Clerkenwell, London. (*Major Heathcote Coll.*)

Celestial equator   Imaginary extension of the Earth's equator into space. As the Earth's axis is tilted, the celestial equator intersects the path of the sun at opposite points, one being the FIRST POINT OF ARIES. See ARMILLARY SPHERE.

Celestial globe or **sphere**   Transparent globe with the Earth in the middle and the moon, sun and planets driven round it by clockwork. See TERRESTRIAL GLOBE and ASTRONOMICAL CLOCK for pictures.

Celestial poles   The two points at which the Earth's axis when extended cuts into the CELESTIAL SPHERE.

Cell   A power cell for a watch usually has a zinc anode and silver or mercuric oxide cathode. High internal resistance gives a long shelf life with a loss of only 1–2 per cent of power a year.

Centaur clock   French Empire (1800–30) ORMOLU clock bearing the mythical part-horse, part-man figure.

Centre arbor   ARBOR normally in the centre of the movement and carrying the CANNON PINION and minute hand.

Centre of oscillation   Time of swing of a PENDULUM depends on its length (only) from the CENTRE OF SUSPENSION to the centre of oscillation (also called the 'centre of percussion'), which is an imaginary point within the BOB below the centre of gravity. Adding a weight above the bob, or raising the bob, makes the clock go faster, as it raises the centre of oscillation.

Centre of suspension   The theoretical point on which a PENDULUM pivots. It is easy to locate with KNIFE-EDGE SUSPENSION, but difficult with a SUSPENSION SPRING.

Centre pinion   Pinion in a GOING TRAIN driven by the BARREL or FUSEE.

Centre seconds hand   Seconds hand of a watch or clock pivoted to be in the centre of the dial. Also called 'sweep seconds'. One not in the centre is called an off-set seconds hand. See TRAIN.

Centre wheel   The wheel to which the CANNON PINION is attached. It is normally in the centre of the MOVE-MENT.

Ceramic clock   Pottery and porcelain cases came into fashion c1750. Pottery is made from baked clay and porcelain is a hard, translucent and usually white type of pottery. Fine porcelain is hard paste made with kaolin. Soft paste is imitation porcelain and rarer. In the Louis IV period, French makers combined ORMOLU scrolling and foliage with ceramic flowers and figures. In the Empire period and later, they set panels in frames in the ormolu clock case. Later whole cases were made in ceramic. Enamelled plaques for clocks were produced by such well-known factories as Dresden and Meissen in Germany, Sèvres in France, and Wedgwood, Minton and Doulton in England. A popular style was a set of two vases and a clock. As pottery and porcelain shrink on drying and firing, cases could not be made accurately, so clamps are used to hold standard DRUM CLOCK movements.

Chain guard   A pin or block fitted inside a watch MOVEMENT which prevents damage to adjacent parts if the FUSEE CHAIN breaks.

Chain wind   Popular name for a clock or watch with a FUSEE CHAIN drive.

Chaise watch   Very large travelling or CARRIAGE WATCH hung from a hook inside a hooded horse carriage (the chaise) by the pendant, which was usually attached to the watch by a universal joint. It was made from the 17th c, and was still being made well into the 19th. It is like a large pocket watch up to about 18cm (7in) across, normally with an ALARM and usually striking the hours (i.e. a CLOCK-WATCH). Some later ones are PULL REPEATERS. Most are elaborately decorated. A few have music and AUTOMATA for diversion. Possibly the REPEATER made them no longer necessary. See REPOUSSÉ for picture.

Chalk   Traditionally used by clock- and watchmakers to clean the brushes used for cleaning movements. Chalk is abrasive and has to be removed entirely before brushing FIRE GILDED cases.

Chamber clock   Earliest form of domestic clock. Made of iron by blacksmiths or gunsmiths, like the first TOWER CLOCKS. Driven by weights and hung on a wall in the hall which was the centre of the medieval home, so that its striking could be heard all round. Also called a 'house clock' or 'iron clock'. See LANTERN CLOCK.

Chamber master   See SIGNATURES.

Chamfer top   Top of a wooden case with a sloping chamfer, popular in Regency times in the UK.

Champlevé   Style of fired ENAMEL where it fills hollows cut in metal, such as silver. Used occasionally for DIALS of earlier watches so that the dial markings and decoration stand proud. See DIGITAL DISPLAY for picture.

A **champlevé** enamelled French clock of c1860. (*Sotheby's*)

Chandelier clock   Clock set in the bottom of a chandelier in the same way as a BIRDCAGE CLOCK. One or two can still be seen in churches in Denmark and Holland. One in the Royal Palace, Madrid, also has a singing bird.

Chapter ring   The circle on a DIAL bearing the hours and minutes and their divisions. Sometimes called the 'hour circle'.

Chapters   The hour numbers on a DIAL. It particularly applies to the separate enamelled plates for the numerals of some early French clocks.

Chariot   Plate to which a CYLINDER ESCAPEMENT is attached, enabling it to be removed for adjustment.

Chariot clock   French 19th c ORMOLU clock modelled on a miniature two-wheeled horse-drawn chariot with the clock as one wheel.

Chasing   Method of modelling a surface in relief from the top by hammer and punch, used for gold and silver watch cases in the 18th c. The chaser filled the (sometimes already embossed) case with pitch to work on it. The design was often in a CARTOUCHE, usually asymmetrical after the 1730s. About 100 watch case chasers have been identified between c1700 and 1770. See REPOUSSÉ.

Chatelaine hook   Very simple chatelaine, formed like a hook from which to hang a watch, for women to wear at the waist. See CHATELAINE WATCH.

Chatelaine watch   Watch with an ornamental, and often enamelled, chain with trinkets, such as a seal, scissors, thimble case, etc., attached. A true chatelaine was the chain holding the keys, worn by the mistress of the medieval castle. Introduced in the 17th c to England, it became popular again in Victorian times as an ornament. Until c1800 some chatelaines were made for men. They were longer and two were worn at the thighs to cover the sides of the breeches flap. One end held a watch.

A **chatelaine watch**, a repeater by Cabrier in a gem-set case.

Chaton   Metal ring in which an early watch JEWEL was mounted before being fitted into the movement.

Cheeks   The short plank or seat of a longcase clock movement rests on two battens called 'cheeks'. Also short for CYCLOIDAL CHEEKS.

Cheese-head screw   Screw with a cylindrical head.

Chelsea clock   An alternative American name for a SHIP'S BELL CLOCK, as many were made by the Chelsea Clock Co., U.S.A.

Chemical clock   Device using chemical cartridges for timing periods of electric current flow. The current 'eats up' the cartridge, the reduced length showing the time on a scale.

Chenier   Tubing used for watch case hinges.

Cherub clock   French 19th c clock of gilded cast metal showing a cherub with drum sticks and a clock in the form of a side drum.

Cherub spandrel   See SPANDREL and BASKET TOP for pictures.

Chess clock   Special TIMER for chess players with two MOVEMENTS and two DIALS, one showing the accumulating time taken by one player in his moves, and the other the time of the other player. As each player makes a move, he presses a knob on the clock which stops the hands of his dial and starts those of his opponent's dial. At each hour a flag appears. Players are usually allowed 20 moves an hour. Time limits were introduced about 1860 and the clock appeared after then.

Chime   Simple melody on BELLS or GONGS at the quarter or half hours and preceding the hour. The earliest was the TING TANG on two bells. Most are on four bells, but there are others on any number. The WESTMINSTER CHIME is a four-bell; Nôtre Dame in Paris is an eight-bell. The WHITTINGTON CHIME of

Bow Church, London, is on eleven bells, but is sometimes modified so that it can be played on fewer.

Chime/chime silent   Auxiliary dial with a hand that can be turned to switch the chime on or off.

Chime corrector   Many quarter chimes are controlled by a mechanism like LOCKING PLATE STRIKING, which means they could get out of phase. If so, at the third quarter a chime-correcting DETENT comes into action. It holds up chiming of the fourth quarter until the clock hands indicate the full hour; i.e. it can only be unlocked by the longest of the four cams on the CANNON PINION.

Chime selector   Auxiliary DIAL with a hand that can be turned to select one or another chime, usually the WESTMINSTER or WHITTINGTON CHIME.

Chiming clock   Clock that CHIMES. TOWER CLOCKS and antique clocks chime on bells. French, American, and German clocks often had coiled ROD GONGS. The TUBULAR CHIME was introduced in the late 19th c. Modern domestic clocks usually have the WESTMINSTER or modified WHITTINGTON CHIME on rod gongs. The hour note is produced by hitting several straight gongs simultaneously. A turning chime BARREL with pins or cams operates gong hammers to produce the tune. Such clocks have three separate MAINSPRINGS (or driving weights) and TRAINS of wheels for timekeeping, striking, and chiming, and are recognised by the three winding holes in the dial.

Chiming watch   Rare watch which chimes, normally striking on ROD GONGS.

China case   See CERAMIC CLOCK.

Chinese bracket clock   Clock just over 30cm (1ft) high on a wall bracket assembled in China in the 19th c from movements with round enamel dials from English workshops. The cases were made from Chinese teak with elaborate

CHASING and engraving on their DIAL PLATES. A later style was smaller.

Chinese clocks   The Chinese produced the transitional clock between the old inaccurate WATER CLOCK and the mechanical clock. A monk, I-Hsing, probably invented the first ESCAPEMENT in 725AD. The Chinese had no part in the development of the mechanical clock, but the present regime has introduced clock- and watchmaking industries. Many clocks (and watches: see CHINESE DUPLEX) of special design including MUSICAL CLOCKS were made in the 18th and 19th c by English (see COX) and Swiss makers for the Chinese market. Usually the movements were imported from England and the rectangular cases made in China of teak wood. The brass DIAL PLATES were elaborately engraved and had enamelled dials. BACK PLATES were often engraved with the buyer's and seller's names and sometimes with imitation English signatures. Smaller BRACKET CLOCKS were available, sold in gilt cases in a European style with AUTOMATA in the arch over the dial. There are English bracket clocks in Chinese museums today with the makers' names painted out. See PEACOCK CLOCK.

Chinese duplex   Swiss watch with a special kind of DUPLEX ESCAPEMENT made for the Chinese market in the Fleurier district of the Swiss Jura in the mid-19th c. This made the CENTRE SECONDS HAND appear to be DEAD BEAT, and move every second. Such watches were usually made in pairs. The MOVEMENTS have elaborately engraved and scalloped-edged BRIDGES, which can be seen through an inside glass cover.

Chinese match   Joss stick marked with hours like a CANDLE CLOCK.

Chippendale case   Clock case, usually in mahogany, based on the drawings of Thomas Chippendale in his book of furniture designs of 1754. Carving was often a feature.

Chops   Two metal blocks clamping the

top of the pendulum SUSPENSION SPRING to hang it onto the SUSPENSION BRACKET. A single bent strip is used in cheaper clocks. See BROCOT SUSPENSION for sliding chops. The term is also used for clams, the two pieces of soft metal, wood, leather, etc. between vice jaws to avoid damaging work.

Chronograph Timepiece that can be started and stopped to measure short time intervals. Usually a watch for timing only is called a 'TIMER' or 'STOP-WATCH' and one that shows the time of day as well is called a 'chronograph'. Wrist chronographs often have special scales such as a TELEMETER and a TACHOMETER. There are also chronographs for technical and scientific uses. The recording chronograph was invented in 1807 by Thomas Young, who used a revolving drum on which a pencil marked the beginning and end of the time interval. The electromagnetic chronograph was invented by WHEATSTONE, or the younger BREGUET. Washington Observatory was the first to use a chronograph for measuring star transits in 1849. See TRANSIT INSTRUMENT. Chronographs for very short time intervals are often electronic and to confuse the name still more, the makers called them CHRONOMETERS.

A **chronograph** by C.F. Hancock, London, being a keyless lever with centre seconds. Hallmarked 1865. (*Sotheby's*)

Chronographer or **chronopher** Apparatus controlled by a clockwork CONICAL PENDULUM used from 1852 by the Electric Telegraph Co., railway companies and the General Post Office to send TIME SIGNALS from GREENWICH OBSERVATORY by wire to some 1,000 towns and to railway stations. Work at telegraph offices was stopped a few minutes before 10 a.m. and before 1 p.m. to receive the 'time current', which moved the telegraph (galvanometer) needles to one side, then flicked them to the other exactly at the hour. Big Ben's timekeeping was originally checked by chronographer.

Chronometer Originally a name for a METRONOME, but applied to a precision timekeeper in 1714 by Jeremy Thacker. Now a general name for a non-pendulum precision clock or a watch, although purists insist that it means a timepiece with a DETENT ESCAPEMENT, such as the MARINE CHRONOMETER. The Admiralty names high precision LEVER WATCHES 'chronometers'. In Switzerland since 1951, no manufacturer has been allowed to call a watch a 'chronometer' unless it has obtained an official RATING CERTIFICATE from one of the testing bureaux. QUARTZ WATCHES were at first disallowed, but later could be so named.

Chronometer escapement Another name for the DETENT ESCAPEMENT.

Chronometer clock One with a DUPLEX ESCAPEMENT.

Chronoscope Name usually given to a continuously running timepiece for recording short intervals by engaging and disengaging a hand. Invented in 1840 by WHEATSTONE, whose instrument was accurate to $\frac{1}{60}$th of a second. Hipp made one accurate to one thousandth of a second a few years later. Today a QUARTZ CRYSTAL CLOCK, AMMONIA MASER or ATOMIC CLOCK is used. See TIMER, CONICAL PENDULUM.

Chuck Lathe accessory for holding

work to be turned. Some hold the work by screws, others by jaws or wax.

Church clock The oldest clocks in England are usually in the towers of cathedrals and churches, although the earliest were in the body of the church itself. On the Continent many were in separately built towers. In Langford Church, Oxfordshire, is a large VERGE clock still working, with its original stone weights. The SALISBURY CATHEDRAL CLOCK in England, dated 1386, is the oldest in the world still working. In France the ROUEN CLOCK is the earliest existing that struck quarters and the STRASBOURG CATHEDRAL CLOCK was the biggest and most elaborate. Often simply referred to as TOWER CLOCK or TURRET CLOCK.

Circular dial Most clocks with wooden cases had doors with square, rectangular or arched glasses (as with the RELIGIEUSE CLOCK) in their case doors to show the rectangular DIAL PLATE. Before the circular metal bezel door holding the glass became popular, there was a transitional period in about the mid-18th c in the English bracket clock when the case door had a circular glass over the rectangular dial plate.

Circular error To remain accurate regardless of the angle through which it swings (ISOCHRONOUS), a PENDULUM should swing in a CYCLOIDAL CURVE. It actually swings in an arc, and takes longer to swing in a large arc than a small one. The circular error is the loss in time caused by swinging in a circular path. At an arc of $10°$ the loss is about 40 seconds a day. Christiaan HUYGENS discovered this and invented CYCLOIDAL CHEEKS to eliminate it. Precision clock pendulums are designed to swing through a total arc of about $1.5°$ so that the error is negligible. The recoil of an ANCHOR ESCAPEMENT tends to compensate for the circular error. See ESCAPEMENT ERROR.

Circular grain Curved pattern of lines produced on a steel watch part by using one side of an abrasive cup wheel. Brass clock plates were STRAIGHT GRAINED

or matt, having no grain direction. Others were polished. Another method was SPOTTING.

Circular pallets Form of LEVER ESCAPEMENT where the impulse face of each PALLET is equidistant from the pallet ARBOR. Employed mainly in American watches.

Circular pendulum See CONICAL PENDULUM.

Civil time Time related to the rotation of the Earth.

Cleaning Misleading term used for servicing a mechanical watch or clock, which actually involves stripping, examination, cleaning of individual parts by CLEANING MACHINE, reassembling, oiling, readjustment, and regulation by RATE RECORDER. OIL dries out after about two years and forms a soap which may act as a grinding paste with dust. After removal of this and reoiling and greasing, the watch usually has a different RATE. Old craftsmen used to clean clocks and watches by hand, starting with cleaning fluids, then a paste of powdered chalk brushed on and off, and finally finishing the PIVOT holes with PEGWOOD, and the pivots with PITH. Silvered dials are cleaned with cream of tartar (potassium acid bitartrate) which is safe and gives a white colour. Brass is polished traditionally with COOMB or more often today with proprietary brass polish. Steel is polished with CROCUS or rouge. Now cleaning machines are usually employed, especially for watches.

Cleaning fluid Dirty clock and watch parts were cleaned by hand using brushes with soft soap, ammonia in water, petrol, benzine, trichlorethylene, sodium cyanide, carbon tetrachloride, etc. The sale of the last two is now proscribed in several countries. All except the first have to be handled with great care.

Cleaning machine Special automatic machine, in which the main parts are placed in a basket and oscillated in a series of fluids, spun dry and finished in a drying chamber. Ultrasonic cleaners with one chamber are commonly used today. See EPILAME.

Cleopatra's Needle On the Thames Embankment in London, this was once the GNOMON of a huge sundial at the Temple of Heliopolos, a sun-worshipping region of ancient Egypt.

Clepsydra (*Greek*: stealer of time). See WATER CLOCK.

Clerkenwell Traditional home of watch and clock manufacturing in London, although many famous earlier clockmakers, such as TOMPION, GRAHAM and MUDGE were in the Fleet Street area. The peak of Clerkenwell's manufacture of ENGLISH LEVERS was in the first half of the 19th c when 20,000 craftsmen were employed. Much of the watchmakers' MATERIAL came from the PRESCOT area. They formed the BRITISH HOROLOGICAL INSTITUTE in 1858 when threatened by cheaper Swiss imports. In the first half of this century many watch and clock traders joined the diamond dealers in Hatton Garden. In the later 1960s there was still a gold pocket case maker, R.J. Oliver at 25 Spencer Street, using POLE LATHES. The business was founded elsewhere in 1845 by R.O. Oliver and fine gold cases are found with the marks R.O., R.J.O., and A.T.O. Turret clocks were made by THWAITES AND REED in Clerkenwell until recent times. The area was named after the old Clerk's Well used by the Brothers of St John of Jerusalem. Guy Fawkes plotted in the house of the printer Sleep in St John Street; two judges at the trial of King Charles I lived in Clerkenwell Close; Izaak Walton, who wrote 'The Compleat Angler', lived in Clerkenwell until 1661; and Dr Samuel Johnson had a room in St John's Gate where he compiled his famous Dictionary.

Click Traditional horological name for the PAWL and RATCHET mechanism permitting a toothed wheel to turn in only one direction. See RECOILING CLICK.

Clinker electric mains clock Non-SYNCHRONOUS clock, but still needing an alternating mains current, invented c1930 by C.H. Clinker, who worked for British Thompson-Houston, Rugby, whose initials appear on the dial. If an alternating voltage through a coil of wire resonates at the same frequency as the mains (50 Hz in the U.K.), the current rises very rapidly. As an iron armature on the bottom of the cylindrical PENDULUM BOB swings over a coil beneath the base, this happens and the pendulum is given an IMPULSE. The same thing happens when the pendulum swings back again. The pendulum has a very wide arc but the clock uses negligible electricity.

Clipper synchronous clock NOVELTY CLOCK driven from the electric mains, invented by J.S. Thatcher and J.F. Summersgill and sold in the late 1940s by Vitascope Industries of the Isle of Man. The cream-coloured case, of the early brittle plastic Bakelite, was 31cm (12.5in) high with an aperture like a small television set, above a clock without a glass. In the 'screen' a four-masted clipper can be seen tossing in a rough sea, while the background lighting keeps changing. Realistic enough to induce sea sickness. Patented in a number of countries.

Clock From *clokka*, a bell. The first mechanical clock of which there is definite evidence was put up in 1335 on the church of Beata Vergine (now San Gottardo), Milan. It struck a bell at every hour up to 24, having no DIAL, and may have been the first public clock. The first printed illustration of a MOVEMENT was in a book by Girolamo Cardan (inventor of the cardan universal joint) in 1557. Earliest references to 'clok' and 'clocke' are in 1371 and 'clokkemaker' in 1390.

Clock salt Traditional name for the ceremonial SALT CELLAR CLOCK.

Clock star The rotation of the Earth, and therefore time, can be measured more accurately from one or more of the 'fixed stars' than from the Sun, so such stars are called 'clock stars'. See TRANSIT INSTRUMENT, SIDEREAL TIME and TIME DETERMINATION.

Clock-watch Early watch that strikes like a clock. Some also sounded the quarters and others had repeater mechanisms, but with an extra train of wheels that had to be wound separately. Popular in the 17th c until the REPEATER WATCH, which strikes when required to, appeared c1690. See CARRIAGE WATCH and GADROONING for picture.

A 16th c **clock-watch**, i.e. a watch that strikes the hours. It has a stackfeed and verge escapement and is in Basingstoke Museum.

Clock winder Man who winds and looks after clocks, either domestic ones in large houses or TOWER CLOCKS, which often took many hours to wind after climbing hundreds of steps. Most tower clocks now have AUTOMATIC CLOCK WINDING.

Clockmaker Once a maker of clocks and watches who was recognised by his craft guild. Now a clock repairer. Clockmaking requires skills and knowledge different from watchmaking.

Clockmakers' Company The Worshipful Company of Clockmakers is No. 61 in the City of London craft guilds, its Charter having been granted on 22 August 1631. The first Master was David RAMSAY. The most famous past craftsmen were Freemen or Liverymen. Its Charter enabled the Company to enter any premises in and around London City to seize and destroy any faulty work, or work done by someone who had not served his apprenticeship. See APPRENTICE, JOURNEYMAN. Clockmakers outside London normally belonged to blacksmiths' guilds and could become brother clockmakers on setting up in London. Foreigners could only work with Company members, and foreign timepieces and sundials had to be approved before sale. It no longer controls the trade, but is involved in education, apprenticeship, encouraging individual skills, exhibitions, etc. It has a fine library in the Guildhall, London as well as the GUILDHALL MUSEUM COLLECTION, publishes lists of past apprentices (useful for tracing makers), and awards the TOMPION MEDAL. The Livery includes well-known horologists. Address: Room 66/67, 29 Queen Victoria Street, London EC4N 4SE.

Clockwise The mechanical clock was invented in the northern hemisphere where the sun appears to move from east to west and the shadow on a horizontal sundial travels clockwise. That movement was copied by the clock hand moving left to right. If the clock had been invented in the southern hemisphere, and the hand made to follow the sun, it would have moved from right to left or contra-clockwise.

Clockwork globes The development of clockwork in the 16th c to revolve celestial globes was probably the earliest development of precision timekeeping. Makers included E. Baldewein (1575), Jost Burgi (1582) and Roll and Reinhold, who made several from 1584 to 1588. See ARMILLARY SPHERE, GLOBE CLOCK, ORRERY.

Cloisonné enamel One of the earliest forms of enamel after CHAMPLEVE, introduced in the 14th c. Enamel is fired in compartments formed by soldering thin bands of metal on a surface. Used for some early watch cases. See ENAMEL.

Club-footed verge   See DEBAUFRE ESCAPEMENT.

Club-toothed lever escapement   Special shape of ESCAPE WHEEL teeth employed with the LEVER ESCAPE-MENT to increase the length of IMPULSE while decreasing wear.

Coach watch   See CARRIAGE WATCH.

Coaching clock   Wall timekeeper with a large DIAL, used by coaching inns in the 18th c, for the benefit of travellers. Also called a TAVERN CLOCK, and today an ACT OF PARLIAMENT CLOCK.

Cock   A bracket shaped like half a BRIDGE, which usually carries a pivot hole or bearing. Typical is a BALANCE COCK. The object is usually to make the part concerned removable without dismantling anything else. It is usually secured by one screw and has one or more STEADY PINS to locate it exactly. Similarly the PALLET cock holds the pivot hole for one end of the PALLET STAFF in a watch. The bracket that supports the PENDULUM in pendulum clocks is usually called a 'pendulum cock', although it also acts as a bridge for the pallet ARBOR. A cock inside a MOVEMENT is called a POTENCE.

Cockerel clock   The famous STRAS-BOURG CATHEDRAL CLOCK in 1354 had a mechanical cockerel (now in the town's horological museum) which flapped its wings and crowed thrice as in the Bible story. A cockerel appeared centuries later from BLACK FOREST makers as an alternative to the cuckoo in CUCKOO CLOCKS.

Cocktail watch   Fancy watch for women. Usually the UNBREAKABLE GLASS is thick and hemi-cylindrical and called a 'cocktail glass'.

Coffin case   One shaped like a coffin, probably based on one of Chippendale's various designs for longcase clocks.

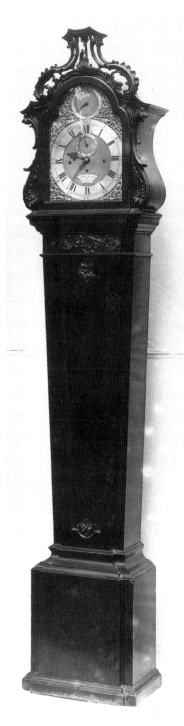

A longcase clock of c1775 by J. Holmes in a **coffin case**.

Coil bound   When a MAINSPRING is wound so tightly that it is held in the wound state by friction. Avoided by STOP WORK or RECOILING CLICK.

Coin watch   Gold coin, usually a Napoleon or a Marie Louise, with an extremely thin mechanical watch movement and dial concealed inside it, made in Switzerland. The coin is hollowed out and hinged, and opened by a hidden catch. Two coins are needed for each watch.

Cole, James Ferguson (1798–1880)   One of the finest makers, known as the English BREGUET, although his own designs and execution were original. It was Coleridge, the poet, who suggested to clockmaker Cole senior that he name his newborn son after the famous James FERGUSON. See RESILIENT ESCAPEMENT.

Collet   Ring-shaped collar to hold something to an ARBOR or shaft, such as the collet soldered on to an arbor of an early clock, and riveted to a toothed wheel. The BALANCE SPRING is attached to its staff by a split collet which grips the staff friction-tight so that it can be rotated to set the ESCAPEMENT in BEAT. The collet for the hands is flat like a washer, instead of cylindrical, and is used with a taper pin to fasten the minute hand to the CENTRE ARBOR. Split chucks used in watchmakers' lathes are often called 'collets' or 'collet chucks'.

Colonial clocks   During the expansion of the British Empire, a number of clockmakers among the emigrants began making clocks locally in the English style as soon as they could obtain suitable materials, particularly in America, and also in Canada, Australia, New Zealand, South Africa and elsewhere.

Colonial Williamsburg   Museum town in Virginia, U.S.A., which managed to acquire the RECORD TOMPION in 1956.

Columbus clock   Souvenir clock made almost entirely of wood, but imitating a 15th c VERGE and FOLIOT iron clock. Probably first made in the BLACK FOREST, Germany, for the Chicago Exhibition of 1892 to commemorate the 400th anniversary of the landing of Columbus and later mass produced in the U.S.A. A picture of Columbus and the date 1492 which are embossed on the wooden dial have misled gullible buyers. Variations have Mozart's picture or a fir tree with the date 1640.

Column clock   Clock with a base like an architectural column, popular in France in the early 18th c. See PILLAR CLOCK.

Column sundial   See ALTITUDE SUNDIAL.

Column wheel   Castle-shaped wheel in a CHRONOGRAPH or timer that, when turned, operates the start, stop and return-to-zero levers.

Comb   The set of reeds tuned to the musical scale in a MUSICAL WATCH or CLOCK.

Compass, watch as a   A watch can be used as a compass because the hour hand turns twice as fast as the Earth rotates in relation to the sun. Point the hour hand at the sun, and a line dividing the angle between this hand and 12 will point south.

The back of a **compass watch**. It is not stated how the magnetism affects the timekeeping.

Compass sundial Type of PORTABLE SUNDIAL similar to a fixed SUNDIAL, which is held or placed in the right direction by use of a compass, usually built in. The shadow of the folding metal or cord GNOMON, then shows SOLAR TIME.

Compass watch Watch with a compass incorporated in the case. Some were COMPASS SUNDIAL watches.

Compensation balance Changes of temperature affect the RATE of a simple balance and spring because the diameter of the balance changes, so that it loses in heat and gains in cold. They also affect the BALANCE SPRING to a much greater extent. See MODULE OF ELASTICITY. About 1765, Pierre LE ROY devised a method of compensation using two thermometers on the balance, the mercury of which expands inwards to compensate. He followed this with a cut balance rim made of strips of brass and steel fastened together. As the brass expands more than the steel in the heat, the ends of the semicircular parts of the rim move in and out with temperature changes to compensate for the expansion of the spokes and, more particularly, for the weakening of the BALANCE SPRING. See BI-METALLIC BALANCE. J. ARNOLD and F. BERTHOUD adopted this, and Thomas EARNSHAW (see for picture) improved it by fusing the two metals together. (Modern thermostats use the same system.) The arms of the balance carry weights to give the right amount of compensation. Chronometer makers had many individual systems, but the principle was the same. Additional compensation was often added for MIDDLE TEMPERATURE ERROR. Compensation balances became normal for all but cheap wrist watches, until the invention of alloys such as NIVAROX and GLUCYDUR made them unnecessary. Millions of cheap mechanical watches were made with useless dummy compensation balances. See ELECTRIC CLOCK for picture.

Compensation curb Attempt at TEMPERATURE COMPENSATION by John Harrison in the mid-18th c. A BI-METALLIC strip effectively shortens the length of the hairspring by moving two CURB PINS along it as temperature rises. As adopted by watchmakers, the bi-metallic strip moved the curb pins closer together to achieve the same result.

Compensation pendulum A PENDULUM that has been compensated for TEMPERATURE ERROR caused by variations in the length of the rod and BOB. In 1721, GRAHAM made a MERCURIAL PENDULUM with a jar of mercury of particular size for its bob. This was followed by Harrison's cheaper version of steel and brass rods, the GRIDIRON PENDULUM ROD. Another combination of metals is zinc and steel (see RIEFLER CLOCK). John ELLICOTT devised a pendulum in 1732 in which the bob was raised or lowered by a brass and steel rod. Pendulum rods were also made of wood as its expansion coefficient is small, although it varies with different woods. Humidity changes the thickness of wood across the grain but not along the length, so the grain is along the length of a pendulum. Woods used include fir and boxwood (dried out and varnished), teak and deal (usually saturated with paraffin wax). Almost perfect compensation, however, was not achieved until GUILLAUME discovered INVAR, a metal alloy that remains the same length at different temperatures.   COMPENSATION PENDULUM rods are made from invar or composite materials. See TEMPERATURE ERROR. See EARNSHAW and ELECTRIC CLOCK for pictures.

Complicated watch Watch with COMPLICATED WORK. The most complicated watch in the world is said to be one, still existing, made by LE ROY in 1896. It has a PERPETUAL CALENDAR giving date, day, month, and year for 100 years, phases and age of the moon, seasons, solstices, equinoxes and EQUATION OF TIME; there is a CHRONOGRAPH with FLY BACK, minute and hour counters, and UP-AND-DOWN DIAL. It will strike GRANDE SONNERIE or ordinarily, or be silent. There is a MINUTE REPEATER on three notes. SIDEREAL gearing operates ASTRONOMICAL CLOCK dials for Paris and Lisbon (where the first owner lived) and LOCAL TIMES are given for 125 of the world's towns. It shows sunrise and sunset (times for Lisbon), and a thermometer, hygrometer, barometer and compass are incorporated. The watch can be regulated without being opened. Only about three manufacturers still make really complicated watches.

Complicated work Any mechanism other than simple time-of-day in a clock or watch, such as ASTRONOMICAL, CHRONOGRAPH and REPEATER. Watches with SELF-WINDING work, simple CALENDAR or ALARM, are not regarded as complicated.

Compound pendulum PENDULUM which has a weight on each end of its rod and is suspended above the centre, on knife edges or the equivalent. It swings

A **compound pendulum** controlling a 20th c clock by E. Dent and Co., London.

very slowly. Several early clockmakers experimented with it. Used in the METRONOME, in a few earlier clocks, and most commonly in SWINGING CLOCKS. If it is horizontal it is an EQUIPOISE PENDULUM.

Compressed air clock See PNEUMATIC CLOCK.

Comtoise or **Comté clock** Alternative name for a MORBIER CLOCK, after the district where the village of Morbier is situated.

Condensation A watch case that is not completely air tight or WATER RESISTANT will 'breathe' as its temperature changes. If it draws in perspiration from the wrist, or other moisture, a drop in temperature will make this condense inside the glass and on the steel parts, causing rust. The air in a water-resistant watch contains so little moisture that sudden chilling can only produce a milky haze on the glass. The cure for mist is to seal the watch in very dry air, although one Swiss maker produced VACUUM-sealed cases to solve the problem.

Cone pivot Strictly, a CONICAL PIVOT has rounded points, but the cruder cone pivot comes to a point.

Congreve clock Rolling-ball clock in which the ball is the timekeeper, invented

A **Congreve clock** of the mid-20th c made by E. Dent and Co., Pall Mall, London.

by William Congreve in 1808. The ball runs down a zigzag track in a sloping metal table (indicating seconds by passing under bridges). The table is tilted the opposite way every half-minute to send the ball back to the other end. Tilting is effected by clockwork, released by the ball striking a catch at each end of the track. Hours and minutes are shown on dials. It has been calculated that the steel ball rolls about 12,500 miles a year.

Conical pendulum   A PENDULUM that swings in a circle was invented by Jost Bodeker in 1587. There is no ESCAPE-MENT. The clockwork turns a horizontal arm which contacts a pin below the pendulum BOB, thus swinging it in a circle. One circular swing equals two swings of a normal pendulum the same length. HUYGENS and HOOKE experimented with it. First used only occasionally, e.g. the QUARTER REPEATER in a long case by Casper Bollerman c1815 in the Manfrankisches Museum, Würzburg. After about 1850, French makers in particular produced them in some numbers and many designs, mostly featuring a cast metal classical woman's figure on top of a marble case, holding the pendulum with a raised arm. The best of them are said to keep time to within 30 sec/week. The most spectacular was 4.15m (13ft 6in) tall and was shown at the Paris Exposition of 1869. E. Farcot, Paris, made the movement, and the statue was by the French sculptor Carrier-Belleuse. In another domestic version, three chains are suspended from the figure's hand, tapering out to hold a clock in a ball-shaped case. A bob hanging on a fine chain (instead of a rod) in the centre of the suspension chains is swung in a circle by a rotating lever on top of the ball case. Some domestic clocks, even alarms, had just a frame to suspend the pendulum. Farcot made one with a band dial in the base that rotated as well as the pendulum. Other French makers were Balliman, Guilmet, Louis Moinet, Antoine Redier and Jean Wagner. The factories of JAPY, MARTI and Vicenti also produced movements. JUNGHANS in Germany made some 'rotaries', with the figure of a child holding a wishbone for the pendulum

suspension, before the First World War. Also used as a speed governor, or CHRONOSCOPE, by Siemens and AIRY for training a telescope on a moving star. It has a large CIRCULAR ERROR. See BRIGG'S ROTARY CLOCK, KROEBER NOISELESS CLOCK, WELCH ROTARY CLOCK.

Conical pivot   Elementary cone-shaped PIVOT used in alarm clocks, cheap watches and meters. Runs in a CUP BEARING and usually employed for the BALANCE only in timekeepers. Wear of these pivots often explains why a worn mechanical alarm will only run dial down.

Constant-force escapement   ESCAPE-MENT for precision clocks in which the force applied to the oscillator at each impulse does not vary. Usually this is achieved by a REMONTOIRE, and the expression is used only when such a device is incorporated. A FUSEE, for example, has the same objective, but does not provide a constant force escapement. On the other hand, a RIEFFLER precision pendulum clock, impulsed by slightly bending the suspension spring, has one, since the suspension spring is 'rewound' at intervals to provide impulse. A GRAVITY ESCAPEMENT is also constant force.

Consular case   Pocket watch case with a double back and a high domed glass.

Contra-enamel   When a sheet of metal is enamelled on one side, the metal will buckle in heat because of differential expansion and may crack the enamel, which could be very costly with coloured decorated work as on watch cases, so in those instances the metal is enamelled inexpensively on the other side as well.

Contrate wheel   Cup-shaped wheel with its teeth cut in the rim of the cup so that they are at right angles to the wheel. Used with a normal PINION (gear) to drive through a right angle. Simple alternative to a BEVEL GEAR. Used with the modern PLATFORM ESCAPEMENT and on some VERGE clocks and watches.

Conversion   As each improvement to timekeeping was invented, such as the

PENDULUM, ANCHOR ESCAPEMENT, HAIRSPRING, LEVER ESCAPEMENT, etc., many older timepieces were converted to incorporate them. This can make it difficult to date antique pieces. As accurate modern timepieces are so plentiful, it is now considered vandalism to convert an antique simply to improve timekeeping. (1) The main conversion of the PULL WIND of hanging (LANTERN) and 30-hour LONGCASE CLOCKS with POSTED FRAMES was from two lines and weights to one line and weight to operate clock and striking. A Huygens ENDLESS ROPE could be applied without mechanical alteration. If the left-hand rear part of an endless rope or chain has to be pulled down for winding the single weight, the clock is early; it has been converted and should have two separate driving weights. (2) The conversion from BALANCE WHEEL to short pendulum (from c1660) required changing the VERGE from vertical to horizontal. Look for signs of apparently useless holes. (3) The conversion from short to long pendulum (from c1670) meant a change from verge to anchor escapement, leaving useless holes. (4) The removal of the alarm leaves unnecessary holes and separate engraving of the dial centre where the setting disc was. (5) Most lantern clocks had one hand originally, so two normally means a conversion. Many other one-hand 30-hour clocks were also converted. It is difficult to tell because original MOTION WORK and the readily available conversion sets were very similar. The DIAL will be a warning if it was not changed also, because it will not have minute markings. However, later two-hand clocks have been converted to one hand to increase the 'antique' value. The presence of minute marks may be an indication. (6) When carriage clocks became fashionable in the 20th c, large numbers of earlier ones with CYLINDER ESCAPEMENT were converted to LEVER ESCAPEMENT to improve their timekeeping. Always look for unnecessary holes in dials, in FALSE PLATES, and in movements. See MARRIAGE.

Coomb Paste for polishing brass parts of a timepiece, made by rubbing together two pieces of bluestone (finely grained WATER OF AYR natural stone) with oil.

Coqueret Steel END PLATE screwed to the BALANCE COCK of a French watch to provide an end bearing for the BALANCE STAFF pivot. Introduced about 1735, it came into general use on the Continent in the third quarter of the century until superseded by English JEWELLING.

Corbel Bracket that projects horizontally to support something else, so any clock wall bracket is a corbel.

Cordless clock American name for a BATTERY CLOCK.

Corinthian pillars A feature of late 17th and much of the 18th c English woodencased clocks was their pillars on at least two corners. Various styles were used, but special clocks usually had the more elaborate Corinthian columns made up of a number of small brass or silver castings.

Corum One of the later Swiss watchmaking firms formed by Gaston Reis in 1955 with his nephew René Bannwart. They specialised in ultra-thin movements as in their COIN WATCHES. All their earlier designs are now collectors' items.

Cottage clock Generic name for any once low-priced popular clock. LONG

A simple **cottage clock** comprising a 19th c verge watch mounted in a plain frame.

CASE CLOCKS with 30-hour PULL-UP wind movements and locally made cases were so called, as were the small wooden MANTEL CLOCKS with VERGE WATCH movements from the 18th to just into the 20th c. They were largely replaced by imported German and American clocks which were cheaper and more varied.

Cothele clock   See VERTICAL FRAME.

Count wheel striking The modern name for what was traditionally called the LOCKING PLATE STRIKING since it counts the strokes of striking. See PILLAR CLOCK, PORK PIE BELL and SALISBURY CATHEDRAL CLOCK for pictures.

Counter-enamel When thin metal is enamelled on one side only, it is liable to warp when fired in the kiln, which is unacceptable for a watch case, so some had a coat of enamel fired on the inside as well as the outside. Often this was white, but it was decorated on more important watches.

Counterpoised pallets LEVER ESCAPEMENT PALLETS that are weighted opposite the pallets to assist POISING or balancing.

Coup perdu escapement A French form of ANCHOR ESCAPEMENT which IMPULSES the swinging PENDULUM in one direction only. The clock ticks but does not tock.

Coventry Important English watchmaking centre with London (CLERKENWELL), LIVERPOOL, and PRESCOT, from about 1860 to 1900. The industry started centuries earlier in London. In 1841, there were 830 watchmakers which swelled to nearly 4,000 in 1861 and had declined to just over 500 in 1901. The industry was organised on cottage lines with as many as 102 branches of the trade, individual craftsmen making and supplying hand-made parts including jewels to finishers for assembly. It was centred on Spon Street, spreading westwards to Spon End and Chapelfields. After the mid-19th c many of the individ-

ual craftsmen had been organised into about 60 primitive factories, the largest of which was Rotherhams in Spon Street, turning out about 9,000 ENGLISH LEVER watches a year. Up to 1860 a big trade was carried on with the U.S.A. RAW MOVEMENTS came from Prescot, and went through the hands of the 'first half doer', the 'escapement doer', the 'finisher', the 'timer' and the 'examiner'. The Coventry trade was killed in the late 19th c by the craftsmen refusing to accept machine finishing methods and only Rotherhams continued until their factory was bombed in the Second World War. Coventry watchmakers were once easily recognised in the street by their top hats, white aprons rolled up to the waist, and eyeglasses hanging round their necks.

Cow's tail WALL CLOCK with a short PENDULUM hanging in front of the dial. This name, or WAG ON THE WALL, remained in use for the later clock with an exposed short pendulum hanging below it. Such BLACK FOREST clocks were made in large numbers in the 18th c and to about the middle of the 19th. They were also produced in Austria and Switzerland.

Cox, James (d.1788) Ingenious London maker of AUTOMATA watches and clocks, large numbers of which were exported to China. Some in Chinese museums which the author saw in 1977 had Cox's name blanked out and were credited to Chinese makers. He made a BAROMETRIC WINDING a feature of a clock; another was wound by opening and closing a door. Cox had a collection of AUTOMATA worth £197,500 in 1773. See PEACOCK CLOCK.

Crank roller lever escapement Type of ENGLISH LEVER for easier manufacture invented by MASSEY in 1814 and used in LIVERPOOL watches. A notch in the end of the lever, like the gap between two gear teeth, engages a tooth on the BALANCE ARBOR to IMPULSE the BALANCE WHEEL.

Crazy dial Popular name for a DIAL on which the numerals (or letters, perhaps of a name) are placed at odd angles.

Creeping record A method of advancing the minute recording hand on the dial of a timer or CHRONOGRAPH. When the timer is started, a finger attached to the CENTRE ARBOR (which holds the seconds hand and rotates once a minute), at each turn of the arbor, advances one tooth of a recording wheel. This turns the minute recording hand, which creeps up to each minute mark before stopping. See INSTANTANEOUS RECORDING.

Crescent hand A MOON HAND.

Cresting Carved wooden strip across the top of a HOOD of an early LONG-CASE CLOCK, introduced in the last quarter of the 17th c. On fine cases it was carried round the sides. The early motif was usually a cherub with scrolling and central ball FINIAL. Few original ones remain as they were only pegged to the case. SWAN'S NECK CRESTING eventually became by far the most popular.

Crocus An oxide of iron used for polishing brass and steel parts. See ROUGE for finer and coarser grades.

Cromwellian clock Misnomer for a LANTERN CLOCK, which was made before and after Cromwell's time.

Cromwell's watch See OLIVER CROMWELL'S WATCH.

Cross-beat escapement A more accurate VERGE ESCAPEMENT having two BALANCE arms swinging across each other on nearly the same centre. Invented by Jobst BURGI about 1586. Also called a 'double balance'.

Crossing The 'spokes' of a clock or watch WHEEL.

Crown wheel ESCAPE WHEEL of a VERGE ESCAPEMENT, which is therefore also called 'crown wheel escapement'. It is a form of CONTRATE WHEEL with pointed teeth, which gives it the appearance of a king's crown. It lasted in clock and watch escapements for 400 years until the ANCHOR ESCAPEMENT made it unnecessary in clocks and the CYLINDER and other escapements

The movement of a Danish clock with **cross-beat** escapement (seen between the two top plates).

ousted it from watches. See HUYGENS and FOLIOT for pictures.

Crucifix clock Clock of the 17th c combined with a model of the Christian crucifixion. Often with figures from the Gospels standing on the base, which enclosed the movement and was pierced when fitted with strike or alarm. A small globe on top of the cross has a band marked with hours which turns against a fixed pointer. Most came from Augsburg.

Crucifix watch CRUCIFORM WATCH with decoration referring to the Christian crucifixion.

Cruciform watch Watch with a case the shape of a cross, i.e. a FORM WATCH, hung from the neck as a pendant. Made in the 17th c mainly in France, but also in Flanders, Switzerland, England and elsewhere. VERGE movement with one hand. The case is of gilt metal (sometimes engraved and pierced), REPOUSSÉ silver, and occasionally of crystal. The dial is of brass or enamel. Many copies were made in 19th c Vienna.

Crutch Connecting member between the ESCAPEMENT of a clock and its PENDULUM, allowing domination by the pendulum. Invented by Christiaan HUYGENS in 1657. The common version is a short descending arm fixed to the end of the PALLET ARBOR outside the back plate. At the bottom end of it is a fork (or slotted piece) at a right angle embracing the pendulum rod. See BACK PLATE for picture. See also ASYMMETRICAL CRUTCH. Another version, has a single pin which fits into a slot in a flat part of the pendulum rod, as favoured by Viennese makers.

Crystal Alternative name for a watch glass or MINERAL GLASS. A plastics substitute is called a 'U/B' (unbreakable) in the trade.

Crystalonic solar watch One of the earliest SOLAR WATCHES. Instead of a power cell needing to be replaced at intervals, a row of solar cells on the DIGITAL dial converts light to electrical energy which is stored in a rechargeable cell to power the QUARTZ CRYSTAL module continuously.

Cuckoo clock Clock in which a wooden cuckoo calls the hours by popping out of a door above the DIAL at the hour, its call being imitated by pipes and air bellows. The earliest extant, c1775, is of wood with a VERGE ESCAPEMENT and PENDULUM in front of the dial. It strikes half hours on a glass bell. The inventor may have been Anton Ketterer, of Schönwald in the Black Forest, some 40 years earlier. Later ones have carved wooden cases like chalets, metal MOVEMENTS, short pendulums, and two metal 'fir cone' weights, and run for 30 hours. Cuckoo clocks are often but quite wrongly supposed to be Swiss in origin and make. See CUCKOO-QUAIL CLOCK.

Cuckoo clock, public The first FLORAL CLOCK with a cuckoo was installed in Edinburgh in 1904 by James Ritchie and Son, using organ diapason pipes and later electronic reproduction. The mechanical cuckoo pops out of a chalet and bows in time with its call.

Cuckoo-quail clock CUCKOO CLOCK which also imitates the sound of the quail at each quarter-hour. Another version has a trumpeter as well as a cuckoo.

A **cuckoo-quail clock** of the mid-19th c from the Black Forest. The second bird sounds the quarters.

Cup bearing Cone-shaped depression (with a convex 'point') in the end of a steel screw or plug, associated with the CONICAL PIVOT of the BALANCE of a 30-hour ALARM clock and cheap mechanical watch. For electric supply and other meters, the cup bearings are often of synthetic ruby.

Cupid ornaments Popular name for the early SPANDRELS with the winged faces of cherubs on bracket clocks, and other clock decorations of complete cherubs in silver or brass.

Cupola top Domed top of a BRACKET or TABLE CLOCK most commonly seen on clocks exported to Turkey and other countries with this type of architecture.

Curb pins or **index pins** To make small changes in the RATE of a watch, the outer end of the HAIRSPRING runs between two closely spaced curb pins on the INDEX so that moving the index in effect alters the length of the hairspring.

Cushion top A shaped top of a LONG-CASE CLOCK HOOD, popular in the 17th c. It has a double curve with a small platform on top, usually with ball or flame FINIALS.

Cut balance Temperature COMPEN-SATION BALANCE with a BI-METALLIC rim. The rim is cut to form two semicircles, each being fastened at one end to the arm of the balance wheel. Larger cut balances which carry weights on the ends of the arms tend to be affected by the weights trying to swing outwards under centrifugal force, so that they are not truly ISOCHRONOUS.

Cut-glass case Some French makers favoured these in the DIRECTOIRE and EMPIRE PERIODS, using DRUM CLOCK movements.

Cuvette Inner hinged and sprung cover of a pocket watch to protect the move-ment from dust. Often engraved with the maker's name and other information. Replaced the earlier removable DUST COVER.

Cycloid suspension spring Triple SUSPENSION SPRING for OBSERVA-TORY CLOCKS that compensates for cycloidal error. The centre spring of the three suspending the PENDULUM buck-les as the pendulum swings. An alternative invention is to suspend the pendulum from a pod with a cycloidal curve that rocks on a fixed flat plate.

Cycloidal curve The arch-shaped curve

made by a point on the rim of a rolling wheel.

Cycloidal cheeks Curved plates each side of the SUSPENSION SPRING of a PENDULUM to make it swing in a cycloid instead of an arc, thus avoiding CIRCULAR ERROR. Invented by HUYGENS. Improved and made adjustable by John HARRISON. See CYCLOID SUSPENSION SPRING.

Cylinder escapement Form of ESCAPE-MENT perfected by George GRAHAM in 1725 with a half-cylinder on the BALANCE STAFF which releases and is IMPULSED by the ESCAPE WHEEL teeth. It replaced the VERGE ESCAPEMENT, and came into its own again in the 19th c for machine-made cheap watches and clocks, until replaced by the PIN LEVER. Also called the 'horizontal escapement'.

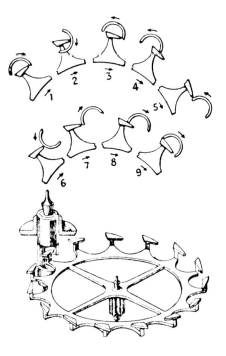

The **cylinder escapement**, in which a part tube forming the axle or staff of the balance wheel is given its recipro-cating motion by the unusual teeth of the escape wheel.

Cylindrical balance spring Early POCK-ET CHRONOMETERS and MARINE CHRONOMETERS have BALANCE

SPRINGS that are helical in shape with in-curved ends (instead of being flat spirals) because makers found these had better RATES. First patented by ARNOLD in 1775. Some Mercer marine chronometers have helical balance springs made of an alloy of the precious metal palladium. There are also marine chronometers with cylindrical QUARTZ SPRINGS. The FLOATING BALANCE (see for picture) is suspended from a helical balance spring, half of which is wound clockwise and half anti-clockwise to prevent the balance from rising and falling. A few pocket watches have also been made with cylindrical MAIN-SPRINGS. See EARNSHAW.

A **cylindrical spring** above a balance wheel. It is made of quartz. (*Société Suisse de Chronometrie*)

D

Daily rate The gain or loss of a time-piece from a certain correct time on one day to the same correct time on the next. The actual RATE may well vary in between.

Damascene In horology, a surface decoration applied to old watch parts, especially winding wheels and BRIDGES. Particularly favoured in the U.S.A. and by the Waltham Watch Co. Produced by abrasive end laps by hand or machine. Some were simply curved lines, others elaborate patterns.

Daniels, George Called the 'greatest living watchmaker', he started as a trade watch repairer in London, and went on to antique clock and watch restoration. He then began making BREGUET-style clocks and watches and developed very special pocket watches of his own, many with TOURBILLON escapements. Believing that the weakness of the LEVER ESCAPEMENT was that it needed lubrication he designed his own and submitted a watch with it to the ROYAL OBSERVATORY, where the chronometer department found it registered zero variation in strict trials. He patented it under the name 'co-axial escapement'. The price of one of his watches can be up to £250,000. His books include one on 'Breguet' and one on 'Watchmaking', and he collects vintage and more recent Bentley and Rolls-Royce cars but frequently rides a motorcycle. He was born in 1926.

Danish clocks The Court of Count William IV in Cassel attracted the celebrated astronomer Tycho Brahe and a school of clockmakers highly skilled in clockwork GLOBES and ASTRONOMICAL CLOCKS. One was Jobst Burgi who invented the CROSS-BEAT ESCAPEMENT. In the Holy Ghost Church, Copenhagen, is a silver and bronze chandelier with a clock in the base originally from the Court. See BORNHOLM CLOCK.

Dart Alternative name for a GUARD PIN.

Date See CALENDAR.

Date aperture Square or round hole in a DIAL through which the date is shown.

Date letter Letter used in a HALL-MARK to indicate the date.

A Viennese **David and Goliath** mantel clock with grande sonnerie and repeater. There are animated figures in the dial with visible motion work. Goliath's eyes move. (*Sotheby's*)

Date line Going westwards round the world, time gets earlier by one hour every 15° of latitude (TIME ZONE), and a day is gained on reaching the starting line. Going eastwards, a day is lost. The place chosen for a change of day is 180° from the Greenwich meridian (0), which fortunately misses most land, and is diverted round what there is, so that date changes are made at sea or in the air.

Date corrector Lever or button to alter the date on a timepiece.

David and Goliath clock One of the many themes of French ORMOLU case makers during the EMPIRE and SECOND EMPIRE periods.

Day-and-night watch One with a DOUBLE TWELVE-HOUR DIAL, half the dial, from 6p.m. to 6a.m., being black to show the night hours, and the other half white.

A silver-cased **day-and-night watch** by Breguet. The subsidiary dial gives the age of the moon. (*Sotheby's*)

Daylight saving The introduction of the Summer Time Act of 1925 putting clocks on in summer to give an extra hour of daylight was almost entirely due to William Willett (d.1915), a London builder. While Britain dallied, Willett's pamphlet on his ideas was translated into French and German and the Germans introduced the system during the First World War from 1914 to 1918 for economy of lighting. The British followed from 1916 to 1918. A sundial memorial to Willett in Petts Wood, Kent, always shows summer time.

De Vick's clock One of the earliest known clocks, made by Henry de Vick, of Paris, for King Charles V of France in 1371. It has been heavily restored and is in the wall on a corner of the Palais de Justice in Paris.

Dead beat Moving in definite jumps without recoiling, as with the seconds hand of a clock with DEAD BEAT ESCAPEMENT, a SLAVE DIAL or an INDEPENDENT SECONDS watch.

Dead-beat escapement More accurate form of ANCHOR ESCAPEMENT that does not RECOIL. Perfected by George GRAHAM (see for picture) in 1719 and still used for REGULATORS and other precision clocks. The PALLETS are often jewelled.

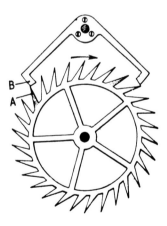

The **dead-beat escapement**, which is more accurate than the recoil escapement. When tooth A drops on the face of pallet B, the pendulum continues to swing to the right, but the pallet does not move the escape wheel backwards.

Dead-beat verge See CLUB FOOTED VERGE.

Dead point   Central (vertical) position in the swing of a PENDULUM.

Deaf piece   Another name for a PULSE PIECE used in certain REPEATERS. When this knob is pressed, blows telling the time can be felt. Useful in the dark as well as for the deaf. See DUMB REPEATER.

Deal case   Actually deal is a plank of sawn fir or pine wood 12ft long by 11in by 2.5in thick in the U.S.A. and 225mm wide and no more than 75mm thick in the U.K. Used loosely for any softwood, particularly for the many locally made LONG CASES in Britain after about 1790, when oak was needed more for building ships to combat Napoleon's attempt to cut off England's trade with India. The softwood case was often finished with a two-tone coat of paint to imitate oak or mahogany. Today, such cases are often stripped of their paint 'graining', then waxed and labelled 'stripped pine'. See PINE.

Death's head watch   See MOMENTO MORI, SKULL WATCH.

Debaufre, Peter (b. Paris 1675; London 1689). French maker and inventor. Patented the first watch JEWEL, with FACIO DE DUILLIER in England, and invented an ESCAPEMENT.

Debaufre escapement   Form of VERGE ESCAPEMENT without the large recoil of the traditional one in which the

CROWN WHEEL is replaced by two escape wheels side by side on the same ARBOR, but out of phase by half a tooth. The teeth alternately IMPULSE, a verge on an arbor in the same plane as the wheels bearing the BALANCE WHEEL. Also known as the 'club-footed verge'. Debaufre invented it before 1704, when Sir Isaac Newton commended it to SULLY, who made a version with a diamond verge. It was virtually forgotten until c1800 when it was taken up almost exclusively by the English watchmaking trade in Ormskirk, Lancashire, and adapted to machine manufacture for middle-priced watches, and known as the 'Ormskirk escapement' and also the 'chaff-cutter' because of its resemblance to a miniature one. Versions were used in French watches by Paul Garnier and others around the mid-19th c. The RACK LEVER followed it.

Decimal time   After the French Revolution, a committee was set up in 1792 to study the most practical way of transforming clocks and watches to decimal time indication. It included famous clockmakers. The revolutionary calendar had months of 30 days divided into three decades of ten days, days divided into ten hours, and each hour divided into 100 minutes. Some decimal clocks and watches were made, but traditional timekeeping survived even revolutionary reforming zeal. As well as the ten decimal hours, decimal timekeepers usually have the 'old' 24-hour dial superimposed. One hand turning once a day shows either

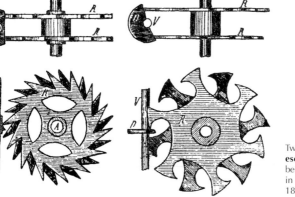

Two versions of the **Debaufre escapement**, that on the left being adopted by English makers in Ormskirk, Lancashire, around 1800.

hour. Another hand shows normal minutes on a 60 scale, and a third shows decimal minutes on a 100 scale. The months were re-named, e.g. November became Brumaire (fog). There are French watches in the Musée d'Art et d'Histoire, Geneva, and one in the Clockmakers' Company collection, Guildhall, London, by two English makers, Richard and Thomas Statter, Liverpool, dated 1862, with hands that move contra-clockwise. X (midnight) is at the bottom of the dial, and V (noon) at the top. Each hour is divided into ten minutes and each minute into 100 seconds, shown by a centre seconds hand. Two more hands show normal hours and minutes on a small normal subsidiary dial. By 1805 nobody used it.

Decimal timer   Modern TIMER with the normal minutes divided into 100 instead of 60 for certain industrial uses where it is more convenient to show elapsed time as, e.g. 4.20m instead of 4m 12s. It is not the same system as revolutionary DECIMAL TIME, although timers were made to show 100 minutes to the hour.

Deck watch   Because a ship's MARINE CHRONOMETER was moved as little as possible to avoid disturbing its RATE, a precision watch (deck watch) was compared with it and used on the deck for observations during NAVIGATION. Early ones have a CHRONOMETER ESCAPEMENT and later ones a LEVER ESCAPEMENT, like a large pocket watch but kept in a special box, and as a result, the deck watch was renamed 'chronometer watch' by the Admiralty, and the HACK WATCH was promoted to deck watch. From about 1850 to 1870, English and Swiss makers produced pocket watches with one dial showing GREENWICH MEAN TIME and the other LOCAL TIME. They had two main purposes, one for sea NAVIGATION, the other to show RAILWAY TIME (GMT) as well as LOCAL SOLAR TIME (sundial time) in the early days of railways before local people got used to GMT.

Declination   The angle of the sun north or south of the Equator, i.e. its latitude. The limits are the Tropic of Cancer 23° 30'

N on 21 June (longest day) in the northern hemisphere and the Tropic of Capricorn 23° 30' S on 22 December (shortest day). Also used for stars.

Defroster time switch   TIME SWITCH driven by a SYNCHRONOUS CLOCK motor that switches off a deep freeze refrigerator for an hour or longer every six hours to keep it defrosted without damaging the contents.

Degree dial   DIAL on a SIDEREAL CLOCK showing degrees of the Earth's rotation instead of time (24 hours = 360°). A clock by TOMPION, designed by John FLAMSTEED, first Astronomer Royal, with such a device, can be seen at the old ROYAL   OBSERVATORY, Greenwich.

Degree plate   Small plate, often made of ivory, marked in degrees and seconds of a degree, and fixed to the back of a clock case behind a pointer on the end of a PENDULUM, to show the amplitude or angle of swing. Used on REGULATORS, TOWER CLOCKS, MASTER CLOCKS and other PRECISION CLOCKS. B-L. VULLIAMY claimed to have invented it, but it was used much earlier by George GRAHAM and John Shelton. Also called a 'beat plate'.

Deity dial   Watch with an aperture in the upper part of the DIAL in which one of seven enamelled figures appears. Pressing the pendant changes the deity for the day. One by Rodet, London, c1700, was shown at a Science Museum exhibition in 1964.

DeLong, Charles E   (b.1871) American originator of the DeLong ESCAPEMENT, a PIN-PALLET with better LOCKING, and a weaker MAINSPRING. Adopted by several manufacturers, but beaten by an increasing demand for thin watches.

Demagnetiser   Workshop tool for reducing the MAGNETISM in an affected watch so that timekeeping is no longer affected. It is a coil of wire in which an alternating current induces a reversing magnetic field. Holding the watch in or over it causes rapid reversals of magnetic polarity in any affected part, the strength of the polarisation being reduced almost to zero as the watch is withdrawn.

Demoiselle clock French provincial longcase style from Calvados and Manche with wider oval middle section in the trunk (like a wide waist) and central glass.

Denison, Edmund Beckett Designer of the Westminster clock. See GRIM-THORPE, Frederick DENT, and BIG BEN.

Dennison, Aaron L (1812–95) Pioneer of machine-made watches in Roxbury, U.S.A., c1850, with E. Howard and D.P. Davis, for which he was named the 'father of American watchmaking'. The Warren Manufacturing Co. followed, then Samuel Curtis and the Boston Watch Co., watches bearing these names in succession. The enterprise moved to Waltham and eventually became the WALTHAM WATCH Co. That struggled on until 1857 when case makers Tracy, Baker and Co. took over and changed the name to theirs, only Dennison staying on as an employee until 1861, when he went to Europe and returned to help set up the Tremont Watch Co. in Boston to make escapements and trains. That failed too and eventually he went to live in England where, in Handsworth, Birmingham, he established a watch case manufacturing factory in 1874 which became the Dennison Watch Case Co. and was a successful business through two generations of his family until it closed in the 1950s. His son Franklin bought the Evan Roberts watch collection and expanded it. It was bequeathed to the Waltham Watch Co. in 1937 and sold by them as the Dennison watch collection at Christie's, London in 1961 for £13,680.

Dent, Frederick (d.1860) Born Ripon, Frederick became the stepson of E.J. Dent (See BIG BEN), and changed his name to Dent. He succeeded to the major part of the Dent business in 1853 including the contract to make the Westminster Palace Clock, or Big Ben. He became a successful businessman, clockmaker to the

Queen, and a drunkard. He died with a fortune of £60,000, £8,000 a year, delirium tremens, and intestate. There followed a squalid legal battle when GRIMTHORPE claimed there was a will in his favour, but he lost the case, his costs, and his reputation.

Depth The amount by which parts intersect each other, such as the depth of WHEEL teeth in PINION teeth.

Depthing tool Formerly called 'depthening tool', introduced in the 18th c for marking out centres for pivot holes. A WHEEL and engaging PINION with their ARBORS are mounted in the tool and adjusted so that they run freely. Points at the end of the tool can then be used for marking the plate with centres for drilling. There are sizes for clock and watch work. The tool is also used for checking the accuracy of wheels and pinions while being made. Clockmakers usually left these curved scribed lines on clock plates. Invaluable for planting a wheel and pinion between two others.

Derby World Clock Modern executive version of the 18th c PICTURE CLOCK made in the 1970s by Ebauches Electroniques, Neuchâtel. The rectangular dial shows a Mercator projection of the world in a single strip. Along the bottom is a moving black and white tape showing 24 hours. The tape is white on black between the hours of 18.00 (6p.m.) and 06.00 (6a.m.) so that the trading hours in any country can be seen at a glance. Time is kept by an ELECTRIC WATCH movement with a FAST BEAT balance. A 1.4v battery powers this and operates a mechanical drive to the hour tape. At opposite ends of the world dial are a normal clock dial and a thermometer.

Desk clock STRUT CLOCK or other small clock with feet to stand on a flat surface introduced in the mid-19th c.

Destroyer clock INDUSTRIAL CLOCK in the form of a destroyer with a clock in one side.

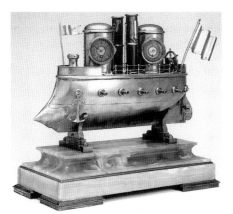

A French industrial automaton **destroyer clock**. The gun turrets and propeller move. The dial on the right is of a barometer. (*Sotheby's*)

Detached escapement One in which the oscillator (pendulum or balance wheel) is entirely or almost entirely free of the mechanism that it controls. English and Swiss LEVER ESCAPEMENTS are detached, but the RACK LEVER is not. The DETENT ESCAPEMENT is detached, so is the FREE PENDULUM. Any escapement with a FRICTION REST is not detached.

Detent The French word *détente* means a trigger and in horology a detent is much the same, being a lever that holds up a spring or weight or locks something. A PAWL or CLICK is one. The term particularly used for the lever associated with the DETENT ESCAPEMENT.

Detent escapement Accurate DETACHED ESCAPEMENT also known as a 'chronometer escapement' since it was developed for the MARINE CHRONOMETER and subsequently used also in precision pocket watches. A tooth of the escape wheel is held up by a DETENT which is moved aside by the BALANCE WHEEL as it swings in one direction only. When this happens, the tooth is released to IMPULSE the balance wheel in the same direction and the next tooth is held up by the detent. On the return swing of the balance, a PASSING SPRING prevents the escape wheel from being unlocked; thus the balance is

impulsed in one direction only. English chronometers generally have SPRING DETENTS and French ones PIVOTED DETENTS. Detent escapements were occasionally used in pendulum clocks, including SKELETON CLOCKS.

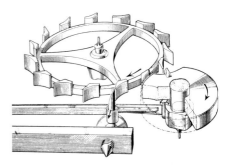

The accurate **detent escapement**, which impulses in one direction only.

Determination of time See TIME DETERMINATION.

Development curve A graph showing the power of a MAINSPRING in relation to the number of turns of winding. Measured on a dynamometer.

Dial Generally a visual display on which the time intervals are indicated by moving hands, or a moving shadow in the case of a sundial. Alternatively, the dial may rotate against a fixed hand, as in an URN CLOCK. Dials of domestic clocks or of watches may be made of iron, brass, copper, zinc-coated mild steel, wood, mineral, card, paper, plastics, ceramic, silver or gold – in fact, almost any material. Public clock dials are made of cast iron, concrete, stone, glass, copper, bronze, aluminium and other materials that will withstand the elements. See ANALOGUE DISPLAY, ASTRONOMICAL CLOCK, AUTOMATON DIAL, AZIMUTH DIAL, BRAILLE DIAL, CALENDAR DIAL, CHRONOGRAPH, CHRONOMETER, COMPASS DIAL, DATE INDICATION, DIGITAL DISPLAY, DISC DIAL, EQUATION DIAL, FLIP-LEAF CLOCK, FLOATING HOUR DIAL, FLOOR CLOCK, FLORAL CLOCK, FRANKLIN CLOCK, GLOBE MOON, GOLDEN NUMBER, JAPANESE

CLOCKS, JUMPING DIAL, MOON DIAL, PLANISPHERE, PULSIMETER, REGULATOR, SHEPHERD'S DIAL, SUBSIDIARY DIAL, TACHYMETER, TELEMETER, TIDAL DIAL, TIMER, UP-AND-DOWN DIAL, VELVET DIAL, WANDERING HOUR DIAL, WORLD TIME DIAL. For styles of dials, see under the type or period of timepiece.

Dial, clock Before c1400, a dial turned against a fixed mark, but a moving hand and fixed dial gradually became almost universal. Some early clocks showed advanced astronomical and calendar indications for special purposes. When they became more available they were simplified for domestic use. English makers favoured brass for dials with separate silvered CHAPTER RINGS. The French enamelled most of theirs, at first in 13 or 12 separate pieces because larger sizes were impossible to enamel. Wooden dials were common on German and early mass-produced American clocks. PAINTED DIALS became almost universal in the later 18th c. Many were attached to a FALSE PLATE.

Dial, degree See DEGREE DIAL.

Dial, diamond In recent years, very small facetted diamonds, up to about 150 per carat, have been glued into watch dial surfaces to cover them completely.

Dial, enamel Enamel was used for watch dials as early as the 16th c. The area of metal that could be covered was initially limited, so the French made clock dials of thirteen separate pieces, twelve for the CHAPTERS and the thirteenth for the centre. See CONTRA-ENAMEL, ENAMEL.

Dial, false See FALSE DIAL.

Dial, painted See PAINTED DIAL.

Dial, paper In the early 19th c, printed paper was used for the dials of many cheap clocks, such as mechanical alarms. Fastened with the glues that were then available, the paper easily peeled off the metal. The problem was solved, it was reported, by dipping the zinc supporting plates into strong, hot washing soda solution, scrubbing them dry, and using onion paste as an adhesive.

Dial, types of Also for indications and markings, see AHAZ, DIAL OF, ANGLE CLOCK, ARCH DIAL, AUXILIARY DIAL, BAND DIAL, BRAS-EN-L'AIR WATCH, BREAK ARCH, CALENDAR, DIAL MARKINGS, DIFFERENTIAL HOUR DIAL, DIGITAL DISPLAY, DOUBLE-DIAL CLOCK, DOUBLE SIX-HOUR DIAL, DOUBLE SUNK DIAL, DOUBLE TWELVE-HOUR DIAL, EQUATION DIAL, EQUATORIAL DIAL, FALSE DIAL, FLIP-LEAF CLOCK, FLOATING HOUR DIAL, FLOOR CLOCK, FLORAL CLOCK, GLOBE MOON, GOLDEN NUMBER, HOUR ANGLE, JAPANESE CLOCKS, JUMP-ING DIAL, JUMPING HOURS, JUMPING SECONDS, LUMINOUS DIAL, LUNAR DIAL, MASONIC CLOCK, MASS DIAL, MERIDIAN DIAL, MONTGOMERY DIAL, MOON DIAL, MOVING ARM WATCH, NIGHT CLOCK, NOON MARK, PAINTED DIAL, PERPETUAL CALENDAR, PILLAR CLOCK Japanese, PLANI-SPHERE, PROJECTION CLOCK, RADIUM DIAL, RECORDING CHRONOGRAPH, REGULATING DIAL, REGULATOR, REVOLVING BAND CLOCK, RISE AND FALL REGU-LATOR, SCRATCH DIAL, SCULLING TIMER, SIDEREAL CLOCK, SIX-HOUR DIAL, SKELETON DIAL, SLAVE DIAL, SMEATON-FRANKLIN DIAL, SOLU-NAR DIAL, STOP WATCH, SUN-AND-MOON-WATCH, TELEMETER, THER-MAL DIAL, TIDAL DIAL, TOUCH KNOBS, TROTTOISE, TRUNK DIAL, UNIVERSAL TIME DIAL, UP-AND-DOWN INDICATOR, VELVET DIAL, WANDERING HOUR DIAL, WORLD TIME DIAL.

Dial, watch Early watch dials were of gilded metal engraved with numerals. Silver or gold were used for very fine watches. BREGUET used both metals ENGINE TURNED. Sometimes the numerals were engraved on a separate silver CHAPTER RING. Occasionally the whole dial was silver. ENAMEL-coated watch dials were introduced in the 16th c, some painted, others CHAMPLEVÉ (inlaid with enamel). Later dials are silvered or gilded brass, with matt, brushed, polished, or other finish. The numerals or BATONS are printed on, embossed, or metal pieces separately made and applied. There can be as many as 40 processes in making a dial. The finest dials are of gold, and for novelty other materials such as gem minerals like malachite, sodalite, tiger-eye, and granite, leather, wood and linen have been employed.

Dial clock Wall or hanging timepiece (i.e. non-striking) with a large round dial for use in offices, schools, halls, and public buildings, based on the ENGLISH DIAL. Later versions were DROP DIALS. All were spring-driven with PENDULUMS and English ones had FUSEES. Later versions were made in large numbers in the 19th and early 20th c in the BLACK FOREST, and in America with GOING BARRELS. Some early German versions have WOODEN MOVEMENTS, or wood and brass ones, with CROWN WHEEL ESCAPEMENTS, but most have ANCHORS like the English and American. The BEZELS are often inlaid with brass or bone. The (normally) white dial has Roman numerals and spade hands.

Dial foot Peg, usually one of four, fixed to the back of a dial for attachment to the MOVEMENT or FALSE PLATE. Older dials usually have taper pins to fasten the feet. Later watch dial feet are notched so that each can be held by a screw in the plate or the EBAUCHE. Cheap watches have copper wire feet that can be bent to hold the dial.

Dial frame Wooden frame around the dial on older clocks, seen when the glazed door is opened. Often called the 'mask'.

Dial markings Early dials were marked by hour divisions only, with 12 Roman or sometimes Arabic numerals. Twenty-four hour dials were often marked I to XII repeated, called a DOUBLE TWELVE-HOUR DIAL. Sometimes Arabic numerals also indicated 1 to 12. Some

early clocks had a small separate quarter-hour dial. Later, to show quarter hours, four divisions were marked between each hour numeral, and also an ornament included for half hours. When minutes were introduced, there was occasionally a separate dial and hand, but numbering from 1 to 60 (1 to 5 between the chapters) with a separate concentric minute hand became orthodox. The HALF-QUARTERS are also marked on some early minute rings. Seconds dials and hands are usually separate on clocks and early watches but concentric ones (centre seconds) were occasionally used on clocks and became standard on watches after the mid-20th c. Individual dials and hands for hours, minutes and seconds were retained for most precision clocks, with the exception of marine chronometers. A clock with one hand and minute markings on the chapter ring, or one with two hands and no minute markings, indicates a conversion.

Dial painter Clock and watch dials have been hand painted from the very earliest times. A number of medieval astronomical clocks exist with elaborately painted wooden dials and 15th and 16th c European iron chamber clocks have painted numerals. Probably in the 18th c, a clear distinction appeared between the dial painter, who was responsible for the dial itself, and the dial decorator, who added designs in the centre and corners, because they used different black paints. In England in the later 19th c, there were at least 80 concerns supplying decorated dials mainly to the English and North American clockmakers. For metal (usually iron) dials, they used a white ground of paint which was varnished after the design was completed. Dutch makers produced very elaborate painted dials, some without the usual white ground. BLACK FOREST makers used painted wooden dials from the earlier 18th c and from about 1780, a DIAL TURNER supplied the shaped wood to the dial painter, who sealed it with size and chalk and smoothed this with TRIPOLI POWDER and pumice, before painting on the ground with white lead paint. The dial painter was also essential to earlier ENAMELLED DIALS used mainly for watches, but also for French and other clocks. See BLOIS, GENEVA, and LIMOGE. Some dial painters used the EGLOMI reverse-painted glass technique, either in a simple way like the numerals of some POSTMAN'S ALARMS, or a more decorative one as in Black Forest PICTURE FRAME CLOCKS and American SHELF CLOCKS.

Dial plate The PLATE of a movement behind the dial. It is the front plate, or is separate and attached to the front plate, in a clock. In a watch it is the bottom plate, being the top plate of a FULL PLATE watch movement at the back. Confusing!

Dial printer Dial transfer press, used for printing the numerals, batons, brand name, etc. (but not the circles and divisions) in slight relief on watch and other small dials. A plate engraved with these markings holds ink, which is transferred to the dial by a gelatine pad on a swinging arm. The process was semi-automatic in a factory, but hand operated for restoration and adding information.

Dial repair The traditional way of filling fine cracks in a white dial was to use a 'putty' made of equal parts of pure white wax and zinc white melted together and used cold.

Dial sink Small cut in the bottom plate of a clock. This compensates for the slight thickening of the enamel or metal at the bottom of a dial foot.

Dial turner BLACK FOREST craftsmen who made wooden dials with convex CHAPTER RINGS for the DIAL PAINTER. A circle of wood was glued with curdled milk and chalk to the wooden DIAL PLATE and turned on a rudimentary lathe.

Dial washer Thin dished or curved washer acting like a spring between the dial and HOUR WHEEL to keep this against the CANNON PINION and engaged with the MINUTE WHEEL.

Dialling Mathematical laying out of a sundial, an art in Greek and Roman days which became a recreation in Europe in the 18th and 19th c. Earlier called 'gnomonics'.

Diamantine Fine white powder much used by watchmakers for polishing, to give a BLACK POLISH to steel in particular. Not diamond powder, as the name suggests, but calcined aluminium oxide (ruby or sapphire powder). Several degrees of fineness are available. See ABRASIVE.

Diamond end stone A rose-cut diamond used as one end bearing of a pocket watch BALANCE WHEEL, particularly by English makers from c1725 through the century. The lower PIVOT of the BALANCE STAFF rests on the flat side of the rose diamond when the watch is dial up. The diamond is set in the decorated BALANCE COCK. See JEWEL.

Diamond watch Any watch of which the case and/or bracelet is set with diamonds for decoration.

Diana clock A swinging MYSTERY CLOCK made by Junghans of Schramberg until about 1935. The small statue of Diana holds a short bar with two jewelled cup bearings in which rest the two PIVOTS of a COMPOUND PENDULUM. The top weight of a pendulum is a clock and the bottom one a ball. The actual pendulum of the clock is a very short BOB PENDULUM behind the MOVEMENT, which keeps the whole arrangement swinging by sympathetic movement. Regulation is by a RATING NUT below the ball at the bottom, but it works the opposite way from a normal nut, i.e. raising the ball slows the clock. An elephant replaced the woman in some models.

Differential hour dial Very rare form of clock dial made c1700. A single hand turns to indicate minutes by its tip on the main dial. A smaller dial marked in hours rotates behind it, so that the lower part of the hand indicates the hour on the rotating dial. The hour dial must rotate one twelfth of a full circle in an hour.

Digital display Indication of the time in figures. Digital displays for timepieces have reappeared in fashion several times every century since the 16th. Until the 1970s indications were mechanical; now most are electronic. See TICKET CLOCK.

A **digital display** on a gold and champlevé watch, a hunter by Jean François Bautte of Geneva, c1830. (*Sotheby's*)

Dijon clock A record of the Montpellier Town Council in 1410 shows they were so dissatisfied with their human clock keeper that they ordered a mechanical one from Dijon. The Gothic Church of Nôtre Dame in Dijon, currently has JACKS which were imported in the 15th c from Courtrai in Belgium.

Dipleidoscope Instrument for determining APPARENT SOLAR TIME by the coincidence of two images of the Sun, patented by J.M. Bloxham in 1843 and assigned to E. Dent and Co.

Diptych dial PORTABLE SUNDIAL comprising two leaves, usually of ivory, hinged together and a cord at an angle between them for the GNOMON. They show EQUAL HOURS in several latitudes by altering the angle of the cord. They also have pin gnomons to show ITALIAN HOURS and BABYLONIAN HOURS. Also called a TABLET DIAL. See also COMPASS SUNDIAL.

Direction hand Some wrist CHRONO-GRAPHS of the mid-20th c were fitted with an extra short hand, bearing the letter 'N', which pointed to the north when the watch hour hand was pointed to the Sun. See COMPASS, WATCH AS A.

Directoire clock French style of clock from 1795–9 before and after the Revolution showing the transition from various restrained neo-classical designs of the LOUIS XIV period to the heavy Roman styles of the EMPIRE period. Includes clocks made to show DECIMAL TIME.

Distribution of time See TIME DISTRIBUTION.

Ditisheim balance BALANCE with a solid rim and small separate bi-metallic blades for TEMPERATURE COMPENSATION, invented by DITISHEIM in 1920 for use with an ELINVAR BALANCE SPRING. Timekeeping was greatly improved by the elimination of the centrifugal problems of the CUT BALANCE and magnetic troubles of the steel balance spring.

Ditisheim, Paul (1865–1945) Eminent French watchmaker who made the smallest watch in the world at the time for the Sultan of Morocco, then turned to the manufacture of medium-priced watches. Collaborated with GUILLAUME in applying the alloys INVAR and ELIN-VAR to timepieces to reduce TEMPERATURE ERROR and also devised the DITISHEIM BALANCE that was responsible for many precision time-keeping records. Developed modern watch OIL and EPILAME in co-operation with Dr Woog.

Diver's watch Watch with a tough water-resistant case for the use of divers and underwater swimmers. The dial is relatively large with luminous hands and numerals. There is usually ELAPSED TIME indication.

Divided lift An ESCAPE WHEEL with pointed teeth depends on the angle of the PALLET ends for the LIFT (i.e. to move the lever). If the tips of the teeth are made flat and angled (club-footed) like the pallets, the lift is divided between the teeth and the pallets and also lasts longer. Introduced by Jean-Moyse Pouzait of Geneva in 1786. Adopted and improved by BREGUET after 1800 and popularised by the Swiss.

Dividing plate Before the mid-17th c, when filing wheel teeth, the circular wheel blank was first marked as accurately as possible. The dividing plate was devised for this purpose. A circular plate, with several series of holes representing different numbers of teeth around it, is pivoted in a frame with an arm, the end of which holds a pin that can be dropped into each hole in turn to lock the plate. The blank to be marked out is attached to the dividing plate and marked by a scriber also attached to the frame. About 1650, the scriber was replaced by a cutting tool and the dividing plate became a dividing engine or WHEEL-CUTTING ENGINE.

Doctor's clock Earlier name for a desk clock because doctors were supposed to find most use for them.

Doctor's watch Pocket watch of the 17th c and onwards with a seconds hand that could be started and stopped at will to time a patient's pulse.

Dog screw Screw with part of its head cut off, or an eccentric head, used as a fastener for fixing watch MOVEMENTS into cases without removing the screws.

Dollar watch In America at the end of the 19th c, a marketing man, Robert INGERSOLL, sold many attractive articles for a dollar each, including a camera and a printing outfit. In 1892, he produced his first watch for only a dollar as 'the watch that made the dollar famous'. Selling in England for five shillings, it was called the 'crown watch'. The so-called dollar watch became so popular in the U.S.A. that in the 1920s about seven million were being made yearly, mainly by Westclox and Ingersoll, compared with about one million jewelled watches.

Doll's head clock See TÊTE DE POUPÉE.

Dolphin fret Common decoration on the top of a brass LANTERN CLOCK and occasionally in the arch of a LONGCASE CLOCK. A grotesque dolphin was a favourite baroque decoration, e.g. on furniture legs.

A typical **dolphin fret** on top of a small lantern clock of c1700 by Ignatius Huggeford. The bell on top has been removed. The dark centre disc sets the alarm. (*Sotheby's*)

Dome For a key-wound pocket watch there is usually an inside back cover with a winding hole, the dome, intended to keep out dust when the back is open.

Domestic clock Any type of clock for the home. The earliest was the HOUSE CLOCK.

Dominical letter Old Babylonian method of reckoning days. The first seven days of January were given the first letters of the alphabet, that falling on the Sunday being the dominical letter. Leap years have two letters. Used by the church with the GOLDEN NUMBER to fix Easter. Some early clocks showed the dominical letter.

Dondi's clock An early astronomical clock of which complete constructional details are known. Built originally in 1348–64 to the design of Giovanni de

Dondi, professor of astronomy, logic, and medicine at Padua University, Italy, it was believed to have been in the Convent of San Yuste in Spain when it was burned down during the Peninsular War of 1809. It had a 24-hour dial with fixed hand and elaborate indications, including the first continuous recording of minutes, and dials showing sunrise and sunset, day of the month, annual calendar, conversion of MEAN TIME to SIDEREAL TIME, trajectories of planets, etc. The Latin description and plans survived. An exact model was first made from these in 1960 by Peter Hayward, then of Thwaites and Reed, London, for the Smithsonian Institution, U.S.A., under the instruction of H. Alan Lloyd. In subsequent years, more were built and are in Zurich, London, Washington, New York, Rockford, Illinois and Bury St Edmunds, Suffolk. An independent version in Milan was constructed by Luigi Pippi of Italy. Another was completed by the French maker Paul Pouvillon in 1939 and in 1995 one was set going in Zurich, commissioned by the watch company of Türler. It was designed by Dr Ludwig Oechslin and completed after nine years in the Jörg Spöring. The gear ratio of one train is near 10^{12} to 1.

Door-frame clock See VERTICAL FRAME.

Dormant jewel False name invented by advertising men to make useless watch jewels mounted or stuck inside watch cases seem important to gullible buyers. See JEWELLING, FALSE.

Double balance Early name for the CROSS-BEAT ESCAPEMENT. Also a COMPENSATION BALANCE with two S-shaped bi-metallic strips, moving weighted rods inwards or outwards.

Double barrel When English makers eventually adopted the GOING BARREL, they replaced the FUSEE by a dummy barrel acting as a transmission wheel, thus preserving contra-clockwise winding. The dummy barrel tended to reduce the damage caused by MAINSPRING breakage.

Double-basket top Decoratively pierced metal top of a BRACKET CLOCK like one inverted basket on top of another, introduced c1680.

This bracket clock by James Markwick of c1700 has a **double basket top**. (*Sotheby's*)

Double-bottom case Most FULL-PLATE watches are in one-piece cases. The movement is on a hinge or joint so that it can be swung out by releasing a latch. The dial fills the case opening. When this case is held in another, with a hinged BEZEL round the glass, the full case has a double bottom. See PAIR CASE.

Double-dial clock Clock with two dials, sometimes at right angles to each other, as in the passenger hall at Charing Cross railway station, or more often parallel to each other facing in opposite directions, enabling one mechanism to show the time in, say, the station booking office and the station platform. See DOUBLE TIME RAILROAD REGULATOR.

Double escape wheel   Charles Fastoldt (1818–98) of Rome, then New York, made a form of LEVER ESCAPEMENT with concentric ESCAPE WHEELS, one smaller than the other. As it IMPULSED in only one direction, he called it a CHRONOMETER ESCAPEMENT. Other escapes had double escape wheels, including the DEBAUFRE or Ormskirk.

Double lunette   Thick domed pocket watch glass.

Double pendulum   PENDULUMS geared together to swing in opposite directions by Jean-Baptiste Dutertre in 1726 in an attempt to solve the problem of clocks at sea. See CHRONOMETER.

Double roller   The ROLLER in the modern LEVER ESCAPEMENT. One roller is of wider diameter and carries the IMPULSE PIN; the other is part of the SAFETY ACTION.

Double six-hour dial   Early attempt, c1700, to show minutes by a watch with one hand. There are six dial divisions and the hand takes an hour to travel from one to the next, each interval being marked with minutes from 0 to 60.

Double spade hand   In a HALF-HUNTER WATCH the SPADE HAND for minutes has another spade near the middle so that it appears to be a complete hand through the small glass in the cover.

Double striking clock   Public and domestic clocks that strike the hour and then repeat it about two minutes later for those who did not hear it the first time have been made in Europe for centuries. AUGSBURG produced such clocks from the mid-17th c. It was also favoured by Italian makers from c1600 to c1750. French provincial MORBIER CLOCKS with double striking were made from the end of the 18th c and some are still made today. The Dutch have a variation, called DUTCH STRIKING, at the half hour.

Double-sunk dial   Watch dial with the centre and the seconds dial at lower levels.

Double summer time   During some Second World War years, double British summer (D.B.S.) time was introduced for the high summer months, but clocks still reverted to GREENWICH MEAN TIME at the end of October. There was an attempt to keep clocks one hour ahead in the early 1970s, to match Central European Time throughout the year, thus giving rise to another form of D.B.S., but this is not quite the same thing.

Double-time railroad regulator   Pendulum wall clock made by the Seth Thomas Clock Co. in the U.S.A. after STANDARD TIME was introduced on 18 November 1883. It has two full-size dials, one above the other, marked Local and Railroad Time. See RAILWAY TIME.

Double three-legged gravity escapement   Escapement invented by Lord GRIMTHORPE for the WESTMINSTER CLOCK (Big Ben).

Double twelve-hour dial   A dial sometimes used on earlier clocks and watches. The hour hand turns once in 24 hours and the dial is divided into 24, marked I to XII then I to XII again. See GERMAN HOURS, ITALIAN HOURS, WHOLE CLOCK.

An early **double twelve-hour dial** in Roman and Arabic numerals with a single hand.

Douzième gauge   Gauge for measuring watch parts in douzièmes. A douzième is the twelfth part of a LIGNE.

Dover Castle clock   Large wrought iron POSTED FRAME clock with its original VERGE and FOLIOT control, once in Dover Castle and now in the Science Museum, London. It is wound by CAPSTAN and has END-TO-END TRAINS with central COUNT WHEEL. The foliot balance makes a double swing in about eight seconds, permitting the main wheel to turn once an hour and let off the striking. Once it bore the fictitious date of 1348. The true date is probably after 1600, as there are similar clocks in northern Belgium and in Holland dated between 1550 and 1730. Many similar central count wheel clocks exist in England, although most have been converted to pendulum. In 1971, Dr C.F.C. Beeson listed 30 of them. The Cassiobury Park Clock (now in the British Museum) has been reconverted to the original foliot. Most are in the southern counties and some may have been imported from the Continent. Some have identical cockleshell smith's marks on their frames.

The **Dover Castle clock**. Note the capstan winder at each end, one for timekeeping and the other for striking.

Dragon boat clock   See FIRE CLOCK.

Draw (U.S.A. **Draft**)   A detached LEVER ESCAPEMENT has to remain in a locked position and be free of the BALANCE WHEEL except for the few milliseconds when IMPULSED during every swing. To keep it locked, the PALLETS are set at such an angle that they are drawn into the teeth of the escape wheel as each pallet DROPS onto a tooth. Mudge's original lever escapement did not have draw, which was added by Josiah Emery. Georges-Auguste Leschot of Geneva introduced it for CLUB-TOOTHED escapements c1825. See RUN TO BANKING.

Draw plate   Hardened steel plate with a series of holes in it of different sizes and shapes for making wire. The original bar or thick wire is pulled through tapered holes of successively smaller size, being annealed from time to time. Small wire is gripped by special pliers and pulled by hand. Heavier wire needs a draw bench, a wooden or steel horse or trestle. The drawplate is held at one end and the wire is gripped by pliers attached to a leather band which is pulled by a windlass at the other end. PINION WIRE was made in the same way with special draw plates, mainly by specialist workshops in Lancashire. So were balance springs, in draw plates which changed a round section to a flat one. Gold balance springs were made in draw plates with adjustable sapphire jaws with a vernier gauge for accurate measurement.

Dresser clock   Simply a clock set in a kitchen dresser. There are probably a few more around than one would expect. Most of the surviving examples are Welsh.

Drop   The action when an ESCAPE WHEEL tooth, released by a PALLET, is moved to the other pallet, or 'drops' on it.

Drop-dial clock   Form of ENGLISH DIAL with a very small trunk below the dial, often with a glass for the pendulum to be seen. Some strike on a bell. Popular around the middle of the 19th c. An octagonal drop-dial clock was made by Chauncey Jerome in the U.S.A. c1850. Copies were mass-produced there later and called 'school clocks' or 'regulator clocks'. They had poor-quality GOING SPRING power compared with the original heavy FUSEE movements. Germany produced them in volume too, sometimes with wooden PLATES.

A **drop dial** on a simple striking wall clock with enamel dial.

Drop-forge clock One of the many types of industrial clock produced during the French Industrial Revolution in the late 19th and early 20th c. The pendulum is U-shaped and swings inside one of the hollow pillars of the case. It is IMPULSED

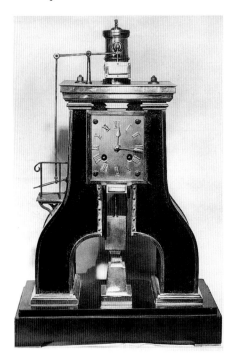

A French eight-day striking **drop-forge clock**. The 'hammer' moves up and down.

by a BROCOT ESCAPEMENT and also counterbalances the rising and falling of the forge hammer. Associated with the Parisian maker Guilmet.

Drum clock Some early clocks of the 16th c were in drum-shaped cases with a hand on top. From the 18th c, French makers put movements in drums with DIAL, BEZEL and glass in front and a lid at the back so that they could be fitted directly into cases of all shapes and sizes. See PENDULE DE PARIS. Cheap alarms of the early 20th c were also fitted into drums or canisters. The earliest watches also had such cases.

An early 19th c **drum clock** on a green marble base. (*Biggs of Maidenhead*)

Drum escapement Alternative name for a TIC-TAC ESCAPEMENT used in some French DRUM CLOCKS.

Drum-head clock LONGCASE CLOCK with a drum-shaped top and round dial instead of the usual HOOD. A fashion for some REGULATORS and French long-case clocks and very popular with Scottish makers.

Drum watch The first portable clocks became watches when they could be made small enough to be carried on the person. The original form of drum case was retained. Earlier ones had separate lids like boxes, but the lid was soon hinged. Some had a metal loop brazed to the side so that a ribbon could be passed through it and hung round the wearer's neck. Also called 'canister' or 'tambour' watches. The front and back became more domed and then the sides were made convex, to arrive over the years at the familiar pocket watch shape.

An oval **drum watch** made in Nuremberg c1600. The hand shows only hours and half-hours. (*Wuppentaler Uhren Museum, Germany*)

Dueber-Hampden John C. Dueber, a German immigrant to the U.S.A. began making gold pocket watch cases in 1864. The business became big and the cases so low-priced that other case manufacturers formed a trust and enforced a boycott. To stay in business, he bought the Hampden Watch Co. of Springfield, Massachusetts. About 3,000 people were employed at the date of Dueber's death in 1907. In 1925, the business was sold by his successors, but went into receivership in 1927. The machinery and tools were sold to the Russian buying agency, Amtorg, for $25,000, to establish watchmaking in the U.S.S.R. under the First Five Year Plan. It was delivered in 28 freight cars. The Russians also made contracts with 21 former Dueber-Hampden technicians to supervise the establishment of the First Soviet Watch Factory in Moscow. The ANSONIA tools and equipment were bought to start the Russian clock industry.

Dumb-bell balance A balance bar or FOLIOT shaped like a dumb-bell used in the earliest German watches. Some versions had screwed nuts on the ends of the bar to adjust timekeeping.

Dumb repeater Pocket watch for deaf people introduced in the 18th c. Instead of indicating the time on demand by striking a bell or gong that could be heard, the hammer strikes a metal block so that the blows could be felt. Also called a tact 'repeater'. A repeater with a PULSE PIECE is also dumb.

Dumb vibration The alternate vibration of a balance with a CHRONOMETER ESCAPEMENT or pendulum with a COUP PERDU ESCAPEMENT, when no IMPULSE is given.

Dummy wind Watch with a GOING BARREL made by the Lancashire Watch Co. to fool customers it is the more expensive English FUSEE, which is wound in the opposite direction. It has a reversing wheel between the BARREL and the CENTRE PINION. See PRESCOT. It is also a term used for the first INGERSOLL pocket watches of 1892, which had a dummy winding hole at the pendant, yet were wound with a key fastened to the BARREL ARBOR inside the case.

Duo-in-uno Early form of chronometer BALANCE SPRING, which is cylindrical but with a flat spiral at the top.

Duplex escapement ESCAPEMENT popular among English makers of good watches from the late 18th to about the mid-19th c, until supplanted by the DETENT and LEVER ESCAPEMENTS. Pierre LEROY is said to have invented it c1750 and in 1782 a patent was granted in London to Thomas Tyrer. It continued to be used in some machine-made American pocket watches. The ESCAPE WHEEL has two sets of teeth at right angles, one for LOCKING and one for IMPULSE, which is given in one direction only to an impulse PALLET on the BALANCE STAFF. Some continental versions have two escape wheels. It is a FRICTIONAL

REST ESCAPEMENT. See CHINESE
DUPLEX.

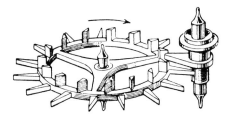

The **duplex escapement** favoured by many English
watchmakers. A slot in the roller on the lower part of
the balance staff on the right, allows a pointed tooth of
the escape wheel to rotate to the next position, where
it is held up. This causes an upright tooth on the escape
wheel to impulse the balace staff.

Dust band   Thin metal band around
some earlier watch movements between
the plates to keep out dust.

Dust cap   Shaped cover used to protect
some 18th c watch movements from dust
when the case proper was opened. It is
made of thin brass and gilded, with a
blued steel sliding spring latch. Often it is
engraved with the maker's name.

Dust pipe   Cup-shaped or tubular brass
piece around and fixed to the winding
and other squares of a marine chronometer or watch to keep out dust. Its top
almost touches the inside of the case
around the winding hole.

Dutch clocks   Until about the mid-17th c,
Dutch clockmakers followed general
European styles of weight-driven WALL
CLOCKS and spring-driven TABLE
CLOCKS. After HUYGENS invented the
PENDULUM they developed their own
Dutch styles. For table clocks they used
GOING BARRELS, instead of FUSEES like
their neighbours, and for wall clocks
Huygens ENDLESS ROPE and later chain.
They also had their own DUTCH STRIK-
ING. AUTOMATA above the dial were
popular. Early makers were concentrated
around Zaandam. Dutch LONGCASE
CLOCKS tend to be variations of English
styles. See STAARTKLOK, SCHIPPERTJE,
STOELKLOK, FRIESLAND, HAAGEK-
LOK, ZANDAAM CLOCK.

'Dutch' clock   Popular but incorrect
name used in the 19th c by English speak-
ers (including Charles Dickens) for the
clocks made in the BLACK FOREST of
Germany, *Deutsch* having been mistranslated.

Dutch striking   As well as striking ordinarily at the hour, the clock strikes the *next*
hour on a higher-toned bell every half
hour. Found in Dutch and German clocks.
Some early TABLE CLOCKS sounded the
previous hour at the half hour.

Dutch wag   See WAG ON THE WALL.

Dwarf tall clock   American name for a
GRANDMOTHER CLOCK, popular
there in the first quarter of the 19th c.

Dynadromic pendulum   High precision
MASTER PENDULUM, invented by Peter
Wills in the 1980s, which is impulsed by
imperceptible vertical displacements of
the support from which it is suspended, so
that no torque is applied.

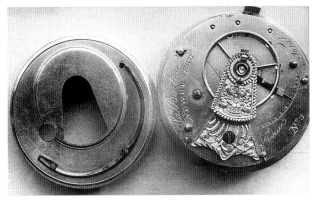

On the left is a **dust cap** of a pair
case for a watch by James Barton of
'Newbrough'. Note the index on
the right of the watch and the end
stone.

E

Early manufacturing centres In very broad chronological sequence the main ones were: Flanders, Burgundy, Nuremberg, Augsburg, Blois, Lyons, Abbeville, Paris, Rosenborg (Denmark), Innsbruck, Prague, London, Geneva, Black Forest (Germany), Philadelphia, Boston.

Ears The BOW of a pocket watch hinges in two BUSHES of this name.

Earnshaw, Thomas (1749–1829) Famous maker born in Ashton-under-Lyne, partly self-taught. Developed the MARINE CHRONOMETER and claimed ARNOLD stole his DETENT ESCAPEMENT. Made pocket chronometers and some clocks. Invented a BI-METALLIC BALANCE of brass fused onto steel.

A **Thomas Earnshaw** chronometer. Note the cylindrical balance spring and the weights on the compensation balance arms.

East, Edward (1602–97) Maker of fine clocks and watches. Probably born at Southill near TOMPION'S birthplace. Followed David RAMSAY as Royal watchmaker to Kings Charles I and Charles II. Lived in Pall Mall near the King's tennis courts. May have introduced NIGHT CLOCKS to England.

Easter Day when the hours of light and darkness are of equal length (vernal equinox), when the rites of spring were celebrated. To the church it was a moveable feast calculated from the GOLDEN NUMBER, DOMINICAL LETTER (which some early clocks showed) and the INDICATION (a Roman calendar period) or EPACT (age of the moon on 1 January). Clockmakers tried to devise mechanisms for clocks to forecast Easter, but only three are believed to have succeeded: DONDI in 1364, Schwiligué with the third STRASBOURG CATHEDRAL CLOCK in 1842, and Jens OLSEN in 1955. The Easter Act 1938 allowed Easter to be fixed but the church blocked this for half a century. There is now a compromise.

Ebauche Unfinished watch frame, now made by machine in special factories. Other specialist factories make mainsprings, escapements, dials, hands, etc. In this century almost all Swiss (but not Japanese, Russian and Chinese) watch factories are FINISHERS and design and manufacture watches based on the parts they purchase. See LEPINE CALIBRE.

Ebonise To imitate ebony by staining wood black. Stained pearwood was commonly used for clock cases because it lacked obvious grain. In Victoria's England, many clocks were blackened by stain or paint after her death.

Eclipse Total or partial blocking of the sun's light by the moon, or of the moon's by the sun. Stars are also eclipsed. Time priests predicted eclipses. STONEHENGE was used for such predictions. About 500BC the Babylonians discovered that the moon can only be eclipsed when it is full and on the ecliptic (the sun's path). Conditions are favourable for eclipses about every 18 years and 10½ days. Clocks with SUN HANDS, MOON HANDS and NODAL HANDS (showing the moon's phase) were used for predicting eclipses. When all three hands came together with the sun hand on top, a solar eclipse was indicated. With the moon hand in opposition (on the other side of the dial) a lunar eclipse was predicted.

Ecliptic The path of the sun around the centre of the Earth. It is inclined to the Earth's equatorial plane (its CELESTIAL EQUATOR) at the same angle of tilt as the Earth's axis, which is approximately 23° 26' and is gradually decreasing. The ecliptic is the centre of the zodiac, the band in which the planets wander. Shown on some ASTRONOMICAL CLOCKS.

Egg watch See NUREMBERG EGG.

Eglisome painting Painting glass executed so that it is viewed through the glass, favoured by American makers of some SHELF CLOCKS.

Eiffel tower clock Clock in a model of the tower sold in two sizes in limited editions during the Paris exhibition of 1889.

Eight-day clock Clock intended to be wound once a week. The extra day is for reserve. Before the pendulum (1658), almost all clocks went for 12, 24 or 30 hours. Some of the earliest week clocks ran for seven days but eight days were quickly adopted.

Elapsed time indicator A MECHANICAL TIMER scaled from, say, 30 minutes to 0, instead of 0 to 30. The hand is turned to 0 and moves back towards 30, showing the time elapsed when stopped. Electronic digital versions are common.

Electric clock General term for a SYNCHRONOUS ELECTRIC CLOCK, MASTER CLOCK, BATTERY CLOCK, or other clock powered by electricity. See BAIN CLOCK, BRILLIE PENDULETTE, CLINKER ELECTRIC MAINS CLOCK, BULLE CLOCK, CORDLESS CLOCK, DERBY WORLD CLOCK, ELEKTRONOM ELECTRO-PNEUMATIC CLOCK, EUREKA CLOCK, ESTYMA ELECTRIC CLOCK, EVERETT EDGCUMBE SYNCLOCK, HETTICH ELECTRIC CLOCK, KUNDO ELECTRIC CLOCK, MAINS CLOCK, MOTOR WOUND CLOCK, MURDAY ELECTRIC CLOCK, PULSYNETIC, SECTICON CLOCK, SELF-STARTING ELECTRIC CLOCK, SHADED POLE, SHORTT CLOCK, SILENT ELECTRIC CLOCK CO., STANDARD TIME CO., SYNCHRONOME, TUNING FORK CLOCK, WARREN MOTOR.

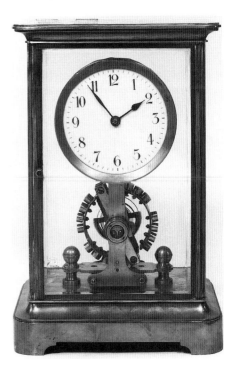

An **electric clock** of the early 20th c with a large compensation balance. (*Phillips*)

Electric clock systems TIME SIGNALS were needed long before there was a public service. In London, the Standard Time Co. supplied hourly time signals over private wires every hour from 1876 until the 1940s, when it was bombed. They provided ENGLISH DIAL clocks that were forcibly corrected at the hour by the signal. One user was the BRITISH HOROLOGICAL INSTITUTE, which still has a clock. The Self-winding Clock Co. of New York installed a similar system on the

London Underground railway, controlled by a master clock at the Lotts Road generating station. The Normallzeit Gesellschaft of Berlin also set up a service in London and checked a clock's gaining RATE by disengaging a one-sided CRUTCH which left the pendulum to idle if it was fast. The First World War brought them to an end in 1914. See MASTER CLOCK.

Electric Telegraph Co. In 1852 the company distributed time signals from GREENWICH to Lewisham, thence over the South Eastern Railway system. They also sent signs via the Electric Telegraph Company at Lothbury for distribution nationwide. See BRITISH AND IRISH MAGNETIC CO.

Electric time switch When first introduced in the early 20th c, this was a clock controlling an electric switch for street lighting. The clock in the lamppost was wound weekly by hand. Later the clock was wound automatically by a SYNCHRONOUS motor. Simpler versions followed, in which the synchronous motor does the switching for central heating control. These do not provide standby operation during power cuts like the earlier versions. The Swiss used a pendulum clock wound by a synchronous motor to power a time switch and provide stand-by power.

Electric watch Wrist watch operated by a small battery in the case. The first on the market came from the Hamilton Watch Co., U.S.A., in January 1957. There is no MAINSPRING and fewer WHEELS than in a mechanical watch. There are French, German, and Swiss versions. The Hamilton has a tiny coil of wire fixed to the BALANCE and a miniature switch operated by it sends a current of electricity through the coil for a few thousandths of a second. This causes a magnetic field around the coil which reacts with two small fixed magnets to give the balance a push every time it swings in one direction. Since the balance has a normal HAIRSPRING, it is kept swinging to and fro. The balance drives the hands by a simple RATCHET system. The 'winding button' is for setting the hands and switching off the battery during storage.

Although so small, the coil has 70m (230ft) of wire. Swiss and French versions have the coils fixed and they attract the arm of the swinging balance. The Swiss produced an ACCUMULATOR WATCH. All are now collectors' items. See LIP ELECTRIC WATCH.

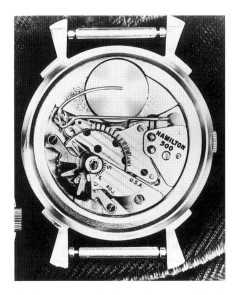

The first commercial **electric watch**. It was made by the American watchmaking company, Hamilton.

Electro-plate Coating of metal (usually precious) on another in an electrochemical bath, invented in 1840 by G.R. Elkington. Cheap alternative which replaced GILDING on watch parts. Also used to deposit silver (usually on nickel) for watch and clock cases. See HARD GOLD PLATING.

Electronic clock Ambiguous name first used for a pendulum BATTERY CLOCK with a transistor instead of a mechanical switch.

Electronic watch Usually called a QUARTZ WATCH. See ACCUTRON, TIMEX QUARTZ WATCH.

Electrotype Reproduction of an article by making a wax model of it, making from this a plaster mould, melting the wax away and pouring in its place a melted lead alloy. In a simpler method, developed in the 1830s, a wax model of the original is heavily ELECTRO-PLATED. Used extensively in the SECOND EMPIRE PERIOD to reproduce earlier ornamental French ORMOLU clock cases.

Elektronom electro-pneumatic clock MASTER-AND-SLAVE CLOCK designed not to magnetise watches and tools. Made for clockmakers in the 1930s by JUNG-HANS. The master clock is spring-driven and operates a switch to send a regular pulse of current through a filament and heat the air in a glass bulb. The bulb is connected by rubber tube to a cylinder in which a piston is moved to rewind the mainspring. Spare energy operated up to six SLAVE DIALS up to about 60m (200ft) away by air pulses.

Elephant clock   One in or on a model of an elephant, sometimes with howdah. Popular during the REGENCY and LOUIS XVI periods. Also a swinging MYSTERY CLOCK made by JUNGHANS in the BLACK FOREST, Germany, until about 1935. A compound PENDULUM, the top being a clock and the lower part a PENDULUM BOB, rests on jewelled cup bearings on the elephant's trunk, and swings from side to side. For operation and adjustment see DIANA CLOCK.

Elgin watch factory   Watch factory for the western states of the U.S.A. founded in Elgin, Illinois, on land donated by the residents. It began producing on 1 April 1867, and was immediately successful. The name was changed from the National Watch Co. to the Elgin National Watch Co. in 1874. Peak daily production was 1,200 watches. It closed in 1964. The patent files (including details of other companies) from 1868 to 1962 are lodged with the Milwaukee Public Museum.

Elinvar   A nickel-steel alloy invented in 1913 by Dr Ch-E. GUILLAUME for use in BALANCE SPRINGS because its elasticity does not change with changes in temperature. The nickel content is susceptible to magnetism, however. The name 'Elinvar' is now used as a generic term for many steel-nickel alloys, some also containing chromium and tungsten, the elasticity of most being almost entirely unaffected by heat within the range of 10–30°C. Alloys developed for watch balance springs

An **elephant clock** of 1610 made in Augsburg by David Haissermann. The figures in the howdah revolve with the striking. (*Sotheby's*)

include Durinval, Isoval, Metelinvar, and Nivarox.

Ellicott pendulum   A COMPENSATION PENDULUM having a rod of brass and steel components which press on levers to raise or lower the bob at different temperatures. John Ellicott (1706–72) was a fine clockmaker with an observatory in his house at Hackney.

Embossing   Decoration for watch cases particularly in the 18th c, formed by a hammer and shaped tools from the back of a surface. See CHASING.

Embryo factories   See FALSE NAME, SIGNATURES.

Empire clock   This name usually refers to a French gilt clock of Greek or Egyptian style made from about 1800 to 1815.

Empire style Usually refers to the French neo-classic style from 1799 to1814. There are other styles, as in the picture with ORGAN GRINDER CLOCK. See SECOND EMPIRE CLOCKS.

Enamel Surface of transparent or coloured glass fused on a surface and used for watch and clock dials and decoration from the 16th c. Transparent enamel (the flux) is a compound of silicon, red lead and potash, which is coloured by the addition of oxides. The constitution of the flux determines its melting point; the higher this is, the harder and longer lasting the enamel. Enamel is most satisfactory on gold and platinum because of their high melting points. Most enamelled watch cases are of high carat gold. Softer enamels are used on silver and copper. Enamelling falls into three main categories. (1) The older methods of using cells to hold the flux. See

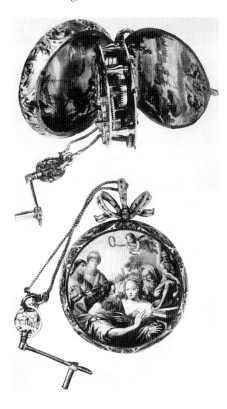

CHAMPLEVÉ, CLOISONNÉ, RELIEF ENAMEL. (2) Painting with different coloured enamels as developed in LIMOGES and used from c1500 to c1600. The only Limoges watch now thought to be extant is in the Metropolitan Museum in New York. (3) Painting in colour with powdered enamels mixed with oil on a white enamelled ground, developed by Jean Toutin (1578–1644). BLOIS was the first centre for enamelled watch cases. GENEVA took over with all kinds of pictures, mostly including people, and still produces some today. Enamelled decoration was used on dials and cases and it was often necessary to enamel and fire the inside as well as the outside of a case to avoid distortion. One form of enamelling outside those listed are BASSE TAILLE and plique-à-jour (like a stained glass window). See FLINQUE, CONTRA-ENAMEL, DIAL (ENAMEL).

End plate Small metal plate, fixed to a clock plate by a screw, to take the end thrust of a PIVOT.

End shake Working clearance at the end of a PINION, PIVOT, shaft, etc., limited in watches by an END STONE and in clocks by a shoulder on the shaft or ARBOR. See END PLATE, SIDE SHAKE.

End stone Flat circular bearing jewel to take the end thrust of a PIVOT. Used

Elaborate **enamelled** watches like this were made in Blois in France and then in Geneva, Switzerland.

A James Whitelaw, Edinburgh, watch with a diamond **end stone** to the balance staff.

particularly for watch BALANCES. Made of synthetic ruby or, in the past, a rose-cut diamond or natural gemstone, because of their hardness. See JEWEL, SHOCK ABSORBER. See DUST CAP for picture.

End-to-end movement Ancient arrangement, particularly for TOWER CLOCKS and LANTERN CLOCKS, of having the driving BARRELS or pulleys for the timekeeping and striking, end to end instead of side by side, as in later clocks. They were weight- and rope-driven. Another construction, known as the 'double-plated frame', was used by the French clockmakers who were incorporated in Paris in 1544, and consisted of an upper compartment for the going train and a lower for the striking train.

Endless rope or **chain** Arrangement to provide MAINTAINING POWER for weight-driven clocks. Invented by HUYGENS about 1656. Used particularly on LANTERN CLOCKS (many of which were converted from the original simple pull winding), 30 hour LONGCASE CLOCKS, and modern TOWER CLOCKS with AUTOMATIC CLOCK WINDING. The endless rope or chain passes over two parallel pulleys so that two loops dangle. The driving weight hangs in one loop and drives the clock through one pulley. The other pulley has a RATCHET so that the weight does not drop. Pulling on one line of the slack loop turns the ratchet pulley backwards and winds the clock by raising the weight. A small weight on this loop, often a lead ring in THIRTY HOUR longcase clocks, is merely to keep the lines in slight tension.

Endless screw Another name for a TANGENT SCREW, the screwed rod for regulating timekeeping by setting up the MAINSPRING in early watches. See BELL for picture. Also the speed regulating device in musical clocks, where the fly or fan is so driven.

Engine turning Geometrical patterns of cuts made by a special lathe. It replaced the hand-engraved patterning called *guilloché*. Invented c1670 but not used in watch cases until c1770. Popular after 1790. Used on cases and, particularly by

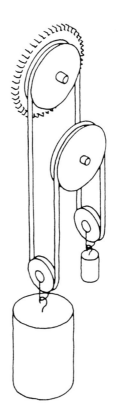

The **endless rope** or **chain** drive invented by Huygens and used in virtually all thirty-hour longcase clocks.

BREGUET, on dials. Barleycorn was a popular pattern and also a rose. Often covered by transparent ENAMEL and called 'BASSE TAILLE'.

English Clock Systems Subsidiary of SMITHS. See QUARTZ MASTER CLOCK.

English dial Wall timepiece of which only the large silvered, or later painted, DIAL and circular wooden BEZEL are visible. Introduced about 1780 or earlier with mahogany bezels about 30cm (12in) across. The most popular clock of any quality throughout the 19th c when there was a huge demand because GREENWICH MEAN TIME had been introduced and was used by the railways, mail coaches, telegraph services and new factories working shifts. Their diameters became standardised at 8, 10, 12, 14, 16, 18 and 24 inches. The makers of nearly all of them were the embryo clock factories, such as those listed under FALSE NAME. Many were of excellent quality with FUSEE movements and kept good time. VERGE ESCAPEMENTS were used in 18th c clocks, usually with plates tapering towards the top, the movement being housed in a wooden box, sometimes called a 'salt box', which it resembled. The ANCHOR ESCAPEMENT was not introduced until c1800–20 and the shape of the case had to

The **English dial**, a popular style of clock in the 19th c. It is about 38cm (15in) in diameter.

be altered to accommodate the PENDULUM, being rounded at the bottom following the bezel curve, with a little trap door to reach the RATING NUT. At the same time the dial was made of wood in one piece with the bezel. Later, the pendulum was lengthened and the DROP DIAL case was developed, and eventually the TRUNK DIAL CLOCK. Around the same time, minute numerals around the edge of the dial were abandoned but the Roman chapters remained. Early clocks had matching pierced hands and almost all later ones SPADE HANDS. Also called 'school clock' or 'station clock'. A few early clocks were striking, some ONE-AT-THE-HOUR, and very few were SHIP'S BELL CLOCKS. Mass-production makers in Germany and America eventually turned out huge quantities of DIAL CLOCKS, most now collectable.

English horological industry See BRITISH HOROLOGICAL INDUSTRY.

English lever General name for the English watch made in the 19th c with a pointed toothed ESCAPE WHEEL (as opposed to the Swiss CLUB-TOOTHED) and LEVER ESCAPEMENT. Regarded at the time as the Rolls-Royce of watches. See BRITISH HOROLOGICAL INDUSTRY.

Thomas Cummins made this **English lever** watch, hallmarked 1825. He was the first maker of highest quality detached lever escapements. (*Sotheby's*)

Engraving All apprentices were once taught engraving, so that they could cut dials and decorate clock and watch parts, but gradually work was put out to specialist engravers. Back PLATES of clocks were once elaborately engraved, as were the DIALS, BOTTOM PLATES and COCKS of watches. Sometimes practice cuts are found on the back of MOON DIALS. Also commonly used for decoration on precious metal watch cases.

Entablature Part of a clock HOOD above the dial and under the dome or cresting at the top.

Entry pallet The PALLET first met by each tooth of the ESCAPE WHEEL.

Epact The number of days that must be added to a lunar year in order to find the age of the moon in a solar year. In 19 years, new moons repeat themselves.

Ephemeris second The fundamental unit of time adopted by the International Committee of Weights and Measures in 1956. Since 1964 it has been based on the vibration of the caesium atom, 9,192,631,770 cycles a second. The standard is broadcast by WWYB at Fort Collins, Colorado, U.S.A., M.S.F. at Rugby, U.K., and D.C.F. 77 Mainflingen, Germany, on a 60kHz carrier, with a pulse each second.

Ephemeris time (E.T.) Time calculated from the Earth's orbit around the sun, instead of its rotation. In 1956 it was agreed to bring together E.T. and G.M.T. (now U.T.C. – see entry) as zero at the year 1900 so that they could be kept in step. Adjustments are made when needed during TIME DETERMINATION. Atomic clocks keep E.T., so the broadcast SIX PIPS, for example, have to be made to catch up, which is achieved by inserting an extra pip when needed, a LEAP SECOND on the last day of the year.

Epicyclic train Gears engaging and travelling round a fixed gear. Found in KARRUSEL and TOURBILLON watches and behind some UP-AND-DOWN DIALS.

Epicycloidal teeth Form used for most domestic clock and watch wheels, based on a curve traced by a point on a circle rolling on another circle. It provides adequate clearance with small teeth. Almost all other machines use the flatter curve of involute gear.

Epilame After parts of a watch have been submitted to an ULTRASONIC CLEANER, they are so chemically clean that oil may spread, so they are given a coating of a patent epilame (stearic acid) to act as a barrier, a treatment devised by Dr Woog of Paris and Paul DITISHEIM before ultrasonic cleaning was invented.

Equal hours After about 1350–1400, the varying TEMPORAL HOURS were largely replaced by equal hours, each hour being of the same length whether by night or day. The use of mechanical clocks caused the change. JAPANESE CLOCKS were still made to show temporal hours, however, until 1873. Some SUNDIALS were also made to show equal hours. See EQUATION OF TIME.

Equation dial An extra dial on a clock showing the EQUATION OF TIME, so that a SUNDIAL can be used to set the

An **equation dial** on a watch of c1750 by John Ellicott.

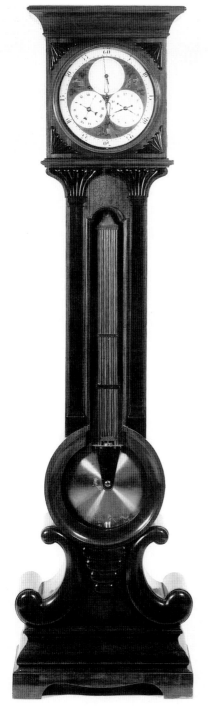

clock to MEAN TIME. First made by TOMPION and by QUARE about 1695, but see FERGUSON. The accuracy of the ANCHOR ESCAPEMENT made the difference between sundial and clock apparent. The equation hand indicating how much the clock should be fast or slow of the sundial was usually operated by a large kidney-shaped cam.

Equation of time The difference between apparent solar time (time shown by the sundial) and mean solar time (time shown by accurate clocks). The sundial sometimes appears fast and sometimes slow according to the clock. Before time signals, clocks without equation dials had to be set by sundials, and a table of differences for different days of the year was often fastened inside a clock or watch case and sometimes engraved on sundials. The equation figures for the year are published in the *Astronomical Ephemeris*. If sundial time is subtracted from clock time, it varies from a maximum of nearly +14.5 minutes in February to nearly -16.5 minutes in November. Four times a year it is zero. The equation of time is caused by the elliptical orbit of the Earth round the sun and the angle of its axis. See EQUATION DIAL.

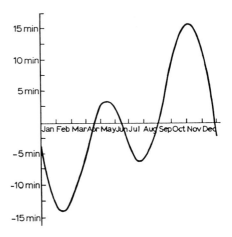

A graph of the **equation of time** through a year, showing how sundial time varies against mean solar time, shown by timepieces. Tables with the variation in minutes at different times during the year were provided with some early longcase clocks as they had to be set against a sundial.

An unusual longcase clock of 1825–50 with another form of **equation dial**. Note the gridiron pendulum through the glass.

Equatorial clock   Clock, usually with a CONICAL PENDULUM, for driving an equatorial telescope to keep it pointing at a star.

Equinoxes   Start of spring and autumn when the days and nights are of the same length, i.e. when the sun crosses the CELESTIAL EQUATOR. See FIRST POINT OF ARIES.

Equipoise pendulum   One with a horizontal rod and a BOB at each end. Because gravity is not the restoring force, is is not a pendulum but a form of BALANCE used in a clock. There is a 19th c version in the ILBERT COLLECTION, now in the British Museum.

An **equipoise pendulum** clock that goes for a year at a winding. It has a modified chronometer escapement but is not a good timekeeper.

Ermeto watch   One of the first watches that folded into a small case, made by the Movado Watch Co., Switzerland.

Escape wheel   The last toothed wheel in a GOING TRAIN, controlled by the ESCAPEMENT.

Escapement   The vital mechanism in a timepiece that controls the rate at which it runs, by allowing a measured amount of power (provided by weight, water, spring, electromagnetism, etc.) to 'escape' at regular intervals to keep an oscillator (PENDULUM, BALANCE, spring, etc.) in motion. The earliest known, made in 725 AD by a Chinese monk, I-Hsing, was called a 'celestial balance' and controlled a WATER CLOCK. A rope escapement to control a falling weight that turned a model of an angel pointing to the sun was devised by a French architect, Villard, and illustrated between 1240 and 1251. The first mechanical escapement in general use was the VERGE and CROWN WHEEL, which appeared in the second half of the 13th c and is still made today for some MORBIER clock movements. For clocks, the verge was followed by the ANCHOR, which became almost universal. For watches, the DUPLEX and the CYLINDER were most common after the verge until the appearance of the DETACHED LEVER, which became universal until the electronic watch. The lever is similar in appearance to an anchor and is called an *ancre* on the Continent. Many classifications of escapement, some of which overlap, are FRICTIONAL REST, DETACHED and CONSTANT FORCE (remontoire). The main escapements are: crown wheel and verge (with BAR or WHEEL BALANCE, FOLIOT, PIROUETTE, or PENDULUM); ANCHOR (of American, English, French, or German style, TIC TAC, LE ROY); DEAD BEAT ESCAPEMENT (BROCOT visible, GRAHAM, Thiout, VULLIAMY, PIN-PALLET); CROSS BEAT (with bar balances or pendulums); spring and pivoted DETENT (for CHRONOMETERS by ARNOLD, BERTHOUD, EARNSHAW, and for pendulum by Berthoud, Reid); GRASSHOPPER (HARRISON, Vulliamy); PIN WHEEL (Amant, LEPAUTE, Vergo or COUP PERDU); CONSTANT FORCE (GRAVITY) (Brocot coup perdu, Charpontier, Fleury, GRIMTHORPE, THWAITES AND REED, MUDGE); electrically reset gravity (BOWELL/ HOPE-JONES, DENT, Froment/Gill, GENT, Gillett, Johnson, Pariss ROLLING-BALL, RUDD, Shepherd, SHORTT/ Synchronome, Standard Time, STEUART); CONSTANT FORCE (SPRING) (BREGUET, COLE for TURRET CLOCKS, Garnier, Le Roy, Lowne, Princeps, RIEFLER); CONICAL PENDULUM

(HUYGENS, Thiout); TORSION PENDU-LUM (FOUR-HUNDRED DAY); MAGNETIC (Breguet, Clifford, Japanese Accutyne); RACK LEVER (HAUTE-FEUILLE, Huygens, LITHERLAND); DETACHED LEVER [RIGHT-ANGLE (English and Swiss), STRAIGHT-LINE (Swiss), pin-pallet (ROSKOPF, Riefler), D-pin-pallet (*De Long*), PIN-WHEEL, spring-tail, Cole repellent, Cole resilient, Savage two-pin, Breguet, Emery, Mudge]; horizontal CYLINDER (Graham, Breguet); DUPLEX (in English and Chinese or Fleurier styles); VIRGULE (single or double); TOURBILLON (Breguet); KARROUSEL (Bonniksen); LOBSTER CLAW; TWO PALLET (Chevalier, Thiout); club-footed verge or double escape wheel (DEBAUFRE ESCAPEMENT, Garnier, SULLY, Lepaute dead-beat, ORMSKIRK chaff-cutter); SILENT ESCAPEMENT with pendulum made for night clocks in Rome. See ELECTRIC CLOCK and ELECTRIC WATCH (ATO, BAIN, BULLE, Diehl, EBAUCHES, EUREKA, Fery, HAMILTON, Hipp, Kiezle, Lip, JUNGHANS, MAGNETA, TIMEX); FLYING PENDU-LUM CLOCK, MYSTERY CLOCK (figure-holding pendulum etc.).

Escapement error As soon as a PENDULUM or BALANCE is given an IMPULSE to keep it swinging, its time-keeping is interfered with. The difference in RATE is the escapement error. It was analysed by AIRY. It and CIRCULAR ERROR are sometimes opposite in effect, tending to cancel each other.

Escutcheon Shield-shaped ornament on clock DIALS, arches, HOODS, etc., often with a maker's name or protecting a keyhole.

Essen ring Quartz crystal cut to a ring shape and used for high-accuracy QUARTZ CRYSTAL CLOCKS. Developed by Louis Essen of the National Physical Laboratory. At the Post Office Research Laboratories in Dollis Hill, London, one was buried 20m (65ft) down in London clay in a sealed canister in 1955 for use as a frequency standard.

Estyma electric clock Small transis-

torised electric battery pendulum clock of c1972 about 23cm (9.5in) high. The bar magnet PENDULUM BOB passes through a coil at each end. There are no electrical contacts. In one direction, the bar magnet swings through the trigger coil, causing the transistor to send a heav-ier current through the drive coil and return the pendulum in the other direc-tion. Although the pendulum is so short, the AMPLITUDE is controlled, which improves timekeeping.

Etablisseur Name used in Switzerland and France for the watchmaker or manu-facturer who issued parts to outworkers for assembly into complete watches. Still used for a manufacturer who buys from movement (EBAUCHE) factories.

Eterna This factory was set up in 1856 in Grenchen in the foothills of the Jura moun-tains by a local doctor and a farmer's son to reduce unemployment there. Their fame came from an AUTOMATIC WATCH with ball-bearing-mounted rotor. In 1962 they were producing the world's slimmest automatic watches.

Eureka clock Electric BATTERY CLOCK, invented in 1906, which has a

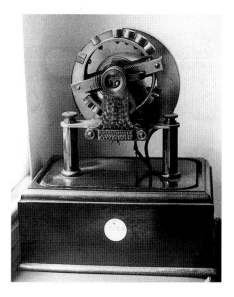

The **Eureka clock** with a huge balance wheel, that runs for 1,000 days, being powered by a battery in the box under it.

very large and heavy BALANCE WHEEL driven by an electromagnet. There is an electromagnet across the balance, which is mounted vertically on ball bearings with glass END PLATES. Close below it is a soft iron armature. Current from a cell passes briefly through the coils of the electromagnet when the balance swings in one direction and brief contact is made with a pin. This IMPULSES it by pulling one end towards the armature.

Evan Roberts collection A Welsh farm boy, Evan Roberts (1836–1918), who could neither read nor write, became a watchmaker and eventually a famous watch and clock collector. In 1916–17 his collection was broken up among several museums including the Victoria and Albert and Science Museums in London and the Welsh Folk Museum.

Everett Edgcumbe Synclock One of earliest British SYNCHRONOUS CLOCKS, introduced c1931 in a normal wooden case. If the power failed, it was self-starting but a red indicator appeared in the dial to show it was wrong.

Exeter Cathedral clock Ancient iron tower clock now restored and in the north transept of the cathedral. The iron VERTICAL FRAME going train is 15th–16th c and the striking side of BIRDCAGE design of the 17th c. The large astronomical dial (worked by a more recent FLAT BED movement) is almost identical to that in Ottery St Mary Church, Devon. It has the Earth in the centre with the moon moving round it and showing its phases. Hours are indicated on a DOUBLE TWELVE-HOUR DIAL. A separate minute dial was added above it at a later date. Records of a mechanical clock date back to 1284.

Expanding bracelet Early versions have expanding spring links; later ones usually have a spring scissors action. A good one is precision made and may have over 100 parts. Some have latches for removing single links for length adjustment. Often made of gold, or base metal such as stainless steel, covered with ROLLED GOLD or GOLD or HARD GOLD PLATING. See FLEXIBLE BRACELET.

Expanding hand Five examples are known of 18th c watches with oval dials and metal hands, shaped like antique carpet beaters made of cane, that expand and contract according to where they are round the dial.

Explorer's watch Watertight English pocket watch made by the firm of DENT with a DENNISON case at the end of the 19th c for use by explorers. The winding button and the dial are covered by screw-on caps with cork washers, which was the first successful WATER RESISTANT case.

Export, earliest A clock was referred to in a prosecution concerning the cargo of a galley leaving for the East in 1338.

F

F.B.H.I. Fellow of the BRITISH HORO-
LOGICAL INSTITUTE.

Face Layman's name for a dial.

Facio de Duillier, Nicolas Swiss mathematician who corresponded with
HUYGENS and Newton and came to live
in London where, in 1704 with two
French watchmakers, Peter and Jacob
DEBAUFRE, he obtained the first ever
patent for watch JEWELS, which gave
English makers the ascendancy for nearly
a century because the method of piercing
was kept secret. Many gem minerals were
used, including garnet, rock crystal (See
LIVERPOOL WINDOW), ruby, sapphire,
and a surprising amount of chrysoberyl.
Synthetic ruby and some synthetic
sapphire later became universal.

Fake The most usual way of faking an
original clock is by a MARRIAGE of parts
without disclosing the fact. A tell-tale sign
is often that the winding squares are not
in the middles of the holes of the dial.
Valuable ancient clocks have been forged
with great skill and knowledge. Some of
these may, however, have originated as
genuine reproductions. Currently it is
possible to order, say, exact reproductions
of Rolex Oyster cases in Hong Kong.
They are made in China, fitted in Hong
Kong with cheap movements, and the
well known brand name added in
Bangkok or elsewhere. See FORGERY,
FALSE DIAL, FALSE JEWELLING,
FALSE NAMES.

Falling-ball clock Form of GRAVITY
CLOCK invented in the 17th c. The spherical brass case has a MOVING BAND
around its 'equator' that does one rotation in twelve hours. The time of day is
indicated by a small brass figure, such as

that of a cherub, fixed to the case. A cord
wound round a BARREL in the ball
emerges from the top of the case. The
clock is suspended from this and slowly
descends (like a money spider on a
thread), being driven by its own weight.
When it hangs low, it is raised by hand
and the cord 'disappears' inside the clock,
being wound back onto the barrel by a
light spring.

A **falling-ball clock** by J. Schlemmer of Schleswig. The
cut-out putto points to the time in Roman and separately in Arabic hour notation. (*Sotheby's*)

False balance BALANCE WHEEL of cheap watches of the 1880s onwards – even as late as the 1940s and 1950s – slotted to imitate screws round the rim like a COMPENSATION BALANCE.

False bob Another name for a MOCK PENDULUM. Also currently for a pendulum attached to some QUARTZ CLOCKS and driven by the clock.

False dial Human vanity has created a demand for articles that look expensive or up-to-date, but are relatively low-priced, such as clocks and watches with extra dials, but no mechanisms to operate them. False winding holes and squares, as well as calendars and moon dials appeared on some 19th c THIRTY-HOUR English LONGCASE CLOCKS to make them look like EIGHT-DAY clocks. A cheaper method was to paint on false winding holes and squares. German BLACK FOREST makers also employed false dials.

False jewelling Practice of adding extra JEWELS with no working purpose to impress purchasers. The first known instance was to impress Parliament when an old watch by Ignatius Huggeford with a jewel was produced by the CLOCK-MAKERS' COMPANY in a petition against the granting of the first watch jewel patent in 1704. The jewel was later found to be a decoration. The modern practice began in the U.S.A. after a 50 per cent increase in the tariff on Swiss watches in 1954. It was rife in the U.K. in the early 1960s when watches with 41, 57, 77 and up to 85 jewels were advertised. The extra jewels were mounted in or stuck on bridges and wheels and even inside cases. A court decided in 1962 that such statements were illegal, being false trade descriptions.

False name There were once genuine makers in very many towns, but from the later 18th c on, many of them started buying complete clock movements from embryo factories, but still used their own names on the clocks. See SIGNATURES. Regretfully there are still a few dial painters today who, when restoring a worn dial, add the name of a real deceased maker in the district where the clock is to be sold, obtained from 'Watchmakers and Clockmakers of the World' (N.A.G. Press). False names are also found on many Swiss pocket watches imitating American brands such as 'Walham' (for Waltham) and 'Rochford' (for Rockford), etc. See FORGERIES.

False pendulum or false bob. Another name for a MOCK PENDULUM.

False plate An extra plate pinned or screwed to the front plate of a clock movement. Introduced about 1770 when a variety of painted iron dials became available to longcase clockmakers. The false plate, instead of the clock plate, could then be drilled to accommodate the differently spaced feet of any dial. See DIAL FOOT.

False watch From 1760 to 1830, the enamellers of Bilston, Staffordshire, produced boxes looking exactly like expensive enamelled watches with glasses and real hands but no movements. The cheapest had hands painted on the dial.

Farmer's watch Large pocket watch with a VERGE ESCAPEMENT and an enamelled dial showing a farming scene, made from about 1820 to as late as 1880.

Farouk collection Exceptional collection of watches, including some with pornographic AUTOMATA, sold by Sotheby's after Farouk was deposed as King of Egypt in 1954. He also collected watches with IV instead of IIII on the dial (BIG BEN has IV).

Fast beat The faster the beat (tick) of a watch, the less likely is its accuracy to be affected by sudden jerks. Makers from the 17th to the 19th century usually used a beat of 16,200, which is the number of ticks an hour. During the first half of the 20th century, the beat was increased to 18,000, or a tick every fifth of a second, and after that some watches had trains of 36,000, or ten ticks a second. For comparison, a marine chronometer has a beat of 14,400.

Father Time Traditionally, an old man with a long beard holding a scythe in one hand and an hour glass in the other to symbolise Time. Although rather obvious, used very occasionally as a clock theme.

Federal clock American SHELF CLOCK made in the period after the Civil War of 1861–5.

Fellows Watch Collection Antique watches bequeathed to the British Museum in 1874 by Sir Charles Fellows. Lady Fellows made water-coloured drawings of the watches before restoration, which are exceptionally beautiful and accurate and now belong to the Royal Institution, London.

Ferguson, James (1710–76) Eminent London astronomer and mathematician who designed special clock mechanisms such as ORRERIES, EQUATION DIALS and TIDAL DIALS.

Ferguson's clock Three-wheel, two-pinion clock devised by James FERGUSON. A central hand fixed to the second wheel indicates minutes on a dial. The first wheel carries a weight pulley and a disc showing hours through the DIAL. The third, or ESCAPE WHEEL, has a disc with 180 divisions showing seconds through the dial.

Ferrule Small pulley in a bearing rotated back and forth by a bow string, with one turn around the pulley, and used as a primitive lathe. Alternatively it is turned one way only by a cord from a hand wheel, pedal wheel or electric motor. Work to be turned is fastened to it, or a tool is held in it. Types used by makers are: friction, with a tapered hole to grip a drill shank; screw, with a clamp to fasten it to work; wax (commonly made of bone) with a rough face to shellac small parts to.

Fiddle-case clock Case with a waist like a fiddle or cello, introduced in France in the Louis XV period for WALL and LONGCASE CLOCKS and adopted by country makers for longcase clocks in the Comtoise district of France (see MORBIER CLOCK) from the mid-18th c. Later the Swiss (NEUCHÂTEL CLOCK), the Austrians and the English (BALLOON CLOCK) adopted it. The Swedes and Finns followed with longcase versions and the Americans with their BANJO, FIGURE-OF-EIGHT and GIRANDOLE CLOCKS.

Figure-of-eight clock American WALL CLOCK with round DIAL and round face like the GIRANDOLE but joined by a fiddle waist. Introduced about 1870 by the Howard Clock & Watch Co.

Figure plate See INDEX DIAL.

Finding the longitude A ship has to know its position east or west by 'finding the longitude'. It is relatively easy to find the position north or south by the sun or stars; that to the east or west is complicated by the rotation of the Earth and ships often sailed thousands of miles off course and were wrecked. The Spanish, Dutch, Venetians and British (in 1714) offered big prizes for methods of finding the way at sea. The British one of £20,000 was the only one ever paid, to John HARRISON for his marine timekeeper. An accurate timekeeper was set to the time at the port which the ship left, say Bristol. Suppose the ship sailed west: The captain would compare his LOCAL TIME, obtained from observations of the sun, with the clock's time. If there was an hour and a half's difference, he was 22.5° w of Bristol because the Earth turns 15° in an hour. The MARINE CHRONOMETER is kept to UNIVERSAL TIME (Greenwich Mean Time) by RADIO TIME SIGNALS and compared with local time. See NAVIGATION.

Finial Decoration on the top of a clock case, or old iron TURRET CLOCK, to 'finish it off'. Common types in brass were balls with points on top, flambeaux (flames), acorns, pineapples, urns, spikes. They were used singly (and also called 'terminals') or in groups. Dutch clocks often had more elaborate ones showing figures of deities such as Mercury and Bacchus, and others like Atlas, angels blowing trumpets, bowmen, etc.

Finisher A divison of the old hand-made watch trade. The finisher worked on an EBAUCHE until it was ready for the ESCAPEMENT to be planted.

Fire clock In Tibet and China, joss sticks were once used for timekeeping. The stick was a strip of cane coated with a dried mixture of clay, sweet burning sawdust and gold dust. Lit at one end, it smouldered for several days. Marks along the stick showed the hours. A fire stick was used as an alarm by hanging a thread with a little weight at each end over it at the appropriate place. When the stick smouldered to that point, the thread burned and the weights dropped with a clang into a copper bowl. Some made in the 18th c were in the form of a long metal trough with a Chinese dragon's head one end and tail the other, called a 'dragon boat'. Across the trough were threads and weights and in it a fire stick. See CHINESE MATCH, INCENSE CLOCK, INCENSE SEAL.

A dragon boat of lacquered wood, a form of Chinese **fire clock** or more accurately **alarm**. (*Wuppentaler Uhren Museum, Germany*)

Fire gilding Another name for MERCURIAL GILDING. See also WATER GILDING.

First point of Aries Position of the sun at the vernal EQUINOX, the point from which movements of the stars, sun, and Earth, and therefore SIDEREAL TIME (despite its name referring to the stars) are measured.

Fishtail fret A pierced fret of metal or wood comprising a series of semicircular curves displaced by half a circle in each row. Commonly used in the sides of 18th and early 19th c English clocks to allow the sound of striking to escape.

Metal **fishtail frets** backed by fabric in a **quarter repeater** bracket clock. The cord on the right is pulled to operate this pull repeater.

Five-minute repeater REPEATER clock or watch that sounds the previous hour on a low note, the last quarter on a TING TANG, and one blow on a higher note for each five minutes past the quarter. Operated by a slide on the side of a watch and a pull cord on the side of a clock. First introduced c1700. Some were made in the second halves of the 18th and 19th c.

Flag The PALLET of a VERGE ESCAPEMENT.

Flagellation clock One of various clocks with religious themes made during the Renaissance. A German version has a metal figurine of Christ chained to a post on top of which is a globe with rotating hour band turning anti-clockwise against a pointer. The movement is in the square wooden base.

Flambeau   See FINIAL.

Flamsteed, John   First ASTRONOMER ROYAL, appointed in 1675, and originator of the *Nautical Almanac*, now published as *Astronomical Ephemeris*. See ROYAL OBSERVATORY.

Flanders   Former territory on the North Sea ruled by a Count, which may have been the original source of clockmaking. It passed to the house of Burgundy from 1384 to 1482, during which time industry and art flourished. Courtrai had a public clock with JACKS in 1382 by Philippe Hardi. It disappeared after 1600. The names of the jacks, Manten and Kalle (and an added one) still appear in German nursery rhymes.

Flat-bed movement   Type of construction for TURRET CLOCKS with the ARBORS (axles) in a row across a horizontal frame of steel or cast iron. Popularised by LORD GRIMTHORPE in BIG BEN in 1859, but used as early as 1763 in the church of Nôtre Dame, Versailles, France.

The **flat-bed movement** of a turret clock by Dent. Note the fly and the leading-off work to the hands at top centre.

Flexible bracelet   The first modern flexible metal watch bracelet was introduced after the Second World War by Rodi and Weinenberger of Pforzheim, West Germany. It comprises spring-loaded, flattened O-shaped links so this is also an EXPANDING BRACELET. Many other versions followed. One form of flexible and expanding band is simply a flattened

coil spring. Later ones are brick or pavé, in the form of closely fitted and jointed links and made of gold, stainless steel or gold-plated stainless steel. Another construction is Milanese, woven gold wire. Some have closely fitting short rectangular tubes fitted over the Milanese which gives the impression of a flexible metal strip. Some bands or bracelets are soldered to the watch case, but most are held in place by LUGS. Earlier versions have to be altered for length in a workshop but later ones have built-in adjustment.

Flinqué enamel   Transparent enamel over an engine-turned pattern used on some watch case backs from c1670.

Flintlock alarm   Alarm which fired a small charge of gunpowder to awaken the sleeper. See ALARM-AND-CANDLE CLOCK.

A German **flintlock alarm** or pistol alarm of c1600.

Flip-leaf clock   Carriage clock with the hours and minutes on a pack of cards that flip over. Made in the U.S.A. by Ansonia and in France and Germany. See PLATO CLOCK.

Flirt   Lever or other mechanism to cause a sudden movement, e.g. as used in a

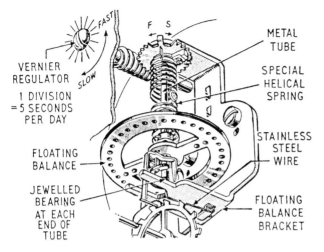

The **floating balance** where the balance wheel is supported by the cylindrical spring.

clock with JUMPING SECONDS and some English and French clocks to release striking and/or chiming trains.

Floating balance BALANCE system for spring-driven clocks invented by the German firm Blesch und Hettich in 1950 as a better alternative to the short PENDULUM, but used mainly in British clocks by SMITHS. The BALANCE WHEEL is mounted on a hollow tube with a jewel hole at each end through which a taut stainless steel wire passes. The balance on its tube is suspended part-way up the wire by its CYLINDRICAL BALANCE SPRING, the top half of which is wound in one direction and the bottom the other. Thus, when the balance swings round the wire, it remains at the same height. In early versions, the balance is FREE SPRUNG and regulation is made by moving small balance weights on it, by a lever. In later ones a regulator is applied to the spring and operated from outside the case. In a later battery-powered version a weighted arm drives the clock and is reset by a solenoid. All have PIN-PALLET ESCAPEMENTS.

Floating hour dial See WANDERING HOUR DIAL and NIGHT CLOCK.

Floor clock Clock set flush in the floor. One is installed in a mosaic sunburst in the centre of the Gothic entrance hall of

the Sydney State Theatre, Australia, opened in 1929.

Floral clock Large public clock set out in bedding plants in a garden. A buried movement turns the hands, some of which are also troughs for plants. Some strike and a few are cuckoo clocks. The Swedish botanist, Carl Linne, invented a non-mechanical one, each hour being planted with flowers that opened about that hour of the day.

A **floral clock** by Smiths of Derby.

Flotation effect See BAROMETRIC ERROR.

Fly Governor or rotating fan used to slow down a striking or chiming mechanism to a constant rate. To avoid damage through sudden stops, it incorporates an elementary clutch, the fan being made only friction tight on its ARBOR by the pressure of a short length of flat spring; a RATCHET freewheel is used on TURRET CLOCKS. That on a LONGCASE CLOCK is about 3.8cm, (1.5in) across and that on BIG BEN's clock about 4.5m (15ft). Some later ones have centrifugal blades that decrease the area of the fan as the speed falls (i.e. as the MAINSPRING runs down) to keep the intervals between blows on the bell constant. Also used on some REMONTOIRES and GRAVITY ESCAPEMENTS. The rate of striking is increased by changing the fly PINION for one with more LEAVES and vice versa. See FLAT-BED MOVEMENT for picture.

Fly back   Returning a hand instantly to zero as in a TIMER or CHRONOGRAPH action. Also called zeroising. The first was made in 1862 by Nicole and Capt, a Swiss concern in England. H-F. Piquet was the inventor. A heart-shaped cam is attached to the ARBOR of the hand. When a flat-ended lever is pressed on the cam, the hand is returned by the shortest route. The gear train is connected to the hand only when it is running.

Flying pendulum clock   Novel and very inaccurate clock invented in 1883 by an American, A.C. Clausen, and produced by Jerome & Co. in the U.S.A.. The movement, in a wooden case with a dial, has a rotating rod of inverted L shape projecting from the top. A thread with a light ball on the end is suspended on the end of the top bar and is swung round by the clock. At each half-turn, the cord is interrupted by a vertical rod on the end of the case. The cord winds round each post until stopped by the ball, then unwinds to release the moving arm until arrested at the other side. It is a crude escapement. Reintroduced in Germany as a novelty for the Horolovar Co. in the U.S.A. in 1959.

Fob watch   Now a watch hanging on a short strap or chain, usually combined with a brooch and often worn by nurses. The watch dial is upside down so that it can be read when lifted. Originally a fob watch was a pocket watch on a short chain, named after the word *fuppe*, Low German for 'pocket'. Also a CHATE-LAINE WATCH. See ALBERT.

A **fob watch** in the form of a book, which also makes it a form watch.

Foliot   Swinging horizontal bar with an adjustable weight on each end. First used

The restored **foliot** (at the top) of the famous Salisbury clock. Note the crown wheel, the lantern pinions and the wedges holding the frame together instead of nuts.

as a time controller with a VERGE ESCAPEMENT in the later 12th or early 13th c, at about the same time as the BALANCE. The bar is twisted first one way and then the other and its RATE can be increased by moving the weights on the ends towards the centre, and also by the driving weight, which sometimes had a cup on top to receive lead shot. The name, first used by Jean Froissart, the French chronicler, in 1369, means 'to dance about madly'. See SALISBURY CATHEDRAL for picture and VERTICAL FRAME for underslung foliot picture.

Follower Any WHEEL or PINION that is driven.

Forgery English watches were often forged on the Continent during the 18th c and falsely signed 'TOMPION', 'QUARE', 'GRAHAM' et al., some names being misspelt. The MOVEMENTS inside were cheap and not even imitations. BREGUET's work was often forged, which made him devise his SECRET SIGNATURE. On the Continent, old German STACKFREED watches have been faked earlier in at least three places, and again in the 1940s and 1950s in Belgium. Clocks have been forged, but much more realistically. Not infrequently a case became separated from its original movement and both were later built into complete clocks in the style of the maker, so that there are two 'genuine' antiques instead of one. DIALS with famous names faked on them have been given to inferior movements and existing movements given new 'antique' cases. An original engraved name is sometimes scraped off and a famous one engraved in its place. The word 'forgery' implies intent to deceive so the situation is further confused by the fact that in the 19th c many genuine makers – Barraud, Perrigal, Dwerrihouse and others – bought their 'bread-and-butter clocks' from EMBRYO FACTORIES and had their own names engraved on dials and movements. Thousands of retailers, middlemen and even customers also had their names engraved to appear as makers. As the name affects the price, identical clocks were often sold for differ-

ent prices. Many ELECTROTYPE copies of old AUGSBURG clocks have been produced. In the later 19th c, Viennese makers produced reproductions of various 17th c watches. Many MOVING ARM WATCHES were made in the 19th c by French makers in imitation of an earlier period. Although not forged, these are sometimes sold as genuine. Huge numbers of electrotype copies of earlier French ORMOLU clocks were made during the SECOND EMPIRE from 1852 to 1870. Made as reproductions, they were often sold as genuine ormolu. Until about 1914 various WATER CLOCKS were listed in the catalogue of Pearson-Page, a Birmingham brass and pewter manufacturer. Some bear the date 1640. None were copies of originals yet they are sometimes bought as genuine even today. In the 1960s a hitherto unknown style of Italian monastic clock was discovered by Antonio Simoni, an antiquarian. It was still thought to be original, and dated 15th c. At a Bonham (London) auction in the 1960s an identical clock was offered but then withdrawn. Quite often changes were made to timepieces when a contemporary invention improved the timekeeping or another function, the best examples being ENDLESS ROPE or CHAIN and the ANCHOR ESCAPEMENT. Large numbers of LANTERN and other clocks with VERGE ESCAPEMENTS were converted; for improved accuracy, many verge watches were converted to more modern escapements. Such changes were not made for forgery purposes and today reconversion to the original escapement is not considered as faking as long as any changes are identified. More recent faking includes the conversion of quarter striking CARRIAGE CLOCKS to GRAND SONNERIE, not a difficult operation. A converted clock will not strike through eight days like a genuine one. There was an ASTROLABE forgery 'factory' run by two Englishmen in Mexico in the 1960s and some of these Arab instruments are still regarded as genuine, although certain star calculations were impossible at the dates attributed to them. See CONVERSION, FAKES, FALSE DIAL, FALSE JEWELLING, FALSE NAMES, MARRIAGE.

Fork Forked end of a LEVER ESCAPE-MENT engaging with the IMPULSE PIN on the BALANCE.

Form clock or **watch** One made in the shape of something else such as an animal, BOOK, CRUCIFIX, mandolin or SKULL. Most are Swiss and enamelled.

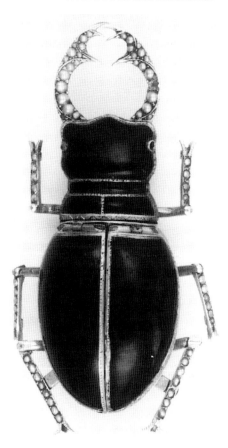

A **form watch** in the shape of a gold and enamel beetle. The wings fold back to reveal the dial. (*Sotheby's*)

Fountain oiler Fountain pen with an oil reservoir and hypodermic needle, instead of ink and knib, for oiling watches.

Four-post frame One in which the top and bottom PLATES are held together by four corner posts. Very occasionally there are six posts.

Four-glass clock Form of MANTEL CLOCK with a short PENDULUM fitted in a frame case of brass with four sides of bevelled glass. Made in several countries but especially France in the 18th and 19th c, first with high quality movements, later with standard DRUM MOVEMENTS. The name was not used at the time.

Four-hundred-day clock (U.S.A., **anniversary clock**). A year clock with a TORSION PENDULUM below it, invented by Aaron D. Crane in America c1829. Later introduced as the Four-hundred-day clock in Germany by Anton Harder. Early versions had a brass disc loaded with lead as the BOB. Later versions (except the ATMOS CLOCK) have four brass balls mounted together. The pendulum oscillates once in 7.5 seconds and has a DEAD-BEAT ESCAPE-MENT. The case is a glass dome. The pendulum is not easy to regulate and modern battery versions have a false pendulum that does not control the clock.

A typical German **four-hundred-day clock**. (*Charles Terwilliger Coll., U.S.A.*)

Fourth wheel The WHEEL in a watch that drives the ESCAPE WHEEL. Sometimes it carries the seconds hand.

Frame The structure in which the wheels and other parts of a clock or watch are mounted. In early TOWER CLOCKS, VERTICAL FRAMES or POSTED FRAMES were used, and all later ones FLAT-BED. Early domestic clocks had post frames or horizontal PLATE frames. After the invention of the PENDULUM, vertical plate frames became almost universal. Early watches had two brass plates held together by pillars, the FULL PLATE. Various forms of HALF PLATE, THREE-QUARTER PLATE, and BAR MOVEMENTS led to the 20th c EBAUCHE.

Franklin clock One with a single hand showing hours and minutes. The hand rotates once in four hours. Each quarter of the dial is divided into 60 minutes and at each quarter there are three hour marks, viz:

XII	I	II	III
IIII	V	VI	VII
VIII	IX	X	XI

It was assumed that whoever wanted the time would know which hour to choose. One later version moved a ball in a spiral to indicate the hours. Some showed minutes in an arch above the main dial. Benjamin Franklin, the American philosopher, was a friend of James FERGUSON, the English astronomer and clock designer, hence his interest in clocks.

Free pendulum The less interference with a PENDULUM, the more accurate it will be. The first practical free pendulum was invented by W.H. SHORTT in 1921. His free pendulum controlled a SLAVE PENDULUM CLOCK which did the work of counting the time to operate the dials. He used as the basic mechanisms two modified Synchronome electric clocks invented by F. HOPE-JONES, who helped him develop his ideas. The free pendulum clock is kept in a vacuum case on a heavy base. At every 15th swing (30 seconds) of the free pendulum, the slave clock allows it to be given a gentle IMPULSE. When this happens, an electric impulse is sent to the slave and a device called a 'hit and miss' synchroniser gives a slight impulse to the

A longcase wall clock with a **Franklin dial**. It was made by Porthouse of Penrith, c1810. (*Christie's*)

slave if it is slightly slow, and nothing if it is slightly fast. All the world's OBSERVATORY CLOCKS were Shortt clocks until the QUARTZ CLOCK.

Free sprung BALANCE and SPRING assembly that has no REGULATOR. Adjustment is by changing the configuration of the assembly by altering the position of the screws mounted on the rim of the balance. Used in precision watches in the late 18th and early 19th c.

Freemen See CLOCKMAKER'S COMPANY.

French horological industry One of the world's oldest and perhaps the first. The earliest known maker was Julien Couldray, who made two watches set in dagger handles in 1518. Early centres were Blois (see ENAMEL), Paris and Rouen, with smaller ones at Dijon, Grenoble, Lyons, Angoulême, Sedan, Autun and Lorches. When the Huguenots were persecuted, many watchmakers went to Geneva, which greatly strengthened the SWISS HOROLOGICAL INDUSTRY. After the French Revolution, Laurent Megevard, backed by the government, set up an industry in Besançon. Other pioneers were JAPY and SULLY. The present industry is organised like the Swiss. It is currently centred in the Doubs, the Haute-Savoie and the Seine. The French firm of Lip produced one of the first ELECTRIC WATCHES. The clock industry was also very old. The first maker may have been Phillipe le Bel (d.1314). Renaissance clocks had small two-tier horizontal PLATE frames with FUSEES. Distinctively French ornate clocks were introduced during the Louis XIV period (1643-1716), flourishing from then onwards in very many styles. The development of a standardised movement for DRUM CLOCKS in the 19th c enabled large numbers of clocks of many earlier styles to be made and exported. See CARRIAGE CLOCK, CARTEL CLOCK, MARBLE CLOCK, MORBIER CLOCK, RELIGIEUSE CLOCK. The industry still flourishes, making alarms and domestic clocks.

French plate An early attempt at plating base metal. It was covered with silver foil which was heated to near melting point and burnished on with a heated iron. Close plate is a similar process, the metal first being dipped in molten tin. Rare for clock cases.

French provincial clock In earlier times, these were different in style from those from clockmaking centres, being more extravagant in shape and decoration. LONGCASE CLOCKS usually had almost violin-shaped cases and PENDULUM rods were extravagant similar shapes in REPOUSSÉ metal. See MORBIER CLOCK.

French Revolution dial The effects of the French Revolution even reached the decoration of enamel watch dials in the later 19th c. Some bore slogans such as *Liberté*, and *Vie Libre*. There were also those supporting the king, like *Vive la Nation et le Roi* and *Obéir au Roi*. Many had illustrations on a white ground showing the tools of labour, such as spades and rakes, the female figure symbolising France and the scales of justice. Most were relatively crude. Most had twelve-hour dials but a few showed ten-hour DECIMAL TIME.

French silvering Uses 'flake silver' (finely divided silver) rubbed on to the carefully prepared brass PLATE with cream of tartar and considerable friction. Used for the CHAPTER RINGS of LONGCASE CLOCKS and BRACKET CLOCKS with brass DIALS. The finished surface is usually lacquered to prevent tarnish.

Frequency (Hz or Hertz) Cycles per second. A cycle is the start of one to the beginning of the next. Makers of mechanical timepieces use half-cycles. An 18,000 watch TRAIN has a frequency of 9,000Hz and a seconds pendulum of 0.5Hz. The average quartz clock has a frequency of 1,200Hz and quartz watch 31,768Hz.

Frequency comparison meter Special meter used at electricity power stations to compare mains frequency with a MASTER CLOCK, so that SYNCHRONOUS CLOCKS are kept to MEAN TIME.

A typical hanging **French provincial clock** with its ornate exposed repoussé sheet-metal-covered seconds pendulum. (*Hagans Clock Manor Museum, U.S.A.*)

Fret A pierced panel of wood or metal in a case to allow the sound of striking and chiming to be heard. Usually used on the sides or back of a clock case and covered with silk. The most common design is FISHTAIL.

Friction Mechanical clocks and watches work in frequent small jerks instead of continuously, and incorrect lubrication affects the timekeeping. The object is to keep friction as low and as constant as possible except in places where it is needed. For very small parts such as watch PIVOTS, solid (dry) friction is negligible but oil is necessary to reduce wear. However, the viscosity of the oil can create more drag than friction. Similarly, oil or grease on GRAVITY ESCAPEMENT parts that touch the PENDULUM will reduce wear, but may cause enough drag to slow, even stop, a large TOWER CLOCK. The choice of a lubricant in relation to the bearing load is very important. Some makers discovered that if a greater bearing area is needed to increase the life of a pivot, lengthening it will do this without increasing friction. Pivot friction is much reduced by JEWELS. With gearing, friction is normally greater when teeth mesh than when they disengage. Air is also a cause of friction, affecting the pendulums and timekeeping of precision clocks. See FRICTION SPRING, FRICTION REST, OIL, STACKFREED.

Friction roller Method of reducing the friction on PIVOTS. Instead of working in a hole, a pivot is surrounded by rollers so that it runs in roller bearings. SULLY was probably the first to use them c1700, followed by HARRISON (see for picture), MUDGE, LE ROY, and BERTHOUD. In the 1950s, the Swiss company, Eterna Watches, used special three-ball bearings for some wrist watch pivots.

Frictional rest An ESCAPEMENT in which the balance or pendulum is never free, such as the CYLINDER, DUPLEX, DEAD-BEAT and PIN WHEEL.

Friction spring A curved strip of spring with a square hole in the centre to fit on to the CENTRE ARBOR. The ends press against the CANNON WHEEL and drive the hands, but at the same time provide a form of CLUTCH to allow the hands to be set.

Friesland   Clockmaking area of Holland that produced STOELKLOKKEN and a newer style of hanging long pendulum clock called the STAARTKLOK.

A Dutch 18th c thirty-hour **Friesland** bracket clock. The pendulum hangs from the backboard. (*Christie's*)

Fritillary watch   In the 15th and 16th c, some enamel watch cases had snake skin patterns like the fritillary lily or fritillary butterfly.

Fromanteel   Famous family of clockmakers in London, who have been traced to Norwich. They were named Ahasuerus, John and Abraham. Ahasuerus introduced PENDULUMS into England, advertising them in 1658.

An early longcase clock by A. **Fromanteel**. The very earliest had short pendulums. It is 1.9m (6ft 3in) tall. (*Christie's*)

John, while an apprentice, had been sent to The Hague in Holland and learned from Saloman Coster how to make HUYGENS pendulum clocks. Evelyn (1620–1706) refers to 'our famous Fromantil' in his 'Diary'. They worked at Mosses Alley, Southwark and at The Mermaid in Lothbury. Abraham worked in Newcastle.

Front wind   Clock wound through the DIAL.

Frosting   Grey matt finish given to steel parts of watches, particularly KEYLESS WINDING parts, by rubbing them with oilstone dust in olive oil, cleaning them and finishing by rubbing in circles with PITH. The same mixture is used to give a matt finish to brass before GILDING. DUST CAPS and PLATES of watches were frosted by another method, by dipping them in strong acids for a few seconds, scratch brushing, then gilding.

Full plate   Circular BACK PLATE of earlier PLATE and PILLAR watch MOVEMENTS with the BALANCE WHEEL outside it.

Fully adjusted   Mechanical watch ADJUSTED for accurate timekeeping in dial up, dial down, and three of the four edge positions. The words were sometimes engraved or stamped on movements.

Fully jewelled   Mechanical watch with at least 15 jewels. If the CENTRE WHEEL is also jewelled it becomes a 17-jewel watch. Normally AUTOMATIC watches must have 21 jewels to be considered fully jewelled. See FALSE JEWELLING.

Fusee   Pulley with a spiral groove that increases in diameter, used in conjunction with a MAINSPRING in a BARREL to provide even power output for driving a clock or watch. A gut line or chain is wound round the spring barrel and the free end attached to the largest groove in the fusee. When the fusee is wound, the line is drawn off the barrel, thus winding the spring. When the spring is fully wound, it drives the fusee, and therefore the timekeeper, by pulling the line from the

smallest-diameter groove. As the spring runs down, losing power, the line acts on a larger and larger diameter of pulley, thus increasing the mechanical advantage and maintaining the initial power output. Who first applied the fusee to a clock is unknown, but it made spring-driven clocks and watches competitive in time-keeping with weight-driven clocks, and remained in use from the first quarter of the 16th c until the last quarter of the 19th. Its last use was in the MARINE CHRONOMETER. The principle was known to Leonardo da Vinci, who sketched it about 1490, and there are three sketches in the ALMANUS MANUSCRIPT of c1477, but the earliest illustration is in that of a Burgundian miniature clock movement in a manuscript of c1450–60 in the Bibliotheque Royale, Brussels. Its origin was probably a mechanism for winding a giant catapult used as a war engine. The name is from the Latin *fusata*, a spool filled with thread. The earliest clock still extant with a fusee was made by Jacob Zech (Jacob the younger) in 1525. A fusee should be matched to the spring used with it. See ADJUSTING ROD and SETTING UP. As springs improved, fusees became less tapered. Because a fusee has to be turned backwards to wind the timepiece, time-keeping will be affected, so the so-called 'going fusee' was provided with MAINTAINING POWER. See PURITAN WATCH for gut fusee and MARINE CHRONOMETER for chain fusee pictures.

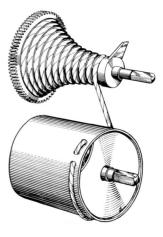

The **fusee**, which evens power supplied by the main-spring in its barrel.

Fusee cap   Thin metal plate with a projecting nose, which chronometer makers called a 'poke'. The plate is fastened over the small end of the fusee. As the line is wound onto the smallest groove, it makes contact with a lever (the stop finger or FUSEE IRON) pushing it into the path of the nose and preventing the fusee from being overwound.

Fusee chain   Chain followed gut line from about 1600 for the connection between FUSEE and spring BARREL. Gruet, a Swiss living in London, is supposed to have invented it. It comprised alternate single and double links and was stronger, safer, and more accurate than gut. Chain was made for both clocks and watches, the earliest for watches having links about twice as long as became normal.

Fusee chain makers   Little is known about early fusee chain makers; the first published information appeared in Diderot's 'Grande Encyclopedie' of 1755. There were two makers in La Chaux de Fonds and one at Le Locle in Switzerland in 1750. Some must have existed in other centres, including London, but after 1790 the main English industry was in Christchurch, Hampshire, which also exported to other countries. It was started there by Robert Harvey Cox (1755–1815), who trained many children from local workhouses. A cottage industry grew up rapidly so that 125 fusee chain makers were listed in the 1851 census, all but ten of them women, ranging in age from 14 to 61. The main subdivisions of labour were: wire drawer, wire cutter, tool maker, link cutter, chain riveter, chain finisher, chain polisher and chain examiner. From about 1875, Swiss GOING BARREL watches were competing so successfully with English fusee watches that the industry declined and, by about 1905, fusee chains were only needed for repair work on earlier watches.

Fusee engine   A kind of screw-cutting lathe introduced in the early 18th c to form the spiral groove in a FUSEE. It is held in a vice and hand-driven. After a fusee was cast, it was turned up in an ordinary lathe, then mounted in a fusee engine. Turning the engine handle rotated the fusee and also moved the carriage of the cutter sideways. The cutter itself, a form of graver, was in a slot and pressure was applied to it by a lever.

Fusee gut line   Animal gut was used as the line that linked the FUSEE with the spring BARREL for about a century before the introduction of the FUSEE CHAIN. One disadvantage was that it expanded and contracted with varying humidity. Some watches were converted from gut to chain, but the fusee itself, with its rounded instead of square section grooves, was retained and became badly worn. Gut continued to be used for clocks long after it had been abandoned for watches.

Fusee iron   Hinged piece that prevents overwinding. Also known as the fusee stop iron. See FUSEE CAP.

Fusee maintaining power   Extra small spring fitting into the MAINWHEEL and DETENT to keep a FUSEE clock going while being wound.

G

Gadrooning Decoration of convex ridges or fluting often applied to edges. For watches it was used in straight lines or a radial pattern in the late 18th and early 19th c, and made by casting or embossing. Wooden gadrooned decorations were sometimes applied to clock cases.

Gadrooning on the silver case of a clock-watch by Cameel, Strasbourg, c1610.

Gaining rate   See RATE.

Galileo Galilei (1564–1642)   Pioneer of experimental science who first noticed that a PENDULUM appeared to swing in the same time regardless of the AMPLITUDE (but see HUYGENS). He invented a pendulum clock with a simple ESCAPEMENT before Huygens, but it was kept secret and constructed by his son after his death, too late to influence the history of horology.

Gallery clock   In the U.K., one used on the balcony in a church or hall. An American name for a BRACKET, DIAL, or DROP-DIAL CLOCK, often with an ornamental case and carved eagle ornament, also used in other public buildings like banks and railway stations.

Gallows tool   Clockmaker's tool for holding a PINION in order to file the teeth. The lower part of the tool is held in a vice and the upper can rock to guide the file.

Garter back   A pattern like an old-style garter commonly used to complete the centre of an ENGINE-TURNED pattern on the back of a watch case.

Gas clock   Clock made by Pasquale Andervalt of Italy c1835 that runs on gas. Pellets of zinc are dropped automatically at intervals into diluted hydrochloric acid to produce hydrogen, which raises a piston and weight to power a clock. One in the GUILDHALL MUSEUM is about 1m (3ft) high and has a pin-pallet escapement with ornate French PENDULUM. A coiled brass tube on top of the clock holds the pellets.

Gas controller   The first form of TIME SWITCH, invented by Dr Thurgar, of Norwich in 1867, for gas street lamps. A Bournemouth builder, John Gunning, first used them in 1897 when he installed street lighting to new houses. The controllers were spring-driven and hand wound weekly. A pilot light remained on and the clock turned the mains gas supply on and off. Later they were made to adjust on and off times automatically through a year. See SOLAR TIME SWITCH.

Gathering pallet   A single tooth or pin on an ARBOR in a striking train that, when allowed to revolve, moves the striking rack (See RACK STRIKING) one tooth at a time to determine the number of blows struck.

Gear train   See TRAIN.

Gearing   See WHEEL.

Gem-set Pocket as well as wrist watches were sometimes set with gemstones, usually on the back of a pocket watch.

Geneva movement Watch in which all the PIVOT bearings on the opposite side from the dial are in BRIDGES or COCKS for easy dismantling. See BAR MOVEMENT.

Geneva stop work Maltese stop work. See STOP WORK.

Gent, John T. Firm of TURRET CLOCK makers founded in Leicester in 1872, taken over in 1894 by Parsons and Staveley. Produced electric MASTER CLOCKS under the name 'Thornbridge' from 1904. See WAITING TRAIN.

Genta, Gerald Current watch designer for some of the big Swiss firms who set up his own business in Geneva and Le Brassus producing complicated and high quality watches. The Quantième Perpetuel wrist watch is a MINUTE REPEATER, has a TOURBILLON, and shows UNIVERSAL TIME.

Georgian Auctioneers sometimes use the furniture specialists' method of dating for later clocks. Georgian is an umbrella term for the large number of styles from 1714 to 1811, during the reigns of the Georges I, II and II until the Regency. During the period mahogany and satinwood became popular. See REGENCY CLOCK and VICTORIAN CLOCK.

German horological industry South Germany and Austria had a big lead among the earliest clockmakers from the 16th to the second half of the 17th c. The main centres were NUREMBERG and AUGSBURG. Makers there produced an astonishing variety of clocks. See ANIMATED CLOCK, CENTAUR CLOCK, CRUCIFIX CLOCK, GLASHUTTE, HENLEIN, HOG'S BRISTLE, JOKELE CLOCK, MONUMENTAL CLOCK, MUSK BALL WATCH, SCHILD CLOCK, SCHOTTENUHR, STACKFREED, STOCKUHR, TELLERUHR, ULM and ZAPPLER. Competition from

A **Georgian** (actually George II) **bracket clock** by Jackson, Merton. (*Sotheby's*)

elsewhere gradually strangled the early centres, but what eventually became the world's biggest clock industry grew up in the BLACK FOREST in the 18th c. See JUNGHANS. A watchmaking industry was established in Pforzheim, the jewellery centre, after the Second World War. See also HETTICH ELECRIC CLOCK, MEISSEN CASE, NORMALLZEIT GESELLSCHAFT.

German clockmakers In medieval days, Germany included the northern and southern Low Countries, Alsace, Lorraine, Austria and the Tyrol. Very early German clockmakers could have come from any of these areas.

German hours See WHOLE CLOCK, ITALIAN HOURS.

Gilding Coating another metal with gold. Sometimes gold itself is gilded to change the colour. Gilded silver is called 'silver gilt' and if partly gilded, 'parcel gilt'. Methods used are MERCURIAL

GILDING, GOLD DIPPING, ELECTRO-
PLATE and GOLD LEAF. See GOLD
DIPPING.

Gilt Earlier alternative word for gilded,
covered with gold, e.g. silver gilt. See
GILDING.

Gimbal See GYMBAL.

Girandole clock Very rare American
eight-day HANGING CLOCK like a
BANJO CLOCK but with a circular base,
for the PENDULUM BOB, and circular
DIAL. Scrolled brackets flank the tapering trunk and a carved eagle is mounted
on top. Designed by Lemuel Curtis of
Concord, Massachusetts, and made
during the first third of the 19th c. A
girandole is a mirror with ball decoration
round the frame.

Girard Perregaux This firm's origins
were in 1791 under another name and it
passed from one generation to another
until inherited by Constant Girard-Gallet,
who married Marie Perregaux in 1854 and
renamed the firm. In 1867 it introduced a
TOURBILLON and still has a reputation
for high precision wrist CHRONOME-
TERS. In 1887 it received an order from the
German Navy for 2,000 of the new 'wrist
watches', the first to be mass produced.

Girocap Swiss system of mounting a
JEWEL HOLE and END STONE for a
watch TRAIN in a small tube so that they
could be fitted into the EBAUCHE as a
single unit.

Glashutte Very early centre of German
watchmaking in Saxony, founded c1510
by Peter HENLEIN (1480–1542). It never
fully recovered from the Thirty Years War
of 1618–48 and French competition. With
government help, Adolf Ferdinand Lange
(1815–1875), established a pocket watch
industry there in 1845. He adopted the
metric system 30 years before France and
Switzerland. A horological school was
founded in 1878. His first watches used
PIN PALLETS, but later JEWELS. From
1862 he started producing MARINE
CHRONOMETERS. His son Richard
developed a SELF-WINDING WATCH in
1885.

A **Glashutte** quarter repeating watch by A. Lange and
Achne with day and date and moon dial. (*Christie's*)

Glass The watch glass appeared in the
18th c, although some dials were
protected earlier by faceted rock crystal.
In this century almost all 'glasses' are
unbreakable, i.e. plastics (such as Perspex
or Plexiglas) and known to the trade as
'U/Bs', but also called 'crystals'.
Transparent synthetic sapphire, often
faceted on the edge, is used for some
high-quality wrist watches, as it does not
become scratched. Both old glasses and
U/Bs are 'sprung in' from the front, using
a special tool for U/Bs to dome them.
Springing in domed pocket watch glasses
by hand was once a skill of many watchmakers and jewellers. From 1920
onwards, transparent celluloid was also
used, although in time this discolours.
Today, 'mineral' glasses are true glass,
SiO_2. In WATERPROOF watches extra
sealing or pressure rings are often
employed with the glass. Clock glasses
are flat or often domed if circular.
Original glass adds value to such clocks
as real VIENNA REGULATORS.

Glass bells Used in early BLACK
FOREST clocks. One of the last made was
the case as well as the bell of a clock with

ship's watch striking, produced for the Festival of Britain in 1951. See SHIP'S TIME.

Glass brush Bundle of fine glass bristles used for de-burring after cutting watch wheels, matting silver watch dials and removing fine rust and other blemishes.

Glass plate Thickish piece of glass polished absolutely flat and used for finishing brass watch parts including END STONE settings and for polishing and FROSTING steel parts. Plates are made in threes, to avoid dishing (hollows forming), by rubbing the surface of each against the others using emery powder in finer and finer grades and finishing with putty powder.

Globe clock Globe of the Earth which turns or has a moving band or hand around it to show the time. Some were made on the Continent in medieval times for astronomical use and at intervals later. Some were intended to show the differences between the Ptolemaic and Copernican systems. All can provide world time. Most were individual productions but two makes were available in the later 19th c: the EIGHT-DAY Timby is a rotating globe mounted on a case with separate dial, adjustable for any longitude, and the Juvet with a larger globe on a stand has a THIRTY-HOUR movement.

Globe moon Sphere divided vertically into black and white halves. Rotated once in 29½ days in a circular hole displaying half the globe, it represents the phases of the Moon. Used since the 16th c.

Glossing Another name for BLACK POLISHING of steel parts.

Glucydur A bronze (i.e. copper and tin alloy) with the addition of 2–3 per cent of glucinium (beryllium). It is hard, non-magnetic, stainless, and highly elastic with a low coefficient of expansion and in considerable use for BALANCES and BALANCE SPRINGS, having superseded ELINVAR. Also known simply as beryllium alloy.

Gnomon The wedge-shaped plate, rod or pin of a SUNDIAL that throws its shadow on the dial. In the usual garden sundial (COMPASS DIAL) the angle of its edge should be the latitude of where it is sited. Also called a 'style'.

Gnomonics See DIALLING.

Goddard, Luther First American to produce watches in quantity by machine from 1809 to 1817 in Shrewsbury, Massachusetts.

Going barrel Most common spring motor for watches and clocks. It contains the MAINSPRING, of which the outer end is hooked inside the barrel. The inner end is hooked to the BARREL ARBOR (i.e. the shaft through the barrel). The winding button or key turns this arbor, which winds up the spring. As the spring uncoils, it turns the barrel, which has teeth around it to drive the train of gears. The barrel turns in the same direction as winding, so providing its own MAINTAINING POWER. The English industry continued to make watches with FUSEES while the Swiss adopted the cheaper going barrels and gradually took over from the English from the 1850s.

Going train Train of gears in a timepiece controlled by the ESCAPEMENT and responsible for indicating time. It is normally on the right of a striking clock (from the front) and in the centre of a striking and chiming clock.

Gold, rolled A thick, small sheet of gold is fused onto the same sized sheet of a base metal such as nickel. The doubled sheet is then passed backwards and forwards through polished steel rolls so that it becomes thinner and thinner and larger and larger. The final product is used for manufacture; used for earlier pocket and wrist watch cases and expanding bracelets.

Gold dipping Simple method of applying a non-corrosive coating to brass parts by dipping them in a solution containing gold fulminate.

Gold filled In the U.S.A., the best quality rolled GOLD. Not accepted as a term in the British Standard for watch case finishes because it is misleading.

Gold leaf Gold that is rolled to a sheet and beaten into a film only a few molecules thick. Often used for the numerals of outside clock dials.

Gold plating Covering of pure or alloy gold applied by an electrochemical method. A British Standard of 1960 requires gold-plated watch cases to be marked 'P/' followed by the thickness of gold in microns (thousandths of a millimetre), thus P15M. See ELECTRO-PLATE, rolled GOLD and HARD GOLD PLATING.

Gold spring See PASSING SPRING.

Gold watch case Gold is used because it is unaffected by acids from the skin and corrosion, as also are cases of platinum, rolled gold, gold plate, stainless steel and tungsten carbide. Silver was once commonly used for watch cases, partly for the same reason, but it tarnishes. Goldsmiths have been associated with watchmaking for 400 years.

Golden number New and full moons return on the same days every 19 years. The number of the year of this cycle is calculated automatically by some early clocks. The Greeks thought so much of Meton, who in 433BC discovered that there were 235 lunations in almost exactly 19 years, that they had the numbers representing these years carved in temples and gilded. To find the number for any year, e.g. 2000AD, add one and divide by 19. The remainder five is the golden number.

Goldsmiths' Company The City livery company in London responsible for HALLMARK.

Golf watch Reichenberg and Co. of Hatton Garden in London, advertised golf wristlet watches for men and women in 1928, but the term is used today for a stroke recorder that looks like a watch.

Goliath A large pocket watch with EIGHT-DAY or THIRTY-HOUR MOVE-MENT which is more than 5cm (2in) in diameter. Used as a clock. See CHAISE WATCH.

Gong Metal rod, either straight or spiral, on which chimes or hours are struck. Made of steel or phosphor bronze. May have been invented by Julien LE ROY in the last quarter of the 18th c. BREGUET used them in REPEATER watches. Straight ones (rod gongs) are used in most domestic striking and chiming clocks. Early American WALL CLOCKS and French CARRIAGE CLOCKS have spiral ones, and REPEATER WATCHES curved ones made of steel. Modern chiming clocks have a set of gongs for the chime, two of which, in harmony, are struck to provide the strike. Some CARILLON CLOCKS were provided with rods although most had bells. A set of gongs is mounted in a solid metal block anchored to the case to provide resonance. See TUBULAR CHIME.

A large spiral **gong** on a skeletonised cathedral clock.

Gothic This description is used very loosely in horology. It means Germanic or related to the Middle Ages (12th–16th c), or to the pointed arches and other architectural features of that period. The original arched shape appeared in some early iron movements and was continued in wooden cases until present times. The pointed Gothic arch is also called the sharp Gothic or steeple and sometimes the top forms a triangle as in some American wooden cases. The rounded Gothic arch is also called the beehive.

Gothic hands on a large silver gilt split-seconds duplex watch of 1840 by Widenham and Adams, London. (*Christie's*)

A **Gothic clock** of c1840 in mahogany with quarter-hour striking on eleven bells. A strike/silent dial is at top left and a tune selection is at top right. (*Sotheby's*)

Gothic hands A style with two opposite comma shapes towards a pointed end.

Gothic-on-frame clock American SHELF CLOCK like a sharp Gothic clock on a rectangular base for the WAGGON

SPRING movement. First made by Bridge and Fuller of Bristol, Connecticut, c1844.

Gould, Rupert T. (1890–1949) Lieutenant-Commander Gould, author and broadcaster, was an authority on the MARINE CHRONOMETER (on which he wrote the standard book), typewriters, and the Loch Ness monster. He was the first restorer of HARRISON'S four famous timekeepers.

Governor See FLY.

Graham, George (c1673–1751) One of the greatest of all makers of clocks, watches and scientific instruments. A friend of, relation by marriage and successor to TOMPION. Invented the practical CYLINDER ESCAPEMENT for watches in 1715, and MERCURIAL PENDULUM (see for picture) for pendulum temperature compensation in 1721. Made nearly 3,000 watches, about 175 clocks and various astronomical instruments. Known as 'Honest George Graham'. Buried in Westminster Abbey with Tompion.

George **Graham** made this regulator c1722–3 with one of the earliest of his dead-beat escapements, seen at the top. (*Christie's*)

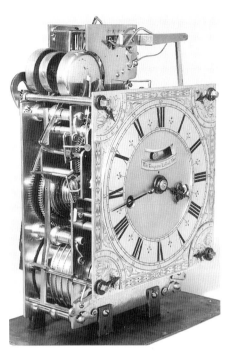

The grande sonnerie striking movement of an ebony **bracket clock** by Thomas Tompion c1676–80. Spring- and fusee-driven, it has a mock pendulum and the corner dials include a pendulum regulator, one for strike/silent, and pendulum locking. (*Christie's*)

Graining   Finish applied to metal parts after they have been filed or worked on with an abrasive. Clock plates were often straight-grained instead of being polished. The steel parts of fine watches were straight-grained using a fine emery stone, and their bevelled edges BURNISHED. Some parts were CIRCULAR-GRAINED and others had SNAILING. ELGIN and WALTHAM in the U.S.A. made a feature of graining their watches.

Grande sonnerie   Clock or watch which strikes the hour before chiming each quarter of an hour, e.g. at 3.30 it would strike three, then two quarters. Normally EIGHT-DAY.

Granddaughter clock   Clock of GRANDFATHER style standing under about 1.4m (4ft 6in) high. Almost all are relatively recent.

Grandfather clock   Name for a LONG-CASE CLOCK which originated from a song written by the American Henry Clay Work in 1876, beginning, 'My grandfather's clock was too tall for the shelf. . . .' The clock he wrote about is claimed to be that in the George Hotel, Piercebridge, North Yorkshire, but a relative, Mrs Randolph Parker, is another claimant for her clock in Granby, Massachusetts.

Grandmother clock   Like a GRAND-FATHER, but under about 1.9m (6ft) high. Antique ones are extremely rare. The first LONGCASE CLOCKS from 1657 to c1660 had short BOB PENDULUMS and were little more than this height.

Graph drum clock   One that turns a drum carrying graph paper for recording

A mahogany **grandmother clock** in Lancashire style with a moon dial and swan's neck cresting. It is 1.36m (4ft 5½in) tall. (*Christie's*)

events in relation to time, like the BARO-GRAPH CLOCK.

Grasshopper escapement Accurate wooden ESCAPEMENT not needing oil, probably designed and first used by James Harrison in a TURRET CLOCK, who later joined his brother John HARRISON. John claimed that his clocks with a grasshopper (it looks a little like one) kept to a second a month. Modified and used later by VULLIAMY.

Graver Small hand tool with a (usually) square section steel shaft and half ball wooden handle. It is ground at an angle at the end to give a V-point with cutting edges. Used for engraving dials, BACK-PLATES, etc., but especially for turning work held in TURNS and some watch-makers' lathes.

Gravity arm A small lever of certain weight, pivoted at one end, for giving IMPULSES to a PENDULUM. It is normally held horizontal and released to rest on a projection on the pendulum. After impulsing the pendulum, it is reset electrically or mechanically. See MASTER CLOCK and GRAVITY ESCAPEMENT for picture.

Gravity clock Clock driven by its own weight. Two early forms are the INCLINED PLANE and the FALLING-BALL CLOCK. Another, made as early as 1600, is the RACK CLOCK.

Gravity escapement Accurate clock ESCAPEMENT in which the MAIN-SPRING or driving weight lifts a small lever, which drops to give IMPULSE to the PENDULUM or BALANCE, and is thus independent of the driving force. Invented by Thomas MUDGE and by Alex Cumming around 1760–70, but not really successful until the DOUBLE THREE-LEGGED ESCAPEMENT made by GRIMTHORPE about 1852 for BIG BEN. Employed in most accurate TURRET CLOCKS, ELECTRIC MASTER CLOCKS and the FREE PENDULUM. See GRAVITY ARM.

A **gravity escapement**, which impulses the **pendulum** rod (*left*) by the weight of the two gravity arms whose pallets are one each side of it.

Great clock Early name for a TOWER CLOCK. 'Great clockmaker' meant a maker of big clocks, not a famous maker.

Great Tom The bell of a clockhouse built at Westminster after the Commonwealth, which was removed to St Paul's Cathedral by Sir Christopher Wren when the Westminster tower was pulled down in the 18th c. The present Great Tom is a replacement. The original one saved a soldier accused of being asleep on sentry duty at Windsor Castle from court-martial sentence. He said he heard the bell strike 13. Unlikely as this was, it proved to be true.

Great wheel The principal driving wheel of a clock or watch gear train, whether weight- or spring-driven.

Greenwich Civil Time After 1925, GREENWICH MEAN TIME was reck-

oned from midnight instead of noon. American astronomers called this 'Greenwich Civil Time'.

Greenwich Mean Time (G. M. T.) Mean SOLAR TIME at the ROYAL OBSERVATORY, Greenwich. Solar times vary across the country, e.g. when it is 12 noon at Greenwich it is 11.40 at Pembroke. In 1880, G.M.T. was established by law as official time all over Great Britain. In 1884, an international conference adopted the line of longitude through Greenwich as ZERO MERIDIAN and the basis of TIME ZONES (on the proposition of the U.S.A., only France and Ireland voting against). Replaced by UNIVERSAL TIME.

Greenwich Observatory See ROYAL OBSERVATORY.

Gregorian calendar In 1582 Pope Gregory XIII advanced the calendar by ten days to bring dates in line with seasons. He introduced leap years to keep it that way. Catholic countries adopted the reform quickly, England did not do so until 1752 and Russia not until 1923. The changes help in dating some early calendar clocks.

Grey, in the A steel part said to be 'in the grey' if finished except for the final BLACK POLISH.

Gridiron pendulum rod A PENDULUM rod compensated for TEMPERATURE ERRORS, invented by John HARRISON in 1726. A grid of alternate brass and steel rods is arranged so that in temperature changes the expansion of one metal upwards in one direction is equal to the expansion of the other in the opposite direction, so that the pendulum remains the same length. See COMPENSATION PENDULUM. Used subsequently in many English LONGCASE precision clocks and in a number of French ordinary MANTLE CLOCKS. See EQUATION OF TIME and PILLAR CLOCK for pictures.

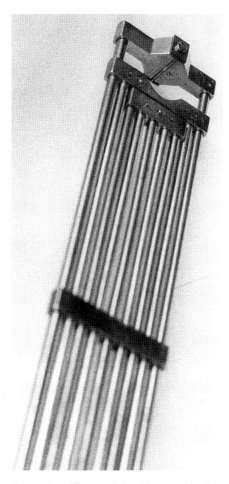

A **griffon clock** from the famous Russian jeweller Fabergé's workshops. The clock was made by Julian Rappoport, St Petersburg, sometime between 1800 and 1908. (*Sotheby's*)

The top of a **gridiron pendulum**. The second bar from the top slides over the outer rods and is moved up by the second inner rods as they expand. The bottom works the other way.

Griffon clock   One of the earliest clock designs from AUGSBURG. A model of the legendary griffon holds the clock dial between its paws.

Grimthorpe, Lord (E.B. Denison, M.A., Q.C. 1816–1905). Irascible lawyer and brilliant amateur clockmaker who designed BIG BEN, the WESTMINSTER PALACE CLOCK, to which he applied his GRAVITY ESCAPEMENT, as well as to other clocks. The clock was made by E. Dent of the Strand, and successors from 1852 to 1859. Grimthorpe upset clock makers by instructing that non-working parts be left rough, but Big Ben proved not only bigger, but much more accurate than any clock previously made.

Grisaille enamel   Pattern produced by laying down a white ground on a dark one and removing parts of the white to form shapes and textures, like drawing on scraper board.

'Groaner'   Nickname for an all-wooden American clock for farmers made by Jerome of Bristol, Connecticut c1830. The gears and pulleys of the striking train caused the groaning noise.

Grollier, Nicholas (1593–1686) Famous maker of ROLLING-BALL CLOCKS in which the ball is the timekeeper. The invention of the practical PENDULUM clock virtually ended attempts to make the rolling ball an accurate time standard. See CONGREVE CLOCK.

Guard pin Part of the safety action of the LEVER ESCAPEMENT, preventing the lever from disengaging.

Guild Mutual-aid society. Many craftsmen's guilds were formed in feudal times to set standards and control apprenticeship, although many villages developed crafts without them. The earliest known clockmakers' guild was formed in Annenberg in Saxony in 1543. Nuremberg's guild started in 1565. Some early clockmakers belonged to blacksmiths' guilds and watchmakers' to locksmiths' guilds. In England, guilds were called 'companies'. See CLOCK-MAKERS' COMPANY.

Guildhall Museum London clock and watch collection and library of the CLOCKMAKERS' COMPANY with many fine specimens including a MARY QUEEN OF SCOTS WATCH and the HARRISON wooden precision clock.

Guillaume,   Charles-Edouard (1861–1938) Director of the International Bureau of Weights and Measures, Paris, who won the Nobel Prize in 1920 for inventing INVAR and ELINVAR, which revolutionised precision timekeeping.

Guillaume balance A COMPENSATION BALANCE that overcomes MIDDLE TEMPERATURE ERROR by using a special nickel alloy (instead of steel) with brass for the bi-metallic rim of the CUT BALANCE. Introduced by GUILLAUME for use with a steel HAIRSPRING in 1899, and used through the first half of the 20th c. Also called the 'integral balance'. Weaknesses are the spring's susceptibility to magnetism and the tendency of the cut arms of the balance to fly outwards on heavy balance wheels. See COMPENSATION BALANCE and DITISHEIM BALANCE.

Guilloché Continuous scroll pattern produced by two or more plaited bands, usually with rosettes or domes in spaces. Copied from the classical frieze for 16th c clock cases. Favoured by engravers and ENGINE TURNERS for watch cases.

Guinness clock Large public clock with AUTOMATA representing various zoo animals in Guinness advertising. Made for the Festival of Britain Gardens, Battersea, in 1951. Eight copies were constructed followed by a number of simplified versions.

Gunmetal Dark grey metal, fashionable for a time after the First World War for pocket watch cases. Originally a bronze of nine parts copper and one of tin for casting cannon, it was later copied by coloured plating. This term is frequently misapplied to blued/oxidised steel watch cases.

Gut line Cord of cured sheep or cattle gut used for weight-driven clocks and earlier spring FUSEE drives. Clockmakers would soften them by soaking them in a dish of sperm oil.

Gut pallet Short, tightly stretched lengths of gut used as PALLETS instead of metal in some SILENT ESCAPEMENT clocks with CROWN WHEEL and with ANCHOR ESCAPEMENTS.

Gymbal Universally jointed frame that allows a MARINE CHRONOMETER to remain level in its box on a rolling or tacking ship. Invented by Cardano (1501-76) for ship's lanterns and adapted by HUYGENS.

H

Haagse Klokje Dutch 17th c spring-driven WALL CLOCK with VERGE ESCAPEMENT and short PENDULUM

A **Haagse Klokje** by Jean Vrijth Jaune, Maestrich. Note the silk suspension of the pendulum.

in a rectangular box case with framed glass door. The MOVEMENT is attached to the hinged dial plate which is covered with velvet and has a pierced chapter ring. Usually with a bell on top. Now very rare.

Habrecht Famous clockmaking brothers, Isaac and Josias, who completed the second STRASBOURG CATHEDRAL CLOCK in 1575. A 1.2m (4ft) high clock made by Isaac in 1589 in imitation of the Strasbourg clock is in the BRITISH MUSEUM COLLECTION.

Hack watch Watch with a good RATE introduced by the Admiralty in 1914 to carry time from one place to another without having to disturb a shore or ship's chronometer. Most were Swiss lever watches. Later renamed DECK WATCH. In the U.S. Navy the term seems to have been used for a precision watch in which the seconds hand can be 'frozen' by engaging the set-hands position of the winding button, then released to synchronise the watch exactly with the standard timekeeper.

Hairspring Flat spiral fine spring attached to the BALANCE in a mechanical watch. The invention was claimed by both HOOKE (in 1664) and more correctly by HUYGENS (in 1675). At its inner end, the hairspring is fixed to the BALANCE STAFF by a small ring or COLLET and a very tiny taper pin. At its outer end, it is fixed to the BALANCE COCK by a stud. For simple timekeeping adjustments, two CURB PINS are moved by the INDEX to alter the length of the active part of the hairspring (see REGU-LATION and REGULATOR). Made of steel until ELINVAR and other temperature compensating, non-magnetic springs

133

were invented (see COMPENSATION BALANCE). Usually made now by winding four together as a 'nest' and separating them. See BALANCE SPRING. CYLINDRICAL SPRINGS are also employed. The outer end is sometimes raised and curved towards the centre. See BREGUET SPRING and FREE SPRUNG.

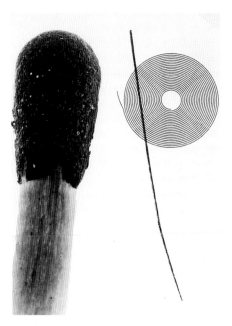

The **hairspring** of a watch of the 1960s compared with a matchstick and a hair.

Hairspring vibrator A standard BALANCE and spring in a glass-topped box, used for checking another balance and spring. That being tested is held with watchmakers' tweezers by the end of the hairspring so that the lower PIVOT rests on top of the box. Now virtually replaced by a timing machine, the RATE RECORDER.

Half-chronometer Old expression for a pocket watch with LEVER ESCAPEMENT adjusted to near-chronometer standards.

Half dead-beat escapement Compromise between a RECOIL and DEAD-BEAT ESCAPEMENT.

Half-hour ornaments Diamonds, clover leaves or other ornaments engraved between the hours on the brass dials of most English clocks up to c1720. Most had disappeared by 1750 except on provincial clocks.

Half-hunter See HUNTER.

Half-plate Watch movement with about half the plate at the top (back) in one piece, the FOURTH WHEEL and ESCAPEMENT parts being planted on separate cocks. See FULL PLATE.

The **half-plate** movement of an **English lever** watch of 1828 by Joseph Penlington, Liverpool. The balance is of gold. (*Sotheby's*)

Half-quarter marks From about 1690 to 1710, some London clockmakers introduced four ornaments (e.g. diamonds or fleurs-de-lis) outside the minute ring between XII and III, III and VI, VI and IX, and IX and XII, to indicate half a quarter of an hour by the minute hand.

Half-quarter repeater A REPEATER WATCH or CLOCK which, when operated, strikes the last hour on a low note, the last quarter on a TING TANG, then either nothing or a higher note to indicate that 7½ minutes (a half-quarter) has passed since the last quarter. For example, at 3.38 there would be three strokes of the lower note, two ting-tangs on the two notes, and one stroke on the higher one.

Half timing Running a fine LEVER ESCAPEMENT pocket or DECK WATCH without the hairspring to check escapement action. If the balance wheel is the correct weight the watch should show half the time it would with its balance spring. The system can equally be applied to the VERGE ESCAPEMENT, but to no other.

Halfpenny moon Another name for a HALIFAX MOON.

Halifax moon Moon dial based on contemporary calendar practice, favoured by Halifax, Yorkshire, makers around the mid-18th c. See MOON DIAL for operation.

A **Halifax moon** on an oak longcase clock of c1750 by Edward Barlow of Oldham. Minute figures got smaller over the years. It has locking plate striking, but see rack striking.

Hall clock American name for a LONGCASE or GRANDFATHER CLOCK.

Hallmark Silver and gold watch and clock cases are assayed in Britain to determine the quality and stamped with: (1), the mark of the assaying hall (e.g. Goldsmiths' Hall); (2), a quality mark; (3), the maker's mark; and (4), a date letter. The latter is useful for accurately dating antique watch cases. The Goldsmiths' Company, London, marked gold cases from about 1685 and silver ones from about 1740 and still do. Case makers, although not members of the Goldsmiths' Company, often struck their initials on cases from 1680 on. See SILVER WATCH CASE.

Hamilton electric watch First practical ELECTRIC WATCH.

Hamilton metal American version of PINCHBECK, a brass imitating gold.

Hammer, striking Hammer to strike a clock, bell or GONG. Early ones were operated by AUTOMATA. The first for BIG BEN weighed 408kg (8cwt) and cracked the bell. The hammers of present domestic striking and chiming clocks have leather or plastic ends to improve the note. They are operated by a PIN WHEEL or BARREL with cams or pins which press on the tails of the hammers to lift and release them.

Hammer-hardened Hammering some metals such as brass, copper, gold, silver, some others, and certain alloys when cold on a STAKE hardens them to make them more springy.

Hampton Court clock Large ASTRONOMICAL CLOCK originally made c1540, at Hampton Court Palace, Middlesex.

Hand, clock Until about 1400 a clock had a rotating dial and a single fixed hand, usually of iron, steel or hammered brass. The first moving (hour) hands were like short arrows, with a pointed tail to make it easier to turn them for setting. The arrow head on LANTERN CLOCKS later became heart-shaped, then for LONGCASE CLOCKS it was pierced and elaborated. The minute hand came into general use after the mid-17th c and seconds hands became popular after 1660 when the longcase clock came into use, the first of these having no tails. Both minute and seconds hands are, however, found on some very early special clocks (see DONDI'S CLOCK). The finest were of steel, pierced and carved by hand and blued by heat. Late clock hands are stamped out and coloured chemically. Hands of big public clocks were made of copper and bronze and are now often of aluminium alloy.

Hand, watch Before about 1700 watches had one thick hour hand, which was adjusted by pushing it. The accuracy of the HAIRSPRING encouraged the addition of a minute hand, and that of the CYLINDER ESCAPEMENT a seconds hand. Early English hands were 'beetle' (like a stag-beetle) for the hour, and 'poker' for the minute. French ones were often pierced. A fine steel or gold hand for an early 20th c watch required over 20 manufacturing operations.

Hand setting Many early public clocks had no means of setting the hands to time. If the clock ran slow, the escapement was disengaged to run through to the correct time. If it was fast, it was temporarily stopped. This feature is still found in Italian domestic clocks of the mid-18th c. Watches were set to time by moving the hands themselves. Clock hour hands had tails making them like turnkeys. Next the square on which the minute watch hand was mounted was extended so that a key could be used on it after opening the glass. In the later 19th c, the square was situated on the back of the movement of small portable clocks as well as watches to provide back setting. Next for watches, the winding PENDANT was given the task. A button was added near it which, when held down, engaged the hand setting wheels. Finally the button had to be pulled out slightly to engage the winding work. See WINDING BUTTON.

Handley and Moore See SIGNA-TURES.

Hanging ball clock Mid-17th c ball-shaped clock hanging from a cord coming from inside it. Its own weight powers it as it slowly descends. There is a spring inside, however, to rewind the cord as the ball is raised by hand. The time is shown by a rotating hour band round the circumference. Reproductions are also seen.

Hanging barrel One in which only the upper end of the BARREL ARBOR is supported. Invented by J.A. Lepine, Paris, c 1760. Used in ultra-thin Swiss watches.

Hanging clock Weight-driven clock that is hung from the wall, such as a GOTHIC iron clock or a LANTERN CLOCK. The earliest clocks had an iron hoop at the top back to hang on a hook and two sharp spurs at the bottom back to stick into the wall and stop the clock from swinging when pulling up the weights while winding.

A **hanging clock** by Joseph Knibb of c1680.

Hare and snail Some early batch-produced watches had these symbols engraved on the regulator scale instead of the F and S on English watches and A and R on French ones.

Hare's foot Used by watchmakers to remove dust in the early 20th c before bristle brushes were introduced.

Hard enamel Form of glass, usually coloured, powdered and fused on to metal for decoration. Used on watch and small clock cases. Not a glaze as in pottery. See ENAMEL.

Hard gold plating Method of plating watch cases with a gold alloy (instead of pure gold) that can be hardened by heat treatment to make it more durable.

Harmonic motion Repetitive motion with a sinusoidal component as with a PENDULUM and BALANCE and spring.

Harp watch One with a harp-shaped case.

Harrison, John (1693–1776) Self-taught son of a carpenter from Foulby, Yorkshire, who, with his brother James, made extremely accurate clocks with wooden wheels (to avoid oiling). When the British government offered a £20,000 prize for 'solving' or FINDING THE LONGITUDE to help ships' navigation, he devoted the rest of his life to this, visiting London where GRAHAM lent him money. During the next six years he built his No.1 timekeeper, which showed seconds, minutes, hours and days, and worked very well on a sea voyage to Lisbon on test. Eventually his No.4, a big watch, qualified for the prize by being only 15 seconds slow after five months at sea. The BOARD OF LONGITUDE refused to pay him fully and it was only after many years of dispute and the intervention of the King, that Parliament overruled the Board, and Harrison received the remaining money, at the age of 80! Invented GRIDIRON compensation, the GRASSHOPPER ESCAPEMENT, TEMPERATURE COMPENSATION and a form of MAINTAINING POWER. Worked in later years in Red Lion Square, London. Buried in Hampstead churchyard.

A close-up view of part of John **Harrison's** third marine timekeeper. Note the anti-friction rollers on the pin wheel at just above centre left. (*National Maritime Museum, Greenwich*)

Harwood, John Twentieth-century English inventor of the first SELF-WINDING WRIST WATCH. One model had no winding button; turning the BEZEL moved the hands. His several inventions included a self-winding car clock. See BLANCPAIN, ROLEX.

Hatton Garden Traditional home of the diamond merchants in London and once the garden of Sir Christopher Hatton's Ely House. It became a centre of much of the clock and watch trade, which moved from CLERKENWELL, but now is mostly occupied by retail jewellers.

Hautefeuille, Abbé (1647–1724) Parisian inventor of the RACK LEVER ESCAPEMENT.

Heart cam Heart-shaped cam that returns a hand of a CHRONOGRAPH to zero by the shortest route. Invented by Adolphe Nicole in 1862.

Heart watch   Pocket watch with a heart-shaped case.

Heel ball   Inferior substitute for black enamel used to fill indications on brass clock dials. It is a hard black wax.

Hele, Petras.   See HENLEIN.

Helical gear   Toothed wheel with the teeth at an angle. Used in SKELETON CLOCKS for novelty, in music boxes for the worm gear driving the governor, and in some early watch escapements. See WORM ESCAPEMENT.

The **helical gears** in a skeleton clock in the British Horological Institute Museum.

Helical spring   Another name for a CYLINDRICAL SPRING.

Helio-chronometer   Very accurate COMPASS SUNDIAL.

Heliotrope clock   Name for a flower that faces and follows the sun and can therefore indicate the time. See FLORAL CLOCK.

Helmsman clock   French INDUSTRIAL CLOCK modelled on the bridge of a ship with a steersman at the helm who rocks from side to side, turning the ship's wheel.

A **helmsman clock** on which he is rocked by the pendulum to mimic sea motion.

Hemicyclium   Sundial shaped like quarter of a sphere and thought to have been invented by Berosus, the Chaldean astronomer, about 300BC. There is one at Pompeii.

Henlein, Peter   German clockmaker traditionally supposed to have invented the MAINSPRING for clocks and thus made the first portable clock or watch about 1510 (see NUREMBERG EGG). It is more likely that the first watches were made in Italy, Burgundy or Flanders, before 1488.

Hertz   Unit of frequency; number of cycles per second. Most quartz watches have a frequency of 32,768Hz. A seconds pendulum oscillates at 0.5Hz.

Hettich electric clock   Electric clock under a glass dome, at first sight like a FOUR-HUNDRED-DAY CLOCK but actually with a large FLOATING BALANCE suspended under the dial. A weighted arm drives the clock for about 50 seconds as it falls; the arm is then reset by a solenoid operated by a battery.

Heuer At the age of 20 in 1860, Edouard Heuer started making CHRONO-GRAPHS in St Imier, Switzerland, and the business has become associated with major sporting events, including the Olympic Games, and more recently Formula 1 Grand Prix motor racing. But it makes other watches and in 1949 invented the Solunar, a TIDAL DIAL watch. Taken over in 1985 by the French concern Techniques d'Avant Garde, it is now known as TAG-Heuer.

High brass Brass of higher than normal tensile strength used for clock wheels and other stressed parts comprising 66 per cent copper and 34 per cent zinc.

High frequency See FAST BEAT.

Highest clock This is said to be one in Brooklyn, New York, 131m (430ft) up.

Hindley, Henry (1701–71) Notable York maker of watches, clocks, and turret clocks who invented a WHEEL-CUTTING ENGINE and, in 1740, a screw cutting lathe.

Hipp trailer, toggle, or **butterfly** Device for electric clocks to supply driving IMPULSES on demand. As the PENDU-LUM swings, it drags a loose toggle over a switch. If the AMPLITUDE of the pendulum drops, on the return swing, the toggle does not clear the switch and presses into a notch to close the switch momentarily and impulse the pendulum.

Hit-or-miss synchroniser Means of synchronising a slave pendulum with a FREE PENDULUM. The SLAVE has a slight losing RATE and when the AMPLI-TUDE falls, a toggle catches on a switch to cause a small IMPULSE to be given to the slave.

Hoadley, Silas (1786–1870) Greystone, U.S.A. Early maker, first of clocks with wooden movements. Became TERRY, Thomas, and Hoadley in 1809, and just Thomas and Hoadley from 1810 to 1813. Then he worked alone until 1849.

Hog's bristle See BRISTLE REGULA-TOR.

Hole-closing punch Special punch used for reducing the diameter of PIVOT holes in brass clock PLATES that have become larger or oval through wear. The correct-sized punch is positioned in the hole. There is a concave grooved part around the punch, so that, when the punch is hammered, the metal of the plate closes round it. Considered to be very bad prac-tice by professional restorers.

Hong Kong industry From making watch bracelets in the 1960s, by the 1980s Hong Kong became at one time the world's biggest exporter of watches and electronic clocks. It manufactures for most of the world brand names and the parts are often assembled in mainland China. Before China took over in 1997, it had large numbers of small watch companies who bought quartz watch modules from Japan and also clock modules, which were turned into complete watches and clocks to the designs of the 'manufacturers' in other countries. It produced few of its own designs and had no known brands. A number of watches were made to order in Hong Kong with cases similar to those of well-known Swiss watch manufacturers, which was quite legal there. These became forgeries when the well-known names were reproduced on the dials in Thailand.

Hood The top of a LONGCASE CLOCK case enclosing the MOVEMENT. The earliest hoods were 'rising hoods', lifted up to reach the dial and locked up by a spring catch, the 'spoon'. After about 1685 clocks became taller and the hood was designed to be pulled forward to remove it. It has a glazed door to reach the dial, unlike the fixed glass of the rising hood.

Hooded clock WALL CLOCK enclosed in a case but with the weights and pendulum hanging below it. Often at first it was a LANTERN CLOCK in a wooden case, then a clock in its own right made from the late 17th and through the 18th c.

A George III mahogany **hooded clock** with pierced cresting by John Ellicott, London, with anchor escapement.

Hook escapement   Another name for a VIRGULE ESCAPEMENT.

Hooke, Robert (1635–1703)   An eccentric genius, first experimenter of the Royal Society, horological inventor and pioneer of the microscope. Discovered the law of springs. Invented various HAIRSPRINGS in 1664 which may have included a spiral one. In answer to HUYGENS' counter-claim, he declared 'Zulichem's spring not worth a farthing!' Designed a toothed wheel cutting engine for clockmakers in 1670. Dr Hooke may have invented the ANCHOR ESCAPEMENT made by CLEMENT. Collaborated closely with TOMPION.

Hooke's Law   The law of springs discovered by HOOKE which states that the force produced by a spring is proportional to its tension.

Hoop wheel   A WHEEL in the striking TRAIN of an old clock disc with a wide rim to one side. The rim has a gap for about seven-eighths of its circumference into which a DETENT can drop to allow the WARNING, then striking.

Hope-Jones, Frank   Pioneer and historian of electric and MASTER CLOCKS ('Electrical Timekeeping', N.A.G. Press, 1940). Invented in particular the Synchronome detached GRAVITY ESCAPEMENT, which greatly improved timekeeping by using an electric solenoid to raise a lever. The lever, released by the pendulum, IMPULSED it at an exact moment and was reset. It was a REMONTOIRE. The electric solenoid impulsed the PENDULUM directly in earlier clocks.

Horizontal escapement   Alternative name for the CYLINDER ESCAPEMENT, because the ESCAPE WHEEL was parallel to the other wheels and not at right angles to them, as in the VERGE.

Horloge   Name given to both water and mechanical clocks in the Middle Ages, which makes it difficult to decide which is meant in ancient manuscripts.

Horloge de Sapience   See WISDOM CLOCK.

Horned cresting   See SWAN'S NECK CRESTING.

Horns   A LEVER ESCAPEMENT has a notch at the end with 'horns' each side of it, which form part of the SAFETY ACTION.

Horologium   Medieval name for a timekeeper of any kind – sundial, water clock or mechanical clock – which makes it difficult to interpret some ancient writing.

Horological Institute of America   Founded in 1921 by the National Research Council, Washington, D.C., to control standards and encourage recruiting. Superseded by the AMERICAN WATCHMAKERS' INSTITUTE.

Horology The study of time and time-keeping.

Horology in art Timepieces shown in paintings of well-attested date have been useful for confirming styles and dates. An example is a VERTICAL FRAME alarm clock with crown VERGE in Botticelli's painting of St Augustine in 1480.

Horse Wooden jig to hold a clock while repairing it. Also a trestle. Horse hair from the tail was used in the bows used with the TURNS because it did not fray like string.

Horse timer Old name for a CHRONO-GRAPH.

Hour Twenty-fourth part of a day, equivalent to 15° of rotation of the Earth. In the past, hours were often of variable length (see CANONICAL HOURS, TEMPORAL HOURS, JAPANESE CLOCK). The division of 24 may have come about as described under MINUTE. An hour is now based on the definition of one SECOND. BABYLONIAN HOURS were based on the 24-hour system and the Italians used the 24-hour system (as opposed to two 12s) from the 14th c. See DECIMAL TIME.

Hour angle The angle (time elapsed) through which a star has passed since it crossed the MERIDIAN. Shown very rarely on a clock dial.

Hour glass A SAND GLASS arranged to time an hour's interval.

Hour-glass clock American THIRTY-HOUR clock of hour-glass shape by Joseph Ives c1840 with a round dial and painted glass trunk with a pillar each side. Unusual FUSEE and spring drive. Now very rare.

Hour wheel The wheel in the MOTION WORK to which the hour hand is attached.

House clock Early name for a domestic or CHAMBER CLOCK, when there was usually only one in the home.

Huaud Three Geneva painters, Pierre, Jean, and Amy Huaud became famous for ENAMELLED WATCHES from about 1679.

Huguenot makers It is known that in the 17th c watch and clockmakers had a higher than average degree of literacy and the Reformation converted an exceptional number of them so that they rivalled Catholic makers in numbers. France's Revocation in 1685 of the Edict of Nantes caused many Protestant craftsmen to flee, fearing persecution. Skilled watchmakers went to Geneva and London, which also received clockmakers. Skilled silversmiths went to Cheapside in London. They were the seeds of English and Swiss dominance in these trades later.

Human clock See BIOLOGICAL CLOCK.

Humidity error Change of RATE caused by the amount of moisture in the air.

Hunter Normally a pocket watch with a hinged lid over the dial, but wrist watches are occasionally made hunter-style. A half-hunter has a hole in the centre of the lid to read the time. Supposedly Napoleon's idea. See DIGITAL DISPLAY and PERPETUAL CALENDAR for pictures.

Hunting tooth An extra tooth added to a WHEEL or PINION so that the number of teeth is not an exact multiple of an engaging wheel or pinion, thus spreading any wear.

Huygens, Christiaan (1629–95) Dutch scientist who invented the first practical PENDULUM clock in 1657, which was made for him by Salomon Coster. He discovered CIRCULAR ERROR and wrote the first accurate treatise on the pendulum, 'Horologium Oscillatorium'. A handsome and gifted man who was given an English title. Probably the inventor of the spiral BALANCE SPRING, 1675 (but see HOOKE). Often referred to as 'Zulichem'. See THURET.

Hydraulic clock Clock in which the power is supplied by water or one in which the ESCAPEMENT is water controlled. The Frenchman Bernard Gitton has made sophisticated public hydraulic clocks using coloured antifreeze liquid in syphons of glass tubing and bulbs as 'liquid gears' and escapement. Sixteen of them from 2 to 8m (6ft 6in–26ft) high are working in different countries.

Hydrogen clock 19th c clock in which zinc pellets are released from time to time to drop into hydrochloric acid to generate hydrogen gas to wind the weight, after which the hydrogen was released. Explosive timekeeping! There is one in the Guildhall Museum, London.

A replica of the first pendulum clock by Christiaan **Huygens**. He soon eliminated the gearing seen here between the pendulum and crown wheel. It is in the Science Museum.

I

Iatromathematical dial Form of early ASTROLOGICAL DIAL indicating the 'best' times to carry out certain medical operations, such as bleeding, as well as personal needs, such as cutting toe nails.

Idler, or **idle wheel** One used to link others or change their direction of rotation without altering the gear ratio. They tend to wear out sooner than others.

Ilbert Collection One of the most famous collections of clocks and watches and horological books ever assembled, by Courtenay A. Ilbert (1888–1956), who lived in south-west London. He left to the nation a TOMPION clock that came from the ROYAL OBSERVATORY (see FLAMSTEED). Almost all the clock collection was bought in 1958 by public donation, organised by the Worshipful Company of Clockmakers to be added to the BRITISH MUSEUM COLLECTION to form the most important historical collection of clocks and watches in the world. Selected items from it, most of them going, are presented with historical and technical details in a remarkable permanent exhibition. There is a students' room, the Ilbert Room, for serious students of horology, opened in 1963 as a condition of the donation.

Ilbert Library A famous library of books and leaflets left by C.A. Ilbert in 1957 to the BRITISH HOROLOGICAL INSTITUTE, Upton Hall, Newark, Nottinghamshire, where it is now housed.

Illuminated clock NIGHT CLOCKS for domestic use are of 17th c origin, and illuminated public clocks much later. London's first was at St Giles-in-the-Fields church in 1827 although they were previously introduced in Liverpool, Manchester and elsewhere. A gas flame

with a reflector was stationed behind the skeleton cast-iron dial of the clock, which was over opal glass.

Imitation compensated balance See FALSE BALANCE.

Imitation material Replacement parts for watches made by suppliers other than the original makers.

Impulse Small force applied at intervals to a PENDULUM or BALANCE to keep it swinging.

Impulse dial Another name for a SLAVE DIAL, which is operated by a MASTER CLOCK. The master clock sends electric IMPULSES at intervals, usually of half a minute, which operate a solenoid and RATCHET to advance the hands, hence the name.

Impulse pin Small pin by which an IMPULSE is given to a BALANCE. See RUBY PIN. See LEVER ESCAPEMENT for illustration.

In beat When IMPULSES have the same power, and therefore swings of an oscillator are the same in both directions. Clockmakers gauge this by listening to the intervals between succeeding ticks and tocks. Adjusted in PENDULUM clocks by bending the CRUTCH or by a BEAT ADJUSTER. Altered in BALANCE and spring by the PINNING POINT or a beat adjuster.

Incabloc The first universal SHOCK ABSORBER system for watches, made by a Swiss firm. The JEWELS and END STONES are also shock-absorbers.

Incense clock The Chinese laid a trail of powdered incense in a groove in wood ash and set light to one end. Bamboo pegs marked with the hour and placed along the groove showed the time as the incense burned. The 'clock' is a pan into which the ash is tamped. The groove forms a pattern. It is made by placing a perforated lid over the ash and running the handle end of a small shovel along the slots, like using a stencil. Incense placed in the groove burns at an even rate without a flame. After lighting the perforated cover was replaced to protect the clock from draughts. See CHINESE MATCH, FIRE CLOCK.

Incense seal Like an incense clock but using a flat piece of stone or metal instead of ash with a channel on the surface to hold the powdered incense. Tracks are simply up and down, spiral or in maze form. Made for many centuries, into the 20th. Usually wrongly described as 'opium stoves' or 'hand warmers' in antique shops. They were used in China and also Japan, where they were made of wood lacquered in red and black and larger than the Chinese versions.

Inch, Paris See PARIS INCH.

Inclination test Rating test for a marine chronometer by locking the GYMBALS and testing it at an angle.

Inclined plane clock Form of GRAVITY CLOCK made in the 17th c. The clock is in a drum case which rolls very slowly down a sloping wooden track. It is restrained by a heavy weight on the end of a lever attached to the ARBOR of the CENTRE WHEEL, thus powering the clock as it slowly descends. The time is shown by a single hand attached to the CENTRE ARBOR which points upwards against the turning dial. Sometimes the inclined plane is marked with days of the week. Also called a 'rolling clock'.

Independent seconds The seconds hand of a CHRONOGRAPH or STOP WATCH that can be stopped for reading (e.g. a lap time) and released to catch up. Also used for a clock or watch seconds hand, usually a CENTRE SECONDS HAND, which jumps from one second to the next, i.e. it is DEAD BEAT, although the other hands are not. Sometimes called 'jump seconds'. BREGUET invented a jumping hour hand.

Index Part of a watch REGULATOR which effectively alters the length of the HAIRSPRING for final timekeeping adjustments. The outer end of the spring is fixed and the index, which is a lever, moves two CURB PINS (one each side of the spring) around a short arc of the spring. See DUST CAP for picture.

Index dial Small numbered dial on a winding square at the back of an early watch. Also called a 'rosette', or 'figure plate' because of the numbers engraved on it. Turning the square alters the effective length of the HAIRSPRING, like the later INDEX.

Index pins See CURB PINS.

India oilstone Manufactured abrasive material available in various shapes for shaping metal parts or tool sharpening. It is soaked in light oil before use.

Indian case Case of a LONGCASE CLOCK made by a local craftsman for a movement exported to the British in India. The case was often carved.

Indiction A cycle of 15 years, shown very occasionally on early clocks. It may have originated from the taxation census carried out every 15 years in Egypt from about 300AD. See JULIAN PERIOD.

A 20th c **inclined plane clock** by Dent, London. The position of the clock on the ramp down which it rolls gives the day of the week.

Indicator Hand for indicating the time an alarm clock is set to ring.

Indirect seconds See INDEPENDENT SECONDS.

Industrial clock French and German makers, during their Industrial Revolutions in the 1800s, produced many clocks in cases representing power-driven machines and other artifacts, some of them automated. Examples are the autocar, BATTLESHIP, BEAM ENGINE, DESTROYER, DROP FORGE, Eiffel Tower, HELMSMAN, LIGHTHOUSE, LOCOMOTIVE, motor car, RAILWAY ENGINE, PRINTING PRESS, stationary STEAM ENGINE, SUBMARINE, TORPEDO, WATER WHEEL, WINDMILL, WINE PRESS, even the BOMB! Many were made by Diette et Hour, Paris, 1890–1910.

One of the many styles of **industrial clocks**, this depicting a stationary steam engine.

Industrial Revolution The main impact of this on clockmaking was on the brass plates which provided sheets of brass of even thickness. Previously the clockmaker had to cast the brass into sheets, which were flattened by trip hammers operated by water mills. At this time, brass was called 'latten'. Hammer marks on the back indicate an early plate.

Industrial timer One for timing individual actions or processes in factories and with some models also adding up series of operations.

An **industrial timer** of 1964, the first to give the total time of operations as well as individual times.

Ingersoll Two brothers Robert H. (1859–1928) and Charles H. (1865–1948) started a mail order business and decided to have some cheap watches made by the WATERBURY CLOCK CO., first the Jumbo, then the Columbus. They sold so well that the business became a watch supply company in New York, manufacturing from 1890. In 1898 they sold a million watches. They opened in Britain in 1899, later offering a Boer War commemorative watch. The American company went into liquidation in 1922 and then became part of Waterbury, which was bought by the U.S. Time Corporation, which produced Ingersoll watches until the name TIMEX was adopted. The British directors bought Ingersoll in 1931, when it became a British public company. See DOLLAR WATCH.

Ingold, Pierre-Frederic (1787–1878) Pioneer of mechanized watchmaking from Bienne, who worked for BREGUET in Paris, introduced JEWELS to Switzerland, entered negotiations with the JAPYs, but could not agree and tried to set up a watchmaking factory in France. He transferred to London, where his Soho factory was damaged by workers who made watches by hand, so moved to the U.S.A. and became a U.S. citizen. There his ideas were adopted and the first factories set up in Boston, but he personally was expelled without reason. He returned to La Chaux de Fonds and tried, again unsuccessfully, to set up a factory, dying there at the age of 92. In the meantime watchmaking by machinery had been started by Leschot in Geneva. Ingold drills were used until recently.

Ingold fraise Cutting tool shaped like a PINION for correcting inaccuracies in the teeth of wheels. Invented by INGOLD.

Ingraham, Elias (1805–85) Pioneer of the American clock industry who eventually formed the E. Ingraham Co. His sharp Gothic-style case, called the 'steeple case', became one of the most popular small SHELF CLOCKS ever manufactured. Added watches in 1914.

Ink recorder Tracer which makes an ink dot on a dial to indicate the end of a timed event. Literally a chronograph made by BREGUET, L. Fatton and J.W. Benson, London.

Inkstand clock Desk clock incorporated in inkstand.

Inner terminal Inner end of a HAIRSPRING where it is attached to the COLLET. In the past it was given a special curve to improve the timekeeping of precision watches. This is now known to be valueless, but the POINT OF ATTACHMENT is very important.

Inox Stamped on some Swiss watches, meaning 'inoxydable' or non-oxidising, non-rusting.

Inro watch Pockets were rare in Japan before Western dress was adopted. The Japanese carried a stamp and ink, then medicines, in small decorated wooden boxes called 'inros'. They were worn attached by cords and a button (the *netsuke*), to the kimono belt. In the 18th c many inros were converted to watches or CLOCK-WATCHES. There is a small drawer for the watch key.

An early 19th c Japanese inro clock-watch in a Shitan wood case. It has a verge and chain for the going train and going barrel for the striking train. (*Sotheby's*)

Instantaneous recording Jumping action of a minute indicator as each minute passes, as used on high-quality chronographs. In most, the hand creeps round the dial.

Integral balance BI-METALLIC BALANCE, with the two metals of the rim bonded together.

Integrated circuit Electronic circuit with all its transistors, diodes, capacitors and resistors included in one small block, the chip. Used in QUARTZ CRYSTAL watches as a frequency divider, decoder, memory recall system, etc.

Intermediate wheel One interposed between the GREAT WHEEL and CENTRE WHEEL to increase the duration of going. Thus a month-duration LONGCASE CLOCK will have an intermediate wheel, as do most French and German fourteen-day clocks.

Internal gear Wheel with the teeth on the inside of the rim as used in sun and planet gearing and the COUNT WHEEL of some early TURRET CLOCKS as well as in TOURBILLION and KARRUSEL watches.

International Atomic Time English name of the international standard T.A.I. See U.T.C.

International Date Line See TIME ZONES.

International time STANDARD TIME as applied in the different TIME ZONES.

International Watch Co. Founded in the 1860s by an American, Florentine Jones, in Schaffhausen, eastern Switzerland, far from the watchmaking centres of Geneva and the Jura. The object was to export watches to America. In 1875 it failed, was taken over by others and eventually by a German conglomerate. It was a pioneer of KEYLESS WINDING, and I.W.C. pocket watches with this are collectors' items. It was one of the first producers of ladies' wrist watches, based on its ladies' pocket watch and gained a reputation for COMPLICATED WATCHES.

Interrupter Circuit breaker used in some electric clocks.

Interval timer Clock mechanism that can be set to a given time interval and gives a sound or light signal or turns a switch at the end of it, such as a kitchen, parking, PROCESS, TELEPHONE or PHOTOGRAPHIC TIMER. The earliest of fair accuracy was probably invented by HIPP or WHEATSTONE. See PARKING TIMER (WATCH).

Invar Alloy of 35.6 per cent nickel with the remainder steel, invented by GUILLAUME and named from 'invariable' as its expansion at different temperatures is negligible. Invar pendulum rods solve TEMPERATURE COMPENSATION problems. See COMPENSATION PENDULUM.

Inventions The late American clockmaker, Henry Fried, identified clockmakers as responsible for several basic inventions: the thermostat (see BIMETALLIC BALANCE), the oblique drive, the endless chain double pulley (see ENDLESS ROPE), the block chain as used on bicycles (see FUSEE CHAIN), WORM GEARING, differential gearing (see WILLIAMSON), the universal joint (see CLOCK), roller bearings (see HARRISON), cams (see WILLIAMSON), the dividing head for gear cutting, gear hobbing, the friction clutch, the split lathe chuck, programming (see COUNT WHEEL, RACK STRIKING), variable speed gearing, jewel bearings, the oil-retaining bearing (see OIL SINK), the jewel bearing (see JEWEL), gear hobbing, the split chuck for lathes and the feedback principle (See PENDULE SYMPATHIQUE).

Inverted bell top Top of a clock case where, instead of starting convex at the top and becoming concave like the BELL TOP, it does the opposite, starting concave and becoming convex.

Inverted escapement Arrangement with the ANCHOR under the ESCAPE WHEEL instead of on top, as in many earlier American clocks. The purpose on some clocks, such as a few English LONGCASE CLOCKS, was to position the seconds hand below instead of above the centre of the dial.

Iron clock The first domestic clocks (in Italy, Germany and France), early public clocks and watches were made of wrought iron because their makers were blacksmiths and locksmiths. Brass was introduced in the 16th c on the Continent for cases and dials, and spread to England at the beginning of the 17th. See LANTERN CLOCK. It was, however, also used for DONDI'S CLOCK in the 14th c. Wrought iron was retained for TURRET CLOCKS until cast iron was used in the 19th c by GRIMTHORPE.

Iron clock case American makers, particularly the Ansonia company, of quantity-produced 'French marble clocks' made the cases of cast iron or embossed tin plate lacquered to imitate marble. Typical American movements were fitted.

This enamelled American **iron clock case** imitates marble.

Iron front clock In America there was a fashion for cast-iron fronts to clock cases in the 1850s to 1870s. Many were of overornate rococo design and, actually cheaper then, in bronze, presumably because it cast cleaner. It is said that they were a cheaper version of the PAPIER MÂCHÉ CLOCK.

Iron marks POSTED FRAME turret clocks are occasionally found with marks stamped in the iron. Although these are commonly supposed to indicate the clockmakers, they usually indicate the makers of the iron. Much of this came from Sweden.

Isochronism Occupying equal time. Used of a BALANCE or PENDULUM when the time of swing does not vary whatever the ARC of swing. Almost

impossible to achieve in practice (although some MARINE CHRONOMETERS approach it), thus resulting in POSITIONAL ERRORS in watches. Because QUARTZ CRYSTALS vibrate, they can also have positional errors, although very small ones. See CIRCULAR ERROR, GALILEO, AIRY.

Isoval Alloy used for HAIRSPRINGS, said to benefit ISOCHRONISM.

Italian horological industry There is documentary evidence of mechanical timekeepers in use well before 1300 and simple individual clocks by 1305. A public clock by Jacopo Dondi, father of the famous Giovanni, was erected in Padua in 1344. Spring-driven clocks appeared about 1400. Watches seem to

An early product of the **Italian horological industry** in the Ilbert Collection.

have first been produced in the 1480s. Mantua was an important centre in the 15th c. What is said to be the earliest ALARM clock in existence is also Italian, an interesting fact being that it is made of brass. There is, however, some doubt about its authenticity since identical ones came up for auction in London. The Italians eventually lost the lead to the Flemish, French, Germans and English. Clocks of many types, including alarms and TOWER CLOCKS, and some watches, are made today. See ALMANUS MANUSCRIPT.

Italian hours Early Italian method of dividing EQUAL HOURS into one series numbered from 1 to 24, starting at every sunset. DONDI'S CLOCK employed this system. The rest of Europe used the DOUBLE-TWELVE system, starting at midnight and midday. As the main centres of clock and watchmaking were in southern Germany between countries using different systems, many timepieces were adaptable to both. The most common practice was a hand rotating once in 12 hours with a dial divided into 12 from I to XII and also (in Arabic numbers) from 13 to 24.

Ithaca Co. New York firm that made clocks with two large dials, the lower one being a PERPETUAL CALENDAR, in the 19th c. The Seth Thomas Co. also made these.

Ives, Joseph (1810–55) American clock-maker who devised a stamping process for brass clock plates and invented the WAGGON SPRING CLOCK.

Ivory Cream coloured tusk of an elephant, walrus, hippopotamus, etc., often used in the past for small decorative inlays in wooden clock cases. Also imitated by bone.

J

Jack Originally a man (the sexton) struck the CANONICAL HOURS on a bell when a small ALARM warned him to do so. Then a mechanical man (AUTOMATON) was invented to strike the bell. One of the earliest, the 1383 clock at Dijon, France, was called 'Jacquemart' (Jack o' the clock) in 1517 records. This became contracted to 'Jack' in England, as with 'Jack Blandifer', who sits above an arch inside Wells Cathedral, one of the oldest jacks still extant. He sounds the quarters on another bell with his heels. The clock was made c1392. 'Jack the Smiter' at Southwold, Suffolk, is in 15th c 'armour', but is now operated by a rope.

Jacobean pillar Twisting wooden pillar used at two or all corners of the HOOD of some LONGCASE CLOCKS.

Some early bracket and longcase clocks had **Jacobean pillars** on the case hood. These are on the ebony case of a Thomas Tompion clock of 1670–5.

Jack Blandifer, an automaton who, operated by the clock, strikes the bell with a hammer in Wells Cathedral.

Jacob's chuck Three-jaw self-centering chuck used in lathes and small drilling machines.

Jacot tool Tool used by repairers to polish PIVOTS.

150

Jacquet-Droz Swiss watchmaking family of La Chaux-de-Fonds. Pierre (1721–90) specialised in musical work and automata, particularly human figures. Two are in the Neuchâtel Museum, a boy making drawings and a girl playing an organ. With them is a writing boy made by his son, Henri Louis.

Jacquemart See JACK.

Jaeger-Le Coultre Charles Le Coultre formed the company in 1833 in Le Sentier, Valleé de Joux, where it still is. The French MARINE CHRONOMETER maker, Edward Jaeger, became a partner in 1937. They specialised in CHRONOGRAPHS, MINUTE REPEATERS and ALARM WATCHES by the end of the century. In 1928 they produced the ATMOS CLOCK (see for picture) and in 1931 the REVERSO WATCH. Today it is the biggest employer in this watchmaking centre.

Jam nut Nut used to lock another one on a thread; what engineers call a 'locking nut'. Used to fasten the RATING NUT on some REGULATORS.

Janvier, Antide (1751–1835) One of France's finest clockmakers, who was a self-taught peasant. At 15 he began making a clock showing the motions of the sun and Earth; sidereal, true and mean times; the length of days, the rising and setting of the sun at any horizon; and the mean motion of the moon, its nodes (when its orbit cuts the ECLIPTIC), its phases, and conjunctions (when it is between the sun and earth). When only 16 he presented it to the Academie des Sciences et Belles Lettres at Besançon. It is still there. He made a number of other astronomical clocks. Was a Member of the Revolution Art Commission and then Horologer du Roi but died in a pauper's home. Few of his 500–600 clocks have been located.

Japanese bell clock Late 18th c clock inside a bell, which it sounded. The rotating dial was underneath, in the bell mouth.

Japanese clocks Dutch traders took VERGE and FOLIOT clocks to Japan in

The complicated train of a **Janvier** planetary clock made between 1789 and 1801. Indications include the movement of Uranus.

1600. The Japanese copied these, but did not follow European trends. Instead, they adapted clocks to show Japanese hours. Until as late as 1873, a day was divided into six night hours and six day hours. The hours were indicated by zodiac symbols: cock (sunset), dog, boar, rat (midnight), ox, tiger, hare (sunrise) dragon, serpent, horse (noon), sheep, monkey. Each hour was divided into ten parts. Since periods of daylight altered through the year, so did the lengths of both day and night hours. Clocks were therefore made to go one RATE in the day and another at night by using two foliots. Hour divisions could be changed by hand, or the dials replaced by others at each month. Each six hour period was numbered backwards 9 (noon or midnight), 8, 7, 6 (sunset or sunrise), 5, and 4, starting from noon and midnight. Striking followed suit. Clocks of the period striking half hours sound them alternately with single and double blows. So a Japanese clock of the period strikes 9 at 12 noon; 1 at 12.30 pm: 8 at 1 pm: 2 at 1.30 pm: 7 at 2 pm: 1 at 2.30 pm, and so on. Collectors divide old Japanese clocks into three varieties: LANTERN, BRACKET (introduced in the 19th c), and pillar, a type not found elsewhere. On a pillar clock a pointer indicates the time on a straight vertical scale, which is changed monthly.

A **Japanese clock** of the 19th c that strikes and has moveable hours. (*Sotheby's*)

Japanese watches The best known to collectors in the West is the INRO WATCH.

Japanese horological industry After being highly specialised for centuries, a modern industry in Japan grew rapidly after the Second World War and was one of the first to produce a QUARTZ CRYS-TAL domestic clock and first to produce a quartz crystal watch.

Japanning Methods of imitating Oriental LACQUER, devised in Europe and North America in the late 17th c and used for clock cases, particularly LONG-CASE, from 1695 to 1715 in London and up to 1775 in the provinces. The ground colour was usually black with decoration or scenes in low relief and gilded with

metal dust. Dark green, red (particularly in England) and yellow or buff were also used for the ground colour. The surface becomes covered in fine cracks in time. A few brass dials of longcase clocks were japanned in the 1790s to 'modernise' them after the white dial was introduced c1770.

Japy Frères Pioneers of the FRENCH HOROLOGICAL INDUSTRY, now a huge French group of clock and watch factories based on a business founded by Frédéric Japy (1749–1812) about 1772 and so named after his five sons had joined him. It made millions of timepieces of every kind including great numbers of French MARBLE CLOCKS and PEND-ULES DE PARIS in the 19th c. Originally it also made many other articles includ-ing toys, and the engine for Peugeot's first motor car. Japy invented the earliest machine tools for making watches, partic-ularly of LEPINE CALIBRE design.

Jar The iron or glass container of a MERCURY PENDULUM bob.

Jean-Richard, Daniel Went to Le Locle in Switzerland in 1700 and, with his five sons, became a pioneer of watchmaking in the Neuchâtel area, particularly by factory methods. There is a statue of him in Le Locle.

Jerome, Chauncey (1793–1868) Clock case maker and deviser of the American BRONZE LOOKING-GLASS CLOCK. Also made a number of GRAND-MOTHER CLOCKS c1823. Became America's largest clock manufacturer by 1850. Movements were made of wood until he introduced cheap brass ones. He exported to England. In his 70s, his companies failed and he ended his life as a factory worker.

Jesuit clocks Striking clocks introduced into China by Jesuit missionaries after 1585.

Jewel Clock or watch bearing made of a gemstone, comprising a ring (the 'hole') with a SINK for oil. The first ever patent was granted in London in 1704 to Nicholas FACIO, and Peter and Jacob

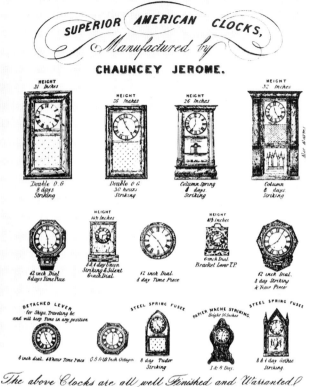

SUPERIOR AMERICAN CLOCKS,

Manufactured by

CHAUNCEY JEROME.

HEIGHT
31 Inches

HEIGHT
26 Inches

HEIGHT
26 Inches

HEIGHT
32 Inches

Double O.G.
8 days
Striking

Double O.G.
30 hours
Striking

Column Spring
8 days.
Striking

Column
8 days.
Striking

HEIGHT
14½ Inches

HEIGHT
10½ Inches

42 inch Dial
8days Time Piece

8 & 1 day Drawn
Striking & Silent
6 inch Dial.

12 inch Dial.
8 day Time Piece

6 inch Dial.
Bracket Lever T.P.

12 inch Dial.
8 day Striking
& Time Piece.

DETACHED LEVER
for Ships, Travelling &c
and will keep Time in any position

STEEL SPRING FUSEE

PAPIER MACHE STRIKING
Height 16 Inches

STEEL SPRING FUSEE

6 inch dial, 48 hour Time Pece

O.S.& 1.0 Inch Octagon

8 day Tudor
Striking

1 & 8 Day.

8 & 1 day Gothic
Striking

The above Clocks are all well Finished and Warranted.

THE PUBLIC ARE RESPECTFULLY CAUTIONED AGAINST COUNTERFEITS.

A page from a **Jerome** catalogue showing American clocks designed for the English market.

DEBAUFRE, who used pierced natural rubies. Many other gemstones have been used including sapphire, chrysoberyl, quartz and garnet (which is too soft) as well as diamond. The jewel patent kept the English industry ahead of the French, their main rivals, for a century. Now synthetic ruby or sapphire is universal. Also an END STONE to take the end thrust of a PIVOT, an IMPULSE PIN, and a PALLET made of synthetic ruby for watches or agate for clocks. Jewels reduce friction and wear. Making them is a highly specialised separate industry. A court case in 1962 established that it is illegal in the U.K. to advertise or sell watches by 'jewels' that are not truly functional. See DORMANT JEWEL, LIVERPOOL WINDOW.

Jewel hole gauge Tapered pin to measure the hole size. Also, a brass plate fitted with a graduated and accurate series of jewel holes acting as standard sizes.

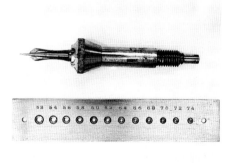

A **jewel hole gauge** with hole gauge plate.

Jewel pin   See IMPULSE PIN.

Jewelled   Fitted with jewel bearings. The most important in a watch are two with holes and two END STONES without holes for the BALANCE STAFF, two PALLETS and an IMPULSE PIN, totalling seven. Better mechanical watches have other train bearings jewelled. Fully jewelled normally means 15 or 17 jewels or 21–25 in an automatic watch. In older watches the jewels were mounted in CHATONS fixed into the watch by screws. Modern jewels are friction fitted. See FALSE JEWELLING.

Jewelled lever Watch of better quality, with a LEVER ESCAPEMENT which has jewelled PALLETS, not pin pallets (see for illustrations of both).

Jockele clock or Jockeleuhr Miniature weight-driven PENDULUM clock devised in the BLACK FOREST by Jakob Herbstreit (d.1801), by whom it is named. Dials were of metal or porcelain. It is halfway in size between the SCHOTTENUHR and the SORGUHR.

Jockey wheel When a belt and pulley are used to drive another pulley, the tension of the belt is often maintained by a third WHEEL or pulley pressing against the belt.

Joker musical alarm A cheap BLACK FOREST alarm in CARRIAGE CLOCK style which plays two tunes for about ten minutes instead of ringing a bell. Seth Thomas supplied an almost identical clock in America in the late 19th c.

Joss-stick alarm See FIRE CLOCK.

Journeyman After seven years, an APPRENTICE clockmaker had to work as a journeyman for two years before he was allowed to submit his MASTERPIECE to the CLOCKMAKERS' COMPANY. If the masterpiece was approved, he was granted the Freedom of the Company and could become a MASTER clockmaker. Apprentices lived on the premises, but journeymen could live out, i.e. they 'journeyed' to work.

Julian calendar Different early civilisations like the Indians, Chinese, Persians, Hebrews, Incas, Aztecs, et al., had different calendars. All varied. Julius Caesar introduced the first calendar of 365.25 days in a year with leap years. The one we now use is the GREGORIAN CALENDAR.

Julian period Because months and years of unequal lengths cause complications, astronomers use a Julian period of years and days, not to be confused with the JULIAN CALENDAR. The Julian era started on 1 January 4713BC, from which days were numbered consecutively and each year comprised 365.25 mean days. The period is based on the INDICTION of 15 multiplied by the lunar or METONIC CYCLE of 19 multiplied by the SOLAR YEAR or cycle of 28, which equals 7,980. They began together on the above date. Its incorporation is extremely rare.

Jump of Mount Street Maker of fine clocks from some time before 1850. The firm was founded by Richard Thomas and Joseph Jump, apprentices of B.L. VULLIAMY, whose business they eventually took over. It was closed in the 1930s. Typical Jump clocks are in the BREGUET milestone shape.

Jumper A wedge-shaped CLICK held between the teeth of a STAR WHEEL by a spring so that the wheel jumps a tooth when turned one way or the other by a pin. Used for calendar indication, JUMPING DIALS, etc.

A **jumping dial** watch with just the hours jumping, and shown in the top aperture.

Jumping dial   Clock or watch dial with DIGITAL RECORDING on which the numerals are seen through apertures, the hours 'jumping' or changing every hour, and the minutes every minute. Such watches go in and out of fashion. Also employed in small public clocks. A variation is the TICKET CLOCK.

Jumping hand   Hour hand that jumps forward at every hour. BREGUET repeating watches often had them.

A **jumping hand** watch of c1850.

Jumping seconds   Seconds hand that is DEAD BEAT, i.e. jumps forward every second.

Jurgensen, Urban (1776–1830)   Celebrated Danish maker of MARINE CHRON-OMETERS and astronomical regulators. Worked in Denmark, Switzerland, France, and England.

Junghans Gbr.   Erhard Junghans made brass pressings for PICTURE-FRAME CLOCKS. His brother Xavier saw new clockmaking machinery in America, so the brothers set up a factory in Schramberg, Germany, in 1870. It became one of the world's biggest, exporting in huge numbers. VIENNA REGULATORS, CUCKOO CLOCKS and many other types were made through the years. Erhard was a pioneer of the BLACK FOREST HOROLOGICAL INDUSTRY.

K

Karrusel Revolving ESCAPEMENT, slower than the TOURBILLON and simpler, intended to reduce POSITIONAL ERRORS. Invented in 1892 by B. Bonniksen, a Dane who was at one time a BRITISH HOROLOGICAL INSTITUTE instructor. Used by the U.S. Navy.

A **karrusel** of 1900–1 by Golay of Myddleton Street, Clerkenwell, London, which did very well in the Kew trials.

Kassel (or Cassel) Seat of the court of Count William IV in Hessen, Germany, which was an important clockmaking centre inspired by Tycho BRAHE. Two famous makers there were Eberhart Baldewin and Jobst Burgi.

Kew A Certificate Performance certificate for timekeepers introduced in 1885 at the Kew Observatory, Old Deer Park, Richmond, and taken over by the NATIONAL PHYSICAL LABORATORY at Teddington in 1912. This, and the lower grade B Certificate tests were superseded in 1951. The Kew Observatory was originally built for King George III, who was keenly interested in timekeepers. It became the Air Ministry Meteorological Office. See RATING CERTIFICATE and TIMEKEEPING TRIALS.

Key Used for winding (or sometimes for SETTING UP) the MAINSPRING. No watch keys before the 17th c have survived. The early crank type in iron or brass was partly replaced by the T-shaped key around 1650, which became elaborately pierced and engraved or set with agate, rock crystal, or cameos after the Commonwealth. The best watches had gold or silver keys from about 1680 to 1770. Around this time simpler brass and steel keys were introduced, but London makers still supplied gilt embossed crank keys with watches for the Turkish market until around 1840. Clock keys were similar but not so decorative.

Key wind Clock or watch wound by a key, as opposed to a clock wound by pulling on a rope or chain and to a KEYLESS WATCH or one with automatic winding.

Keyhole case clock American form of DROP-DIAL WALL CLOCK in which the trunk is long and rounded at the bottom so that the case is reminiscent of a keyhole.

Keyless rack clock RACK CLOCK without a key, the clock being raised up the rack to wind it.

Some unusual watch **keys**. (*Uto Auktionen, Zürich*)

Keyless winding Having to wind a watch by a separate KEY was a nuisance as the key was easily lost. In the 18th c many attempts were made to invent keyless winding but it was not until 1820 that T. Prest, foreman to ARNOLD, produced a successful winding button. Although Louis AUDEMARS and Sons of Le Brassus produced a version in 1838, the mechanism in modern watches was invented by Adrien Philippe in 1843. It was developed from 1846 to 1847 by Antoine Le Coultre. The English trade was wedded to FUSEE watches which did not lend themselves to keyless winding, although Adam Burdess devised a lever winding system for the fusee in 1869.

Kidney piece A cam similar in shape to a kidney. It turns once a year and an arm resting on its edge turns a hand or dial slowly backwards and forwards to indicate the difference between GREENWICH MEAN TIME and SOLAR TIME. See EQUATION OF TIME.

King's death, clock of the From the time of King Louis XIII of France to 1838, a one-hand clock without a movement at Versailles Palace was permanently set to the time of the last king's death.

Kitchen clock Earlier kitchen clocks had the movement protected from steam to avoid rust. Later ones normally do not.

Knibb, Joseph (1640–1711) He and his younger brother John (1650–1722) became renowned clockmakers. Joseph is recorded as 'gardner' to Trinity College, Oxford, as well as a clockmaker. Later he set up at The Dial in Fleet Street, London. He used ROMAN STRIKING and also made NIGHT CLOCKS. The bells on his clocks were often shallow and sometimes had flat sides. He was apprenticed to a cousin, Samuel Knibb (b.1625) who probably co-operated with Ahasuerus FROMANTEEL. Their styles are very similar. Joseph Knibb invented a clock ESCAPEMENT, used with a long PENDULUM, that was similar to, but more complicated than, the ANCHOR ESCAPEMENT and may have pre-dated it. John remained in charge of the family

business in Oxford and was Mayor in 1700. See HANGING CLOCK and PORK-PIE BELL for pictures.

John **Knibb** made this bracket clock with a velvet dial and silver mounts c1675–8. It is a pull repeater. (*Christie's*)

Knife-edge suspension VERGE escapements on most BRACKET CLOCKS had a normal PIVOT at the front and an edge on the ARBOR resting in a V slot at the back near the PENDULUM rod.

Knock-out striking French carriage clock striking system introduced for REPEATING CLOCKS. It was also used for non-repeating clocks, to standardise production.

Koozens's clock Electric clock in which a centrifugal governor switches on and off an electric motor which turns the hands. Invented by Koozen in 1862.

Kroeber noiseless clock Rotary (CONICAL PENDULUM) clock sold in the 1880s by the F. Kroeber Clock Co. of New York, clock distributors. There were six models. The first, 52cm (20.5in) high under a glass dome, has the pendulum suspended from a structure behind and above the dial, and was known as the derrick or oil-well clock. All the others were very similar to the French MYSTERY CLOCK, with a cast-metal classical woman's figure on top holding the pendulum with a raised arm.

Kullberg, Victor (1824–1890) Celebrated maker of MARINE CHRONOMETERS who introduced several improvements.

Kundo electric clock First transistorised electric clock. Made by Keininger and Obergfell, of West Germany c1957 under a glass dome. The forked PENDULUM has a curved bar magnet as BOB, which passes to and fro through a fixed double coil with a resistor and a transistor. As the pendulum swings one way through one coil, the magnet triggers the transistor to send current through the other (the drive coil). This IMPULSES the pendulum the other way. The design is actually French, by the firm of Hâtot, and many clocks were made with the brand name A.T.O.

L

L.C.D. Liquid crystal display, usually digital, as used in QUARTZ WATCHES, in which the numbers or letters are formed in short black (or white) bars.

L.E.D. Light emitting diode, as used for digital display in the earliest electronic or solid-state watches. The figures are formed in bright dots. Replaced by the L.C.D. display.

Label American clockmakers of the late 18th c provided labels with their identity and instructions. Later they pasted these inside the clock cases, many giving only the identity.

Lacquer True lacquer was made in China and then Japan from the sap of a tree. It forms a natural plastic liquid that can be coloured and hardened by polymerising, which allows it to be carved. It is said to have been used for a few special English clock cases lacquered in China in the 17th c. Most were JAPANNED, an imitation. Another type of lacquer is extracted from the lac insect found in India. The result is shellac, which can also be coloured.

Lacquer gilding Gold leaf ground up and added to lacquer is used for protection and decoration of some parts of TURRET CLOCKS.

Lacquered case See JAPANNING.

Lacquering Exposed brass parts of clocks and MARINE CHRONOMETERS are usually given several coats of clear lacquer to avoid discoloration and corrosion. HAIRSPRINGS of marine chronometers were also often coated by special lacquer which was supposed not to flake. That most commonly used by clockmakers for domestic clocks is shellac lacquer applied in a dust-free atmosphere. Sometimes the parts are warmed first. Only brass parts are treated.

Lamp clock German 19th c timepiece comprising a lamp with a glass oil reservoir scaled to indicate time as the oil burned away. In the 19th c the spring driven NIGHT CLOCK had an illuminated oil lamp shade with the hours marked on it revolving against a fixed hand.

Lancashire escapement The DEBAUFRE ESCAPEMENT as used in the Ormskirk (Lancashire) watchmaking industry for about 20 years after 1800.

Lancashire style Many LONGCASE CLOCKS were turned out by Lancashire clockmakers in the 19th c with painted dials and mahogany cases with wider trunks than earlier clocks. See GRANDMOTHER CLOCK for picture.

Lancet clock Wooden-cased clock, shaped like a Gothic arch, popular during the end of the 18th c. Earlier versions were larger than machine-made ones.

Lantern clock Earliest English style clocks, probably named after 'latten' meaning brass or possibly their likeness to ships' lanterns, introduced c1600. All had weight drive, one hand, a large BALANCE WHEEL without HAIRSPRING and a brass case with a bell on top surrounded by brass frets, often with dolphin or heraldic theme. The earliest had a hanging stirrup and two spurs at the back for hanging on a wall and ran for 16 hours at a wind. Some had ALARMS at the back. Most were converted from direct to ENDLESS ROPE winding, from VERGE to

BOB PENDULUM and to two hands. Later some were converted to LONG PENDULUM or made with it. These usually stood on wall brackets or floor stands. The PILLAR FRAME continued in HOODED and county-made LONGCASE CLOCKS. See WINGED LANTERN CLOCK and SHEEPSHEAD CLOCK.

Lantern clock, Japanese The Japanese copied the English lantern clock but with a FOLIOT under the bell. It remained in use until as late as 1875. They were mounted on floor stands because the house walls were normally unsuitable for hanging. See JAPANESE CLOCKS.

Lantern pinion Earliest form of PINION (gear) like a squirrel cage, or cylinder made up of rods fitting into disc ends. Used in TURRET CLOCKS and cheap machine-made alarm clocks. See FOLIOT for picture.

Lap, abrasive Strip of abrasive cloth stuck to a length of wood or metal, the end being left as a handle. Used for finishing clock and watch parts. One cement used for metal laps was resin heated with about three-quarters the weight of paraffin and a little Vaseline.

Largest clock Beauvais Cathedral clock has 90,000 parts and is 12.2m (40ft) high, 6.1m (20ft) wide and 2.75m (9ft) deep. A clock dial 18.3m (60ft) in diameter was exhibited by Synchronome in London in 1959. Milwaukee, Wisconsin, U.S.A., has a clock with four 12.2m (40ft) dials.

Latch Fastening device, such as for holding a BOB PENDULUM for transport.

Latched plates High-quality 17th c clocks had the BACK PLATE fastened by swivelling latches instead of TAPER PINS.

Laternduhr Form of VIENNA REGULATOR that hung on the wall but was shaped more like an architecture style LONGCASE CLOCK.

Lathe A device for rotating workpieces so that they can be rounded when a cutting tool is held to them. The earliest

was the TURNS, operated by a bow, and the POLE LATHE operated by foot. Both revolved the work, which was held between centres, first one way and then the other. Next came the THROW in the later 18th c, where a hand wheel and endless cord turned the work in one direction, then the WATCHMAKER'S LATHE driven by electric motor. The first tool was the hand-held GRAVER, still used when doing restoration work. Special tools are now used.

Leading-off work Shafts from a turret clock driving the hands, sometimes through bevel gearing. See FLAT-BED movement for picture.

The **leading-off work** of a public clock in Bristol.

Leaf Clockmaker's name for a tooth of the small driven gear wheel called a PINION.

Leap second See ATOMIC TIME, U.T.C.

Leclanché cell Early form of electric cell or battery (linked cells), wet or dry. The dry cells with paste electrolyte were used for early electric clocks. Much larger than present cells.

Left-hand screw One that unscrews clockwise. Some have three instead of one slot in the top for identification. Used where a turning action might unscrew it, as in some watch-winding work.

Left-hand fusee FUSEE movement with the third WHEEL on the left and BALANCE on the right, dial down.

Left-handed watch Swiss mechanical wrist watch with the winding button opposite 9 instead of 3 and regulated for wearing on the outside of the right wrist.

Lenticular bob PENDULUM bob of discus shape, traditional on LONGCASE CLOCKS. It takes up less space but is not as effective as the cylindrical bob used on many English REGULATORS.

Lentille Round, oval or BULLSEYE GLASS in an early LONGCASE CLOCK trunk door for seeing if the PENDULUM is swinging. It is in a door forming the front of the plinth in clocks with 1.25 second pendulums. Also used to describe a pocket watch with a shape like a convex lens.

Lepaute escapement A DEAD-BEAT, PIN-WHEEL ESCAPEMENT for accurate clocks invented by Lepaute c1752.

Leschot, Georges-Auguste (1800–84) Inventive genius of Swiss watchmaking. See DRAW, INGOLD, VACHERON & CONSTANTIN.

L'Epée One of the main French factories (the other was JAPY) in the Franche-Comté making CARRIAGE CLOCKS and watches. Some clocks had twin escape wheels.

Lépine calibre Layout for pocket watches to make them much thinner, invented in c1770 by Jean Antoine Lépine (1720–1814). He eliminated the FUSEE and substituted BARS or BRIDGES for the upper (back) PLATE so that the BALANCE and spring could be between the plates instead of on top as previously. French makers adopted it; English ones continued with old ideas for about a century.

The **Lépine calibre** movement of an English lever watch hallmarked 1822 and unsigned although the maker may have been J.F. Cole. (*Sotheby's*)

Le Roy, Julien (1686–1759) Most famous French maker, particularly of REPEATER watches. Horologer du Roi. Perfected the OIL SINK about 1725 and may have

The balance of a marine timekeeper by **Le Roy**. It has mercury temperature compensation. Note the thermometer tubes.

invented the ROD GONG and DUMB REPEATER. Often used the CYLINDER ESCAPEMENT designed by GRAHAM. His son Pierre (1717–85), also Horologer du Roi, became as famous, particularly for MARINE CHRONOMETERS, his finest (now in the Musée des Arts et Métiers, Paris) having one of the first DETACHED ESCAPEMENTS, a temperature COMPENSATED BALANCE, and ISOCHRONOUS hairspring. This had more future influence on marine chronometers than HARRISON'S. See SULLY and MONTRE-À-TACT for watch picture.

Lever escapement Most successful of all ESCAPEMENTS, invented by Thomas Mudge in 1759 for QUEEN CHARLOTTE'S WATCH (see for picture), and improved by Josiah Emery in 1785, who added DRAW. Eventually used in almost all mechanical watches and PLATFORM ESCAPEMENT clocks, in conjunction with a BALANCE WHEEL and HAIRSPRING. Also called 'detached lever' because of the freedom of the balance. Capable of high timekeeping performance. See ENGLISH LEVER and CLUB TOOTHED LEVER ESCAPEMENT. In the sketch, the balance swings clockwise and the RUBY PIN mounted on it enters the lever fork, moving the lever upwards.

This releases the ESCAPE WHEEL tooth marked A, which moves across the end of the exit PALLET stone, pushing it right. This IMPULSES the balance in the same direction as it is swinging, by causing the lever fork to thrust on the ruby pin. The escape wheel (turning under the influence of the MAINSPRING) is stopped by tooth B coming against the side of the entrance pallet. On the return swing of the balance (under the influence of the hairspring), the lever is knocked the other way and the balance impulsed anti-clockwise by tooth B acting on the entrance pallet. From 1842, Antoine Léchaud developed lever escapements for machine manufacture in Geneva which contributed largely to establishing quality watchmaking in Switzerland. Called 'ancor' on the Continent owing to its similarity to the ANCHOR ESCAPEMENT. Various modifications for simpler production included the CRANK ROLLER, RACK LEVER and SAVAGE TWO-PIN.

Lever set Type of hand-setting mechanism used on some American RAILWAY WATCHES. A lever was pulled out from the side of the case to change the pendant from winding to setting. It could not be left out by accident.

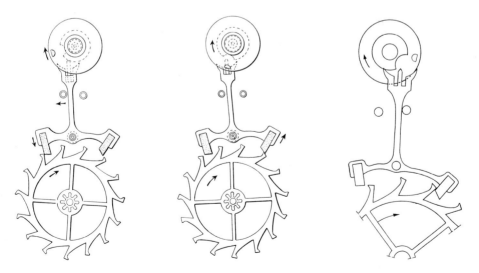

The action of a typical English **lever escapement** releasing the escape wheel. At the top is the roller with the impulse pin of the balance wheel. The escape wheel teeth impulse the balance first one way and then the other, by means of the shaped jewelled pallets in the lever.

Lever watch Watch with a LEVER ESCAPEMENT.

Leichti Famous Swiss family of clock-makers through twelve generations from 1480 to 1857.

Libertine watch See PORNOGRAPHIC WATCH.

Lieutand, Bolthazar (d.1780) Probably the best French clock case maker, using ebony veneers and ORMOLU mounts. Often signed his work.

Lift The action of a tooth moving (lifting) a PALLET in the LEVER ESCAPEMENT.

Lifting piece A double lever which releases RACK STRIKING.

Light clock The first clock driven by light, patented and produced in 1960 by PATEK PHILIPPE in Switzerland. A photoelectric cell on the top powers a micro-motor to wind the MAINSPRING of a LEVER ESCAPEMENT clock through a train of gears. Four hours of light will drive the clock for 24 hours. Later versions operate quartz movements. See SOLAR CELL WATCH.

Lightfoot, Peter Legendary maker of the 14th c elaborate clock at Glastonbury Abbey and WELLS CATHEDRAL CLOCK. However, the latter came from the same workshop as the SALISBURY CATHEDRAL CLOCK which would have been too early for the imaginary Lightfoot. Probably a corruption of Johannes Lietuyt, of Delft, Holland, a clockmaker invited to England by King Edward III in 1368.

Lighthouse clock Tall brass table clock shaped like a lighthouse. In some, the 'lamphouse' is a cylinder made up of glass prisms, which rotates. In others the 'lamphouse' is actually a TORSION PENDULUM controlling the clock. Some have a rotating clock dial in the top under a glass dome. Originally produced in France in the late 19th c. Simon Willard made simpler wooden cased versions in America. See INDUSTRIAL CLOCKS.

One of many styles of **lighthouse clock**. It has a torsion pendulum. Note the cylindrical spring in the 'lamp-house'. (*Sotheby's*)

Ligne Old French measure used by some watchmakers until recent times. See PARIS INCH. About 11 ligne equals 1in. English makers once used the English line, about 12 to the inch or three barley-corns. See SIZES, WATCH. The Swiss introduced metric sizes, which are now universal.

Limoges enamel Painted opaque enamel decoration for watch cases from c1500 to 1600. See ENAMELLED WATCH.

Line Gut lines were used for FUSEE clocks and watches and better weight-driven clocks until recent times when monofilament nylon or fine wire cable have been used to replace them. Wire cable tends to damage the fusee and BARREL unless coated with nylon.

Lip electric watch See FRENCH HOROLOGICAL INDUSTRY.

Litherland Family of watchmakers active in LIVERPOOL in the late 18th and early 19th c. Peter (d.1800) invented the RACK LEVER ESCAPEMENT.

Lithium cell Cell developed for electronic timepieces that lasts for five years and longer. Not corrosive if it leaks like earlier cells.

Little Ben A 9.25m (30ft) high version of BIG BEN outside Victoria Railway Station, London. It was removed in 1965 for street widening but restored and re-erected in 1981. It now has a SYNCHRONOUS ELECTRIC CLOCK movement and the hours are struck by electromagnetic hammers.

Liverpool English batch-production centre for the earliest affordable lever watch, the RACK LEVER from 1791 for c25 years, then of the detached lever, many JEWELLED. See LIVERPOOL WINDOW. The main makers were the LITHERLANDS and Robert Roskell. COVENTRY superseded it. Raw movements came from PRESCOT.

The movement of a typical **Liverpool** lever escapement watch. It is by M.E. Tobias and Co. (*Dr Vaudrey Mercer Coll.*)

Liverpool window Large transparent quartz JEWEL bearing in the top plate of Liverpool watches used as a kind of advertisement. Jewels out of sight were of normal size.

Liverymen See CLOCKMAKERS' COMPANY.

Lobster claw A watch ESCAPEMENT invented by the Swiss Antoine Tavan (1749–1836), recognisable by the heart-shaped part of the lever.

Local solar time Actual local time based on its being noon when the sun is at its highest point (crossing the meridian). The sundial indicates it. Everywhere east or west is later or earlier, so the actual time is different at the eastern and western ends of a football pitch. One degree of latitude equals four minutes. See EQUAL HOURS and MEAN TIME.

Local time clock Before MEAN TIME (equal hours) was established all over a country (G.M.T. in the U.K.), very occasionally a clock was made showing local solar times in various places. JANVIER made a clock in 1791 which could show sundial time instead of mean time by means of a KIDNEY cam that altered the length of the pendulum to change the RATE.

Locking The action of an ESCAPEMENT when it 'locks' or holds up a tooth of the ESCAPE WHEEL, preventing it from turning until the next IMPULSE occurs.

Locking-plate striking Clock with a locking plate, a disc with notches at increasing intervals round the edge that control the number of blows struck at the hour. Introduced c1350. An L-shaped arm, the locking lever, is moved up and down to cause each blow on the bell. If the end of the arm drops into a notch, the striking is stopped. Until c1680 it was on the outside of the BACK PLATE, then was moved inside. It was still being used by county makers in Britain until c1800. The French continued with it until the middle of the 20th c and the newer BLACK FOREST and American industries also adopted it until about the same time for many clocks. London makers adopted RACK STRIKING c1680, but it made slow progress elsewhere, despite its advantages. A locking plate can become out of phase and should be adjusted without touching the hands by lifting the locking lever until the striking and hands agree. The modern term is COUNT WHEEL STRIKING, but the old one persisted for a long time. Continued in use on TURRET CLOCK and domestic striking ones to control the quarter striking. See PILLAR CLOCK, PORK PIE BELL, SALISBURY CATHEDRAL CLOCK for pictures.

Locking-plate striking with the locking plate (on the left) unusually engraved with the hours.

Locomotive clock INDUSTRIAL CLOCK, usually French, showing a steam locomotive with a clock in the side. The loco's wheels are turned by a separate spring drive.

London horological industry Some foreign clockmakers worked in and outside London in the 16th c. See ROYAL CLOCKMAKER. Clockmaking began in London c1600 mainly with LANTERN CLOCKS. In 1622, 16 clockmakers unsuccessfully petitioned the King because they were 'much agreeed both in theire estates credittes and trading through the multiplicity of Forreiners usinge theire profession in London'. They listed 24 'knowne straingers', most French. In 1631, however, they were allowed to form the Worshipful Company of Clockmakers, after an attempt to incorporate clockmakers with the Blacksmiths' Company had failed. The Thirty Years War between

Catholics and Protestants effectively ended the dominance of the earliest centres in Germany, Augsburg and Nuremberg. Clock and watchmakers fled to Paris, London, Geneva and Blois. In 1620 London had 60 master clockmakers and ten years later Paris had 20. Being in general more literate than most of the population, clock- and watchmakers followed the Reformation. HUYGENS invented the PENDULUM clock in Holland in 1657, but the English developed it and were advertising clocks with pendulums the following year. See FROMANTEEL. Through the next century London was the centre of English clockmaking and clock- and watchmakers set up in all towns of any size all over the country as well as in Scotland, Wales and Ireland. The main products were BRACKET and LONGCASE CLOCKS, musical clocks and MARINE CHRONOMETERS (largely for export), ENGLISH DIALS and watches of many kinds. Makers invented the LONG PENDULUM, ANCHOR ESCAPEMENT, RACK STRIKING, INDUSTRIAL CLOCKS, TIME SWITCHES, ELECTRIC CLOCKS, REPEATING CLOCKS, the LEVER ESCAPEMENT etc. and the first JEWELLING patent was English. John HARRISON made the first marine timekeeper and ARNOLD and EARNSHAW pioneered the marine chronometer industry. One of the last products was SKELETON CLOCKS. In watches, the English lever made in London, mainly around CLERKENWELL, dominated other countries' products in the first half of the 19th c. Eventually American machine-made clocks and watches put paid to the London trade. There were attempts to adopt modern methods for watches in PRESCOT, LIVERPOOL and COVENTRY. The last large scale clockmakers to survive into this century were John Smith and Sons, Clerkenwell, until the First World War, and S. SMITH AND SONS, who were very much bigger, until the 1970s. Another survivor until recent years was THWAITES AND REED, Clerkenwell.

London Museum Collection European 16th–18th c clocks with some fine early German examples, at the Museum of London, Barbican.

Long arcs Wide swing of a BALANCE as opposed to short arcs. Term used in adjusting.

Long pendulum PENDULUM that swings from one side to the other in one or more seconds and is therefore 1m (3ft) or more in length (see SECONDS PENDULUM and TWO-SECONDS PENDULUM). The RYE CHURCH CLOCK has a beat of about 2.4 seconds. So do the St Peter and St Paul, Deddington (Oxfordshire) and Ringwood (Hampshire) church clocks. St Peter's Church (St Albans), Retford (Nottinghamshire), and Antrim Parish church (Northern Ireland) clocks have 2.5-second approx. pendulums. There is 3-second pendulum about 8.94m (29ft 4in) long on the clock of Lewknor church, Oxfordshire, and a 4-second pendulum approx 15.9m (52ft 2in) long on that of St Chad's Church, Shrewsbury. La Chaux-de-Fonds clock also has a 4-second pendulum. The longest pendulum known is in Avignon, France at 20.4m (67ft). The pendulum bob weighs 59.9kg (132lb) and the beat is 4.5 seconds with an arc of 2.7–3m (9-10ft). The clock with the longest pendulum in Britain is probably that in St Stephen's Church, Stockbridge, Edinburgh. Dating from 1912, it has a 4-second pendulum.

Long-wind watch Nickname of a cheap watch designed for the Benedict and Burnham Manufacturing Co., Waterbury, Connecticut, U.S.A., by Daniel Buck in 1877. It had a ROTARY MOVEMENT, only 58 parts and no jewels, and took 150 half-turns of the button to wind the 2.74m (9ft) long spring.

Longcase clock Clock in a wooden case, usually over 1.8m (6ft) tall standing on the floor. The MOVEMENT, running for 30 hours or for eight days, has a long PENDULUM ticking seconds, strikes the hours and sometimes also the quarters, and often has a CALENDAR DIAL, sometimes a MOON DIAL, and even a TIDAL DIAL. The first were introduced in England around 1660, perhaps originating from casings put around the weights of HANGING CLOCKS. In the

17th and 18th c, they were made in large numbers, even the makers numbering tens of thousands. At first most of the best makers went to London to work, but Edinburgh was another centre. CASES were often of oak with an ebony, walnut, or mahogany veneer. London set the style; country makers were slow to follow. The DIALS of the best clocks were of brass, silvered on the CHAPTER RING bearing the engraved numbers. After about 1770, painted iron dials appeared and movements were quantity produced. In the 19th c mass-produced MANTEL CLOCKS superseded them. Another 17th c name was 'coffin clock'. They were called 'tall case clocks' in America. The name GRANDFATHER CLOCK did not become popular until much later. They were also made in Holland (where the clock pendulum was invented) and several other European countries, and the then British colonies.

Longitude The angular distance east or west from longitude ZERO through the ROYAL OBSERVATORY, Greenwich, on which LOCAL and STANDARD TIMES, and NAVIGATION depend. See FINDING THE LONGITUDE.

Looking-glass clock Occasionally a looking glass was set in the door of a LONGCASE CLOCK in the first half of the 18th c. One or two are known by Huguenot makers. American makers used them before 1817, but Chauncey Jerome still got a patent in that year for his BRONZE LOOKING-GLASS CLOCK.

Lossier curve OVERCOIL for improving the timekeeping of a HAIRSPRING calculated by Louis Lossier (1847–93).

Louis XIV clocks (1643–1715) Cases of the time have a heavy richness yet classical lines using costly materials, but with the flamboyance of the BAROQUE STYLE period that had spread from Italy to the rest of Europe. BOULLE MARQUETRY (see for picture) was often used with complicated interweaving patterns including acanthus. The period saw the beginnings of

ORMOLU. These were followed by REGENCY CLOCKS.

Louis XIV hinge Prominent decorative hinge on LENTILLE watches of this period.

Louis XV clocks (1750–74) Style after the REGENCY which was a French version of rococo, with ornaments of gently curling foliage and forms and serpentine shapes, sometimes asymmetrical. Much rich fantasy. See MEISSEN CASE for picture.

Louis XVI clocks (1774–93) A reaction against the rococo style that began before the King's reign, with calm and restrained classical designs and neat geometrical shapes. The previous scrolling was replaced by figures and ornaments derived from those of classical Greek and Roman architecture. In the 1770s an Etruscan style began to appear which became DIRECTOIRE, then EMPIRE STYLE. See URN CLOCK for picture.

Loupe Watchmaker's magnifying lens held in the eye. Instead of being marked with the power, e.g. x 5, it is marked with the working distance, e.g. 3in.

Lourdes chime Theme based on a composition by Liszt. Also called 'Ave Maria chime'.

Lubrication See OIL.

Lug Shaped part of a watch CASE to which the strap or bracelet is attached. Some are permanent, others sprung for removal.

Luminous dial The most successful means of making watches and clocks (particularly ALARMS) suitable for night use is to luminise the hands and dials. It was first applied in the U.S.A. at the beginning of the 20th c, when the dangers were not understood and those who licked their paint brushes eventually died from radiation illness. Luminous paint is a mixture of phosphorus and a tiny amount of radium. The phosphorus transforms the invisible radio-active rays

from the radium into visible light. On good watches there are only thin fillings of luminous paint (some 'safer' paint) in the hands and small dots on the dial. Some have the paint under the hands. The colour of the glow is often made green because the eye is most sensitive to this colour. Some SYNCHRONOUS alarms had electro-luminescent dials, the tension of electricity producing a glow without radiation.

A French **lyre clock** in ormolu. It is 39cm (1ft 3½in) high. (*Sotheby's*)

Lunar cycle   See METONIC CYCLE.

Lunar dial   See MOON DIAL.

Lunar distances   Astronomical solution to finding the longitude at sea that was an alternative to using a marine timekeeper, but too complicated in practice.

Lunation   Lunar month of about 29 days, 12 hours, 45 minutes, normally approximated in a clock with a moon dial to 29.5 days.

Lund Cathedral clock   Fine large astronomical clock with AUTOMATA in Lund, Sweden, the original going back to 1380.

Lunette   Watch glass with greater doming near the edge than at the top.

Lyre clock   Elegant mantel clock inspired by the stringed instrument and invented by Kinable of Paris (d.1825). The curved frame of the 'lyre' is of marble or bronze with the clock dial near the bottom. A GRIDIRON PENDULUM above the clock (suggesting the strings) is connected through its BOB to the clock ESCAPE-MENT. The French made other versions including even REGULATORS in wood. Copied in large numbers in the U.S.A. after the Civil War, in wood and usually called BANJO or GIRANDOLE clocks.

M

M.S.F. transmissions Standard of frequency by the ATOMIC CLOCK, transmitted from 1950 and currently by the Post Office radio station, Rugby, for the NATIONAL PHYSICAL LABORATORY.

Magic lantern clock Form of NIGHT CLOCK that projects an image of the dial on the wall. Invented in France in the 18th c and made in the 19th c in various styles projecting the image from the front or back of the clock. The idea was revived in the early 20th c when electric and electronic clocks were made to project the dial and hands on the ceiling.

Magneta clock Electric MASTER CLOCK for operating SLAVE DIALS made by the Magneta Time Co. The system was invented by Martin Fischer of Zürich in 1900. It eliminated contact points, a previous source of breakdown. It provided electric IMPULSES by making a coil of wire oscillate over the poles of a permanent magnet. These impulses, sent to slave dials, advanced the hands every minute. In later versions, however, a HIPP TOGGLE was used with contacts and a device to advance or retard the dials.

Magnetic balance BALANCE used in some early ELECTRIC CLOCKS and the first ELECTRIC WATCHES in which the IMPULSE is given electromagnetically instead of mechanically. The balance incorporates a coil moving over a fixed permanent magnet or a magnet moving over a coil. Adam Kochanski used a lodestone in place of a HAIRSPRING in 1659.

Magnetic click RATCHET using a powerful small magnet instead of a spring click, first employed in ELECTRIC WATCHES.

Magnetic clock See TORTOISE CLOCK.

Magnetic correction Means of correcting the rate of a PRECISION CLOCK PENDULUM probably first suggested by Sir George AIRY. An electromagnetic coil is fixed below the pendulum, which itself carries a permanent magnet below the BOB. Activating the coil effectively speeds or slows the pendulum.

Magnetic escapement Invented by C.F. Clifford in England in 1948, this ESCAPEMENT has no physical contact between the ESCAPE WHEEL and the controlling element. Friction is extremely low and the action is silent. Used for German and Japanese clocks and British TIME SWITCHES. The control element is a short length of spring which vibrates. On the end of this is a small horseshoe magnet. The specially shaped escape wheel teeth pass between the poles of the magnet which release them one by one as the magnet vibrates up and down.

Magnetic suspension A BALANCE WHEEL introduced in the 1950s which carries a small ring magnet under it. This is oppositely magnetised to a fixed ring magnet around the lower PIVOT so that the balance assembly 'skates' on a magnetic field, considerably reducing friction. Another version uses a magnet a short distance above the steel BALANCE STAFF (axle) to lift it and reduce friction. Used by British and German makers.

Magnetised Steel parts of watches, especially the HAIRSPRING if of steel, can become magnetised from TV circuits, magnetic kitchen and tool racks, generators, radar equipment, etc., and behave erratically. They can usually be demagnetised without difficulty. 'Anti-magnetic' watches are partly protected by having vital parts NON-MAGNETIC. The best protection is an anti-magnetic screen around the MOVEMENTS of special watches. ELECTRIC WATCHES can be affected and also demagnetised. The DEMAGNETISER is not strong enough to damage any magnets in them. Largely avoided in electronic timepieces.

Mahogany case Spanish mahogany, heavy and deep brown, was introduced to England when import regulations were relaxed in the 1720s. First used for furniture, it did not influence clock case makers except in isolated cases until the 1760s. By then Cuban mahogany, with a wavy grain, had largely superseded Spanish, followed by Honduras mahogany (bay wood) before the last quarter of the century. Very popular with Yorkshire LONGCASE clockmakers, it was often used solid, being difficult to veneer. A high surface finish was obtained by using fire-brick dust and linseed oil.

Mail guard's watch A few years after the introduction of the mail coach services in 1874, a clerk at the General

The **mahogany** case of a chiming longcase clock of c1790 by J. Gray.

A **mail guard's watch** by Edward Smith of Dublin, c1930. (*H.M. Post Office*)

Post Office (G.P.O.) was charged with handing a special watch locked in a rectangular case to each mail guard. The guard passed it on to his successor if he did not complete the run himself. At every post stage, when the horses were changed, the postmaster entered the time of departure on a time bill, together with the local (sundial) time. The watch was collected by the G.P.O. and the time recorded at the end of the run.

Main wheel Driving first WHEEL in a clock or watch, usually attached to, or part of, the BARREL. In a FUSEE time-piece it is attached to the fusee and often called the 'great wheel', which strictly applies to a FUSEE.

Mains clock Clock powered by the electric mains supply. See SYNCHRONOUS CLOCK and MASTER CLOCK.

Mainspring (U.S.A. **Motor spring**) Coiled flat spring for driving a clock or watch. The inventor is unknown, but may have been a swordmaker and clockmaker of about 1450. The mainspring made the portable clock and the watch possible. Early springs were hammered out of steel or brass. They gave much more power wound than partly wound, which affected timekeeping. Attempts were made to compensate for this by STOP-WORK, the STACKFREED, forms of FLY, and particularly the FUSEE. Modern springs are made of tempered carbon steel, stainless steel and various alloys; the unbreakable mainspring (for watches) is an alloy steel containing iron, carbon, nickel, chromium, cobalt, molybdenum, manganese and beryllium. It is non-magnetic and was introduced in 1947. Some springs are set to a reversed curve like a figure 8 when free. Such alloy springs give more power as they age, not less, like steel springs. The power output of modern mainsprings is fairly even at different tensions, which improves time-keeping performance. Mainsprings break through fatigue, no lubrication and sudden changes of temperature (see GOING BARREL and SETTING UP). One form of mainspring (the Tensator) for clocks running a month at a winding and for early cine cameras is coiled round a

free-running ARBOR when unstressed. It is wound in the opposite direction round an adjacent arbor. It then runs back on to the first, giving very even power output, but not MAINTAINING POWER, like a going barrel. Springs are normally contained in a SPRING BARREL, which is usually going but can be a RESTING BARREL, when the arbor revolves. Some early clocks and many cheap alarms of the earlier 20th c had open springs which were anchored at the inner end to a pillar and were wound back when run down.

Mainspring barrel See GOING BARREL.

Mainspring bridle An automatic or SELF-WINDING WATCH can wind the mainspring until it can go no further. To save damage to the ROTOR or oscillator, which does the winding, the spring inside the BARREL is allowed to slip. A thicker spring called a 'bridle' fastened to its outer coil is friction tight in the barrel.

Mainspring gauge Simple gap gauge for measuring the thickness and height (width) of a mainspring in order to estimate its strength.

Mainspring hook Projection on the end of a mainspring to fasten it to the inside wall of the BARREL. Sometimes the barrel has a hook and the spring a hole.

Mainspring winder Tool with which to wind a mainspring through a slot into an appropriately sized false barrel. A sliding bottom is then used to press the mainspring into the barrel itself.

Maintaining power A clock without a GOING BARREL loses time while it is being wound because there is temporarily no power to drive it. Maintaining work provides this power during winding such as by an extra weight or spring. A HUYGENS ENDLESS CHAIN in THIRTY-HOUR GRANDFATHER CLOCKS and AUTOMATIC CLOCK WINDING in TOWER CLOCKS automatically provides maintaining power. Some of the best weight-driven LONGCASE CLOCKS have BOLT AND SHUTTER maintaining power. A similar arrangement for tower clocks is a weighted lever which has to be moved before the winding handle can be turned. Moving it applies power to a clock wheel through a RATCHET. For FUSEE clocks and watches, and MARINE CHRONOMETERS, a spring-driven maintaining power invented by John HARRISON in 1735 is employed.

Make and break Simple electromechanical switch used in early electric clocks and even some later ones.

Maker to the Admiralty Title assumed by some suppliers as well as chronometer makers in the 19th c. Also used as sales promotion, as in 'John Forrest, maker to the Admiralty' found on ordinary pocket watches. He died in 1871 having never made a chronometer for anyone according to evidence in a court case over the right to use the qualification in 1891.

Maltese clock WALL CLOCK with a wooden frame dial based on the Italian standing altar clock. The dial and case are gilded and painted. It has a driving weight inside the case with pendulum and escapement at the bottom of the movement. Made in the villages of Siggiewi and Zebbug in the early 19th c. The earliest had one hand and ran for 12 hours only.

Maltese cross stopwork See STOP-WORK.

Mandrel An accessory for a lathe, being a circular plate (faceplate) with three clips (dogs) to hold irregularly shaped items when turning or boring holes in them. Some mandrels are self-contained, being driven by hand using an endless cord, or through gears (Geneva mandrel). A mandrel upright tool was used by Lancashire watch finishers. This was a mandrel that could be used as a lathe, driven by an endless cord round a wooden wheel.

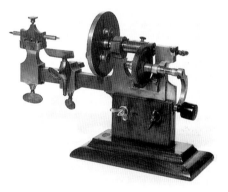

A Geneva style clockmaker's **mandrel** of brass and steel. (*Phillips*)

Mantel clock Clock intended to be placed on a mantelpiece; otherwise similar to a BRACKET CLOCK. Later ones were made thin to suit mantels over electric and gas fires.

Mantel clock set French makers in about the first quarter of the 19th c offered three-piece sets with two ornaments to flank a central clock. Most were very elaborate following the fashion of the time.

Marble clock Although some marble clock cases were used by makers in other

An early 19th c **Maltese clock** with a painted dial, signed Caicedonio Mizzi Melita. It has an English fusee movement. (*Sotheby's*)

countries, they are particularly associated with the French, who made them in large numbers from c1850 to 1914. Most cases came from Belgium and are found in many styles but almost invariably in black (calcareous) marble, sometimes inlaid with a pattern of coloured marble, although there are white and coloured marble cases. The French movements are usually drum-shaped and of good quality. They strike the hours on a bell and also sound the half hours with one blow. BROCOT and SILK SUSPENSIONS are associated with them as is the VISIBLE ESCAPEMENT. The main movement makers were Vincenti, Marti and particularly JAPY. They were so popular that they were copied by English makers, and with cheap movements in huge numbers by the factories of America (ANSONIA in particular) and Germany (the firm of H.A.C. in particular). American cases are usually of wood or iron imitating marble. A large marble clock in a Victorian household kept good time because it was rarely moved because of its weight. Many clocks were made with ORMOLU classical figures modelled on top like the true ormolu clock. Small chips in a marble case were repaired with a mixture of five parts resin and one part beeswax. Some were made as MYSTERY CLOCKS.

An elaborate French late 19th c **marble clock** and barometer with a calendar and moon dial. A Brocot escapement can be seen at the top of the dial. The black marble has red marble panels.

Marie Antoinette watch The French Queen was a customer of BREGUET. One watch he made for her, delivered in 1787, was self-winding with a platinum weight. All parts were of gold except where steel was essential. It was a MINUTE REPEATER with PERPETUAL CALENDAR, EQUATION OF TIME, UP-AND-DOWN DIAL, INDEPENDENT SECONDS with DETACHED LEVER ESCAPEMENT, and was fully sapphire jewelled. Breguet made her one of his commercial repeaters while she was in prison awaiting execution and charged her for it.

Marine chronometer Chronometer designed for use at sea. The traditional mechanical version is mounted in a heavy brass case held in gymbals in a stout brass-bound mahogany box so that it remains level regardless of the position of a ship such as a sailing vessel on a tack. Normally it has a two-day MOVEMENT with CHRONOMETER ESCAPEMENT, but is wound daily and kept in one place, time being carried around by a DECK WATCH or HACK WATCH. Eight-day chronometers were normally for depots but also used at sea. Originally the chronometer was the personal property of the navigation officer, whose initials often appear on a brass plate let into the top of the box. The box has a double lid, the inner one with a glass so that the chronometer can be read in wet conditions. The dial normally has concentric hour and minute hands, a small seconds hand and an UP AND DOWN DIAL. The FUSEE movement has Harrison MAINTAINING POWER and is wound by turning the movement upside down in its gymbals and turning a dust cover to insert the key which is kept in the case. The gymbals can be locked for transport. QUARTZ CRYSTAL modules are used for many modern chronometers, but frequently fixed in similar boxes.

Marine clock Spring-driven, electric, or electronic, clock for general use in a cylindrical brass case with a flange at the back for mounting on a bulkhead. The more accurate MARINE CHRONOMETER or DECK WATCH was used for NAVIGATION.

A **marine chronometer** by Parkinson and Frodsham, London. Note the up-and-down dial. The key is housed at top left and the lever at bottom right locks the gymbals for transport.

The movement of a **marine chronometer** showing its detent escapement. Note the cylindrical balance spring.

Marquetry Elaborate patterns of holly, boxwood, ivory, etc. veneers, usually in a background of walnut or ebony veneer. Used mainly on LONGCASE CLOCK cases, first in panels from 1675 to 1700, then all over from 1690 to 1725. Superseded largely by overall burr walnut veneer. (See CASE, CLOCK.) BOULLE work is also a form of marquetry.

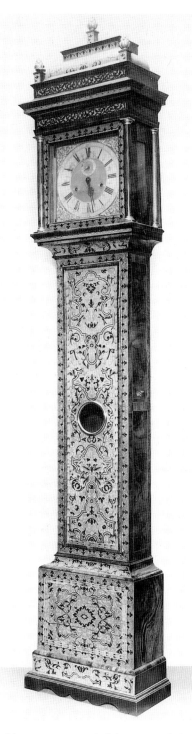

An elaborate **marquetry** clock by Oosterwijk dated c1710.

PARQUETRY is a simple geometrical form of it. Cutting out a veneer pattern with straight instead of bevelled edges to the cut leaves a veneer 'negative' of it, so two veneered cases could be made at a time, light wood in dark and dark in light.

Marriage Trade term for fitting a MOVEMENT into a CASE that does not belong to it. A classic example was when the collector Courtenay ILBERT found a miniature TOMPION BRACKET CLOCK with a wrong movement, and, quite separately, the missing Tompion movement in a wrong case. Immediate visual indications of some are the top of a lantern clock dial flattened because the dial has been changed, winding squares not in the centre of holes in the dial of a bracket or LONGCASE CLOCK because the dial or movement was changed; a soldered date disc because the mechanism is missing on the wrong movement; a pendulum too long for case (sometimes the bottom of the wooden case was scooped out); a marquetry hood not the same pattern as the longcase, and a one-hand clock with minute divisions on the dial. See CONVERSION.

Marti Name often stamped on the back plate of PENDULE DE PARIS clock MOVEMENTS, made particularly for French MARBLE CLOCKS, from 1841 to 1912. The main company was Samuel Marti et Cie.

Martin screw plate SCREW PLATE by Martin, a famous early maker of such dies. Sizes of threads were not standardised then. A later form for metric thread is the Progress.

Martin, Vernis See VERNIS MARTIN.

Mary Queen of Scots' watch Large SKULL WATCH incorrectly believed to have been given by the Queen to Mary Seton, one of her Maids of Honour. The forehead of the skull is engraved with a figure of death between a palace and a cottage, and a quotation in Latin meaning 'pale death visits with impartial foot the cottages of the poor and the castles of the rich' (Horace). The skull is held upside

Marriages may not be obvious. The Vulliamy movement of this clock does not belong to the earlier case of c1750.

The famous **Mary Queen of Scots' watch** of c1585 in a memento mori case. To see the time, it is inverted and the jaw lifted.

down and the jaw is lifted to read the silver dial. The hour is struck on a bell. Made by Moyant à Blois (1570–90). The ESCAPEMENT is unfortunately a CONVERSION to lever.

Masonic clock One showing masonic symbols as a form of decoration.

Masonic movement American watch with a bridge shaped like a square and compasses made by the Dudley Watch Co., Pennsylvania, in the 1920s.

Mass dial Ancient vertical sundial to remind churchgoers of times of Mass. Usually seen today as a little group of radiating lines marking the TIDES, scratched on the stonework on one side of the south porch of the church. Originally there was a rod sticking out from the centre. Also called a SCRATCH DIAL.

Massachusetts shelf clock American THIRTY-HOUR CLOCK with a two-part case. The top is a BRACKET CLOCK with a larger than usual PENDULUM that hangs down into the lower section on which it stands. Made at the turn of the 18th–19th c by Simon and Aaron Willard. Also called a 'case-on-case'.

Massey, Edward (1772–1852) Inventor of a DETACHED LEVER ESCAPEMENT in 1814 known as the 'crank roller lever', which was subsequently used in all standard English watches during the 19th c by such makers as Barwise, Henry Russell, Gravell and

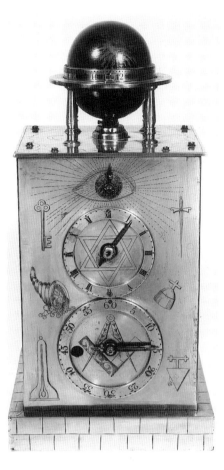

A **masonic clock**, actually a timepiece, with a rotating Earth on top. (*Sotheby's*)

Son, and, in LIVERPOOL, James Hornby, Litherland Davis and Co., and Robert Roskell. The ESCAPE WHEEL has pointed teeth and the lever is at a tangent to the wheel. Also called a 'club roller lever'. It was the forerunner of the ENGLISH LEVER. Massey also invented PUMP WINDING.

Master Clock or watchmaker who had served an APPRENTICESHIP, become a JOURNEYMAN and eventually had his MASTERPIECE approved by the Court of the CLOCKMAKERS' COMPANY. He could then take an apprentice himself, but only one, a ruling broken by several prominent London makers. After the Worshipful Company of Clockmakers obtained the right to bear arms in the City of London, some master clockmakers were appointed liverymen and could carry arms. A guild of master craftsmen was ruled by a court of elected wardens, itself ruled by a Master. About 1550, Paris had 20 master clockmakers and Lyon had ten in 1570. The numbers multiplied over the years. In 1575, Geneva had 17 French masters, and 100 masters with 800 other workers by 1686. Augsburg had 43 masters and 43 journeymen in 1615 and London 60 in 1620. Innovation came from London and Paris and production from Geneva. Other small centres of master craftsmen were in the Low Countries, Austria (then part of Germany), Italy and Copenhagen, with 13 masters in 1635.

Master clock Clock which controls SLAVE DIALS, a TOWER CLOCK dial or a PROGRAMME CONTROLLER. Invented by Carl Steinheil in 1839 and Alexander Bain in 1840. Most electric master clocks have a SECONDS PENDULUM impulsed by a GRAVITY ARM. Each time it swings to the right, the pendulum turns a 30-toothed wheel one tooth. At each full turn (half-minute), a lever on this wheel unlatches a gravity arm which gives an IMPULSE by pressing on an arm fixed to the pendulum. The gravity arm then drops onto an electric contact which operates an electromagnet to reset the arm and also to provide a brief current to operate slave dials or other device. See SYNCHRONOME CLOCK. Modern master clocks have QUARTZ CRYSTAL time controllers operating slave dials and programme by electronic means.

Masterpiece Special clock or watch that an APPRENTICE, after a period as a JOURNEYMAN, had to submit for approval (to the Worshipful Company of Clockmakers if he were English) before he could set up on his own. See CLOCKMAKERS' COMPANY and NUREMBERG.

Matching hands Before about 1770 the hands of English clocks were pierced for the hour with a pointer for the minute hand. Then clockmakers started using hands of similar patterns for BRACKET and LONGCASE CLOCKS. In the 19th c SPADE HANDS and BREGUET HANDS gradually superseded most others.

Matchlock clock Form of novelty clock made in the early 17th c in Augsburg incorporating the flintlock mechanism of a pistol which was released by the clock. See FLINTLOCK ALARM for picture. Used as a PISTOL ALARM or to light a candle. Also called 'tinder lighter clock'.

Material Originally, parts for a hand-made watch or clock produced by separate trades. See CLERKENWELL, FINISHER. Today, replacement parts for clocks and watches. A few material dealers remain in their traditional home, Clerkenwell, but many are now outside.

Matted dial Centres of brass antique clock dials were often given a rough matt surface, originally by using a single- or multi-pointed punch, then by rolling them in all directions with a matting tool – a knurled and hardened steel roller in a handle. This was done by hand. Today the finish is copied by acid etching.

McCabe, James (c1748–1811) One of the finest London makers of both watches and clocks, many of which were exported. His sons and Robt. Jeremy continued under the same name until 1883.

Mean daily rate The daily RATE of a timepiece over a number of days divided by that number.

Mean solar time The time shown by clocks. Days and hours shown by a SUNDIAL vary in length. When time was averaged into EQUAL HOURS, this was called 'mean time'. Mean time is the same all over the world, so is the mean solar day of 24 hours. A year has 365.25 mean days. See SIDEREAL TIME.

Mean time See MEAN SOLAR TIME.

Medieval clock General term applied to the large wrought-iron clocks of the period. Britain is especially rich in larger medieval clocks such as the SALISBURY CATHEDRAL CLOCK, the EXETER

CATHEDRAL CLOCK, the WELLS CATHEDRAL CLOCK (movement in the Science Museum), the Sherborne Abbey clock, RYE CHURCH CLOCK, Sussex, the one at Cothele House, Cornwall (National Trust), and the one at Sydling St Nicholas Church, Dorset. See VERTICAL FRAME.

Meissen case Made in porcelain by the Meissen factory founded in 1710 at Meisse near Dresden, Germany, the first in Europe and said to be the best for a quarter of a century. Favoured by many French makers in the Louis XVI period in the mid-18th c. Often very decorative with colourful foliage, flowers, birds, human figures etc. The Meissen mark is crossed swords. Similar rococo cases were made by other German porcelain works such as Hochst c1750, Berlin c1751 and Frankenthal c1751. See CERAMIC CLOCK.

Meissen-cased ormolu mantel clock of the **Louis XV** period, showing Scaramouche and Columbine. (Christie's)

Memento mori Reminder of a certain person's death, usually in the form of a skull for a watch or clock case. See MARY QUEEN OF SCOTS' WATCH. A number of 17th c clockmakers incorporated skeletons, such as one by Leloutre, Paris, with two, which danced at the hour and struck their skulls at the ring of a bell for the number of hours. Towards the end of the 18th c, a Dublin clockmaker, Anthony Kister, made one for the Hell Fire Club with six fully automated skeletons that danced the hours in obscene postures; a cock crowed the watches of the night. An animated skeleton FATHER TIME was another favourite for striking work. Some BLACK FOREST clockmakers in the 1880s incorporated a dance of death in novelty clocks.

Memorandum clock Late 19th c novelty clock about 35cm (14in) high with a horizontal drum on top divided into a number of radial slots marked with the time of day. Appointments are written on small ivory tablets which are inserted in slots of the appropriate times. When that time arrives, the tablet is dropped into a small container below the dial and a bell is sounded.

Mercer, Thomas (1822–1900) Well-known English maker of MARINE CHRONOMETERS. Thomas Mercer and Son continued making chronometers under the same family until 1983, when this part of the business was sold. It closed finally in 1990.

Mercurial gilding Gold finish for brass used on clock and watch dials and cases. Also called 'fire gilding' (or 'water gilding'), it was done by mixing gold powder with mercury (about two parts to one) and nitrate of mercury, to make a paste like butter which was brushed on repeatedly. The brass was next washed, heated over charcoal and brushed, being then left matt (see FROSTING), or alternatively polished and burnished. The process is dangerous to health and is rarely, if ever, done now, although it is the only way to restore, say, French gilt work. Electro-gilding is extensively used today for various watch parts. 'Silver gilt' is sterling silver that has had a gilding treatment.

Mercurial pendulum A form of TEMPERATURE COMPENSATION invented by George GRAHAM in 1721. The BOB of the pendulum is one or two jars of mercury. As the pendulum rod expands downwards in heat, the mercury expands upwards, thus keeping the effective length, i.e. CENTRE OF OSCILLATION, the same. In the RIEFLER CLOCK, the rod of the pendulum is a steel tube almost filled with mercury, which gives better compensation because it is effective over the whole length of the pendulum. Commonly used in the 19th c French clocks, with short pendulums each having two jars of mercury, but only as decoration. LE ROY used mercury temperature compensation on the balance of his marine timekeeper. See REGULATOR for picture.

The **mercurial pendulum** in George Graham's finest regulator, with an engraving of him.

Mercury clock Clock controlled by a vertical drum divided into segments each of which had a small perforation in it. The drum is partly filled with mercury. A rope wound round the drum supports a weight. The drum, being mounted on an axle, slowly turns as mercury leaks through one segment to the next. It turns a simple dial. Invented in Spain in the late 13th c. Revived in the 17th c as a water clock.

Mercury switch Small glass tube in which some mercury is sealed. With one end down the mercury bridges two electrical contact points so that the switch is on. Rocking the other way breaks the circuit. As air is excluded the contacts do not oxidise. Used on some AUTOMATIC WINDING for TURRET CLOCKS.

Meridian The highest position of the sun in the sky, which indicates noon. Also the highest position of a star. The meridian of a particular place is a circle passing through it and the North and South Poles, i.e. its LONGITUDE.

Meridian clock See WORLD TIME DIAL.

Meridian dial See ANALEMMATIC SUNDIAL.

Meridian line The line of longitude zero passing through the ROYAL OBSERVATORY, Greenwich, from which GREENWICH MEAN TIME is measured. It is marked in the forecourt by an illuminated white line so that visitors can stand with one foot in the eastern and the other in the western hemisphere.

Merkhet Ancient Egyptian holder for a plumb line, a cord with a weight at the end. Used to observe the TRANSIT of a CLOCK STAR to determine the hour of the night.

Metonic cycle A cycle of 19 years when the moon returns almost to the same phases on the same days. Discovered in 433BC by the Greek, Meton. See GOLDEN NUMBER.

Metronome Instrument that ticks loudly to time the playing of music when learning. It has clockwork with a form of DEBAUFRE ESCAPEMENT and an inverted pendulum. Sliding the bob up or down alters the beat.

Metropolitan Museum collection Fine New York collection of timepieces includ-

ing the PIERPONT MORGAN COLLEC-
TION of watches.

Microsecond One-millionth (0.000001)
of a SECOND, symbol µs.

Middle temperature error A standard
bi-metallic COMPENSATION BALANCE
with BALANCE SPRING will only
provide accurate correction for errors of
rate at two particular temperatures a
distance apart, e.g. 10° and 26.5°C (50 and
80°F). Between these limits, the
chronometer will have a gaining rate
called 'middle temperature error'. The
maximum gaining rate of, say, 2 sec/day,
will be halfway between the limits.
Outside them, there will be a worse
losing rate. Berthoud, Dent, Ulrich and
Hardy have all been credited with its
discovery. Modern materials have eliminated it; so have QUARTZ CRYSTAL
modules. See AUXILIARY TEMPERA-
TURE COMPENSATION.

Millisecond One thousandth of a
SECOND, contracted to ms.

Mineral glass Watch glass make of a
natural or synthetic (man-made) mineral
such as quartz because it is so resistant to
scratching.

Miniature pocket-watch During the
19th c, some Swiss makers produced
small watches with CYLINDER or
LEVER ESCAPEMENTS in pocket-watch
style, but smaller, about the size of
today's wrist watch. Some cases were
HUNTERS in precious metal engraved all
over. Some early cases were decorated
with Geneva ENAMEL. See SMALLEST
WATCH.

Miniature rotor Very small winding
ROTOR, less than half the diameter of the
SELF-WINDING WATCH itself, which
enables the watch to be made thinner.

Miniature shelf clock Small American
SHELF CLOCK about 55cm (22in) tall.
Probably first made by Curtiss and Clark
c1825.

Miniature watch See SMALLEST
WATCH.

A **miniature watch**, a gold lever, given by the late Queen
Mary to the Science Museum. Centimetre scale above.

Minute Sixtieth part of an hour. The
Babylonians divided the path of the sun
into 360 steps representing days of the
year, which gave us our 360° in a circle.
Since angles of 60° were easily constructed
and the smallest division of 60 by repeated
halving is 15, 360 was divided into 24
angles of 15°. As the Earth turns 360° in a
day, the day was thus divided into 24
hours. The association of 60 with time may
therefore account for the division of the
hour into 60 minutes. (But see SECOND).

Minute counter Small DIAL on the
main dial of a TIMER showing minutes
elapsed.

Minute divisions Because of the accuracy of the pendulum, 60 minute
divisions were marked in a narrow band
round the outside of the dial of early
LONGCASE CLOCKS. Every minute was
numbered inside the band before 1680
but some as late as 1700. Numerals were
moved outside the band c1680–5 and
became larger c1725. BRACKET CLOCKS
generally followed suit. See MONT-
GOMERY DIAL.

Minute hand   Hand indicating minutes, incorporated as early as the 16th c on ASTRONOMICAL CLOCKS, but not in general use for clocks until after the introduction of the PENDULUM in 1657 and for watches until about 1700, after the BALANCE SPRING was invented.

Minute pinion   The PINION attached to the MINUTE WHEEL in the MOTION WORK which gears the hour to the minute hand. It engages with the hour wheel.

Minute recorder   Small DIAL on a STOP WATCH recording minutes the watch has run between stop and start. Seconds and fractions of them are shown by a large SECONDS HAND.

Minute repeater   REPEATER WATCH or CLOCK that will sound the last hour, quarter and minute on bells or gongs, at will. Such clocks were made from the early 18th c and watches from the 19th. The last hour is sounded first in the deeper of two tones, the last quarter is sounded by one, two, or three TING-TANGS on the two gongs, then the number of minutes in the higher tone. The earliest known is by Benedict Felder. Operated by a slide on the side of the case or by pushing in the PENDANT, which winds a spring.

Minute wheel   Wheel driven by the CANNON PINION, which itself drives the HOUR WHEEL.

Mock pendulum   Some pendulum BRACKET CLOCKS, particularly from c1680 to c1770, have a curved slot near the top of the dial in which a disc (the mock pendulum) fixed to the PALLETS swings to and fro, to show the clock is going. Most swing in a curve like a smile, but with some the curve is like a hump. Also called a 'false bob'. See PENDULUM WATCH. See GRANDE SONNERIE for picture.

Module   With the introduction of solid-state electronic timepieces it became inappropriate to call the mechanisms 'movements', so the word 'module' was introduced.

A **mock pendulum** in the dial of an early 18th c bracket clock by Windmills, London.

Monastic clock   To keep a strict routine of prayers, medieval monasteries had elaborate WATER CLOCKS. In the 12th or 13th c, a simple ALARM with VERGE ESCAPEMENT was introduced to warn the sacristan when to sound the hour bell. The few still existing are of iron in GOTHIC style. The earliest of them was long thought to be one made in Italy in the 14th or 15th c of brass with a 24-hour revolving dial and fixed hand, and a castellated wheel type of FOLIOT. However, a duplicate turned up in an auction in London in 1979. It seems that a replica was made in 1972. There are illustrations of such clocks in early tarsia panels.

Monometallic balance   Watch wheel balance made entirely of one type of metal. It is used with a HAIRSPRING of a special metal that hardly varies in its elasticity at different temperatures. The combination is temperature compensating so that it keeps good time.

An iron **monastic clock** with a six-hour dial of the 16th c. The smaller hand is used to set the alarm. (*Bonhams*)

A **monstrance clock** with one hand and a double twelve-hour dial.

Monstrance clock Clock made in Augsburg from the mid-16th to the mid-17th c in the form of a monstrance, the vessel used to hold consecrated bread by the Catholic church.

Montgomerie stone Grey-blue stone used with water for giving a fine finish to brass. It is a fine grade of WATER OF AYR STONE.

Montgomery dial Railroad watch introduced by Chief Time Inspector Montgomery of the Atchison Topeka and Santa Fé Railroad, U.S.A., c1895. It has large hour numerals and every minute numbered on the dial for accurate reading.

Month clock One that runs for about 32 days at one winding. There is an extra wheel in the TRAIN between the GREAT and CENTRE WHEELS, which means most are wound contra-clockwise. A heavier weight of 12.7kg (28lb) rather than one of 5.4kg (12lb) is used, or longer and stronger spring. This applies also to striking work, unless ROMAN STRIKING is employed. Six-month clocks have two

intermediate wheels and are wound clockwise.

Montre-à-tact Pocket watch that can be read by blind people in a pocket or in the

A **montre-à-tact** of 1810 by Le Roy for blind people. It has a Breguet (ratchet) key.

dark by touch, introduced by BREGUET. It has knobs round the case representing hours, the pendant being 12. On the back or front is a large hand which is turned until it is stopped. It was a cheap alternative to a REPEATER. Often called 'tact watch'.

Montre de carosse See CARRIAGE WATCH.

Monumental clock Name given to a style of early clock made in Augsburg and reminiscent of a monument.

Moon dial An engraved or painted moon face in an aperture in a clock dial that shows the current phase of the moon. Some of the earliest on MEDIEVAL CLOCKS showed the attitude as well as the phase of the moon. It was common on clocks from about 1750. The moon was then the only 'street lighting'. For most clocks, the lunar month is 29.5 days (actually it is 29 days, 12 hours, 44 minutes, 3 seconds). Since it is impossible to have a moon disc with 29.5 teeth moved a tooth every 24 hours, one with 59 teeth is used. Moved one tooth daily, this gives two lunations, so the disc has two moon faces, exposed one after the other through a

A watch with a **moon dial** by Breguet.

semicircular aperture, usually in the BREAK ARCH. The aperture is shaped so that the correct shape of moon is shown. The age of the moon is often indicated on the edge of the aperture. Watches also have this kind of moon dial. Some clocks from about the mid-19th c followed printed calendar practice, which showed a new moon as a black disc. One black face (new moon) and one white (full moon) are shown successively in a circular aperture. They are painted on a 59-toothed disk which, moved a tooth every 12 hours, turns once a month. The age of the moon is shown through an adjacent small square aperture. This is sometimes called a 'Halifax moon'. Another form of moon dial is a globe painted half black and half white or silver which is revolved in a close-fitting hole in the dial by gearing during a lunation.

Moon hand Hand with a pierced disc or ring, suggesting a full moon, near the tip. Also called 'Breguet hand'. When the hole is not central, it is called a 'crescent hand'.

Moon's effect on rate In 1927–8, A.L. Loomis compared three FREE PENDULUM clocks with a QUARTZ CLOCK by means of a spark CHRONOGRAPH he had invented. His results showed that during a lunar month the attraction of the moon on the pendulums caused them to vary by 0.0002 second.

Morbier clock Distinctive French clock made for home consumption in Morbier in the Haute-Jura mountains, Franche-Comté, mainly from c1750 to 1900. Output reached a peak of about 80,000 during 1860–90. The main production ended after the First World War, but some clocks were still being made after the Second. The weight-driven MOVEMENT is in an iron POSTED FRAME with brass wheels. The rack for striking is straight and drops vertically. It repeats the hours like most continental clocks. Weights instead of springs are used to return levers. Many have VERGE ESCAPEMENTS with the teeth of the horizontal ESCAPE WHEEL facing downwards. They were sold as movements and are found in locally made straight or viola-shaped long cases of oak, or more often stained pine, with round

The movement of a typical French **Morbier clock** with vertical trains in a metal case.

ENAMEL dials and stamped brass hands. The dial is usually set in a *fronton*, a panel of REPOUSSÉ or embossed brass, probably showing a rural scene. The PENDULUM ROD and BOB are also encased in viola-shaped panels of elaborately embossed brass sheet. The design developed from the earliest Morbiers of the late 17th c which had bronze *frontons* and more orthodox pendulums, but with folding rods to help pedlars carry the clocks. Also called 'Comtoise clocks'.

Morez clock   Clock from an adjacent village to MORBIER, which made similar ones.

Motion arbor   Fitting to hold a wheel or a tube between centres in a TURNS or a THROW.

Motion work   Twelve-to-one gearing driving the hour hand from the minute

hand. Also called 'dial train'. Very occasionally made visible through the dial. See DAVID AND GOLIATH CLOCK for picture.

Motor barrel   See STANDING BARREL.

Motor spring   American term for a MAINSPRING.

Motor-wound clock   Clock in which the MAINSPRING is wound at short intervals by a battery-operated electric motor. Very common between 1950 and 1960.

Moulding   Shaped beading, used round cases.

Movement   The 'works' of a mechanical timepiece.

Moving arm watch   Clock or watch in which a human figure (AUTOMATON) on the dial indicates the time by moving its arms. The arm on the left points to the

The Indian dancer's **moving arms** indicate the time by an early 20th c clock. (*Sotheby's*)

hour on a curved scale marked 12, 1, 2, 3, ...12; the other shows the minutes on a scale marked 0–60. Made in France in the 19th c. Also called a 'bras mobile' or 'bras en l'air' watch.

Moving band Some clocks of urn or ball shape have a fixed pointer indicating the hour on a turning band.

A pointer in front of a **moving band** gives the time by a 19th c marble and ormolu French clock by Robin, Paris. It is 41cm (1ft 4in) high. (*Sotheby's*)

Moving band dial Circular band marked with the hours which rotates to indicate the time against a fixed pointer, for example as used in an URN CLOCK (see picture).

Moving eyes clock Novelty introduced in the early days of clockmaking in AUGSBURG (see picture) that has persisted ever since. The FOLIOT or PENDULUM rocks the eyeballs in an animal, bird or human figure from side to side. They were made in the BLACK FOREST centuries later and in America. The French made some with black

figures. They also appear in a few PICTURE-FRAME CLOCKS. See BLINKING EYE CLOCK.

Mudge, Thomas (1715–94) Made the greatest invention of all, the LEVER ESCAPEMENT, in 1759 in QUEEN CHARLOTTE'S WATCH (see for picture). He thought it capable of extremely good performance, but too complicated to be commercially successful. It was perfected 23 years later by Josiah Emery, who made about a dozen. Billions are in use today. Mudge also invented a REMONTOIRE and DETACHED ESCAPEMENT in a clock made for the Swiss astronomer Huber in 1755. He came from Exeter, was apprenticed to GRAHAM in London, and became perhaps the finest craftsman of all. He left Fleet Street in 1771 to go to Plymouth and devote himself to perfecting MARINE CHRONOMETERS. Developed from the lever escapement for cheap watches was the PIN-PALLET ESCAPEMENT (see for illustrations of both).

Thomas **Mudge**, one of the pioneers of timekeepers for navigation that worked on sailing ships, made this marine chronometer.

Mulberry case Mulberry wood veneered and used for some clock cases in the earlier 18th c.

Muller, Franck Swiss watch designer from 1991 whose work is now collected.

Multiple case   Watch case made of separate parts, e.g. PAIR CASE.

Murday electric clock   Electric battery domestic clock of c1912 of which about 300 were made. It has a large BALANCE WHEEL and steel spring (like an alarm clock MAINSPRING) about 12.5cm (5in) in diameter mounted horizontally below the MOVEMENT. The HIPP TOGGLE principle (normally used for electric pendulum clocks) provides the contacts and IMPULSE is by a fixed electromagnet attracting a soft iron armature.

Music for clocks   Several celebrated composers wrote music specifically for musical clocks. Among them, Haydn (1732–1809) wrote 32 pieces for mechanical organs and Mozart (1756–91) wrote several musical clock pieces for Count Josef Deyn. In *The Magic Flute*, Mozart imitated mechanical music on bells.

Musical alarm   ALARM that plays a tune on a small MUSICAL BOX instead of ringing a bell. Produced in large numbers by the Germans, Americans and Swiss from 1897 to 1914 and still made. A popular one made in the BLACK FOREST was the JOKER in a gilt brass case like a cheap CARRIAGE CLOCK. It was copied and produced in quantity in America by the Seth Thomas Clock Co.

Musical barrel or **cylinder**   Also called a 'pin barrel'. A revolving drum set with projecting pins that operate hammers striking bells or reeds to play a melody. The earliest, used in carillons of bells, were made of wood with wooden pins. In clocks, watches and musical boxes, the barrel is usually of brass, with steel pins. One of the earliest known is in a 13-bell musical clock by Nicholas Vallin, dated 1598, in the British Museum. Pin barrels also operate organ and flute-playing clocks. (SINGING BIRD clocks are normally controlled by a cam.) The great carillon at Delft, in Holland, had a large copper pin-set barrel, operated by weight-driven clockwork. The barrel organ originated in Europe, perhaps in Salzburg. One of the most famous, in a monumental clock, was built by Thomas Dallam of London in 1593. Many barrel-operated MUSICAL CLOCKS were made

in England in the 18th c and MUSICAL WATCHES in France and Switzerland. Clocks were also produced by BLACK FOREST makers, one of whom, Johann Werhle, of Neukirch, constructed clocks with carillons of glass bells. A musical barrel is driven either by a spring barrel and FUSEE, or a GOING BARREL, and normally has a FLY to slow it. When designed to play two or more tunes, it is designed to be slid along its spindle in short steps, each bringing a new row of pins into position to operate the hammer tails, which are spaced at the appropriate distances apart. The cylinder is spring-loaded at one end, and a cam at the other end moves it to change the tune. Pricking cylinders to indicate where the pins were to be placed was a skilled task for which musicians were employed. The Swiss developed a barrel-pricking machine, like a large typewriter, which would hold a barrel and could be 'played' by a musician to prick out the tune. Clock barrels were generally earlier and were pricked individually. The best known makers of such musical movements were James Cox of London in the 18th c and Nicole Frères of Geneva in the 19th c. See MUSICAL CLOCK for picture.

Musical box   Clockwork mechanism playing music on bells or cymbals, or on the steel comb which may have been invented by Antide JANVIER in 1775. Louis Favre of Geneva probably made the first musical box in 1770. Musical movements were fitted into snuff-boxes, jewel cases, even watch and door keys. The best makers of larger ones were Nicole Frères from 1815 to 1903.

Musical clock   Both TURRET CLOCKS and domestic clocks have been made to play tunes at the hour, one of the earliest of the latter by N. Vallin, 1598 (in the BRITISH MUSEUM COLLECTION), having 13 bells. Later ones had steel combs played by a revolving musical barrel or cylinder. Famous English 18 c makers were Robert Philip, Markwick and Markham, David Evans, William Carpenter and Christopher PINCHBECK. In the 19th c the Swiss made many musical clocks employing small musical-box movements. Carillons of turret clocks are played by large revolving barrels operating the bell hammers. Famous composers who wrote for clocks include Bach, Beethoven, Haydn, Kircher and Mozart, who was the most prolific. See ORGAN CLOCK and SINGING BIRD.

A **musical clock** in skeleton form. The pin or musical barrel can be seen over the hammers behind the bell cluster. (*Hagans Clock Manor Museum, U.S.A.*)

A **musical cylinder** plays a comb in a Swiss musical watch. (*Christie's*)

Musical watch Watch playing a tune at the hour and usually also at will, by moving a slide. Invented about 1725 in Switzerland and most popular after 1800. The earliest had separate steel teeth, like the blades of a fan, plucked to give the notes by pins in a rotary disc. A metal comb and barrel or cylinder with pins superseded this. Some had discs with pins instead of barrels. Some were REPEATERS, repeating the tune. See MUSICAL BOX.

Musk ball watch Earliest form of watch still in existence, such as those made by Peter HENLEIN in the 16th c. The case is a metal sphere about 10cm (4in) in diameter. Like a scent 'bottle' of the period, it was hung by chain or cord round the neck. The movement is spring-driven and the dial is a smaller-diameter disc (like a base, for standing) at the bottom with one hand and no glass. Of the six such spherical watches known still to survive, the earliest is German and dated 1525–50. There is a German one of c1550 with CLOCK WATCH movement in the ASHMOLEAN MUSEUM and a French one of 1551 by Jacques de la Garde in the NATIONAL MARITIME MUSEUM. The DRUM WATCH may have been invented about the same time or soon after. See NUREMBERG EGG.

Traditionally the first ever style of watch, the **musk ball**.

Mystery clock Clock which appears to work without any power or, in some cases, wheels. A domestic type has the hand 'floating' in a transparent glass dial. Actually the dial comprises three circular glasses. The hand is fixed to the middle glass, which is toothed round its edge and is rotated by a movement in the base. It was invented in France c1860 and later adapted by Cartier for a series of elegant ART NOUVEAU clocks. More mysterious are two large hands, freely attached to the front of a sheet of glass, with nowhere to hide a movement. Each hand contains a watch movement in its counterpoise which turns a weight to alter the centre of gravity as it runs. This causes the hand to rotate very slowly. This idea was invented by John Schmidt of London in 1808, who made clocks with an open CHAPTER RING and a single counterpoised hand, supported from the tail of a dolphin. Another mystery clock, invented by A.R. Guilmet of Paris in 1872, has a statuette on top of the case. In one hand, this figure holds a PENDULUM which swings without apparent connection to the clock. Actually the statuette is given an almost imperceptible twist in alternate directions. IMPULSING is in principle similar to that in the RIEFLER CLOCK 15 years later, through the SUSPENSION SPRING. There are examples in the VICTORIA AND ALBERT MUSEUM and in the ILBERT COLLECTION. Another clock very popular from c1880 is the SWINGING CLOCK with a COMPOUND PENDULUM which is quite separate from the clock. Examples are an elephant balancing the pendulum, just above the middle of the rod, on its trunk and a woman (the Diana clock) doing the same on one hand. The lower end of the compound pendulum is a normal BOB; the top is a clock. The clock drives a miniature pendulum within its case, which impulses the compound pendulum by sympathetic action. Other forms of mystery clock are the ROLLING CLOCK which goes uphill instead of down and the RACK CLOCK and FALLING-BALL CLOCK that climb up instead of falling. They incorporate hidden MAINSPRINGS to overcome gravity. See ANSONIA, ELEPHANT CLOCK, SWING CLOCK, TORTOISE CLOCK.

A **mystery clock** in the form of a pendulum with a clock on top kept swinging on an elephant's trunk, apparently by itself. Many others were made with the pendulum held by a Grecian female figure. (*Christie's*)

N

Nacre The inside of a pearl oyster shell, mother-of-pearl, commonly used for earlier watch dials.

Name bar BAR carrying the end of a spring BARREL ARBOR furthest from the dial, and the maker's name in U.S. and English full-plate watches.

Nanosecond One thousand-millionth of a second, symbol ns. Used mainly for measuring electronic time intervals.

Napoleon Name for a half-hunter watch, which Napoleon is said to have invented, having cut a hole in the cover of a HUNTER to see the hands without opening the case.

Napoleon clock Mantel clock shaped like Napoleon's hat.

National Association of Watch and Clock Collectors Organisation of collectors in the U.S.A. formed in 1943 to stimulate interest in studying and collecting timepieces. It now has over 170 local, national and international chapters, publishes a bulletin and a 'mart', arranges meetings, and has a library and a museum at its headquarters: 514 Poplar Street, Columbia, PA 17512-2130, U.S.A.

National College of Horology and Instrument Technology College opened in January 1947 at the Northampton Polytechnic, Clerkenwell, London, to re-establish horology in the U.K. after the Second World War. Fuse making depended on watch- and clock-makers and the industry was almost extinct in 1939 largely because of very low-priced imports from Germany. The first head was R.A. Fell. It was closed in 1960 and the courses transferred to Hackney Technical College, London, but these too were closed on 6 October 1997.

National Maritime Museum, Greenwich This administers the old ROYAL OBSERVATORY, which is a museum very interesting to horologists. Both are situated in Greenwich Royal Park.

National Physical Laboratory Tests of timekeepers were once carried out at the Laboratory in Teddington, Middlesex, which superseded the old KEW A CERTIFICATES. The ATOMIC CLOCK was developed by Dr L. Essen at the N.P.L.

'Nautical Almanac' Astronomical tables giving star positions at different latitudes for every hour throughout the year, for NAVIGATION. Compiled by the ROYAL OBSERVATORY and published by H.M. Stationery Office. The title was changed to 'Astronomical Ephemeris' in 1959, but other publishers still use the original name.

Navigation A navigator or surveyor can calculate his position north or south (latitude) by finding the height of the sun or some other celestial body and referring to the 'NAUTICAL ALMANAC' or 'Air Almanac'. Finding his position east or west (longitude) is complicated by the rotation of the Earth. LOCAL TIME becomes earlier to the west and later to the east of Greenwich. As the Earth revolves through 360° in 24 hours, it moves 1° of longitude in four minutes. So if a sailor finds his local time is 5 hours earlier than GREENWICH MEAN TIME, he is 75° west of Greenwich To find local time he must know the date and take a 'fix' (find the position) of a star with a SEXTANT, in order to look up the local time in his almanac. G.M.T. is given by the ship's MARINE CHRONOMETER or RADIO TIME SIGNALS and must be accurate because an error of only four seconds equals one nautical mile. Superseded commercially by radar and satellite systems. See FINDING THE LONGITUDE.

Navigator's watch Precision watch as supplied to the armed forces such as aircrew.

Nef Bowl shaped like a ship used on a top table in the Middle Ages, which became a table ornament in the 16th c, often as a fully rigged ship and sometimes incorporating a clock in Germany and Switzerland. A fine example with a clock is in the BRITISH MUSEUM COLLECTION.

Negative set Form of hand-setting for pocket watches, mainly American. The control for winding or setting the hands is in the pendant of the watch case. See POSITIVE SET.

Negro clock Name originally given to a German 17th c AUTOMATON clock with a ball-shaped clock on a post intended to look like a palm tree. Beside it stand a black man and a dog. The black man has a pointer which indicates the hour against a MOVING BAND around the ball. At the hour, he moves his head and the dog tries to jump. Revived in France during the slavery debate in the DIRECTOIRE period (1795–1800) in ORMOLU cases with black figures, and again in novelty clocks in America in the 19th c.

Neoclassical clocks A reaction from the florid rococo cases of the 1750s led to restrained, geometrical, more architectural shapes by the 1770s in Europe, reaching clock cases later in the century through the influence of the Adam brothers in England and later in France during the DIRECTOIRE and EMPIRE periods.

Neuchâtel clock The Neuchâtelois waisted clock with ORMOLU feet on a bracket was the same shape as the French clock that marked the transition from Louis XIV to Regency styles. See

BALLOON CLOCK. This Swiss town was a clock- and watchmaking centre in Switzerland, from the late 17th c.

Newsam, Bartholomew (d.1593) Clockmaker to Queen Elizabeth I after Nicolas Urseau. Worked in the Strand, having probably come from Yorkshire. There is a fine clock by him in the BRITISH MUSEUM.

Newtonian time Absolutely uniform time. See EPHEMERIS TIME.

Nickel silver Not silver but an alloy of 50 per cent copper, 25 per cent zinc and 25 per cent nickel, looking a little more grey than silver and developed as a base metal for plating (electro-plated nickel silver). Used for some watch cases. Also called 'German silver'.

Nicole Nielsen English firm making the highest quality watches and some

Nicole Nielsen and Co., London, made this grande sonnerie carriage clock of c1900. It has up-and-down dials for both going and striking trains. (*Christie's*)

clocks in the late 19th c in a factory in Soho Square, London. They specialised in TOURBILLONS. Nielson became a director of the London firm of Charles Frodsham and Co. in 1871 after Charles Frodsham died, and later took over the firm, which stopped making watches about 1935. See UP-AND-DOWN DIAL for picture.

Niello Silver inlaid with a black material made from powdered silver, copper, lead, sulphur and usually borax, which fills the incised pattern after being heated. Used occasionally for watch cases.

Night-and-day watch See DAY-AND-NIGHT WATCH.

An Italian **night clock** with a picture dial showing Tobias and the angel. (*Christie's*)

An early 19th c **night-and-day** watch, with moon dial (bottom) and regulation (top). The other side of the watch has sweep seconds and a calendar. (*Sotheby's*)

Night clock The earliest iron clocks had TOUCH KNOBS (see for picture) at the hours for telling the time in the dark. The first known true night clock was said to be by Johann Treffler, or it might have been by one of the three Campani brothers in Italy, who made them for Pope Alexander VII in the 17th c. The successful ones had thirty-hour movements and

a form of SILENT ESCAPEMENT with a continuously revolving ESCAPE WHEEL. There is an ordinary dial for day, and a special one for night with an oil lamp behind it. Clocks with illuminated hour numerals moving past a fixed point were common in Italy at the end of the 17th c. FROMANTEEL, EAST and Joseph KNIBB made some in England. In these an oil lamp in the case shines through a perforated hour numeral and marker hole above it. The numeral moves round a large semicircular slot marked in quarter hours and minutes. Another type is the MAGIC LANTERN CLOCK. The REPEATING clock became the most convenient for night use in the 18th c. Some mechanical alarm clocks have LUMINOUS DIALS. A few announce the time in a synthesised voice. See CAMPANUS CLOCK.

Night silencing On some clocks there is a SUBSIDIARY DIAL that can be set to silence the strike or chimes. Some 20th c mechanical clocks have automatic night silencing. See BARRING-OFF WHEEL.

Nivarox Nickel-iron alloy with a little beryllium, invented by Carl Hass of Germany as an improvement on ELINVAR for HAIRSPRINGS. By heat treatment

A French **night clock** of 1860. The hand shows the time on an illuminated pale blue revolving glass bowl.

during manufacture, its elasticity can be fixed at almost any value required. Thus it can be made to give any TEMPERATURE COMPENSATION desired, to eliminate temperature error in watches and clocks with BALANCE WHEELS. It is non-magnetic, rustless and tougher than steel. Other alloys with similar properties have been developed; they are ISOVAL, Durinval and Nispan-C.

Nocturnal Instrument invented c1520 for measuring the time at night. It is held at arm's length to sight the Pole Star through a small hole in the centre. A lever is turned to line up the Pole Star with two stars in the Ursa Major constellation (Great Bear, Plough, Big Dipper) which

appears to rotate once round the Pole Star in 24 hours; thus the lever can indicate the time on a scale. Incorporated in ASTROLABES.

A boxwod **nocturnal** of 1716. Peer through the hole at the Pole Star and turn the arm to the correct constellation to read the time. (*Sotheby's*)

Nodes When one celestial orbit is at an angle to another, such as the sun's to the moon's, the points of intersection are called the ascending node and descending node. Used for predicting eclipses and shown on some astronomical clock dials.

Noiseless escapement See SILENT ESCAPEMENT.

Non-magnetic Fields of MAGNETISM have most effect on steel BALANCE WHEELS and HAIRSPRINGS. In 20th c watches these are usually made of special alloys for TEMPERATURE COMPENSATION, which are also, fortunately, non-magnetic. Such watches are called 'non-magnetic' and are fairly resistant to magnetism, but not entirely as there are still steel parts that can be affected. Aluminium bronze is sometimes used instead of steel, for the lever in particular. Some special watches have a protective screen over the movement inside the case. Standards have been issued by several countries including the U.K. The U.S.A. standard requires a variation of less than 15 seconds in a field of 60 gauss for 5 seconds in each of two positions. See DEMAGNETISER.

Noon mark The point which a shadow reaches at noon on a particular day. It indicates the MERIDIAN. Early settlers often made a noon mark on a south-facing porch or window. The simplest is a line on a horizontal surface with, perhaps, a disc with a hole mounted above it to show a sunspot instead of a shadow. Also made vertical. Since a clock shows EQUAL HOURS, the noon mark and clock only agree at noon on 15 April, 15 June, 1 September and 24 December. See ANALEMMA.

Normallzeit Gesellschaft See ELECTRIC CLOCK SYSTEMS.

Normande clock French provincial clock made in Normandy from the 17th c, having a great variety of cases. Movements were made locally until the 18th c when COMTOISE movements were increasingly used. See DEMOISELLE CLOCK.

Norwich Priory clock A clock made in 1325 with 35 AUTOMATA figures, bells and astronomical work. No longer in existence.

Nôtre Dame chime The eight-bell chime devised for the clock at Nôtre Dame, Paris.

Nuclear watch Timepiece depending on the half-life (decay rate) of a radio isotope, patented in 1970. The emission is used to trigger integrated circuits and provide IMPULSES for showing the usual watch indications.

Numerals Hour numbers on a dial, once almost universally Roman, now usually Arabic, traditionally called 'chapters'. Batons are most common today.

Nuremberg Town in the Bavarian district of Germany, one of the first centres of clock- and watchmaking, having been a centre of instrument making and sundials since the 15th c. In 1565 the council issued a decree forming clockmakers, firearm makers, and locksmiths into a guild. Masterpieces had to be made by them before they were allowed to practise their trade, those for clockmakers being an iron striking chiming and alarm clock 15cm (6in) high in a brass case, or one of the big striking and alarm watches of the time worn on a ribbon round the neck. An early clockmaker there was HENLEIN. See DRUM WATCH for picture. AUGSBURG outstripped Nuremberg in the 16th c with instruments, then clocks.

Nuremberg egg Some of the earliest watches were made in NUREMBERG in the early 16th c. Doppelmeyer, writing a history of the clockmakers there some 200 years later, called these watches *eyerlein* or little eggs. He had mistranslated *Uhrlein* meaning 'little clocks', but the false name still persists today, although these watches were ball-shaped. A few egg-shaped watches were made in later years. See WATCH and MUSK BALL WATCH.

Nuremberg hours Early system of time reckoning in Nuremberg. The 24 hours in a day and night period were numbered afresh from 1 at each sunrise and sunset.

Nurse's watch See FOB WATCH.

Nutation A slow and slight nodding action of the Earth's axis caused by the moon being below and above the ECLIPTIC at different times, thus pulling differently on the Earth. It affects the time of rotation (i.e. SIDEREAL TIME) to the extent of about 20 MILLISECONDS every 15 days, as well as by about 1.2 seconds over 18 years. Discovered in the 18th c but not applied in TIME DETERMINATION until 1926 when the SHORTT CLOCK could measure it. Sidereal time has to be corrected by a nutation figure to give mean sidereal time, in the same way as SOLAR TIME has to be corrected by the EQUATION OF TIME to give MEAN SOLAR TIME.

O

Obelisk clock French REGENCY clock mounted on a square section column tapering outwards towards the top.

Observatory clock Clock for astronomical TIME DETERMINATIONS. The very first mechanical clocks with VERGE ESCAPEMENT and FOLIOT may well have been those that drove GLOBES and other astronomical mechanisms, which only later were simplified for domestic use. The CROSS-BEAT ESCAPEMENT followed for astronomical use, but as more accurate time measurements were demanded, astronomers employed a weight on a cord and counted the swings. This was developed into the PENDULUM CLOCK which was made more accurate by the ANCHOR ESCAPEMENT and still more by the DEAD-BEAT ESCAPEMENT, in clocks called REGULATORS. The RIEFLER CLOCK improved timekeeping and was itself much improved on by the SHORTT CLOCK, in turn replaced by the QUARTZ CLOCK, which the ATOMIC CLOCK has superseded. Some observatory clocks show SIDEREAL TIME and have TWENTY-FOUR HOUR DIALS. See TIME DETERMINATION, ROYAL OBSERVATORY and OCTAGON ROOM.

Octagon room The original room from which observations were made in the ROYAL OBSERVATORY. It contained two fine year-going clocks with 4m (13ft) PENDULUMS above them, designed to show solar time and commissioned in 1676 from Thomas TOMPION by John FLAMSTEED, the Astronomer Royal. Both clocks were removed by Flamsteed's widow but one was reacquired from Holkam Hall, Norfolk, in 1994. The other on show is a replica made by Dan Parkes in 1955.

Odd beat Used to describe watches with other than 18,000 TRAINS, including older ones with a slower BEAT as well as later FAST-BEAT ones.

Offset seconds Separate small seconds dial which is not in the centre but near one edge of the dial.

Ogee (O.G.) S-shaped moulding. Popular with earlier American makers when each side of the top of a SHELF CLOCK was of shallow S-shape coming to an edge at the top (looking like a point from the front); also called an 'onion top'. Also common on English LONGCASE CLOCKS as a SWAN'S NECK CRESTING shape.

Oignon French watches of the 17th and early 18th c which were larger and thicker than the English and therefore called 'onions'. After 1800, French watches became delicate and original and English ones stolidly reliable.

Large **oignon** verge watch by Fecit of Rouen, with single hand and separate enamel chapters. (*Christie's*)

Oil Problems of oiling have always been of great concern to watch- and clockmakers and still are today. The famous BREGUET said to Napoleon: 'Give me a perfect oil, and I will give you a perfect watch.' This is still true of mechanical watches which, unlike other mechanisms, never stop working. The extremely tiny amounts of oil in them eventually must dry out, become gummy or become a kind of grinding paste with quartz dust from the air. Modern horological oils and greases have considerable scientific research behind them. Some are natural and others are synthetic. Church records of 1498 refer to applying 'cowes fatt oil to the pivotts of the clocke'. Freezing of the oil used to stop church clocks, and various inventions of non-freezing oils included calves' foot oil mixed with Scotch fir tar, fish oil mixed with pepper, and other oddities. The problem still arises during Arctic and space exploration. Most early makers used animal fat oils, such as neat's foot (also called 'cow heel'), sheep's foot, and whale or sperm oil (a famous one, Kelley's, came from the nose of the porpoise) as well as vegetable oils, such as olive and palm, which they filtered and blended themselves. Mineral oils were not used until the end of the 19th c. They spread easily, so usually have to have some animal oil added. The first synthetic oils were developed by the Companie Française de Raffinage, Paris, in 1928–9 and P. Cuypers of Dresden in 1929. The first special synthetic watch oils were produced before 1945 by the American and Swiss watch industries jointly financing research; the Germans joined the Swiss later. Various improvements were made subsequently. Clock oils are different from watch oils, having to withstand greater pressures. Different oils are used in different places. MAINSPRINGS often have a dry lubricant known as P.T.F.E. AUTOMATIC watch BARRELS pose special problems because of the controlled slip on overwinding and are usually given a special grease and sealed. Lord GRIMTHORPE advised neat's foot oil for TOWER CLOCKS. Some clockmakers, including HARRISON, tried to eliminate oils altogether. Oil spread can still be a problem. The tiny drops should be held in place by surface tension, like drops of water in the holes of a tea strainer. This is helped by OIL SINKS, but it is not possible to locate them in a number of places. After ULTRASONIC CLEANING a special coating, EPILAME, is given to the MOVEMENT to avoid oil spread. The oiling of a mechanical precision watch requires considerable skill and knowledge. Too much or too little or oil in the wrong places can affect the RATE of clocks, even large public ones, and stop watches. See FRICTION.

Oil-lamp clock See NIGHT CLOCK.

Oil pot A small pot used on the bench to hold oil which is applied to the clock or watch with a glass dropper.

Oil sink A small well around a PIVOT in a clock or watch PLATE or JEWEL which retains the oil. See SULLY and LE ROY.

Oiler Kind of fountain pen for applying watch oil in measured quantities.

Oilstone A finely textured stone used with some oil for putting a fine edge on gravers, etc. A cutting lubricant used in the past was glycerine thinned with a little methylated spirit, which did not clog like oil. Oil-clogged stones were left in a tin of benzine for a few days.

Oilstone dust Powdered oilstone used for preparing PIVOTS and FROSTING parts such as winding WHEELS.

Old-style calendar Popular name for the JULIAN CALENDAR. The date of introduction of the GREGORIAN CALENDAR in a particular country can give a guide to the date of a calendar clock made there.

Oliver Cromwell's watch A plain PURITAN WATCH on a FOB chain which reputedly belonged to the Protector and is now in the BRITISH MUSEUM COLLECTION. Made in 1625 by John Midnall of Fleet Street.

Omega Louis Brandt was making watches from 1848 and formed Louis Brandt et Fils in 1877 after taking on his son. At the end of the century they were making a striking wrist watch named Omega, and they decided to name the company after the watch! Today it is one of the biggest in Switzerland. In 1969 Neil Armstrong wore an Omega watch to the moon. In the 1970s the company produced a very accurate megaquartz chronometer wrist watch with a QUARTZ CRYSTAL vibrating at 2,359,296 Hz, the highest frequency then used by a watch.

One-at-the-hour strike See PASSING-HOUR STRIKE.

One-hand clock Before about 1400, clocks had one fixed hour hand and a dial that turned (see MONASTERY CLOCK). Then the dial became fixed and a single hour hand turned. Minute hands were introduced soon after on special clocks, but not generally until after the mid-17th c for domestic clocks. Cheaper clocks still continued into the 18th c with one hand. The present Westminster Abbey clock still has only one hand.

One o'clock gun The TIME GUN made for Edinburgh in 1861 and fired by a cord from a master clock. It can be heard about 30km (20 miles) away in good conditions. A TIME BALL also drops and is visible for 8km (5 miles).

One-wheel clock There was much competition at one time to produce clocks with the fewest gear wheels. A one-wheel clock is recorded in 1598. Pierre LE ROY made an astronomical one, and Lepaute one showing seconds in the mid-18th c.

Onion top Style of American SHELF CLOCK with a pointed top, each side of the top being OGEE-shaped.

Open-face watch One without a cover over the dial, as opposed to a HUNTER.

Orange shellac Resin used for setting watch PALLET stones and RUBY PINS.

Organ clock Clock playing a small pipe organ every three hours. The earliest

An **organ clock** by Spencer and Perkins, who worked in Snow Hill, London from 1765 to 1806. (*Christie's*)

automatic organs operated by pin or MUSICAL BARREL were made in AUGS-BURG of which the earliest extant is the Salzburg horn organ of 1502. There is a NEF of 1585 with a small pipe organ in the Vienna Museum of Art History. Organ-playing clocks (usually called 'flute playing') were very popular from the mid-18th c for about a century to the BIEDERMEIER period in the BLACK FOREST. Clockmakers pinned cylinders to customers' choices of tunes. Music was also specially composed for them. Several late 18th c London makers produced such clocks, mainly for export. CUCKOO and TRUMPETER CLOCKS are the simplest form of organ clocks. See MUSIC FOR CLOCKS, MUSICAL CLOCK.

Organ-grinder clock The clock is the 'organ' and a model of the grinder appears to turn the handle of the organ.

A French **organ-grinder clock** in Empire style. He turns the handle. (*Christie's*)

Oris Founded in 1904 in Holstein, near Basel, where the great annual clock and watch exhibition is held, this firm started making watch parts, then watches including jewelled levers and PIN LEVERS, but

the government forced them to make only pin levers, some of which passed official trials, enabling them to be called CHRONOMETERS, to the disgust of the makers of JEWELLED LEVER chronometers. In 1988 they made mechanical alarm clocks, some of which are now collectors' items.

Ormolu Literally 'ground gold'. Bronze that has been cast, chased and FIRE GILT. Used for most French clock cases of the 18th c and some English ones in the French style. Gouthière made the best French and Matthew Boulton the best English ormolu. Superseded in France by ELECTROTYPE cases during the Second Empire period from about 1848 to 1870. In the second half of the 19th c many American firms, especially ANSONIA, made copies of ormolu clocks in wood and in cast iron. See BRONZE CASE, PRIEUR. See LYRE CLOCK for picture.

Ormskirk escapement An ESCAPE-MENT for watches employed by English makers in the Ormskirk area, Lancashire, in the 1800s. Developed from an invention by DEBAUFRE in 1704. Also called the 'club-footed verge' or the 'chaffcutter', because the double escape wheel looks like one.

Orpheus clock Group of remarkable 16th c TABLE CLOCKS each with a cast reproduction of Orpheus charming the animals. Nine are known, one only by photograph as it disappeared after 1900. The Orpheus friezes came from the same workshop. One clock, belonging to the Swiss collector J. Fremersdorf, of the third quarter of the 16th c is the oldest clock known with separate seconds indication.

Orrery Version of the PLANETARIUM showing the motions of the Earth and moon around the sun, sometimes operated by clockwork, from which it could be disengaged for hand operation. TOMPION and GRAHAM first made one c1700, (probably based on that by HUYGENS of 1682). John Rowley made a copy for his patron, the Duke of Orrery, which gave it its name.

An **orrery clock** by Raingo, Paris, now in Windsor Castle. (*The Royal Collection © Her Majesty The Queen*)

Oscillating weight Swinging weight which winds the MAINSPRING in an earlier SELF-WINDING WATCH. In later ones, the weight rotates. See PEDOME-TER WATCH and ROTOR. Also used, when driven, in MYSTERY CLOCKS and to control earlier ALARM mechanisms.

Oscillation, centre of See CENTRE OF OSCILLATION.

Ostrich and bear clock Nuremberg AUTOMATON clock design of c1550 with the figure of an ostrich, which has constantly moving eyes, led by a much smaller bear with a drum. At the striking of the hour, the ostrich flaps its wings and moves its beak. At the quarters, the bear turns its head, and for an alarm it beats the drum. Made of gilt copper with an iron movement.

Out of beat A PENDULUM or BALANCE WHEEL releases a tooth of the ESCAPE WHEEL at the end of each swing. If this action is not symmetrical the clock is 'out of beat'. The TICKS are alternately loud and soft and at different intervals, or the clock stops because a tooth is not released. Altering the angular position of a pendulum clock will set it 'in beat', the simplest method being to raise one side by a wedge under it. A more permanent and professional adjustment is to bend the CRUTCH towards the loudest tick side. Precision clocks, such as REGULATORS, have BEAT ADJUSTERS for more accurate adjustment. In some mantel clocks, the crutch is friction tight on its ARBOR and is self-adjusting. To adjust an out-of-beat LEVER ESCAPE-MENT it is necessary to alter the PINNING POINT of the HAIRSPRING, a job for a good professional unless the watch has a special device to allow the outer point of attachment to be moved without dismantling the balance assembly.

Outer case Separate external case of a PAIR CASE.

Oval watch Following the DRUM or canister cases for the earliest watches, many of those of the 17th c had oval cases, presumably to reduce the size.

Ovalising balance BI-METALLIC BALANCE which is not a CUT BALANCE. The crossing (the two opposing spokes) does not expand in the same proportion as the rim as temperature rises, so the balance becomes oval. Combined with a modern alloy HAIR-SPRING, this can give excellent TEMPERATURE COMPENSATION. First invented by Volet, a Frenchman, in the 18th c. Reinvented independently by Lord Charnwood in the U.K. in 1927, and finally in 1942 by the Hamilton Watch Co.

in the U.S.A., whose MARINE CHRONOMETERS and DECK WATCHES had stainless steel rims and crossings of INVAR. The U.S. Navy specification forbade the use of the AUXILIARY COMPENSATION balances used by most makers.

Over-banking Fault in a LEVER ESCAPEMENT which results in the RUBY PIN passing to the wrong side of the FORK, which stops the watch.

Over-compensation A plain BALANCE and spring will lose time as the temperature rises because of TEMPERATURE ERROR. If it has TEMPERATURE COMPENSATION and gains in heat, it is said to be 'over-compensated'.

Over-sprung When the HAIRSPRING is above the BALANCE, as opposed to when it is 'under sprung'.

Overcoil A HAIRSPRING with the outer quarter turn raised and curved towards the centre. An ordinary spiral spring does not keep good time because the spring becomes lopsided as it opens and closes (breathes) while the BALANCE swings. The overcoil avoids this. See BREGUET SPRING.

Oyster clock case Cutting young olive-wood trees at an angle produces oval or circular pieces of veneer with oystershell-like patterns, used on LONGCASE CLOCKS in the late 17th c.

Oyster watch case The first commercial waterproof wrist watch case (in which the winding button screwed down), patented by Rolex in 1926, based on a patent of 1891 by François Borgel.

OZ balance Plain steel three-arm balance (represented by O) with two outside bi-metallic COMPENSATION CURBS (Z) and a helical BALANCE SPRING, used by John ARNOLD from about 1780 to 1791.

P

Padlock watch One of the FORM WATCHES in the shape of a padlock. It is not one.

Pagoda clock One of James COX's clocks of 1785 in the shape of a very elaborate metal pagoda on a stand. A striking and chiming clock with a simple dial is in the middle. The clock is nearly 1.22m (4ft) high and plays several tunes on an organ with wooden pipes and a separate movement.

Pagoda top Ornamental top of a clock case with four concave sides and sometimes flutes, used on BRACKET and some LONGCASE CLOCKS from 1760 to 1790. A version for longcase clocks with curved sides and a flat front and back appeared about the same time, but earlier examples of both are known.

Painted dial Early iron HOUSE CLOCKS of the 15th and 16th c often had CHAPTERS (numerals) painted in colour. The practice continued with many DUTCH CLOCKS and with BLACK FOREST clocks. The Dutch often repainted old dials. In England, LONGCASE CLOCKS with painted dials (also called WHITE DIALS) were made in huge numbers from about 1770, and specialist dial makers and painters in the Birmingham area also exported them. See FALSE DIAL. Dials painted on metal became almost universal in the late 18th c. Painting fired on ENAMEL was first used for watch dials because they were small. Schools of highly skilled decorative enamel painters emerged in BLOIS, then later in GENEVA and elsewhere. Decorative enamelled watch dials are highly prized. From the Louis XIV period, the French favoured painted enamel clock dials, first using 12 small

The **pagoda top** of a bracket clock by James Cowan, Edinburgh. At the turn of the 19th c, many styles like this were copied from earlier periods.

enamelled plates and then 13 (one for each chapter plus a central one) mounted in the case. As enamelling developed, dials became one-piece. Porcelain dials and cases were also painted and fired. The dial painter's skill lay not only in the decoration but in the delineation of the numerals and time divisions, particularly on watch dials, and is most extreme in the SECRET SIGNATURE.

From the 1770s, **painted dials** on longcase clocks began quickly to take over from brass and silvered brass dials. This is on an early Thwaites and Reed clock in the Ilbert Collection.

Pair case Form of double watch case. The inner one is plain, or pierced if the movement alarms, strikes or repeats. The outer case is separate and decorated with repoussé, engraving, etc. Popular on early continental watches and almost universal in England from c1650 to 1800. Most were

An early **pair case**. The inner case is pierced to allow the sound to escape.

in silver, but some in gold, occasionally decorated with leather PINWORK, enamelled etc. Later outer cases were plain. See DUST CAP for picture.

Pallet Part of an ESCAPEMENT that intercepts the teeth of the ESCAPE WHEEL. Most, such as ANCHOR ESCAPEMENT pallets, are of steel in clocks but agate is used in BROCOT ESCAPEMENTS and some REGULATORS. For watches, various minerals have been used, from quartz to garnet, chrysoberyl, sapphire, ruby and in the 20th c synthetic ruby and sapphire. Steel is employed in most PIN-PALLET ESCAPEMENTS.

Pallet staff The steel axle of the PALLETS.

Paper dial Dials printed on paper or thin card and mounted on metal sheet were common on cheaper watches, alarm clocks, and timepieces of the late 19th and first quarter of the 20th c until printing on metals improved.

Paperweight clock Clock set in a block of mineral, metal or ornamental object intended as a desk paperweight. Also a small 19th c Japanese brass PILLAR CLOCK in a wooden case, which is really a large watch. Sometimes called a 'doctor's clock'.

Papier mâché clock Occasionally clock cases and even movements such as those of skeleton clocks were made of a moulding material prepared from scraps of paper or paper pulp with glue, chalk and occasionally fine sand, which was baked, painted and lacquered. The French sold papier mâché THIRTY-HOUR CLOCKS for 50 francs each in the early 19th c. From 1851, the Litchfield Manufacturing Co. supplied cases painted with black lacquer, colour, gold and mother-of-pearl to clock manufacturers in Connecticut, U.S.A.

Parachute index Combined SHOCK ABSORBER and regulation INDEX for watch BALANCE WHEELS invented by BREGUET in which the END STONE is fitted into a spring. Forerunner of the modern shock absorbers such as INCA-BLOC and PARECHOC.

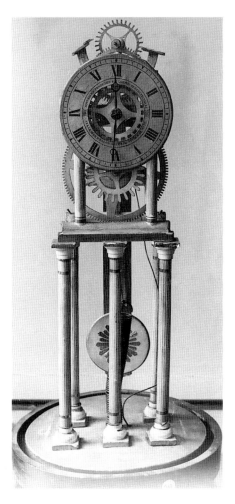

A French clock almost entirely made of papier mâché, including the wheels. The spring and hands are of steel.

Parechoc Shockproofing system where the JEWEL HOLES and END STONES of the BALANCE WHEEL have spring-like settings.

Paris inch Old measure for watch SIZES. One Paris inch measures 12 lignes, and 1 ligne 12 douzièmes. Equal to 27.06mm (1.0654in).

Parking timer, watch After street parking meters were introduced, a Swiss watch was produced with a built-in parking timer which sounded before time was up.

Parliament's clocks Clocks for the House of Commons, restored after damage during the Second World War, were the gift of Northern Ireland. One hundred and seventy-two SLAVE DIALS, split into six groups, were operated from a MASTER CLOCK through a control panel in the switch room. For timing divisions of the House, the Speaker has a special INTERVAL TIMER. The TOWER CLOCK outside is popularly called BIG BEN, named after the bell on which it strikes.

Parquetry Early form of laying veneers in geometrical patterns in small areas used for LONGCASE CLOCKS from 1670 to 1680 when MARQUETRY superseded it in London although it lasted longer elsewhere. Rosette, star and fan shapes in different coloured woods and stained ivory were most common.

Passing hollow See SAFETY ACTION.

Passing-hour strike Striking mechanism providing only one blow at every hour. Also called passing strike and one-at-the-hour strike. Common on SKELETON CLOCKS and occasionally used on ENGLISH DIALS.

Passing spring Thin gold spring fixed to the DETENT of a CHRONOMETER. A PALLET on the BALANCE moves it one way to move the detent and release the ESCAPE WHEEL. On the return swing of the balance, the spring flexes to let the pallet pass without releasing the detent. The IMPULSE is therefore only in one direction.

Patek Philippe One of the finest Swiss makers, which originated in 1832 when a Polish cavalry officer, Antoine de Pradwdzic, fled to Geneva after a revolt against the Tsar. He changed his name to Patek and started making watches with another ex-Pole. In 1844 he met a French watchmaker, Adrien Philippe, who replaced the original partner. The company became strong on innovation and won over 500 international awards. For Ward Packard, the American car magnate, it made over six years a watch with over 20 complications including a

A case with **parquetry** stars and a **marquetry** floral panel on a clock of c1675–80 by Nicholas Coxeter, London.

star map. It repurchased it in the late 1990s for its own museum at $2 million. It claims to be the only watchmaker left in Geneva making its entire watches itself.

Pavement clock   See FLOOR CLOCK.

Pawl   In horology, a CLICK on a lever, preventing reversal of a WHEEL but also allowing it to be moved forwards one tooth at a time.

Pecking pawl   A PAWL that moves to rotate a toothed WHEEL like that which moves the hands in a BULLE CLOCK.

Pectoral watch   Early watch shaped like a cross or skull on a chain to hang on the chest.

Pedestal clock   Clock designed with a separate pedestal on which it stands, favoured particularly by the French from the Louis XIV period. See PILLAR CLOCK.

Pediment   Top portion of a clock case HOOD, especially when triangular.

Pedometer watch   The first SELF-WINDING WATCH was a pocket watch with a weighted lever, like that in a pedometer, which jerked when the wearer moved and wound the MAINSPRING, invented by A.L. Perrelet c1770 and first made in London by L. Recordon. Also made by BREGUET. Used as well for a pocket watch incorporating a pedometer, patented in 1799 by Ralph Gout, London.

Pegwood   Small stick of wood sharpened to a point and used by twirling it for cleaning PIVOT holes in watches and clocks. The point is recut for each pivot hole. Dog wood (*Cornus*), or *bois de fusain* in Switzerland, was considered best and was also turned into charcoal for finishing brass surfaces in a circular pattern. Hornbeam (*Carpinus*) was also long favoured, but has been in very short supply since being made a protected E.U. species.

Pendant   The earliest watches were designed to hang from a cord or ribbon round the neck or waist. The cord passed through a ring fixed to the edge of the watch case. The ring was at right angles to the case so that the watch would hang

An elaborate French **pedestal clock** with Father Time on the top. (*Biggs of Maidenhead*)

A **pedometer watch** of 1831 by E. Fairclough, Liverpool, with a cylinder escapement (*Sotheby's*)

A very early one-hand watch with a **pendant** that is just a ring. It has moon and day and date indication, and an alarm. (*Christie's*)

flat. After the POCKET WATCH arrived, the loop was fastened to the case and hinged in the same plane. Next the loop and its stem were used for PUMP

WINDING. Since KEYLESS WINDING, the pendant position of any watch is where its winding button (also called the 'crown') is fitted. The expression is used when checking POSITIONAL ERRORS, e.g. pendant right. See HAND SETTING.

Pendule, Empire See EMPIRE CLOCK.

Pendule de Paris Standard PENDULUM MOVEMENT which evolved in Paris from the end of the 18th c and was used widely by the French industry until the outbreak of the First World War in 1914. It is of high quality with a short pendulum and circular PLATES and LOCKING PLATE or in some cases, RACK STRIKING. The half-hour is also struck, on a single note. Normally supplied in a brass drum case to be fitted to almost any kind of case, from ORMOLU to MARBLE. Large numbers of them, and of clocks with them, were imported by Britain after a free trade agreement with France in 1860. The largest centres of manufacture were then outside Paris, in St Nicolas d'Ailermont to the north and Beaucourt, Badevel and Montbéliard to the south east. JAPY was the biggest producer. See MARTI.

Pendule de voyage Travelling clock first made in France in the late 16th c. It gradually developed into the French CARRIAGE CLOCK, first made in the early 19th c by BREGUET in Paris. Production centres later were near Dieppe and in the Jura. Very popular in England from c1850. Later made in Switzerland, England, Germany, America and elsewhere.

Pendule d'officier Travelling clock introduced in France c1775 and supposed to have been used on campaigns by army officers. Most typical pieces were made from c1780 to 1820, many in the Louis XVI style. Also made in Austria and Switzerland until c1840. Also called 'Foncine clock' from the village where many were made. See CAPUCINE.

An ormolu quarter striking **pendule d'officier** with pull-repeat. Possibly Swiss c1800. (*Sotheby's*)

Pendule sympathique MANTEL CLOCK devised by BREGUET in 1795 which set a special pocket watch to time and also regulated it to keep better time. The watch was laced in a slot in the top of the clock overnight. Only a few are known. George DANIELS, Breguet's biographer, has examined five and says they are an advanced example of misplaced

A late 18th c French alarm and striking **pendule de voyage** with a calendar and pierced plates to show the action. (*Christie's*)

One of the remarkable **pendules sympathiques** made by Breguet for the Prince Regent in 1814. (*The Royal Collection* © *Her Majesty The Queen*)

ingenuity. They are, however, a clever and very early example of negative feedback, essential in modern control systems.

Pendulette Small clock for travelling or to be kept by the bedside. Examples are a miniature LONGCASE CLOCK a few inches tall, a BOUDOIR CLOCK and a CALOTTE.

Pendulum A weight swinging under the influence of gravity. First it was hung from a thread and the swings counted for astronomical time measurements. GALILEO discovered that the swing or BEAT depended only on the length of the thread or pendulum rod, not on the angle of swing or weight of the BOB. HUYGENS proved this was only true if

the pendulum swung through a CYCLOIDAL CURVE instead of the arc of a circle, the difference being CIRCULAR ERROR. Of several applications of a pendulum to clock mechanisms, that by Huygens was most successful. The RATE of a pendulum depends on its length and the force of gravity, which is different in different parts of the world. The time of one complete vibration (one cycle) T, in seconds, where l is the length and g is the acceleration due to gravity, is:

$$T = 2 \ \frac{l}{g}$$

The exact figure for a SECONDS PENDULUM for London is 993.6mm (39.1393in). This measurement is made from the point of SUSPENSION to the CENTRE OF OSCILLATION of the BOB. The pendulum controls the rate of a clock and is kept swinging by IMPULSES from the ESCAPEMENT. See COMPOUND, CONICAL, ELLICOTT, FREE, GRIDIRON, LONG, MERCURIAL, RHOMBOID, ROYAL, TORSION PENDULUMS and PENDULUM REGULATOR.

Pendulum, compensated One in which changes in length caused by changes in ambient temperature are corrected. See COMPENSATION PENDULUM.

Pendulum, long See LONG PENDULUM.

Pendulum aperture Curved slot in a bracket or table clock dial to show a FALSE BOB.

Pendulum bob LENTICULAR shapes are most common, but cylindrical bobs are more accurate. The weight is only critical for stability. The bob of the two-second pendulum in St Nicholas Church, Bristol, weighed 502kg (12cwt). See PENDULUM, BOB PENDULUM.

Pendulum regulation As well as the formula under PENDULUM, the graph illustrated can be used to calculate BEAT or length. A simple rule for calculating pendulum length is to square the beat time and multiply by the length of a seconds pendulum, e.g. for a half-second pendulum it is a half squared (a quarter) multiplied by 39in = 9.8in. If a nut of 18 threads an inch (e.g. 5/16in Whitworth) is used for the RATING NUT of a seconds pendulum, one turn will equal one minute a day. A regulating weight added to a tray fixed one third of the length of a precision pendulum from the top needs one ten-thousandth of the total weight of the pendulum to make it gain one second a day.

Pendulum regulator Subsidiary dial on some clocks with a square for a key or a hand to regulate it. The SUSPENSION SPRING of the pendulum is raised or lowered between two fixed CHOPS, which effectively alters its length. Occasionally the regulator is on the side of the move-ment. See BROCOT SUSPENSION.

Pendulum regulator dials are usually on the main dial, but this one for a longcase clock by William Clement is on the side of the movement.

Pendulum rod Rod holding the BOB, normally made of brass, steel, or varnished wood. See COMPENSATION PENDULUM.

Pendulum watch After the application of the PENDULUM to clocks, watchmak-ers who did not understand it tried to apply it to watches. A pendulum replaced the BALANCE and the watch was set in GYMBALS so that it would always stay upright. The case was therefore ball-shaped. This did not work well, so a counterbalance was added to the pendu-lum and it really became a DUMBBELL BALANCE again. Most so-called pendu-lum watches were made after about 1700 and are false, being designed to take advantage of the reputation of the pendu-lum. A disc is attached to the balance and can be seen oscillating through a slot in the dial, like the MOCK PENDULUM of a clock.

Petite sonnerie clock Usually a CARRIAGE CLOCK striking TING TANGS at the quarter- and half-hours but not the hours as well, like a GRANDE SONNERIE timepiece.

Perpetual calendar Calendar worked by a clock which corrects not only for months of different lengths (annual calen-dar), but also for leap years. Occasionally incorporated in clocks and watches.

Perpetual motion clock Before it was appreciated that energy must be expended to do work, various futile attempts were made to produce machines, including clocks, that would generate their own energy after being set in motion. Most such clocks of the Industrial Revolution period in fact fake perpetual motion. A French one of c1860, for example, is appar-ently driven by weights on one side of a wheel swinging to a greater radius as the wheel turned. It is actually spring-driven. Perpetual motion was often confused with self-winding (see PERPETUAL WATCH) when energy is drawn from another source.

Perpetual watch (Perpetuelle) Name for the SELF-WINDING WATCHES made by BREGUET.

Phillips curve Special curve or OVER-COIL of the outer end of a HAIRSPRING towards the centre to improve ISO-CHRONISM, worked out mathematically

A **perpetual calendar** on a gold hunter watch hall-marked 1876. (*Sotheby's*)

by Edouard Phillips, a Frenchman, in 1860. The curves were further improved by another mathematician, Lossier of Geneva, around 1907. See BREGUET SPRING.

Phonic clock   See TALKING CLOCK.

Phonic motor   Elementary motor which can be kept in step with an alternating electric current, like a SYNCHRONOUS CLOCK, or the stepping motor of a QUARTZ CLOCK, called a resonant motor.

Phonograph clock   Invented by Bernhaard Hiller of Berlin, this announced the hours recorded on an endless celluloid band driven by a gramophone motor and 'spoken' by a soundbox and horn. The Japanese produced a tape recorder version in the 1970s.

Photographers' clock   ELAPSED TIME INDICATOR with a large luminous dial with luminous centre seconds hand and minute recorder for darkroom use having a mechanical movement with a back or PULL WIND, a SYNCHRONOUS electric one or a quartz module.

Photographic timer   A switching device connected to a photographic enlarger. The dial is set to the time of printing exposure. A switch is pressed which sets the timer going and switches on the enlarger light. The light is switched out automatically at the end of the time set. A simpler form is a TIMER or ELAPSED TIME INDICATOR that rings a bell.

Piaget   In 1874, Georges Piaget started finishing movements for other watch-makers in his farmhouse in the village of La Côte aux Fées. In 1911, his son Timothée assembled and sold complete watches which bore no name. Work was first done on the ground floor of a chapel and then the 'Café Français'. In 1945 a factory was set up and the name 'Piaget' used on the dials. At one time it was making the thinnest watch in the world. The policy is quality before quantity.

Picture clock   Made in the 18th and 19th c in France. At first glance one of these seems to be an oil painting in an elaborate gilded frame, but it is elaborately animated, often with a real clock in a church tower. Examples in the Musée des Arts et Métiers, Paris, include one showing a fortified village with a stream in the foreground, in which a laundress washes linen, a peasant girl is helped by a boy to churn butter, two cocks fight, and a fisherman raises and lowers his line. There is an abandoned drinking bout involving two soldiers and their girls while infantry, cavalry and a carriage and pair cross a bridge. Meanwhile, clouds drift across the sky, occasionally allowing the sun to peep through, and from the church tower comes a full peal of bells. One spring-driven clock movement controls all 15 animations by a simple mechanism of wires and levers.

Picture-frame clock   The round DIAL is set in velvet in a rectangular picture frame with brass SPANDRELS. Made from about 1875 to 1900 in France with green, blue or red velvet background.

Pierpont Morgan collection Magnificent collection of watches, many enamelled, now in the Metropolitan Museum, New York. A superb hand-painted catalogue was originally produced in a limited edition of 46 copies. One is in the ILBERT LIBRARY at the BRITISH HOROLOGICAL INSTITUTE.

Pigeon clock Clock for recording the time of returning racing pigeons. An identification capsule removed from a pigeon's leg as it arrives in the loft is placed through a hole into a drum in the clock. A lever is pressed which moves the drum round a place and stamps the time on a paper chart in hours and minutes. There are several devices to prevent the clock from being tampered with.

A 19th c French **pillar clock** with a gridiron pendulum and outside count wheel. (*Sotheby's*)

Pillar One of the rods which fasten the PLATES together to make a clock FRAME or early watch frame. Formerly they were carved or turned in fancy shapes. Usually they are riveted on the dial side and held by tapered pins, nuts, or occasionally LATCHED, to the BACK PLATE. Also one of the wooden pillars or partly round ones on the sides of a LONGCASE CLOCK HOOD.

Pillar-and-scroll clock American SHELF CLOCK produced by Eli TERRY in 1818 with a CRESTING based on the SWAN'S NECK CRESTING of some English longcase clocks. It has a wooden movement and is more elegant than the 'box cases' of the time.

An American **pillar-and-scroll clock**, a form of shelf clock of c1816 by Eli Terry. (*Hagans Clock Manor Museum, U.S.A.*)

Pillar clock French DRUM CLOCK with round MOVEMENT and DIAL on four vertical pillars standing on a round base. The pendulum hangs in the middle of the pillars. Made in MARBLE, ORMOLU, and wood in the 19th c. Also another name for a PEDESTAL CLOCK.

Pillar clock, Japanese   Long and narrow WALL CLOCK like a pillar, but not one. The time is shown by a short arrow attached to the weight line and moving down a slot as the clock runs down. Most are BALANCE-controlled. Earlier ones had FOLIOTS and a few later ones short PENDULUMS. See JAPANESE CLOCKS.

Pillar plate   The PLATE to which the PILLARS are permanently attached, normally the front plate in a clock and the bottom plate in a watch.

Pin barrel   See MUSICAL BARREL.

Pin lever   Alternative name for a PIN-PALLET watch.

Pin-pallet escapement   One with steel pins instead of jewelled PALLETS, used in cheap, particularly ROSKOPF, watches. The action is very similar to the LEVER ESCAPEMENT, and it is sometimes called 'pin lever'. Also the BROCOT ESCAPE-MENT for clocks, which was not designed for cheapness.

Pin set   Hand-setting by a small pin on the side of a pocket watch with rocking bar KEYLESS WORK which, when pressed, causes the winder to turn the hands.

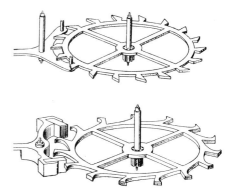

A **pin-pallet escapement** (*top*) compared with a jewelled lever escapement.

Pin-wheel escapement   Popular in France for clocks and also employed in TURRET CLOCKS on the Continent. The teeth of the ESCAPE WHEEL are replaced by pins. A swinging pair of levers attached to the PENDULUM allows the pins to 'escape' one by one, and this also IMPULSES the pendulum. It is accurate and needs only a small pendulum ARC. Invented by Amant of Paris in 1741. Pin wheels were used in the LEADING-OFF WORK of large public clocks.

Pinchbeck, Christopher   (1651–1713) Inventor and maker of musical clocks, which gained world-wide repute, and of the gold-coloured metal alloy still called 'Pinchbeck'. It was gilded but worn gilt

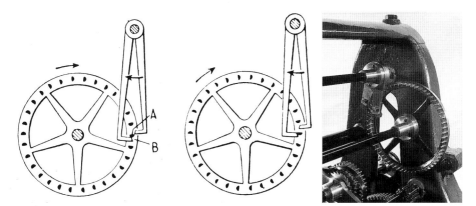

A **pin-wheel escapement** in a turret clock. The French used it in many quality domestic clocks. In the drawing, as the pendulum swings to the left, the escape wheel pin A slides down the impulse face B of the left hand pallet and impulses the pendulum to the left. Then the action is repeated the other way.

did not show. Worked in Fleet Street, 'at the sign of the Astronomico-Musical Clock'. The 'curious secret of new-invented metal which so naturally resembles gold' was four parts copper to three zinc. His eldest son, also Christopher, made an ASTRONOMICAL CLOCK for King George III, which is still in the ROYAL COLLECTION.

Pine Often used for early LONGCASE CLOCK cases and stained to resemble ebony. Clock carcases were often made of pine and VENEERED. County clocks with pine cases were stained or painted. It is doubtful if any were sold in bare wood, i.e. 'stripped', following the modern fad.

Pinion One of the small solid, and usually steel, gear WHEELS in a clock or watch. By convention, a gear wheel with less than 20 teeth. The teeth are called 'leaves'. The large gears are called 'wheels'. See PINION WIRE, LANTERN PINION.

Pinion engine Similar to a WHEEL-CUTTING ENGINE, but for PINIONS. The dividing plate is usually vertical instead of horizontal, and cutting of slots between teeth is done by moving a special narrow file, or cutter, backwards and forwards in a frame instead of by a cutting wheel. See PINION WIRE.

Pinion of report The pinion used to drive either the hour wheel or COUNT WHEEL in clocks and watches. In early work they had two or three leaves, often cut in the solid end of the protruding ARBOR.

Pinion wire PINIONS were filed by hand until steel pinion wire, lengths of wire with the cross-section of a pinion along their entire length, for watches and clocks was invented in Lancashire c1700. England had a virtual monopoly based in Park, near Liverpool, until an Englishman, William Blakey, set up a factory in Paris c1744. London also began making it about the same time. The Swiss began about a century later in Savoy and Fontainemelon village. Pinion wire was made by drawing wire through a pinion-

shaped hole in a DRAW PLATE. Cut to the length of an ARBOR, and with all leaves broken off except those for the pinion, it enabled the arbor, PIVOTS, and pinion to be made as one in a LATHE or TURNS. The leaves were finished by file, then the whole hardened and polished.

Pinning point Usually the point at which the inner end of the HAIRSPRING is fixed to the BALANCE. It is impossible to fix this end on the exact axis of the BALANCE STAFF. The end is therefore slightly out of the centre, which causes movement of the centre of gravity of the HAIRSPRING and therefore small changes in RATE. Manipulation of this end of the balance is one of the fine adjustments carried out by watch ADJUSTERS.

Pin work Outer watch PAIR CASE of leather, studded with silver pins, that was in vogue around 1650.

Pin work on the case of a 17th c watch.

Piqué Tortoiseshell inlaid with a decoration of silver or gold, used for watch PAIR CASES in the 18th c.

Pirouette escapement The earliest type of ESCAPEMENT, in which the BALANCE makes several rotations in one direction and then in the other. HUYGENS used one with the HAIRSPRING which he invented. SULLY and Thiout used it but it was soon superseded.

Pistol alarm   See FLINTLOCK ALARM for picture.

Pistol watch   One set in the butt of a small reproduction flintlock pistol around the turn of the 18th and 19th c.

Pitch   On a screw, this is the distance between a point on one thread to the identical point on the next thread. On a toothed wheel, the pitch is the distance from one tooth to an identical point on the next tooth.

Pitch circle   The circle drawn from the centre of a toothed wheel to where the teeth make contact with an engaging toothed wheel.

Pitching   Setting engaged toothed wheels so that their pitch circles just touch each other.

Pith   The pith of the elder tree (*Sambucus nigra*) is used by watchmakers for cleaning delicate watch parts.

Pivot   The small end of a shaft or ARBOR that runs in a bearing hole. A special contour is necessary for BALANCE STAFF pivots that run in JEWELS, CONE PIVOTS are employed for cheap watches, alarm clocks and many meters.

Pivot-polishing tool   Tool of the 18th–19th c like a primitive LATHE which was held in a bench vice. An ARBOR is held by one end and rotated to and fro by a BOW while the other PIVOT rests in one of a number of grooves of different diameters on the edge of a drum at the other end of the tool. This pivot is polished by using a small hand-held burnisher. It developed into the JACOT TOOL, in use until recent times.

Pivoted detent   A form of DETENT ESCAPEMENT (as used on early MARINE CHRONOMETERS). The lever or detent which releases the ESCAPE WHEEL turns on a PIVOT. Replaced by the SPRING DETENT. See POCKET CHRONOMETER.

Pivoting tool   Primitive LATHE held in a bench vice and used for drilling into the ends of ARBORS to fit new PIVOTS. Operated by a BOW and cord or cord and hand wheel. Although this is called 'pivoting', the name was also used for the work done by a FINISHER, particularly in the Swiss trade.

Planetarium   Representation of the night sky showing the movements of the planets, formerly by mechanical devices. Probably the first was invented by HUYGENS and made by van Ceulen in 1682, very much like the later ORRERY. One 5m (16ft) in diameter showing all the planets and their satellites fluorescing in the dark was the main exhibit in the Dome of Discovery at the Festival of Britain, 1951. More recently optical projection was developed using complicated sets of lenses driven by clockwork, the best known of which in the U.K. is at Madame Tussaud's, London. See PLANETARY CLOCK.

Planetary clock   Clock showing the movements of the planets. Many early European MONUMENTAL CLOCKS were planetary. See ARMILLARY SPHERE, DONDI'S CLOCK, STRASBOURG CATHEDRAL CLOCK. They were also popular in the 18th c. See JANVIER, ORRERY and RAINGO.

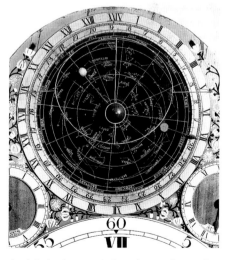

The dial of a **planetary clock** in a longcase by T. Vickers of Bridgnorth, Shropshire, who died in the 1920s. The clock is in the British Horological Institute.

Planishing Flattening and hardening by hammering. Earlier brass clock PLATES were cast and planished until they were superseded by machine-rolled plate in the 19th c.

Planisphere Flat dial in an open aperture showing stars visible at a particular time and place. East is usually shown on the left, i.e. looking south in the northern hemisphere.

Plate A front or DIAL and BACK PLATE of brass are joined by turned PILLARS to make a clock FRAME. In early watches top and bottom (or dial) plates were similarly employed. Early clocks had elaborate engraved decoration, such as TULIPS, over the back plate. The plates of most old American clocks have straight-sided holes in them because of a shortage of brass. Those of many BLACK FOREST clocks, and some early American ones, were made of wood for the same reason. Plates of MARINE CHRONOMETERS are usually decorated by SPOTTING. Those of some watches and small clocks are STRAIGHT-GRAINED or matted and GILDED, and of some machine-made clocks PRINKED.

Plate clock See TELLERUHR.

Plate frame See PLATE.

Platform escapement ESCAPEMENT (usually CYLINDER or LEVER) on a small separate platform, normally mounted across the top of the PLATES, particularly in CARRIAGE CLOCKS. Usually driven by a CONTRATE WHEEL.

Plato clock American name for a TICKET CLOCK.

Pliers Pliers in horology are the same as in other industries and crafts except that many are smaller and finer. Antique versions are collectors' items. The many varieties include flat, round (for forming loops) tapered, parallel-awed, sprung (to keep the jaws open when not being used), copper-jawed (to act as a heat sink to draw off heat from work being soldered), cutting, side-cutting, etc.

Plique-à-jour Enamel in an open metal filigree, like a stained glass window. Extremely rare in horology. See ENAMEL.

Pneumatic clock French mechanical clock of the 19th c that operated SLAVE DIALS by air pressure. Used for public clocks in Paris.

Pocket chronometer High-grade pocket watch with a DETENT ESCAPEMENT and cylindrical HAIRSPRING, made particularly at the end of the 18th and throughout the 19th c (even after the LEVER ESCAPEMENT became general). PIVOTED DETENTS were incorporated before about 1780 and SPRING DETENTS afterwards. The pocket chronometer is liable to POSITIONAL ERRORS and particularly affected by shock, which is why it was surpassed by the LEVER. The seconds hand has DEAD BEAT action. Principal makers included the ARNOLDS, EARNSHAW, DENT, BREGUET, COLE, JUMP and FRODSHAM. The Swiss definition is a pocket watch, with lever or other escapement, or quartz module, that has gained a RATING CERTIFICATE.

Pocket watch Watch introduced after the invention of the pocket in the first quarter of the 17th c and very popular after 1675, when the waistcoat became fashionable. Largely superseded by the WRIST WATCH, except for men's dress wear and precision timekeeping. A mechanical pocket watch is more accurate because of its larger size and reduced liability to POSITIONAL ERRORS, being kept in a vertical position most of the time. A TOURBILLON or KARRUSEL practically eliminates errors in vertical positions. See PAIR CASE.

Point of attachment See PINNING POINT.

Pointed pallets PALLETS of a LEVER ESCAPEMENT in which all the lift is imparted by the ESCAPE WHEEL teeth and none by the pallets. Used in the early ENGLISH LEVER and by the Swiss maker Sylvain Mairet.

Poising Adjusting a BALANCE (without HAIRSPRING) so that the centre of gravity is exactly on the axis of the staff. Screw balances are adjusted by moving certain screws in or out. A plain balance is adjusted in the factory by milling off part of the rim. A POISING TOOL is used to find the heavier parts of the rim. For static balance, the orthodox method is to adjust the balance and staff without the spring; i.e. a balance may be in poise so that it comes to rest in any position, but may not be in poise when it is moving. See POISING, DYNAMIC.

Poising, dynamic A balance and spring may be in static poise when at rest but continuously changes its centre of gravity as it swings because the spring opens and closes (breathes) on one side only. To bring the centre of gravity on the centre of the axis it needs to be poised dynamically. (See also PINNING POINT). To do so precisely requires a precision watch and the skills of a watch ADJUSTER, but high-quality watches can be satisfactorily poised by a method suggested in 1960 by the Swiss firm, Greiner Electronics, using a watch RATE RECORDER with the MAINSPRING almost run down (so that the balance arc is between 150° and 180°) in a series of vertical positions. The rate recorder will indicate the position of the heavy spot, which is corrected by the poising screws and washers or by light drilling of a plain balance.

Poising tool Pair of parallel jaws, like small open vice jaws, with levelling screws. A BALANCE and STAFF is rested on these by its PIVOTS so that it rolls until the heaviest part of the rim is at the bottom.

Poker hand Straight minute hand like a poker, used with a BEETLE HAND.

Pole lathe Form of LATHE used by earlier watch case makers. A wooden pole acting like a spring reaches over the lathe. A cord from the end of the pole passes round a driving pulley and ends by being attached to a treadle. See CLERKENWELL.

Polishing A special art in horology, where high degrees of finish are demanded. A polishing medium is used on a polisher, a simple tool made of a material softer than that being polished. Such materials are, in order of hardness, mild steel, iron, bell metal, tin, zinc, boxwood and cork. Steel surfaces are prepared by using emery, carborundum, or oil stone dust, and left grey or given a polish with DIAMANTINE or RED STUFF (rouge). All are mixed with oil. Brass is normally stoned before polishing using WATER OF AYR STONE or BLUE-STONE with water or oil to remove file marks. Polishers used are of tin or boxwood, and willow for a fine finish. Another polishing medium is Vienna lime mixed with spirits of wine (undiluted ethyl alcohol). For polishing particular parts there are jigs known as 'swing tools', which fit between lathe centres. See BLACK POLISH, BURNISHING, CIRCULAR GRAIN, CLEANING, GREY, SNAILING and SPOTTING.

Porcelain case See CERAMIC CLOCK.

Pork-pie bell Hour bell with almost straight sides used almost exclusively in England by the KNIBB family of clockmakers.

This clock with a **pork-pie bell** is by Joseph Knibb. Note that the numbered count wheel is also slotted for quarter-hours.

Pornographic watch ANIMATED WATCH showing a pornographic scene, often hidden under a back cover. Usually Swiss or French. Farouk, the last King of Egypt, collected them (and also watches showing IV instead of the more common IIII). The collection was sold in London after Farouk's death in 1965 and at least one innocent clerical buyer had an unpleasant surprise when by chance he touched an unknown release.

A Swiss **pornographic watch** with an inoffensive picture of a courting couple on the dial, but this scene inside it. (*Uto Auctionen, Zürich*)

Portable clock Truly portable clocks did not arrive until the invention of the MAINSPRING made it possible to eliminate driving weights. Special wooden carrying cases were made for some early German, Flemish and French brass-cased clocks. To secure the short BOB PENDULUM, and prevent damage to the SUSPENSION of some English LANTERN CLOCKS and BRACKET CLOCKS when carried, a hook was provided on the BACK PLATE. Later bracket clocks had a fitting with a thumb screw to secure the flat-section pendulum rod. A bracket clock has a handle on top for carrying, but it is very unwise to trust

it today without support underneath the clock.

Portable sundial Portable sundials were valuable to military leaders and others before the portable clock was invented. There are two types, COMPASS DIAL and ALTITUDE DIAL. One of the earliest known is a silver and gold Saxon pocket sundial of label shape on a chain of the 10th c found in 1939 in the soil of the Cloister Garth of Canterbury Cathedral. It is an altitude dial showing TIDES.

Portico clock Clock case in the classical Greek temple style, perhaps with columns each side and a triangular top, e.g. French Empire PILLAR CLOCK.

Positional errors A mechanical watch runs at different RATES in different positions owing to ESCAPEMENT ERROR, lack of ISOCHRONISM, changes in the centre of gravity of the BALANCE and HAIRSPRING and so on. The rate in wear is an average of these errors and therefore varies with different wearers. A good wrist watch is tested and regulated in six positions, dial up, dial down, pendant (button) up, pendant down, pendant right, pendant left. The worst errors are kept to the pendant left position, which occurs rarely with the watch on the outside of the left wrist. (A precision watch on the inside of the left wrist will give its worst performance). A good watch which is a few seconds fast can be brought to time by leaving it on edge overnight as it loses slightly in this position. Cheap mechanical wrist watches are checked and regulated in two positions. Positional errors have much less effect on POCKET WATCHES, are much smaller with TOURBILLON and KARRUSEL movements, and do not occur with clocks. See REGULATION.

Positive set The normal form of hand-setting for pocket watches. The one-piece winding stem projects into the movement to operate the mechanism. See NEGATIVE SET, ROCKING BAR.

Posted frame The earliest TURRET CLOCK frame, from the 14th to the 17th c, made of strips of wrought iron in the shape of a cage, held together by mortice and tenon joints or rivetted. The earliest still working is the SALISBURY CATHE-DRAL CLOCK. PIVOTS for the ARBORS are in the vertical straps. The earlier the clock, the more robust the frame, the finest having heavy corner posts set at 45° and forged in the shape of cathedral buttresses at the bottom, with large knobs (FINIALS) at the top, usually turned outwards in English clocks, but often straight in continental ones. The knobs may have been used to raise the clock by ropes. Frames became lighter and less decorated and the finials often became other shapes, such as spires or tulips (as seen on William Monk clocks of the early 18th c), then disappeared in the late 17th and 18th c. Threaded ends and nuts began to replace some morticed joints from the mid-17th c. WHEELS were of wrought iron with shaped teeth, engaging LANTERN PINIONS. Driving BARRELS were of wood, often with stone weights. Two layouts were used for striking clocks. The earliest is the END-TO-END trains lay-out, which continued to be made in some local areas for over 300 years. One in original condition, with CROWN WHEEL and VERGE, is in Hanborough Church, Oxfordshire. An early COUNT WHEEL has a rim with the notches controlling the number of blows on the outer edge, and teeth on the inner one. Spokes are offset to clear the driving PINION within the wheel. Such count wheels are found on medieval clocks in all parts of Europe. The count wheel is outside the frame in the Salisbury and other clocks, but the so-called DOVER CASTLE CLOCK group has the COUNT WHEEL in the middle of the frame. The other layout is the SIDE-BY-SIDE TRAIN, adopted at the same time as the introduction of the ANCHOR ESCAPEMENT to them in c1670–75. An end-to-end train is wound from both ends by capstans or wheels fixed to the barrels. Side-by-side trains could be wound from one side by a winding handle. All posted frame clocks had VERGE and FOLIOT control before the PENDULUM, to which most were converted after 1658. Some still exist on the Continent and in the U.K., with crown wheel and pendulum, but most were converted to anchor. The

BEDPOST FRAME existed alongside the BIRDCAGE frame then superseded it, and was itself replaced by the FLAT-BED MOVEMENT. Continental birdcage frames usually have the corner posts cranked outwards at the bottoms to form prominent feet and raise the clock well off the ground, but otherwise are generally similar.

Postman's alarm Alarm DIAL CLOCK, with PENDULUM and weights hanging below it, a bell on top, and often with no glass. Made originally in the BLACK FOREST in the 1860s. The dial is about 25cm (10in) across and in a round wooden BEZEL with the movement in a wooden frame at the back. Some had a glass with the numerals painted on the inside of the glass. Versions were made in England and were popular until 1939. The origin of the name is unknown.

A **postman's alarm** made in the Black Forest.

Potence Form of COCK used between watch or dock plates as a lower bearing, as in a VERGE watch.

Potence plate Old name for the TOP PLATE of a watch which carried a POTENCE for the VERGE ESCAPEMENT.

Power cell For some of the earliest electric clocks such as EUREKA and BULLE, Leclanché wet or dry cells were used. For the ELECTRIC WATCH and then the ELECTRONIC WATCH, a small power cell was developed, such as the mercury cell. Early ones lasted only about six months. Later a year, two years and longer became common, even up to seven years (See LITHIUM CELL). The shelf life (the time for which it can be stored and still run a watch for the specified time) was once short and currently is about the same as the running time. Normally cells should be stored in a cool, dry place. Heat and refrigeration can cause deterioration. A well-sealed cell is vital as leakage can corrode a watch. Used cells should always be removed.

Power reserve The amount of power deliberately left after fully winding to avoid stoppage, i.e. about six hours in a clock wound daily and about a day in one wound weekly. Many automatic SELF-WINDING WRIST WATCHES have 45-hour power reserves. In use, the MAINSPRING is nearly fully wound all the time, which improves timekeeping accuracy.

Power reserve indicator Subsidiary dial showing the hours left before the clock or watch runs down. See UP-AND-DOWN DIAL.

Power sources The earliest timepieces were driven by weights. The LANTERN CLOCK had a heavy weight on one end of a cord or chain passing over a pulley, with a smaller weight on the other end to keep it in the pulley groove. Then came the pull-up ENDLESS ROPE or CHAIN after 1656 for THIRTY-HOUR CLOCKS, and the weight wound on to a drum for EIGHT-DAY LONGCASE CLOCKS. The MAINSPRING wound by a key was introduced about 1450 and the FUSEE from about the same time.

Prague Town Hall clock One of Europe's finest astronomical clocks. Built in 1490, renovated in 1866, destroyed in the Second World War and reconstructed after it.

Precession of the equinoxes Slow circular motion of the Earth's pole, like a dying top, caused by the moon pulling on the bulge around the equator. This causes a gradual change in the time of the seasons. It results in a day of SIDEREAL TIME being 9 MILLISECONDS shorter that the true period of rotation of the Earth. Discovered in 130BC by Hipparchus. NUTATION is another disturbance in rotation. In 1953, it was disclosed by QUARTZ CLOCKS and confirmed by the ATOMIC CLOCK, that the Earth is slowing down, now corrected by leap seconds at intervals (see UNIVERSAL TIME.)

Precious metal watch cases Most surviving watches of the 16th c have cases of gilded brass. Some gold and silver watches were made, but it is thought that resistance by the goldsmiths' guilds made it difficult for precious cases to be used by the members of locksmiths' or (in England) blacksmiths' guilds who made watch movements. See SILVER and GOLD WATCH CASES.

Precision clock Any clock made for very accurate timekeeping, such as a REGULATOR, a FREE PENDULUM CLOCK, an electric MASTER CLOCK, a QUARTZ CLOCK or CHRONOMETER, a clock with CONSTANT FORCE ESCAPEMENT or DEAD-BEAT ESCAPEMENT, an OBSERVATORY CLOCK, etc.

Precision watch Quality watch which has been individually adjusted and holds a RATING CERTIFICATE. Seen CHRONOMETER.

Prescot About 13km (8 miles) east of Liverpool, centre of an area making most parts of watches (and the best files in Europe) by hand methods from the 17th c for FINISHERS in COVENTRY, CLERKENWELL and Birmingham. In 1866, John Wycherley started a small steam-powered factory making standardised parts, but these were resisted by finishers. In 1882 he sold it to T.P. Hewitt, who later founded the British Watch Co. and then set up the Lancashire Watch Co. (1889–1910) on American lines. In 1893 it employed about 1,000 people, being the first in Prescot to take on women. In its declining years it also made DIAL and DROP-DIAL CLOCKS in seven sizes from 8 to 20 in dials and five grades in mahogany and walnut. There is a fine museum of horology at Prescot now.

Prieus, Jean-Louis French bronze founder around 1765–85, who made some fine ORMOLU clock cases.

Prime meridian ZERO MERIDIAN LINE which passes through the old ROYAL OBSERVATORY in Greenwich is the line of longitude on which the world's time measurements and TIME ZONES are based. A move to Sussex, which is not on the meridian, was officially announced on 12 April 1946, but not completed until 1948, when corrections had to be made for TIME DETERMINA-TION. See ROYAL OBSERVATORY.

Prinked A prinked clock PLATE has small dots impressed in rows on it to flatten the surface after stamping.

Printing press clock French INDUS-TRIAL CLOCK showing a rotary printing

A very rare French rotary **printing press clock** in which most parts move. (*Mr Barney Collection*)

press in some detail and incorporating a clock in the end of a roller.

Process timer Clock for timing a manufacturing process. Sometimes a separate large TIMER, at others an ELAPSED TIME INDICATOR or TIME SWITCH, which actually controls the process.

Production timer TIMER used to measure the time of making a single article and indicate the rate of production per hour.

Programme controller Large cam which turns under the control of a clock to ring bells, such as for school lesson changes, operates switches to carry out other programmes, etc. Today this is done electronically.

Projection clock See MAGIC LANTERN CLOCK.

Provincial makers Name once current for the thousands of clock- and watchmakers spread over the British Isles, particularly during the 18th c. Gradually embryo clock factories took over MOVE-MENT making but cases continued to be made locally. Eventually many former makers became retailers but continued to call themselves 'watch- and clockmakers'. See THWAITES.

Pull repeater A REPEATER CLOCK with a cord from one or both sides which is pulled to make it sound the time. Replaced the NIGHT CLOCK and continued in use until matches were invented. RACK STRIKING made it possible. There were also clocks that did not strike the quarters except when the cord was pulled.

Pull wind Winding a clock by pulling on a cord or chain to raise the weight, as with most THIRTY-HOUR LONGCASE CLOCKS, or to wind a spring as with some WALL CLOCKS. In this case the cord is drawn back into the case. See BLACK FOREST for picture.

Pulpit clock Late 18th c reminder for preachers. Some sounded the quarters. Original ones were large sand glasses and boring preachers would destroy the congregation's hope of an early end to their sermons by turning it over, remarking, 'Brethren, let us take another sand. . . .'

A **pulpit clock** of the 18th c which has an iron movement and strikes four times every quarter of an hour. The dial just shows quarters and half quarters. (*Deustches Museum, Munich*)

Pulse meter TIMER calibrated to give pulse rate per minute by timing 30 beats.

Pulse piece Button in the side of a DUMB REPEATER. Instead of the time being sounded, the pulse piece is tapped and the time is felt by its pulsing.

Pul-syn-etic System of a MASTER CLOCK controlling SLAVE DIALS made by Gent and Co.

Pump clock What some people call a BEAM ENGINE CLOCK.

Pump winding Early form of KEYLESS WINDING in which the spring was wound by pumping the pendant up and down with the thumb. Introduced c1790. Various forms were patented in France and England and used as late as 1860.

Puritan watch Oval-shaped pocket watch with rounded edges and plain case only about 5cm (2in) long and made in England in the 17th c.

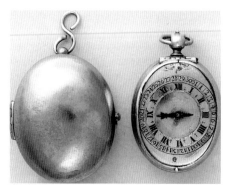

A **puritan watch** of c1630 with a three-wheel train, gut fusee, and worm and wheel set-up. (*Sotheby's*)

Push-button regulator Mechanical watch with a small push button on the case to alter the REGULATION without opening the case. One version has a button which puts the watch to time on the TIME SIGNAL and regulates it automatically at the same time. See also PENDULE SYMPATHIQUE.

Push piece Press button on a watch case for operating additional mechanisms such as an AUTOMATON, CHRONOGRAPH, SPLIT SECONDS HAND, WINDING etc.

Q

Quail clock Similar to a CUCKOO CLOCK but its bellows imitate the quail.

Quaker clock Clock in a very plain wooden case, as in the American Shaker furniture and clocks.

Quality standards The quality of a timepiece depends on good technical and artistic design, sound construction, finish, timekeeping abilities, etc. Most tests are for timekeeping only (see RATING CERTIFICATE), but quality standard tests are applied to some manufacture. The best known was the French Cétéhor standard. There are certain British standards, but they are not compulsory. The Japanese have export standards.

Quare, Daniel (1649–1724) A Quaker who refused to take the oath of allegiance to become clockmaker to George I, but nevertheless was granted the office and permission to use the back stairs! Invented a REPEATER WATCH (now in the ASHMOLEAN MUSEUM) about six years before BARLOW and successfully opposed his patent application. Also made fine barometers, and thin watches only 31mm ($^1/_5$in) between PLATES.

Quarter boy The JACK that strikes the quarter hours on a clock with AUTOMATA.

Quarter repeater Clock or watch REPEATER that repeats hours and quarters, but not minutes. Thus four strokes followed by three TING TANG notes indicates three quarters after four, i.e. 4.45.

Quartz clock The first was the QUARTZ OBSERVATORY CLOCK.

Domestic quartz clocks were developed in the 1960s by the Japanese, Americans and Swiss.

Quartz crystal Quartz is a crystalline form of silica with the chemical formula SiO_2, called 'rock crystal' in its single crystal form. A machined piece is used as the resonator in quartz timepieces because of its piezo-electric properties, i.e. it vibrates when a suitable electric field is applied. Synthetic quartz is usual in bar, plate or tuning-fork shape. The frequency depends on the crystal orientation, shape, size and mounting. The most common frequency for timepieces, 32 kHz is produced by flexing. See AGEING, TRIMMER, QUARTZ CLOCK, QUARTZ WATCH.

Quartz master clock MASTER CLOCK controlled by a QUARTZ CRYSTAL. A pioneer system sold by English Clock Systems c1962 had a master module designed by Patek Philippe of Switzerland which generated 1-amp pulses for a second every minute to operate up to 125 SLAVE DIALS. If the power failed, the slaves were cut off but the master continued by battery. On restoration of power, the master sent stored pulses to the slaves to advance them to the correct time indication.

Quartz observatory clock Electronic clock accurate to the equivalent of about one second in 30 years, invented by W.A. Marrison in the U.S.A. in 1929. A slice of quartz or ESSEN RING given alternate charges of electricity at the appropriate frequency resonates like a piano string. This is known as the piezo-electric effect. Such a crystal cut to vibrate at 100,000 cycles a second controls an oscillating circuit with extreme accuracy, acting like the ESCAPEMENT of a mechanical clock. The frequency is broken down by frequency dividers to 100 cycles per second and this operates a PHONIC MOTOR to show time or operate TIME SIGNALS. Small quartz clocks (ELECTRONIC CHRONOMETERS) are used for measuring short time intervals in industry and in RATE RECORDERS for checking watch RATES. See ATOMIC CLOCK.

Quartz spring The CYLINDRICAL SPRING for a MARINE CHRONOMETER was very rarely made of quartz.

Quartz watch The first commercial quartz watches were made by the Japanese under the Seiko name in 1969. Several Swiss firms first produced them in 1970. The Americans became the biggest producers in the 1970s with new brand names, largely because the microcircuits were developed in the U.S.A., but a reconstructed Swiss industry with their long-established Swiss brands, plus the Japanese, gradually eliminated the new quartz watch divisions of American electronic component manufacturers despite their multimillion-dollar advertising campaigns. The cheapness and availability of quartz watches has brought the mechanical watch back into favour and far higher prices are now paid at auction for good 1930s watches than for genuine historical timepieces. See OMEGA, TIMEX QUARTZ WATCH.

Queen Charlotte's watch Most influential watch ever made, as it incorporated the first LEVER ESCAPEMENT, which

eventually revolutionised watch and clock accuracy and manufacture. Made by Thomas MUDGE in 1759. He thought little of his lever escapement, and it was very difficult to make. After about 1825, however, it gradually became universal. The original watch, made to the order of King George III, is in the ROYAL COLLECTION and kept at Windsor Castle. (The King was very interested in horology, had lessons in repairing, and had his own observatory in Richmond Park.) The watch is in a gold PAIR CASE about 16cm (2.5in) in diameter and 3cm (1.25in) thick, with enamelled dial and CENTRE SECONDS HAND. There is a SOLID BALANCE wheel with TEMPERATURE COMPENSATION.

Queen Charlotte's watch, the most famous of all watches with the first lever escapement ever made, by Thomas Mudge. (*The Royal Collection © Her Majesty The Queen*)

R

Rack clock (see overleaf) GRAVITY CLOCK in which the whole clock is the driving weight as it slowly slides down a toothed rack hung from the wall or mounted on a stand. A PINION in the clock is driven by engaging the rack. They were made as early as c1600. The Kee-Less Clock Co. in England made them in the 1920s. See SILENT-KEELESS CLOCK for picture.

Rack lever A transitional LEVER ESCAPEMENT invented by the Abbé d'HAUTEFEUILLE in 1722, before MUDGE'S detached lever. Many were made in England by Peter LITHERLAND, ROSKELL and others in Liverpool after 1791. It lent itself to early mass production methods, being simpler than the CYLINDER and DUPLEX ESCAPEMENTS and a cheaper alternative to the VERGE. A toothed rack on the end of the lever engages a toothed PINION on the BALANCE STAFF to swing the balance to and fro. It is not DETACHED. See QUEEN CHARLOTTE'S WATCH.

invented by William BARLOW c 1676 and now universal. At the hour, a toothed arm (the rack) drops onto a cam and is wound back a number of teeth equal to the strokes. The cam is snail-shaped, having 12 steps decreasing in height. It rotates with the hour hand, therefore striking cannot get out of sequence, as with the earlier LOCKING PLATE. It may be damaged by turning hands backwards in older clocks, but in later ones there is provision for avoiding damage. It made REPEATING WORK possible in clocks and watches.

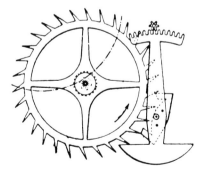

The **rack lever escapement**, popular with English makers interested in quantity production in the late 18th and early 19th c.

Rack striking Method of 'counting', i.e. controlling, the strikes of a clock,

Rack striking with the rack raised to the non-striking position. The snail-shaped cam below determines the number of blows.

223

An Austrian **rack clock**, or actually in this case timepiece, wound by raising it on the rack. (*Sotheby's*)

Radio-controlled clock Before 1914 a German company obtained a government concession to install a nationwide system of wireless-controlled clocks called the Tel system. The war cancelled it. Thiesen and JUNGHANS developed a similar one in 1925 and the Frenchman Marius Lavet introduced one based on the SIX PIPS about the same time. See TIME DISTRIBUTION for modern versions.

Radio time signal The first were from the Eiffel Tower, Paris, in 1913 and from Nordeich, Germany. Clockmakers received the signal (rip, rip, rip, rip. . . .) by headphones from a special crystal set named a Horophone fastened to the wall. There was a hook for a pocket chronometer. The Greenwich time signal began in 1923 along a wire from the ROYAL OBSERVATORY, Greenwich, to the BBC's Savoy Hill Studio, but was later sent from the Observatory's time department at Dollis Hill to BBC headquarters, and in 1990 transferred to the BBC itself. See SIX PIPS. Signals are corrected for land line delay BIG BEN'S first stroke at the hour was also used from 31 December 1923 until after the Second World War. The Post Office began broadcasting an international time signal from Rugby Radio Station (now M.S.F. Rugby) in December 1927, later monitored by ATOMIC CLOCK. See TIME SIGNAL.

Radium dial From c1900 until the 1930s, watches for use in the dark and alarm clocks had luminous numerals and hands, coated with a radioactive material. Abolition of the luminous watch painting industry was recommended in 1929 by the U.S. Department of Labor when it became evident that a number of workers had died from radium poisoning.

Railroad watch Pocket watch of a type and standard specified by various railway authorities in the U.S.A. for the use of employees concerned with train operation. A maximum weekly error of not more than 30 seconds was usually specified. The dial had to be very readable with spade (pear-shaped) hands.

Railroad clock American name for a type of DIAL CLOCK made in the

BLACK FOREST in the latter part of the 19th c. It is actually a THIRTY-HOUR weight-driven timepiece with PULL-UP WINDING and an alarm, set by a small central disc on the dial and stopped by unhooking a small weight from its chain. Said to have been for the railwayman operating level-crossing gates. See POST-MAN'S ALARM.

Railway alarm   BLACK FOREST WALL CLOCK of the early 20th c.

Railway engine clock   French INDUS-TRIAL CLOCK in the shape of a locomotive with a clock mounted in the front or elsewhere. Another version shows a mountainous scene with a model train with trucks or carriages running round a track with a tunnel.

A **railway engine clock** of the industrial revolution period.

Railway time   When railways spread over a country in the 19th c, they had to keep their own MEAN TIME because places through which they passed used LOCAL TIMES. They issued leaflets giving conversion figures from local times to railway time. Eventually both became GREENWICH MEAN TIME in the U.K. Some railway companies shared lines and timetable mistakes caused head-on crashes. Schwiligué, maker of the STRASBOURG CATHEDRAL CLOCK, built a clock in Benfeld, Bas-Rhin, France, which was modified in 1870 to show railway time (Paris time) as well as local time. In the 1880s, before America was divided into seven TIME ZONES,

double time railroad hanging clocks showed local and railway times on two identical dials, one above the other, driven from the same movement. See TAVERN CLOCK.

Railway watch   The same as the American RAILROAD WATCH. GREEN-WICH MEAN TIME was eventually adopted by the railways, but not by all local communities where the trains stopped, so a form of DECK WATCH made c1850–70 by English and Swiss makers showing LOCAL TIME and G.M.T. was useful.

Raingo, Z.   French maker of fine ORRERY clocks in the 19th c. Five are in England, at Windsor in the ROYAL COLLECTION, in Soane's Museum, London, in the Glasgow Art Gallery, and in private collections. One is in the Paul Chamberlain Collection, U.S.A., and others in Paris, Madrid and Brussels.

Ramsay, David   (d.c1654) Chief clock-maker to King James I. First Master of the Worshipful Company of Clockmakers, 1631–32. Probably came from Dalhousie, Scotland. In the VICTORIA AND ALBERT MUSEUM are a watch and clock by him. He appears with a shop near Temple Bar in Sir Walter Scott's novel 'The Fortunes of Nigel'. See ROYAL CLOCKMAKER.

Ratchet   Mechanism comprising a RATCHET WHEEL and a PAWL or CLICK, allowing the ratchet wheel to be moved in one direction only.

Ratchet drive   When a PAWL or CLICK is moved to turn the RATCHET WHEEL, normally one tooth at a time.

Ratchet key   See BREGUET KEY.

Ratchet set-up   See SETTING UP.

Ratchet tooth   Saw-like tooth of a RATCHET WHEEL. The ESCAPE WHEEL of the LEVER ESCAPEMENT also has ratchet teeth.

Ratchet tooth lever   English LEVER ESCAPEMENT. See MASSEY.

Ratchet wheel Toothed wheel allowed to move in one direction only by a CLICK. It may have ratchet teeth (like saw teeth) or they may be normal as in a watch winding wheel. See SETTING UP for picture.

Rate Difference in time shown by a clock and a standard time, e.g. gaining rate and losing rate. Usually but not necessarily given in seconds a day. The worst fault for precision purposes is a variable rate, but not for a domestic clock or watch if it is 'about right' most of the time. For navigation, a constant rate, whether gaining or losing, is much more important. QUARTZ CRYSTAL timepieces have eliminated many earlier rate problems.

Rate recorder A 'timing machine' for printing the instantaneous RATE of a watch or clock. It comprises a QUARTZ CLOCK which controls the feed of a paper tape. The ticks of the timepiece are amplified and printed on the tape to produce a dotted line. The slope of the line gives the exact rate of the timepiece in a few seconds in relation to the quartz watch and is used for bringing them to MEAN TIME and for checking POSITIONAL ERRORS. Also used for fault-finding, since OUT OF BEAT, MAGNETISED, and other conditions are shown at once. Without a machine, each daily check takes 24 hours. Some versions are for QUARTZ WATCHES and show time variations by digital display.

Rating certificate There are two main classes of testing. Tests for special timekeepers were formerly carried out at the NATIONAL PHYSICAL LABORATORY, England, the Geneva Observatory, Switzerland, the German Hydrographic Institute and elsewhere, and special certificates issued. Swiss production watches of high performance are sold with rating certificates issued by one of the official bureaux for testing watches. See KEW A CERTIFICATE.

Rating nut Nut below a PENDULUM BOB for screwing it up or down to alter the clock's rate. Sometimes there is a locking nut below it. Earlier, the pendulum bob itself was screwed up or down the rod. See PENDULUM REGULATION.

Ravrio, Antoine-André (1759–1814) Bronze worker of the French EMPIRE period specialising in ORMOLU clock cases, lamps etc. Left 3000 francs for someone who could protect workers when MERCURIC GILDING.

Raw movement Unfinished MOVEMENT or EBAUCHE.

Rebush To replace a worn bearing with a bush, i.e. inserted tube.

Recoil escapement Another name for the ANCHOR ESCAPEMENT because the wheels turn back a little after every jump forward. This recoil can be seen by watching the seconds hand of a LONGCASE CLOCK.

Recoiling click Form of STOP WORK applied particularly to watches to prevent them being overwound. In the simplest version, the CLICK (ratchet PAWL) which holds up the MAINSPRING has a slot instead of a hole for its bearing. Thus when a watch is wound up as far as it will go, the click will recoil and let down the spring a little to avoid its becoming coil bound, as soon as the winding button is released. There are many other versions.

Record Tompion Magnificent LONGCASE CLOCK made about 1699 for King William III by Thomas TOMPION, probably for Hampton Court Palace. It has a fine case with gilded mounts and a figure of Minerva on the top. The plinth base is of cast and chased metal, the only other Tompion clock with this being in Buckingham Palace. The clock runs for three months at a winding and has a PERPETUAL CALENDAR. Given by Queen Victoria to the Duke of Cambridge, it was sold at Christie's in 1904 for 125 guineas, reappeared in the Dunn Collection and was sold in 1911 for 380 guineas, appeared in the WETHERFIELD COLLECTION and was sold across the Atlantic in 1928. It was brought back by an English collector, J. S. Sykes, for £4,000. In 1956 it was sold again to the U.S.A., when Williamsburg Museum, Virginia bought it for £11,000, despite attempts to stop the sale because of the clock's historical value. Currently it is not on exhibition. The origin of the name 'Record' is not known.

Recorder See TIME RECORDER. Also an extra dial on a CHRONOGRAPH WATCH showing elapsed time.

Recording chronograph CHRONO-GRAPH that records time intervals by marks on a moving strip of paper. Used for making comparisons of timekeepers or recording astronomical events.

Recordon, Louis (1778-1824) Successor to EMERY and the first to patent a self-winding PEDOMETER type watch in England in 1780.

Red stuff Watchmakers' name for ROUGE.

Referee's stop watch A timer that is scaled for football or other team sports and is hung round the neck.

Regency clock A neo-classical style of the early 19th c not actually confined to

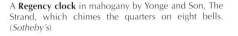

A **Regency clock** in mahogany by Yonge and Son, The Strand, which chimes the quarters on eight bells. (*Sotheby's*)

the Regency (1811–20) but spanning the period from the 1790s to the early Victorian days of the 1840s. Similar to the French EMPIRE style but without gilt bronze mounts and any symbols, especially Napoleonic ones. Mahogany was the favourite wood for clock cases. There was a small revival of JAPANNING. See GEORGIAN.

Regulating dial Small DIAL with a hand that is used to regulate the length of a PENDULUM (see RISE-AND-FALL REGULATOR) or length of a BALANCE SPRING. The clock version is also confusingly called a 'clock REGULATOR'.

Regulation Adjusting the RATE of a timepiece. Precision of regulation depends on the design, quality and condition of the timepiece. Accurate regulation of a clock is much easier than of a watch (see POSITIONAL ERROR) because it is normally stationary. A high-grade mechanical watch will go about ten seconds a day slower in wear and has to be adjusted to suit the wearer. After a major repair (or manufacture), the BALANCE is POISED, and HAIR-SPRING timed, and the assembly itself timed by rate recorder before being mounted in the watch. Then the outer end of the hairspring is 'pinned up' and the assembly set IN BEAT. Next adjustments are made to reduce positional errors as much as possible. The watch should now have a good rate so that final regulation to bring it to MEAN TIME can be done by moving the INDEX. High-precision watches are sometimes FREE SPRUNG which means they have no index, being regulated by TIMING SCREWS or nuts on the BALANCE WHEEL. A non-precision clock with balance and spring is regulated similarly except that positional errors are not now important. A PENDULUM CLOCK is regulated by moving the BOB up or down by a RATING NUT. With some early pendulum clocks, the pendulum was effectively shortened by a RISE-AND-FALL REGULATOR. Precision pendulum clocks have a tray part way down the pendulum rod on which small weights can be placed to raise the effective height of the bob and make the clock gain. An old halfpenny on the tray of BIG BEN for 24 hours, makes it gain one fifth of a second. Very early clocks were regulated by moving the weights on the FOLIOT in or out. If they had balance wheels without springs, they were adjusted by BRISTLE REGULATOR and by SETTING UP the MAINSPRING, or by adding lead shot to a cup on the driving weight. Early watch balances with hairsprings had a regulator turned by a key. See TEMPERATURE ERROR, BAROMETRIC ERROR, CIRCULAR ERROR, ISOCHRONISM.

Regulator Very accurate LONGCASE CLOCK usually with DEAD-BEAT, PIN-WHEEL or GRAVITY ESCAPEMENT, TEMPERATURE COMPENSATED PENDULUM and no striking or other complication. The dial usually has three separate CHAPTER RINGS, for the long central minute hand, the shorter hour hand below it, and seconds hand above it. The case is usually plain.

Regulator, American Usually an ordinary WALL CLOCK to which the name 'regulator' was given to upgrade it falsely in the last half century before 1900 and for about 30 years after. Some true REGULATORS were made.

Regulator, clock See RISE-AND-FALL REGULATOR and REGULATION.

Regulator, watch Device for regulating the timekeeping of a watch. Before the HAIRSPRING was invented this was done by SETTING UP the MAINSPRING by a RATCHET and DIAL provided, and by BRISTLE REGULATOR. The first to adjust the effective length of the hairspring was TOMPION in the 1660s. A dial on the back of the MOVEMENT is turned by a key. The dial is geared to a segment carrying CURB PINS each side of the hairspring near the end. This idea persisted until nearly 1800. About the same time, the BARROW REGULATOR employed a threaded rod which moved a nut carrying curb pins, but it did not become popular. On the Continent, Tompion's scheme was favoured except for the use of a moving pointer and fixed dial. The next development was a

A carved mahogany 19th c **regulator** by James McCabe, Royal Exchange. It has jewelled pallets and a mercurial pendulum. (*Christie's*)

movable ring, carrying curb pins and a pointer, fitted round the hairspring. This developed into the INDEX on the BALANCE COCK, a pointer fitted friction tight round the JEWEL or SHOCK ABSORBER, which carries the curb pins. It is used on modern mechanical watches, and has been developed into the auxiliary regulator or index, which has an additional friction ring carrying the index (curb) pins, so that after the watch is adjusted by the factory the index pointer can be set to a central position.

The small dial of this watch by Charles Goode, London, is the *regulator* of the watch, setting up the mainspring.

Regulator clock American name for a type of DROP-DIAL clock.

Relief enamel Usually the ENAMEL on CLOISONNÉ and CHAMPLEVÉ cases is ground flat. Occasionally the cells were overfilled so that the surfaces of each small patch of enamel was in relief like a bead.

Religieuse clock Style of pendulum BRACKET or TABLE CLOCK developed during the reign of Louis XIV (1643–1715) after the invention of the PENDULUM in 1657. The style is architectural with a wooden case often heavily inlaid with

ivory. Early ones have convex tops with flat fronts, and the glass is also of arched shape. There is an ornament, often with figures, below the dial. Some have barley-twist columns.

A French **religieuse clock** of c1700 by P. le Maire, Paris, with a case veneered in red tortoiseshell with engraved Boulle work. (*Christie's*)

Remembrance watch A watch in which the numerals 1 to 12 are replaced by the letters of a person's name or a message.

Remontoire From *remontoire d'egalité*. Device which applies a controlled force to IMPULSE the PENDULUM or BALANCE to overcome variations in timekeeping caused particularly by variations in the driving motor. One way (invented by HUYGENS in 1659) is to wind up a small weight. Another keeps 'reloading' a small spring, usually every 15 minutes. John HARRISON used this method in 1739. The SECTICON battery clock has a spring remontoire. The

GRAVITY ESCAPEMENT and the GRAVITY ARM of a MASTER CLOCK are both forms of remontoire, but not a FUSEE. Also called a 'constant force escapement'.

Removable barrel A BARREL that can be removed without dismantling the rest of the MOVEMENT. This is achieved by having a separate BRIDGE holding one end, an ARBOR bearing that is in a slot, or a special split arbor.

Renaissance clock 15th c clock in the style of the period when there was a rejuvenation of interest in ancient Rome. Often in the form of a MONUMENTAL CLOCK with a wooden or metal case in Europe.

Renaissance watch Name of skeletonised pocket watch by Dominique Loiseau of Neuchâtel, shown at the Basle Fair in 1982, which has a minute TOURBILLON, GRANDE SONNERIE or PETITE SONNERIE striking, PERPETUAL CALENDAR, EQUATION OF TIME, moon phases, indication of first evening and morning stars, signs of the zodiac, power reserve indicator and detent escapement.

Repair mark Mark scratched on the inside of a case by a repairer identifying him, with a date. Police make much use of these in tracing the owners of stolen watches and also criminals.

Repeater alarm Mechanical alarm clock that rings in short bursts with an interval of about half a minute between them. A SYNCHRONOUS version allows the sleeper ten minutes' dozing time. Also made in electronic versions, some being voice activated to silence them until the next alarm.

Repeater clock Before the days of artificial light, it was difficult to read a clock at night without the performance of lighting a candle with flint and tinder. Some of the best BRACKET CLOCKS could therefore be made to repeat the time on bells. Usually there is a cord with a button on the end from each side of the clock which is pulled to load and operate the REPEATING WORK. This is called a PULL REPEATER. Most clocks are QUARTER REPEATERS, invented by Edward BARLOW in 1676; some are HALF-QUARTER REPEATERS, and a few FIVE MINUTE REPEATERS. MINUTE REPEATERS are known from the 18th c. Many repeater CARRIAGE CLOCKS were made. The system began to go out of fashion after matches were invented in the first quarter of the 19th c.

Repeater watch Pocket watch which will repeat the time on a bell, a GONG or the watch case itself. Intended mainly for use in the dark. The first, QUARTER REPEATERS, were invented by Edward BARLOW and Daniel QUARE near the end of the 17th c. BREGUET employed wire gongs in 1789. Other types are HALF-QUARTER and FIVE-MINUTE REPEATERS before 1730 and MINUTE REPEATERS c1830. There is no special winding button for the REPEATING WORK; on earlier watches the PENDANT of the watch is pressed and on later ones a slide on the side of the case is moved (which loads a spring). When released the pendant or slide sets the repeater going. See DUMB REPEATER, STAR WHEEL.

Repeating work Form of COMPLICATED WORK enabling a REPEATER CLOCK or WATCH to strike the time at will. In watches this is complex and involves separate RACKS for repeating the hours, quarters, half-quarters, five minutes and minutes.

Repoussé Designs, usually on silver or gold, embossed from the back and most popular for gold watch cases in the mid-18th c. When similar decoration is worked from the front it is done by CHASING, popular at the same time. See FRENCH PROVINCIAL CLOCK for picture.

Reproduction clock Clock made for honest purposes to appear just like one of an earlier period. The best are not infrequently passed as genuine after their provenance is forgotten. Many French SECOND EMPIRE clocks were reproductions of those of the EMPIRE period, but

The **repoussé** case of a large silver chaise watch by Miroire, London, with a verge movement, hour and quarter hour strike, and alarm. (*Sotheby's*)

made in electrotype instead of ORMOLU. See FAKE.

Republican time   Attempted decimal division of the hour into 100 minutes by the French Revolutionaries. See DECIMAL TIME.

Resilient escapement   LEVER ESCAPEMENT invented by J.F. COLE which omitted BANKING PINS and relied mainly on the force of the MAINSPRING as a cushion if the balance swings too far and the IMPULSE PIN hits the outside of the FORK.

Resilient hook   Turned-back end of a MAINSPRING, with a short length of spring in it to hook it to a projection on the inside of the BARREL. Formerly a T-piece was riveted to the end of the spring.

Restauration clocks   French styles, mostly flamboyant, during the short time from the Bourbon monarchy restoration

in 1815 to the July Revolution in 1830. TARDY includes it in the EMPIRE period.

Resting barrel   The resting barrel is fixed to the movement and does not rotate, as do plain and GOING BARRELS. The driving wheel (the GREAT WHEEL) is connected to the BARREL ARBOR by clockwork (RATCHET and PAWL). The MAINSPRING can therefore be wound in the direction allowed by the ratchet and, when winding ceases, will drive the great wheel in the opposite direction. There is no MAINTAINING POWER.

Restoration   How much a clock or case should be restored is a matter of debate. For example, the British do not normally repaint painted scenes on 18th c clock dials; the Dutch do so without question. It is normal to replace missing parts of a MOVEMENT, but when the SALISBURY CATHEDRAL CLOCK was restored from PENDULUM to VERGE ESCAPEMENT there was controversy, so the new parts were painted a different colour. In the 1940s to 1950s one restorer of Tompion clocks made plates by the original method and went to the length of reproducing tool marks from other Tompion clocks on new parts. It is not easy to draw a line to which everyone would agree. For the collector with a damaged or incomplete valuable clock it is important to have new parts in as near as possible the same material and identical to the old ones and to keep original parts. See FAKE, REPRODUCTION CLOCK.

Reverse fusee   FUSEE turning in the opposite direction from normal. The gut or chain passes between fusee and BARREL. It reduces wear on the fusee PIVOT holes.

Reversible case   Pocket-watch PAIR CASE. The outer case has a hole on one side and hinged lid on the other. The watch in the inner case can be placed with dial showing, or reversed so that the dial is under the lid, as with a HUNTER.

Reversing wheel   A FUSEE watch (the high-quality article) was wound contra-clockwise and a GOING BARREL watch (the cheaper one) of the late 18th to early 19th c was wound clockwise. Many going barrel watches were fitted with reverser wheels between the BARREL and the CENTRE WHEEL to reverse the winding direction to the same as the fusee watch.

Reverso watch   Rectangular watch by JAEGER-LE COULTRE, which can be flipped over in its case to protect the dial and movement. It was designed for polo players. There were even TOURBILLON and CHRONOGRAPH versions.

Revolution timepiece   See DECIMAL TIME.

Revolving band clock   Clock in which a band, in the form of a circle and marked with 12 or 24 hours, revolves to indicate the time against a hand or fixed pointer. Some have similar minute bands. Popular in France in the 18th and early 19th c and used on clock cases shaped like urns, vases, globes, etc. Most had a moving hour band only. Later versions sometimes had minute hands too. See URN CLOCK for picture.

Rhomboid pendulum   One for which four lengths of steel are joined at the ends in elongated diamond shape to form the rod. Holding the sides of the diamond apart is a horizontal strip of brass. As the brass expands or contracts in different temperatures, it shortens or lengthens the pendulum to provide some TEMPERA-TURE COMPENSATION. Sometimes used on TURRET CLOCKS, rarely on domestic ones.

Richard of Wallingford (1292–1336) Abbot of St Albans Abbey, who designed the earliest recorded English ASTRO-NOMICAL CLOCK, then the most advanced in Europe. It struck the hours from 1 to 24 and had a unique form of escapement. Once known as his ALBION, it no longer exists.

Riefler clock   Precision PENDULUM clock invented by Riefler of Munich in 1889 and adopted as the standard OBSERVATORY CLOCK. The pendulum is almost FREE. It is IMPULSED by an arrangement that flexes the suspension

spring of the pendulum first one way then the other. The TEMPERATURE COMPENSATION is by a mercury-filled pendulum rod. This was later replaced by an INVAR rod; rewinding by electricity was introduced and the clock mounted in a vacuum chamber. Its best timekeeping was about +/-0.01 sec/day. It was the finest of the precision REGULATORS before the FREE PENDULUM.

Right-angle   escapement   See STRAIGHT-LINE ESCAPEMENT.

Ring dial   Portable sundial in ring form. The sunlight passing through a pin-hole produces a spot of light on the the inside surface opposite, the time being read on the internal scale. See UNIVERSAL RING DIAL.

Ring watch   Watch mounted in a finger ring. Guido Ubaldo della Rovere, Duke of Urbino, is recorded as having had a CLOCK WATCH so mounted in 1542! John ARNOLD made a very small ring watch with 120 parts in 1764 for King George III. The movement was only 48mm (⅓in) across. It had a CYLIN-DER ESCAPEMENT with a ruby cylin-der, the first known, only 2.8mm (0.0185in) in diameter, and was a HALF-QUARTER REPEATER. It probably still exists although its present whereabouts are not known. Later ring watches were made in quantity. See SMALLEST WATCH.

Ringed winding holes   Turned rings around winding holes intended to disguise any bruising around them, appeared on LONGCASE and BRACKET CLOCKS at most times, but particularly from c1690 to c1710.

Rise-and-fall regulator   Early arrange-ment for adjusting the length of a PENDULUM from the top, by moving the SUSPENSION SPRING in a slot. An alternative to screwing the BOB of a pendulum up or down for timekeeping. Operated by a hand in a small auxiliary dial on 18th c English clocks and by a clock key on French ones.

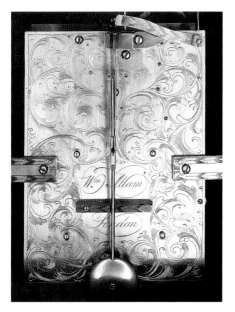

At the top of this movement of c1760 by William Allam, London, the **rise-and-fall regulator**, which alters the effective length of the pendulum, can be seen. (*Sotheby's*)

Ritchie's synchroniser Device to regulate an electric pendulum clock by giving it a gaining RATE. At a given time the minute hand is stopped momentarily and restarted by the properly synchronised IMPULSE.

Rittenhouse, David (1732–96) Best-known Pennsylvanian clockmaker, particularly for his complicated ASTRO-NOMICAL CLOCKS. Also a pioneer astronomer and honorary Fellow of the ROYAL SOCIETY.

Robin, Robert (1742–99) Fine French clockmaker, appointed to Louis XV, Louis XVI, Marie Antoinette and later to the Republic, when he made some DECI-MAL CLOCKS. He invented a single-beat lever CHRONOMETER escapement.

Rock crystal Transparent quartz used for decoration, 'glasses', CASES, and even PLATES, of clocks and watches from the earliest days. See ABBESS WATCH.

Rocking bar KEYLESS winding mechanism with a bar holding a wheel at each end, one for engaging winding and the other for hand-setting work. Operated by a push piece at the side of the winding button. Universal for later mechanical watches until POSITIVE SETTING.

Rocking ship clock Around the mid-19th c the French made some clocks with a model sailing ship on top which rocked on a billowing sea, under a glass dome. The rocking mechanism had three levers, two operated from wheels and the third by gravity.

Rococo Free style of elegant curves and clear colours with much white and gold, between the BAROQUE and NEOCLAS-SICAL periods. Often asymmetrical as with French CARTEL CLOCKS and many CERAMIC CLOCKS of the 1750s.

Rod gong Straight steel bar used as a gong in striking and chiming clocks. Screwed with others into a cast iron block fastened to the case to provide resonance. See GONG.

Rodico Trade name of putty-like material which is the modern substitute for pith. Used to remove dirt, grease, swarf, lint, finger marks etc. from watch parts, dials etc. Also useful for holding small parts to tools, and avoiding pieces from falling while being cut or removed.

Rolex Hans Wilsdorf, a Swiss aged 24 who had married an English girl, and his friend Davis formed a partnership in London in 1905 to assemble Swiss movements. The performance of these watches was so good that in 1910 one gained a chronometer certificate, the first ever awarded to a wrist watch, and in 1914 they won a KEW A CERTIFICATE, again unique. In 1919 Wilsdorf moved to Switzerland and became Montres Rolex, a name he had registered in 1908. He was very keen on waterproofing (see OYSTER WATCH CASE) and thought the solution was a SELF-WINDING WATCH in a sealed case. He made a series of HARWOOD watches but decided there was a better solution, so produced 360° rotation in 1931. Rolex persisted in improving waterproofing and one of their watches was taken down to nearly

11,000 m (27,900 ft) on the outside of Jacques Picard's submarine *Trieste*.

Rolled gold Thin layer of gold which has been soldered to a base metal such as nickel and rolled out very much thinner. A British Standard of 1960 required rolled gold watch cases to be marked 'R' followed by the thickness of gold in microns (thousandths of a millimetre) thus 'R20M'. Cases used to be stamped with the number 5, 10, 15 or 20 according to how many years the rolled gold was expected to last.

Roller Disc in a LEVER ESCAPEMENT which holds the IMPULSE PIN. See LEVER ESCAPEMENT for picture.

Roller jewel American name for IMPULSE PIN or ruby pin.

Roller pinion See ROLLING PINION.

Roller suspension Form of KNIFE-EDGE SUSPENSION for PENDULUMS in which, instead of a blade resting in a V-groove, a circular surface rests on a flat one. If a CYCLOIDAL surface replaces the circular one, it will correct a precision pendulum for CIRCULAR ERROR.

Rolling-ball clock See CONGREVE CLOCK.

Rolling clock Form of GRAVITY CLOCK (without MAINSPRING). The earliest still existing was made c1600 by Isaac HABRECHT. The clock is drum-shaped and rolls slowly down an inclined board. The hand remains still and hour numerals turn with the case. Made earlier this century by Gübelin in Switzerland and Garrard in England, but the dial remains stationary and the hands turn normally. When the clock reaches the bottom of the inclined plane it is replaced at the top by hand. The inclined track is often marked with days of the week. See MYSTERY CLOCK.

Rolling friction The friction resulting from one surface rolling against another, rather than sliding. Gear designers try to achieve it to reduce friction. See ROLLING PINION.

Rolling pinion LANTERN PINION (with rods instead of teeth) in which the rods are free to turn, to reduce friction.

Rolls watch Early SELF-WINDING WRIST WATCH invented by Hâtot in c1930 and used in BLANCPAIN watches. The movement moves up and down against spring buffers in the rectangular case as the wearer moves his arm, and a CLICK moves the winding RATCHET. A knurled gear projects from the side of the case for hand-winding.

Roman numerals These still persist on clock dials because of their symmetry, which is why IIII is usually used for 4 (to balance the VIII) instead of IV. However Big Ben has IV.

Roman striking Method of striking by Roman numerals instead of Arabic, invented by Joseph KNIBB to reduce the number of blows by the STRIKING TRAIN in month clocks. A high-pitched bell represents 1, a low-pitched one V and two blows on the low pitched one X. Thus IX is sounded by a high-pitched note followed by two low ones.

I	•	VII	● • •
II	• •	VIII	● • • •
III	• • •	IX	• ●●
IV	• ●	X	●●
V	●	XI	●● •
VI	● •	XII	●● • •

• = I   ● = V   ● ● = X

The sequence of **Roman striking** on two bells. The smaller dot indicates the higher-pitched bell.

Roof clock One set in a ceiling, sometimes the inside of a church roof. There is one in Volendam, Holland, in the same church as the famous early Swallow organ.

Rose engine turned See ENGINE TURNED and INDEX PLATE. The guide producing the geometrical pattern on watch cases is called a 'ROSETTE'.

Rosette Ornament which is circular or oval and decorated with rose-like petals. Used on some clock cases. See ENGINE TURNED.

Roskell, Robert (1798–1830) One of the best Liverpool makers of watches, some having CHRONOMETER ESCAPEMENTS, and many with the RACK LEVER. Also worked in London.

Roskell hand One with a serpentine (wavy) stem used on ROSKELL watches. A similar clock hand is sometimes called a 'Dutch hand'.

Roskilde Cathedral clock Early Danish 24-hour clock in Roskilde, with two jacks and St George slaying the dragon, which utters agonised cries.

Roskopf First cheap watch, a pocket watch made in 1865–7 by G.F. Roskopf, a German who settled in Switzerland. He eliminated the CENTRE WHEEL, which allowed him to use a big BARREL overlapping the centre of the watch. The ESCAPEMENT was a separate PINPALLET unit; the winding button could be turned only one way; there was no STOP WORK; the MOTION WORK turned on the BARREL ARBOR; and the hands were set by turning them with one's finger. This 'people's watch' was steadily improved until many millions of cheap wrist watches were made on a modified Roskopf layout (many still are).

Rotary clock American EIGHT-DAY or THIRTY-HOUR novelty clock with a CONICAL PENDULUM in front of the DIAL, the clock being under a glass dome. Made in the 1870s by E. N. Welch Manufacturing, in two models, it was possibly based on a French design made by Antoine Redier between 1840 and the 1870s. Reproductions of it by Horolovar, New York, U.S.A., appeared in 1975.

Rotary movement Pocket watch in which the whole movement rotates slowly in the case to improve accuracy (see POSITIONAL ERROR). The first was American, made by the Auburndale company in 1877. Also made by WATERBURY. Now a watch trade name.

Rotary pendulum clock See CONICAL PENDULUM CLOCK, BRIGG'S ROTARY CLOCK, KROEBER NOISELESS CLOCK, WELCH ROTARY CLOCK.

Rotary printing-press clock French INDUSTRIAL CLOCK of the 1870s in the shape of one of the new rotary presses then being used by newspapers.

Roth, Daniel Individual French maker of COMPLICATED WATCHES still working in Le Sentier, close to Lake Geneva. He uses MOVEMENT from suitable firms and makes the complications.

Rotherham and Sons Coventry, England, firm founded in 1747 by Samuel Vale which became the largest and first to use steam power. Longest of the earlier firms to survive, until destroyed by a bomb in the Second World War.

Rotor Eccentric weight which winds the MAINSPRING of a SELF-WINDING WATCH, and can turn through a full circle, as opposed to the PEDOMETER WATCH weight, which has a limited swing. Many rotors wind the watch while turning either way.

Rotton stone A natural stone (tripolite) from Derbyshire which is crushed, mixed with oil and used as an abrasive for cleaning clock parts, which it dulls. They are polished with ROUGE.

Rouen clock One of the earliest medieval clocks to survive and the earliest with quarter hour striking. Installed in the Rouen, France, city belfry in 1389. The MOVEMENT no longer works and the dials are controlled by a FLAT-BED movement.

Rouge (Red stuff) Finest form of abrasive powder produced from iron oxide. Scarlet in colour. Used for polishing gold and silver in particular. The next grade (fine) is used on steel and the next (medium) for steel to be BLUED. There is crocus, which is bluish-purple, for brass as well as steel, and clinker, the coarsest, for steel. There is also a 'white rouge'!

Rough movement An EBAUCHE.

Round dial The traditional English BRACKET CLOCK and LONGCASE CLOCK had a square or BREAK ARCH dial but some makers introduced round silvered dials or enamel ones in the late 18th c.

Round Gothic Popular shaped case by Elias Ingraham c 1840, which was widely copied. Also called a 'beehive case' because of its likeness to the old straw beehive in silhouette because it has curved sides, unlike the sharp or STEEP GOTHIC.

Round-head clock Another name for a TETE-DE-POUPÉE CLOCK and also for a round-head dial instead of DROP-DIAL CLOCK.

Roundel Another name for a BULLS-EYE in a longcase clock door.

Rounding-up tool Another name for a TOOTH-TOPPING TOOL.

Rowing timer Timer used to measure ten rowing strokes and indicate the strokes per minute. Also called a 'sculling timer'.

Roxbury Watch Co. Fictitious name used on some early mass-produced Swiss watches to mislead buyers into thinking they were American. Other such names were Brooklyn Watch Co., Bristol Watch Co., and New England Watch Co. See also MAKER TO THE ADMIRALTY.

Royal Clockmaker Such appointments provide useful historical information. The first, to King Henry VIII, was Nicholas Cratzer who came to England from Bavaria c1517, worked at Oxford and never learned English. Nicholas Urseau was French and worked at Hampton Court from 1538 and in Westminster in 1568 as clockmaker to Queen Elizabeth I, being followed in London by Bartholomew Newsam, probably a Yorkshireman, who was in the position from 1572. The Scotsman King James I chose another Scot, David Ramsay of Dundee, whom he brought back from France c1610. Ramsay became first Master of the Clockmakers' Company in London. One of the most versatile was Peter Auguste Caron, who made watches for the French King, invented a VIRGULE ESCAPEMENT in

1753, and was a musician and author, writing the libretti for *The Marriage of Figaro* and *The Barber of Seville* under the name of Beaumarchais. The appointment is still made in Britain, but to a retailer. There were sometimes separate appointments of Royal Watchmaker, but earlier makers produced both watches and clocks.

Royal collection This contains many magnificent clocks, most of which are in use in Windsor Castle, Buckingham Palace, St James's Palace and Hampton Court. They include the ANNE BOLEYN CLOCK, an early Augsburg MUSICAL CLOCK by Jacob Mayr; and ASTRO-NOMICAL CLOCKS by Julien LE ROY, RAINGO, PINCHBECK, LEPINE, and Eardley Norton, whose version has four dials, one on each side. There are many fine French clocks, some with fine BUHL cases, including a SYMPATHETIC CLOCK, a REGULATOR PENDULE, a two-pendulum (one for metronome use) clock by BREGUET and a YEAR CLOCK by Lepaute. Other clocks are by TOMPION (one has a 24-hour dial and shows both EQUAL HOURS and APPAR-ENT TIME), QUARE (a year clock), Isaac Duhamel, John Barwise, Richard Vick, Alex Cumming (a month clock) and VULLIAMY. There are SKELETON CLOCKS designed by CONGREVE, a Negress-head clock with hours and minutes in the eyes by Lepine, and even a TAVERN CLOCK (at Windsor Castle).

Royal Observatory Established in Greenwich Park, east of London, in 1675, it was to provide a means of navigation at sea. King Charles II set up a committee to examine the idea of using the stars. A young astronomer, John FLAMSTEED, called in by Sir John Moore, declared that star positions were not well enough known. He was appointed to have them 'corrected' and the building of the Observatory was trusted to Sir Christopher WREN for no more than £500, to be financed by the sale of gunpowder. Flamsteed had to teach and beg for money to buy instruments, including two precision clocks from TOMPION. The next ASTRONOMER ROYAL, Edmund Halley, received a grant of only

£1,000 for new instruments in 1720, although the government had offered £20,000 in 1714 to anyone FINDING THE LONGITUDE. The Observatory soon became responsible for TIME DETERMINATION and TIME DISTRIBUTION. In 1948, the Astronomer Royal, followed by the chronometer department, the 'NAUTICAL ALMANAC' office, solar and stellar observation and the time department moved to Herstmonceux Castle in Sussex, remaining there until 1990, when the Observatory was removed again, this time to Cambridge. In 1998 it was finally closed in favour of the Royal Edinburgh Observatory on Blackbird Hill. The old Observatory buildings in Greenwich Park, including the OCTAGON ROOM, became a museum showing fine examples of CHRONOMETERS, including HARRISON'S, and many other timekeeping instruments from SAND GLASSES and SUNDIALS to TRANSIT INSTRUMENTS and telescopes, together with the world's second largest collection of ASTROLABES. The old Observatory is administered by the NATIONAL MARITIME MUSEUM, also in Greenwich Park. See AIRY, GREENWICH MEAN TIME, PRIME MERIDIAN, SIX PIPS, TIME BALL.

Royal pendulum   Contemporary name in the 17th c for a SECONDS PENDULUM.

Royal Society   Society for the promotion of scientific research founded in London in 1660 and granted a royal charter in 1662. The first experimenter was Robert HOOKE, prominent in horological matters in the 17th and early 18th c. HUYGENS was elected a Fellow as were some eminent horologists such as GRAHAM.

Ruby cylinder   High grade cylinder of a CYLINDER ESCAPEMENT made of ruby. BREGUET often used them.

Ruby pin   Pin made of synthetic ruby through which the lever of a LEVER

ESCAPEMENT gives IMPULSE to the BALANCE. Also called an 'impulse pin'. In PIN-PALLET ESCAPEMENTS it is often of steel.

Rudd clock   First FREE PENDULUM clock, invented by R.J. Rudd in 1898. Now in the Science Museum, London.

Run to banking   After a LEVER ESCAPEMENT has IMPULSED the BALANCE, a little extra movement takes the lever to its BANKING PIN. This is necessary for safe action, to avoid damage.

Runner   Accessory used as a centre in TURNS, JACOT TOOL or LATHE when polishing PIVOTS. Also any IDLER (idle wheel) and the TRAIN of gears in a REPEATING WATCH that slows the speed of striking.

Russian horological industry   In 1929 the Soviet government started an industry by buying two complete American watch factories, the Dueber Watch Co. and the Ansonia Clock Co. to set up the First and Second Moscow Watchmaking Plants respectively, which were extended and reconstructed in 1934–5, when two extra plants were set up in Kuibyshev and Prenza. During the Second World War watchmaking plants were set up in the east at Christopol, Chelyabinsk, Zlatoust and Serdobsk, then mainly for fuse making, and after the war others at Oryol, Yerevan, Minsk, Rostov-on-Don, Petrodvorets, Uglich and elsewhere. The Russians only made JEWELLED LEVER watches. Clocks include all types. The industry has the world's biggest output after Switzerland. Technical control of the whole industry is under a single organisation in Moscow.

Rye Church clock   One of the oldest English clocks still working in its original place, in Sussex. Made in 1561 and later converted to very LONG PENDULUM, which hangs down inside the church and takes over two seconds for one swing.

S

S-balance COMPENSATION BALANCE by John ARNOLD in which two S-shaped bi-metallic strips moved weights in and out as the temperature changed.

Safety action Interaction of the GUARD PIN and fork in a LEVER ESCAPEMENT which prevents the ESCAPE WHEEL from becoming unlocked except when IMPULSE is being given.

Safety barrel Spring BARREL with the MAIN WHEEL fastened to the ARBOR instead of being the toothed barrel. If the MAINSPRING breaks, the 'explosive' force does not then damage the main wheel teeth because the barrel becomes free to revolve.

Safety pinion Device mainly in American watches to avoid damage to teeth should the MAINSPRING break. The PINION of the CENTRE WHEEL is screwed on instead of being riveted. A breaking mainspring will unscrew the pinion instead of damaging the wheel train.

St Dunstan's clock Clock in Fleet Street, London that operated the JACKS, Gog and Magog, which struck the hours and quarters on bells. Made by Thomas Harrys of Water Lane and erected in 1671. Removed to near Regents Park in 1830 when the church was demolished. The figures are back in Fleet Street.

St Marie church clock Astronomical clock of c1400 in Rostock, Germany, with a DOUBLE-TWELVE DIAL and calendar dial below indicating the GOLDEN NUMBER, DOMINICAL LETTER, EASTER, sunrise, saint of the day, etc.

St Mark's clock Magnificent astronomical clock with AUTOMATA in St Mark's Square, Venice. It has a 24-hour dial, with XXIIII on the right and was completed in 1499.

St Paul's Cathedral clock May have been England's first public clock. Records show that in 1286 the clock keeper, Bartholomo Orologiario, was entitled to a loaf of bread daily. This clock was probably inside the nave and was replaced in 1344. Such clocks had no dials or hands, but JACKS which struck bells. They were illuminated with candles for services. The present clock by J. Smith of Derby was installed in 1893 and strikes on GREAT TOM, which was designed as a rival to BIG BEN.

Salisbury Cathedral clock Oldest clock (1386) still working. It was originally in a

The **Salisbury Cathedral clock** of 1386 showing the count wheel and winding wheel just behind it. The weights are hung from pulleys above.

13th c bell tower in the Close, and re-installed in the cathedral in the 18th c when the bell tower was demolished. Replaced by a new clock in 1884, it was 'lost' until discovered by T.R. Robinson in the tower in 1928, and cleaned and put on show in 1931. Many years ago it was converted to PENDULUM. In 1956 it was restored to FOLIOT, with four-second ticks, and set going again inside the cathedral. There is no dial. The FRAME and WHEELS are of wrought iron, the frame being held together with mortice and tenon joints with wedges like early furniture. See FOLIOT for picture.

Salomons collection Famous collection, mainly of BREGUET'S work, by the late Sir David Salomons. Unfortunately it was stolen from a special museum in Jerusalem.

Salt-cellar clock 'The salt' a container holding salt, was often large and of gold or silver in the 17th c and of special import at state banquets, unimportant people being put 'below the salt'. A clock was occasionally incorporated in it. The Worshipful Company of Goldsmiths owns the Royal Tudor clock-salt referred to in the 1550 inventory of Henry VIII.

Sand clock A vertical drum is partly filled with sand on an axle. Inside there are radial partitions with holes in them. A rope wound round the drum has a weight at the end. The drum revolves slowly as the sand runs from one compartment to the next and indicates the time. The earliest reference is in a book of 1665. See MERCURY CLOCK.

Sand glass Early interval TIMER, comprising a glass globe with a narrow waist, partly filled with sand (often powdered egg shell). When up-ended, the sand passes from the top to the bottom globe in a fixed time. If the time is an hour, the device is an hour glass. It was developed after WATER CLOCKS, having the advantage of not freezing. The earliest have two open glass bulbs with a pierced brass diaphragm between them. Sand was placed in one and the parts sealed by wax and bound with thread round the joint. The next type was intro-duced in the late 17th c and has two bulbs blown and drawn in one piece, one left with a hole at the top for insertion of the sand. The hole is stopped by a cloth-covered cork. (Many have a copper diaphragm pressed into the waist). A third type, from the early 19th c, is similar but the filling hole has been sealed by the glassblower. Some were constructed in batteries of three or more with different time intervals. Large ones were commonly stood on pulpits in the past to time sermons and called 'sermon glasses'. Used on ships as late as 1839 to calculate speeds. A float or 'chip' at the end of a long line with knots at fixed intervals was thrown over the side. The number of knots that ran out as timed by the sand glass gave the speed in knots. The House of Commons has a two-minute glass formerly employed for timing division bells calling members to vote.

Sandstrom clock BALL CLOCK made by S.E. Sandstrom of Pasadena in 1901. It has two sloping fixed trays with tracks, one above the other, and a tube connects the two. A weight-driven vertical wheel with 60 holes holds 30 balls on the up-moving side. A ball released from the top takes a minute to complete the double track, when it falls through another tube into a hole at the bottom of the wheel. This releases a latch, allowing the wheel to move forward to the next hole and to release the next ball from the top hole. Thus the wheel rotates once an hour. The clock therefore has no GEARING and no PENDULUM or BALANCE WHEEL.

Sapphire 'glass' Synthetic transparent sapphire used as the 'glass' of some 20th c watches because it is virtually scratch-less. 'Portrait' diamonds (very flat natural diamonds) are very rarely used too.

Satellite laser ranger Very short pulses from a green laser are bounced off special reflectors on artificial satellites and the time taken for individual photons to return gives the satellite's position to about a centimetre, from which the Earth's rate of rotation is calculated.

Satellite timer Electronic (originally mechanical) TIME SWITCH for switching on and off the radio transmitter and receiver and other instruments in artificial satellites.

Savage two-pin escapement Development of the English LEVER ESCAPEMENT of MASSEY by George Savage c1818 with two IMPULSE pins instead of the usual one. Improved efficiency but caused wear. Used on clocks as well as watches but not widely adopted.

Savonette French name for a watch with a front cover to protect the glass, as with a hunter.

Saw clock American name for a RACK CLOCK.

Scandinavian clocks Sweden had clockmakers from the early 17th c and Denmark some half-century later. Both later adopted English LONGCASE styles and occasionally French provincial ones. Finland produced a few. In Helsinki is a LONGCASE CLOCK like a woman in a flared dress with arms akimbo and shoes below the skirt. See BORNHOLMER.

Scarab watch Watch in the form of the sacred beetle of ancient Egypt.

Scent clock In 1664 Gaspar Schott invented an attachment for clocks that squirted jets of different scents at different hours.

Science Museum collection Very interesting collection of timekeepers for the mechanically minded, covering not only a comprehensive historical range of instruments and inventions but the history up to recent developments in electric clocks, MASTER CLOCKS, TIME SWITCHES, GAS CONTROLLERS, TIME RECORDERS, STOP WATCHES, QUARTZ CRYSTAL and ATOMIC CLOCKS, etc., not shown by other collections. At South Kensington, London.

Schild (shield) clock Style much favoured by BLACK FOREST clock makers from c1740 to well into the 19th c. There are also modern German versions. Only the BREAK-ARCH-shaped dial is visible, apart from the PENDULUM and

weights hanging below it. The case is hidden behind the dial. There is no glass and the earliest clocks had very decorative DIAL PAINTING on paper stuck on wood. From c1775 relief was provided by painted plaster gesso. Enamel followed c1800. See SCHOTTENUHR.

School clock American DROP-DIAL CLOCK.

Schottenuhr Small SCHILD CLOCK with a dial of about 15cm (6in) introduced by J. Dilger of Schottenhof, near Neustadt, Germany. Sometimes wrongly called 'Scotch clock'.

Scratch dial Primitive SUNDIAL scratched on the south porch of a church.

Scratch mark The repairer of a watch or clock sometimes scratched his initials and the date he repaired it on one of the PLATES or EBAUCHE. This may be useful in dating a MOVEMENT. Currently it is useful in helping the police trace stolen goods.

Screw Metal screws came into use on clocks about 1500 on the Continent, but not until nearly a century later in England. Previously, slots and wedges (as in early wooden furniture) were employed for joints that had to be dismantled. They were in use for TURRET CLOCKS long after domestic ones. Permanent joints were usually fire-welded. Some in watches are so minute that they are not easy to see with the naked eye.

Screw plate Hardened steel plate with a series of threaded dies of different sizes in it for making screws. See MARTIN SCREW PLATE.

Screwback Watch case where the back is screwed on. Also used for some BEZEL rims.

Sculling timer See ROWING TIMER.

Seal watch Watch in a seal. Some Swiss seals for fastening to a pocket-watch chain contained musical MOVEMENTS.

Seatboard Shelf in a LONGCASE CLOCK on which the MOVEMENT is mounted and to which the ends of the weight lines are fastened. It should be level. See SETTING UP A CLOCK.

Seaweed marquetry Complex MARQUETRY design of interwoven foliage and stems popular for longcases in the years around 1700. Also called 'arabesque marquetry'.

Second The International Committee of Weights and Measures defined the second as one 31,556,925.9747th part of the year 1900 based on EPHEMERIS TIME. A second measured by the ATOMIC CLOCK was adopted as the international standard in 1967. It equals 9,192,631,770 vibrations of the caesium atom. The name was originally a 'second minute', i.e. the second division into 60.

Second Empire Period of design during Napoleon III's regime (1852–70) when fine EMPIRE (1799–1814) ORMOLU clock case designs were copied in inferior metals such as ELECTROTYPE. The great majority of French 'ormolu' clocks seen today in antique shops and at sales are of this type and were made from 1850 to 1870. Original ormolu versions command very high prices. American clocks of the 1825–40 period, particularly Connecticut SHELF CLOCKS with upper and lower glazed doors in the front, are called 'American Empire' clocks. The top door encloses the dial and has an EGLISOME PAINTING. The lower one usually held a mirror.

Seconds bit Small circular plate for the small seconds dial of a pocket watch fastened behind an opening in the main dial. Also called 'sunk bit'.

Seconds hand Hand of a clock or watch showing seconds. One of the earliest is on BURGI'S ROCK CRYSTAL clock made just after 1600, but they did not come into general use on clocks until the LONG PENDULUM was invented and on watches until after the application of the BALANCE SPRING.

Seconds pendulum PENDULUM taking a second to swing from one side to the other and therefore theoretically 0.9942m (39.14in) from CENTRE OF SUSPENSION to CENTRE OF OSCILLATION.

Secret signature Extremely small signature (sometimes with the number and type of watch) used by BREGUET to distinguish his work from that of forgers. Can only be seen by magnification, under the XII on enamel dials and on each side of the XII on silver ones. Applied by a small pantograph invented in 1794. Also used by others to give a date or the name of the dial painter.

Secret spring Hidden spring that causes a HUNTER case to fly open when the winding button is pressed.

Secticon clock Unique Swiss precision clock by The Universal Escapement Ltd introduced in 1960. The mechanical movement has a high-quality CONSTANT FORCE escapement like a DETACHED LEVER but impulsing only in one direction. The power is supplied not by spring but transistor-controlled electric motor. One model has a case shaped like a ship's binnacle, about 25cm (10in) high.

Sector V-shaped gauge like two rulers hinged together at one end, used for matching WHEELS to PINIONS. If a pinion of eight leaves (teeth) is placed in the V where 8 is marked, and the V closed, the diameter of a wheel of 32 teeth, say, will be where 32 is marked. Thomas JUMP of Prescot was a well-known maker in the earlier 19th c.

Sector watch Early 20th c wrist watch with a semicircular dial and hands that spring back after each 60 minutes or 12 hours.

Sedan clock Small clock with a VERGE watch MOVEMENT and often a circular wooden case about 15cm (6in) across, reputedly for hanging in a sedan chair. Made in the late 17th c and 18th c. Also a clock mounted in the side of a small metal model of a sedan chair.

A 19th c sedan clock with a verge escapement.

Seiko quartz watch In 1895, a Tokyo jeweller and clock and watch repairer, Kityaro Hattori, started producing pocket watches, and in 1918, wrist watches, mainly exported to China. In 1936 he launched his first wrist watches under the name of Seiko and only 13 years later had taken 60 per cent of the Japanese market including ALARM and MANTEL CLOCKS. In 1963 Hattori and Co. announced a portable quartz chronometer and in 1969, the Astron, the world's first mass-produced QUARTZ WRIST WATCH. They produced a TV watch in 1982 and the first computer wrist watch in 1984. One of their quartz CHRONO-GRAPHS includes a world time alarm that can be set for any TIME ZONE. In 1994 they introduced their kinetic generating system, a watch with an oscillating weight like a SELF-WINDING WATCH except that it generates electricity which is stored in a capacitor to drive the quartz movement - a quartz watch without a battery.

Self-correcting chimes Automatic arrangement on most domestic chiming clocks by which the chimes, if out of sequence, are held up at the hour and released when again in step.

Self-starting electric clock A SYNCHRONOUS ELECTRIC CLOCK that starts when switched on. A shaded pole (one pole piece covered by copper or other non-magnetic metal) causes one pole to be stronger than the other when switched on and the slight IMPULSE given to the rotor starts it running either way. A spring stop sends it the right way if it reverses. Some manufacturers preferred the clock to stop if there was a mains cut.

Self-winding clock Perhaps the first was driven by a fan in a kitchen chimney, as recorded by Gaspar Schott in 1664. Very many types have been invented. See ATMOS CLOCK, AUTOMATIC WIND-ING, BATTERY CLOCK, LIGHT CLOCK.

Self-winding Clock Co. New York company that installed clocks on the London Underground railway

Self-winding pocket watch The first suggestion for one probably came from David Schwenter, a German scholar, in the mid-17th c for a watch on a belt wound by the movement of breathing. The practical solution was invented by A.L. Perrelet the elder (1729–1826). The movement of the wearer causes an eccentric weight to bounce, like that in a pedometer, to wind the watch. Developed by BREGUET in his PERPET-UAL WATCH. Perrelet's friend Louis RECORDON patented it in London in 1780. Breguet found them hard to sell and stopped production in c1817. His weights were of platinum because of its high density. Spencer and Perkins as well as Cabrier made them in London between c 1780 and 1830; Jaquet-Droz and LeSchot in Neuchâtel, Switzerland (who supplied to James Cox, London, who in turn sold them to China), Colladon in Geneva, several makers in Le Locle, Le Roy in Paris, etc. See PEDOMETER WATCH.

Self-winding wrist watch Technical problems delayed fitting a pedometer style of winding (see entry above) to wrist watches until 1922 when Le Roy produced one. The most successful was by the Englishman John Harwood, who patented his AUTOWRIST design for factory-made watches in Switzerland in 1924. The hands were set by rotating the BEZEL. A limited number were produced in 1926 by BLANCPAIN (who produced 14,000 up to 1932), A. Schild and others. Later the Selza Watch factory had some success, but acceptance had to wait until Hans Wilsdorf of ROLEX made them and then patented and launched his own design with a 360° oscillation rotor in 1931 which surpassed all others. Later a slipping clutch was added to avoid overwinding damage. The patent ran out in 1945, when almost every other maker of automatic watches adopted the Rolex system. Eterna S.A. introduced a ball-bearing winding rotor, and then Universal a half size 'micro-rotor'. Other early self-winding systems were the ROLLS WATCH and WIG-WAG. Subsequently Swiss and Japanese factories and others elsewhere made 'automatic watches', as the Swiss called them, in millions. Many later versions have a 45 hour power reserve, which improves timekeeping as the mainspring is kept nearly fully wound.

The first **self-winding wrist watch** by John Harwood.

Separate alarm   Owners of the earliest TABLE CLOCKS could sometimes buy an alarm attachment to be fitted over the dial which, when set to the time required, the clock's hour hand would set off.

Serial numbers   Many makers of clocks and watches used serial numbers that can help collectors in dating. Some were consistent, others not. TOMPION'S numbers are well recorded as well as those of some others. The task of correlating many remains to be done. American serial numbers on factory-made watches are more consistent.

Sermon glass   See PULPIT CLOCK.

Serpentine hand   Clock minute hand which is wavy instead of straight. Introduced about the mid-18th c.

Set hands   Clutch mechanism in every timepiece that allows the hands to be set to a new time without damaging the movement.

Set hands dial   A conveniently placed small dial on a TURRET CLOCK which repeats the time shown on the main dial(s) so that the clock minder can reset the time or regulate the main turret.

Set in beat   See OUT OF BEAT.

Setting up   Pre-tensioning a spring, i.e. fixing the lowest tension to which it can run down. In early spring-driven timepieces, the MAINSPRING could be RATCHET SET UP to different tensions to adjust the power output and therefore the timekeeping. With the FUSEE, the mainspring has to be set up to keep the gut taut. STOP WORK is necessary with such a mechanism. See BELL for picture.

Setting up a clock   After TRANSPORTING A CLOCK, it must be set up. Spring-driven clocks without PENDULUMS present no problem. If the clock is spring-driven with a short pendulum, as with French ORMOLU or MARBLE CLOCKS, first rehook the pendulum at the back and remove the wedge under the CRUTCH. If the clock is on a mantel or shelf with its back to a wall, lift up one side a little to start the pendulum swinging. If the clock is in beat, the ticks will be evenly spaced and the clock will not stop, unless it has run down. If there is no BEAT ADJUSTER, the crutch will have to be bent, as explained under IN BEAT. Marble clocks present a problem because they are so heavy. The only way is to leave a space between the clock and the wall and do the adjustment 'blind', with hands round the clock. In some cases a mirror against the wall can help. One end of the clock can be left wedged up to bring the clock into beat, but this is a make-shift. LOCKING-PLATE STRIKING may become out of phase. Reset it by lifting the locking lever to let it strike until it is in phase again. Setting up a LONGCASE CLOCK correctly is a longer procedure. Choose a floor which is firm and level if possible. If there is a flat wall behind, it is best to anchor the case about halfway up to the wall with a screw and plug to stop it from swaying. Even slight sway will cause it to stop when a weight has run down to the length of the pendulum. For a corner site, make a wooden wedge to anchor the clock to the walls. Next refit the SEATBOARD and MOVEMENT if they were removed and check with a spirit level. Replace the HOOD to make sure the dial is in the centre of the frame and, if not, adjust it

An early form of **setting up** a mainspring by ratchet wheel and click (at top) of a watch of c1615 by Antoine Arlaud.

with wooden wedges. Rehang the weights. Resuspend the pendulum and swing it to see if it is in beat and if not, bend the crutch until it is. Watch the pendulum BOB to see that it does not twist. If it does, the SUSPENSION SPRING has been bent and will have to be replaced. A VIENNA REGULATOR, and other HANGING CLOCKS with long pendulums, like many Dutch clocks, need a wall that is strong and vertical to take a substantial hanging screw and wall plug. Genuine REGULATORS have screws to adjust uprightness if the wall leans, and usually a beat adjuster. It is wise to turn the hands only forwards.

Sèvres clock   18th c French clock with a Sèvres porcelain case or ORMOLU case with Sèvres panels.

Sextant   Instrument for measuring angles used in NAVIGATION for finding LOCAL TIME by star observations. The height of a star is found by turning a knob of the marine sextant so that a mirrored image of the star is brought down to the horizon. A scale then gives the angle, from which local time can be calculated. The bubble sextant, which has an artificial horizon, was used in aircraft.

Shaded pole   See   SELF-STARTING ELECTRIC CLOCK.

Shadow clock   Ancient Egyptian device like a wooden T with a right-angled crank a short way below the bar. Laid with the stem flat on the ground, bar towards the Sun, the shadow of the bar shows the hour by notches in the stem. There is one in the Science Museum, London.

Shagreen   Shark skin used for 19th c watch cases. Imitated also by other fish skins and leather, dyed green.

Shake   Watch- and clockmakers' name for play in a bearing, thus 'side shake' and 'end shake' for 'side play' and 'end play'. In a LEVER ESCAPEMENT, it is the working gap between a tooth of the ESCAPE WHEEL and one of the PALLETS, in a CYLINDER ESCAPEMENT, the gap caused by an escape wheel tooth being slightly less in length than the inside diameter of the cylinder.

Shaker clock Very plain LONGCASE CLOCK made by a Quaker community in the U.S., who did frenzied dancing, called the Shakers. Their other furniture was also very plain.

Sharp Gothic clock An American case style devised by Elias Ingraham c1843 and extensively copied. It is rectangular, long dimension up, with a sharp triangular top. Each side is a cylindrical column topped by a tall cone. It became very popular. Also a neo-GOTHIC style used on some English BRACKET CLOCKS in the early 19th c. The top is triangular with an acute top angle. See WAGGON-SPRING CLOCK for picture. Also called 'steep Gothic'.

Shears Commonly used for thinner metals by watch- and clockmakers, case makers and jewellers. Small sizes are almost identical to modern metal shears. One type has one handle at right angles so that it can be held in a vice.

Sheepshead clock LANTERN CLOCK with a particularly large dial, supposed to make it look like a sheep's head. Introduced at the beginning of the 18th c but not popular until the second half.

Shelf clock Style that became the traditional American one. First applied to Massachusetts CASE-ON-CASE clocks, but later took in the various Connecticut styles made to stand on a shelf. The case is normally rectangular with a framed glass front, the dial at the top and a scene or design in EGLISOME at the bottom. The brass MOVEMENT strikes on a spiral wire gong and the weights hang down each side, inside, the lines being taken over pulleys at the top corners. Also made in other centres from after 1800 to c1840. See BRONZE LOOKING-GLASS CLOCK, OGEE, PILLAR-AND-SCROLL CLOCK (picture), STEEPLE CLOCK, WAGGON-SPRING CLOCK.

Shelton clock Loud-ticking pendulum instrument used during astronomical observation and invented by John

An American **shelf clock** of 1820–30 in mahogany and maple veneer, by Ephraim Downs, Bristol, Connecticut. (*Christie's*)

Shelton of London, a maker of fine regulators, about the mid-18th c.

Shepherd's dial See ALTITUDE SUNDIAL.

Sheraton style Thomas Sheraton (1751–1806), although giving his name to the elegant style of English furniture after Hepplewhite and before Regency, had virtually no influence on clocks, although clocks with simple inlaid motifs such as shells and fans are called 'Sheraton clocks'. See CHIPPENDALE.

Shield clock See SCHILD CLOCK.

Shifter Clock weight like the slotted weights used on large weighing machines, sometimes used on TURRET

CLOCKS. A disc has a rod from the centre attached to the line. The shifters are piled one above the other on the disc. Also used for a PENDULUM BOB. Such a pendulum bob was fitted to St Peter's Church, St Albans.

Ship's bell clock Clock striking SHIP'S TIME. Often a BULKHEAD CLOCK.

Ship's time Three systems of time are used on board ship. A sailor's day is reckoned from noon and divided into a series of 'watches'. Each is of four hours except the two dog watches of two hours each. During a watch the ship's bell is struck once at the end of the first half-hour, twice at the second, and up to eight times at the end of the four hours. A passenger's day is the normal 24 hours, as shown on SLAVE CLOCKS on the ship operated from a MASTER CLOCK, which is advanced or retarded at night, according to whether the ship is going west or east, to adjust approximately to LOCAL TIME. The third time reckoning was for navigation, GREENWICH MEAN TIME shown by the ship's CHRONOMETER. Time signals and satellite navigation replaced this.

Shock absorber Arrangement to protect the delicate PIVOTS of a jewelled BALANCE WHEEL from damage if a watch is knocked. The JEWELS are carried in special self-centring, spring-loaded seats which will absorb blows from various directions. The first was Breguet's PARACHUTE INDEX. Present systems are more precise and efficient. See INCABLOC.

Shockproof Term once commonly applied but now banned in most industrial countries in favour of 'shock-resistant'.

Shortt clock Most accurate form of PENDULUM clock ever made, superseding the RIEFLER CLOCK. Invented by W.H. Shortt in 1921 for use as an OBSERVATORY CLOCK. See FREE PENDULUM CLOCK.

Side-by-side trains Normal arrangement of two or more gear TRAINS in all except very early clocks.

Side shake Freedom of a PIVOT in its hole.

Sidereal clock or **watch** One keeping SIDEREAL TIME, used in observatories for star observations and TIME DETERMINATION. Some clocks show MEAN TIME as well as sidereal. Some mathematicians have spent years calculating gear TRAINS to convert sidereal to solar time (and planetary ratios) and have come close to the true ratio, but they cannot achieve perfection because it is not constant.

Sidereal time The time of rotation of the Earth as measured from a CLOCK STAR, instead of from the sun. This is more accurate but ignores daylight, giving a MEAN SOLAR TIME day of 23 hours 56 minutes 4.1 seconds. It is thus impractical for ordinary use, but employed in TIME DETERMINATION. OBSERVATORY CLOCKS are made (with shorter pendulums when mechanical) to show sidereal time. A more accurate timekeeper, a pulsar (twin stars) rotating at 642 times a second, was identified in 1983. See NUTATION, PRECESSION OF THE EQUINOXES and TRANSIT INSTRUMENT.

Sidereal time as well as the time of day is shown by this large watch by George Margetts, London, of c1790.

Sidewalk clock Clock with two or four dials on a post like that of a lamp-post. The style was first used in Paris and centrally controlled (see PNEUMATIC CLOCK). They were copied by the E. Howard Clock Co. of Boston, U.S.A., c1870. Each had an EIGHT-DAY, weight-driven pendulum MOVEMENT in the base. Other makers followed. Many lamps were electrified later. See PAVEMENT CLOCK.

Signatures The makers of old clocks and watches engraved their names on the dial and BACK PLATE. In the 18th c, they continued to do so because they were the designers and finishers, although much work was put out to makers of parts, called 'chamber masters'. In the late 18th and 19th c more and more clockmakers, including famous ones, bought complete MOVE-MENTS and sometimes complete clocks from embryo factories in CLERKENWELL and elsewhere for their regular cheaper lines, but still had their own names on them. The embryo factories sometimes supplied to retailers who had *their* names engraved or painted as makers. Some such clocks even bear customer names! So for many 18th and 19th c clocks, the true maker is sometimes not the person named on the dial. There may be a punch mark somewhere in the movement revealing the real maker. THWAITES AND REED, London, used 'T & R' stamped on the edge of a PLATE or under the anchorage of a BRIDGE or COCK, often with a number such as '36', which would indicate 1836. Embryo movement factories also included Handley and Moore, London, Whitehurst of Derby, Walker and Finnimore, Birmingham and Matthew Boulton, also of Birmingham.

Silberstein, Alain French designer with Bauhaus inspiration and a company in BESANÇON. He uses Swiss movements to design watches for collectors.

Silencing chimes and strike See NIGHT SILENCING.

Silent Electric Clock Co. See BOWELL.

Silent escapement The noisy ticks of the VERGE ESCAPEMENT was an objection to NIGHT CLOCKS, so some clockmakers introduced a form of silencing, including

P. and T. Campanus, Rome, with their 'silent crank' escapement in the 1680s. Justin VULLIAMY in the mid-18th c intro-duced lengths of taut gut to replace the metal PALLETS, mainly for library and bedroom clocks. Some mechanical ALARMS have a form of silencing. The DROP which causes the tick tock is elimi-nated in the INGERSOLL alarm by another ESCAPE WHEEL around the normal one with teeth pointing inwards. This is free but linked to the first by a spring which acts as a SHOCK ABSORBER. Each is IMPULSED alter-nately. Mauthe of Germany made an alarm in which the escape wheel and lever are of reinforced synthetic resin (instead of brass) and the PIN PALLETS long and springy. The tick is twice a second and almost silent. The MAGNETIC ESCAPE-MENT and QUARTZ CLOCK are silent. See NIGHT CLOCK.

Silent-Keeless clock (see overleaf) RACK or gravity clock made by the Watson Clock Co. in London c1925. The company name was later changed to the Kee-Less Clock Co.

Silk line For REGULATORS, red silk weight lines were commonly used instead of GUT LINES.

Silk suspension Method of suspending a pendulum from a loop of silk thread,

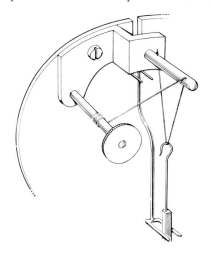

The timekeeping of a pendulum clock with **silk suspen-sion** is adjusted by winding the silk thread to raise or lower the pendulum.

This **Silent-Keeless clock** is actually a form of rack clock.

opposition of the Goldsmiths Company to the use of precious metals by members of the Locksmiths and Blacksmiths Companies, although GOLD WATCH CASES were marked earlier. Silver was regarded as second grade. During earlier times, cases usually had a brass frame with a silver band round the sides and two silver covers. Later they were made wholly of silver with inner and outer cases now called PAIR CASES. A hallmark is an excellent guide to the date of the watch. See GOLD WATCH CASE.

Silvering Fine matt or grained silver finish of brass CHAPTER RING of most antique clocks with brass dials, protected by a coat of lacquer. Before the invention of FRENCH SILVERING, about 1660, decorative clock parts and chapter rings were sometimes in solid silver. One paste for restoration is made from some silver chloride, twice as much potassium bitartrate (cream of tartar), and three times (all by weight) of common salt, adding water to form a creamy paste. This is rubbed onto the cleaned ring with a clean brush in a circular motion by revolving the ring. Alternatively a straight grain can be produced by using a clean linen rag or a cork. Wash in running water and LACQUER.

Singing bird Clockwork mechanism with bellows imitating bird songs, usually associated with AUTOMATA of birds. Some are in snuff-boxes, which reveal a miniature 'bird' when opened, others are life-sized 'birds' in cages which move and sing so realistically it is difficult to believe they are not alive. Made by early English clockmakers such as PINCHBECK and later in large numbers from the mid-18th c by the Swiss, French and Germans, until the 1920s. Famous makers were the Bruguier family (c1770–1886), Jacquet-Droz, the Rochat family, Lami, Jean David and Auguste, and the Maillardet brothers, all of Geneva; and the firms of LE ROY and Blaise Bontemps, of Paris.

Single-beat escapement One in which IMPULSE is given at every other beat as in CHRONOMETER, DUPLEX, and COUP PERDU ESCAPEMENTS.

the pendulum having a hook at the top. Timekeeping is adjusted by winding the thread up or down by a small wheel. Often seen on 18th and 19th c French clocks and also other continental clocks. See HAAGSE KLOKJE or SKELETON CLOCK for picture.

Silver watch case Silver cases were only rarely assayed and hallmarked in London before the 1740s, because, it is said, of the

Single-plane escapement   One basically on a single level like the LEVER ESCAPE-MENT. The VERGE is two-plane.

Sinking bowl   Bronze bowl with a hole in it which sinks in a given time when floated in water; used by the Saxons as a WATER CLOCK, or more accurately, a TIMER. Still used today in Algeria to time the irrigation of land.

Six-hour dial   Rare type of ONE-HAND watch dial of c1700 with I to VI round the dial and also 7 to 12. The purpose was to make the hand move further so that it was more accurately read.

Six-month clock   One that runs just over six months at a winding. See MONTH CLOCK.

Six pips   The familiar RADIO TIME SIGNAL said to originate from a talk on the BBC given by HOPE-JONES on 21 April 1923, two years after the DAYLIGHT SAVING act, when he vocalised the last six seconds to the hour. The electrically produced 'pips' started in August 1923, provided by the ROYAL OBSERVATORY for the BBC. On February 5, 1990, the BBC took over, providing U.T.C. with an uncertainty of under 0.05 seconds in the U.K. with a delay of 0.25 seconds abroad because of the satellite link. On December 31, 1923, BIG BEN striking was broadcast. Its popularity encouraged its use as a TIME SIGNAL.

Size of watch parts   Some mechanical watch parts, hand-made and machine-made, are so small they are nearly invisible. George DANIELS, the finest current maker by hand, relates how he mislaid a tiny screw he had made and found it under his thumbnail. Even in the early 1900s, the smallest screws in pocket watches made in quantity in CLERKEN-WELL 680 to the gram (weighed 19,250 to the ounce).

Sizes, watch   A watch movement was gauged by measuring the diameter of the dial side. If it was not round, the narrowest width was measured. French and Swiss watches were based on the LIGNE, one-twelfth of the PARIS INCH. English and American watch sizes were based on the full diameter of a round movement of 0 size, which is $1\frac{5}{30}$in. Each progressive size was $\frac{1}{30}$in bigger.

Skeleton clock   One in which the plates and other parts are pierced by fret work. Used as early as the mid-16th c on DRUM CLOCKS and WATCHES but first popu-larised as spring-driven MANTEL CLOCKS by French makers in the 1750s. Taken up enthusiastically by English makers from c1820 and became a princi-pal product from centres in London, Birmingham, Liverpool, Derby, Prescot and elsewhere. The most prolific London makers were JOHN SMITH AND SONS of CLERKENWELL. The clocks are spring-driven with FUSEES running for

A dramatic French **skeleton clock** of c1810 that runs for fourteen days at a winding. The pendulum has silk suspension.

eight days although some month, three-month and year clocks were made. RACK STRIKING or ONE-AT-THE-HOUR were favoured for striking and some have CHIMES too on four to eight bells or, later, ROD GONGS, with a variety of peals. ANCHOR ESCAPEMENTS are common but a great variety of others is also found. Many clocks were made by individual makers. Victorian English skeleton clocks invariably have heavy cast frames. They stand on wooden or marble bases under glass domes. An ultra-simple skeleton clock was built in 1981-2 at the La Chaux-de-Fonds Watchmaking School. It has a four-second 15.9m (52ft) pendulum with a 0.45mm (0.11in) wide rod and LEPAUTE ESCAPEMENT.

Skeleton dial Fretwork dials appeared on LONGCASE CLOCKS from c1670 to 1690 and had a short vogue on REGULA-TORS in the early 19th c before being fairly common on SKELETON CLOCKS. They were also used occasionally on watches.

Skeleton watch Skeletonised pocket watches were made occasionally in the 18th to 20th c as a novelty. The PLATES of the MOVEMENT as well as the dial were cut away as fretwork. The fretwork was engraved or had an overlay of filigree work set with real or imitation gems. They have been made at intervals ever since and skeleton wrist watches still are by the Swiss, many being exceptional examples of the watchmaker's art. BRIDGES, BARRELS and COCKS are skeletonised as well as the PLATES or EBAUCHE.

Skull watch Watch made mainly in the 17th c in the form of a skull, sometimes of silver or wood, as a *memento mori*. Read by opening the jaw. See MARY QUEEN OF SCOTS' WATCH for picture.

Slave dial Clock dial in which the hands are operated by an electromagnet from electric impulses sent every half minute from a MASTER CLOCK elsewhere. Also called an 'impulse dial'.

Sleeve Spring clutch in the PENDANT

of a pocket watch set by pulling out the winding button.

Slide-up hood The earliest type of HOOD used on LONGCASE CLOCKS from c1660 to c1700 before they became taller. It is slid upwards to wind the clock through the dial, also called a 'rising hood'. It is locked when down and released by a 'spoon' inside the case door.

Smallest watch Small watches for their time, such as PURITAN WATCHES, have been made since early days. An amazingly small and complicated RING WATCH was made by John ARNOLD for King George III. He refused to make another for the Empress of Russia. The smallest watch in quantity-production was made by Jaeger-Le Coultre. The MOVEMENT has 74 parts including 15 jewels and measures just over 1.28 by 0.5cm (½ by ⅕in). In the first half of the 19th c, the Swiss made some small watches of pocket-watch style, 1.25cm (½in) and less in diameter, with CYLIN-DER or LEVER ESCAPEMENTS. Perhaps the most remarkable technically is the MINUTE REPEATER by BLANCPAIN, made at the rate of about 50 a year from 1985. The movement is 21mm (0.83in) in diameter and 3.2mm (0.13in) thick with 300 parts including over 30 jewels. The smallest component is only 0.06 by 0.03mm (0.002 by 0.001in) in size. See THINNEST WATCH.

Smeaton-Franklin dial A dial arrange-ment devised independently by John Smeaton in the U.K. and Benjamin Franklin in America c1750. A single hand turns in four hours. The dial is divided into four sectors of 60 minutes each and the user has to know which hour is indi-cated. Useful for REGULATORS as there is no motion work.

Smith and Sons, John Clockmakers of the 19th c in St John's Square, CLERKEN-WELL, who made all types of clock, including TURRET CLOCKS, and huge numbers of English SKELETON CLOCKS. Their last remaining stock of wheel blanks and PINION WIRE were sold in the 1950s, after which they concentrated on non-ferrous metals. Their headquarters are now in

Biggleswade, Bedfordshire, with a retail outlet in Kingsland, London.

Smiths (S. Smith and Sons) Samuel Smith, watchmaker and jeweller, had a business at 12 Newington Causeway, London. His son, also Samuel Smith, opened a business in the Strand by 1973, with branches in Piccadilly and Trafalgar Square. By 1900 he claimed to have watch and clock factories in Clerkenwell and Bienne and also at 13 Soho Square and Coventry. Substantial catalogues of clocks and watches were issued in 1900. By then his firm was importing foreign clocks and watches from France, Switzerland, and Germany. Smiths English Clocks Ltd., was formed in the late 1920s in Cricklewood, London, with retail premises at 179/185 Great Portland Street. Allan Gordon Smith (1881–1951), the son of Samuel, had become very active in the business, eventually taking over from his father, and was later knighted. The All-British Escapement Co. was set up in 1928. Smiths English Clocks introduced the SYNCHRONOUS CLOCK under the brand name Sectric. About 1935 they introduced a synchronous electric MYSTERY CLOCK. A year before then, they had absorbed Richard and Co. (importers) and the rump of the Williamson Clock Co., both of whose London premises were used for wholesale and retail distribution. A lack of many imported goods during the Second World War resulted in a new factory, Chronos Works, being set up in 1940 making industrial instruments, timers, etc. By 1947, Smiths were making alarm clocks in large quantities in a modern factory in Wishaw, Scotland, time switches and timers in Brighton, East Sussex, and clocks and watches in Cheltenham, Gloucestershire. Then, with government backing (because of the national interest in having a potential fuse industry) they joined forces with Ingersoll and Vickers (the armaments firm) to build a large modern factory at Ystradgynlais, in Wales, to produce watches which included the first British self-winding wrist watch. By 1963, Smiths Industries had six divisions with over 30 premises in London and the provinces, Australia, Canada and South Africa. After 1966, the organisation gradually ran down its horological activities, although at this time producing TUNING FORK battery-driven WALL CLOCKS, and by the early 1970s seem to have abandoned them. Smiths Industries is now an aerospace and medical group. Collectable items include pre-1939 alarm clocks, especially the Robin and Wren models, some pre-1939 synchronous clocks, especially striking/chiming and Wren models and original 1946 Victory alarm clocks with lead bases. It has been suggested that an interesting collection could be formed of early examples of these brands: Clarion, Tower, Enfield, Duvall, Empire and Astral movements, all but the last having been absorbed by Smiths. Other brands by B.U.C.C. (British United Clock Co.), Caledonian Registered, E. J. Lovely (Eastbourne, East Sussex) and other minor firms, too early to be absorbed by Smiths or beneath their notice, are correspondingly rare.

Smuggling Watch smuggling is caused by high import duties, taxes, and quotas, which make it profitable. It is also associated with cheap watches faking well known brands such as Rolex, Omega, etc., which have penetrated the U.S.A. in particular in alarming numbers. They are commonly made in Hong Kong and China to a recognised style and the brand names applied in Thailand or elsewhere.

Snail Cam shaped like a snail's shell. Used particularly for the hook holding the end of the MAINSPRING to the ARBOR of the BARREL, which avoids breakage by following the spiral of the spring. Also essential to RACK STRIKING (see for picture), where a snail controls the number of blows struck.

Snailing Curved lines radiating from the centre of the polished steel winding wheels in a watch, or the steel small end (the cap) of a FUSEE, used for decoration.

Snap-on cannon pinion See CANNON PINION.

Snap-on back Watch case back that snaps on. Some BEZELS are fastened similarly.

Snap-on cover   One end of a MAIN-SPRING BARREL, actually a lid that snaps into place.

Snuff-box, musical   Swiss 19th c product, very occasionally with a watch. Usually with a singing bird.

Solar-cell clock   See LIGHT CLOCK.

Solar-cell watch   In the 1970s some Swiss manufacturers made watches with silicon solar cells on the dial or nearby that kept the rechargeable power cell topped up to provide a long lasting source of power. In 1984 the Japanese-owned company Pulsar introduced an amorphous solar cell which, with a few minutes' exposure to light, charges a capacitor instead of the usual silver-oxide power cell to run the watch, calendar work and other functions, for 50 hours when fully charged. It is applied like a paint and the energy from it is stored in solid-state capacitor instead of a chemical cell. See CRYSTALONIC SOLAR WATCH.

Solar cycle   Every 28 years, the days of the month fall on the same days of the week, and this 28-year period is the solar cycle. DOMINICAL LETTERS, shown by some early clocks, indicate the first Sunday in a year and each year in the solar cycle has its dominical letter.

Solar time   Time measured by a SUNDIAL. A solar day is from the sun's highest point (MERIDIAN) on one day to its meridian on the next. Solar days vary in length throughout the year. To simplify timekeeping, the average solar day over the year, called the 'mean solar day', is taken as a standard and divided into EQUAL HOURS. MEAN SOLAR TIME at Greenwich is GREENWICH MEAN TIME. See EQUATION OF TIME.

Solar time switch   Street-lighting TIME SWITCH with a solar dial, invented by Horstmann of Bath, England, in 1904, which switches lights on and off and adjusts the switching times according to the time of year. The dial carries two cams to operate the on and off switches and is revolved by a clock. The position of the cams is altered daily by an automatic indexing arrangement. Later versions had SYNCHRONOUS MOTORS, then spring-driven again, but with automatic electrical rewinding.

Solid   balance   Straightforward BALANCE WHEEL normally made of a single metal, and therefore without BI-METALLIC COMPENSATION. Not a CUT   BALANCE.   TEMPERATURE COMPENSATION is usually effected by making the HAIRSPRING of NIVAROX or a similar alloy.

Solid banking   Instead of a BANKING PIN, part of the BOTTOM PLATE or EBAUCHE of the watch is used.

Solid-state timepiece   Electronic watch or clock with no moving parts at all, the time being shown by L.E.D. or L.C.D. numerals or light indication on a dial.

Solunar dial   From sol = sun, lunar = moon. Daily tidal times on some wrist CHRONOGRAPHS are combined with 'solunar tables' compiled by J. Alden Knight to forecast feeding times of fish and game for sportsmen. Can be set for different places. See TIDAL DIAL.

Sorguhr   Very small BLACK FOREST weight-driven PENDULUM clock with a porcelain dial 3–4cm (1.02–1.06in) in diameter. An extension on the top often bears the maker's name. Josef Sorg invented it c1800. See JOCKELE CLOCK and SCHOTTENUHR.

Souscription watch   The famous watchmaker BREGUET never made two watches alike, except for this series, which were claimed to be the cheapest very high quality watches made. They were produced in batches and subscribed for in advance. They have large enamelled dials and single hands.

Spade hand   Hand with an end like the Ace of Spades.

Spandrel   English   BRACKET   and LONGCASE CLOCKS have a circular CHAPTER RING on a square DIAL, the corners of which were at first engraved

A **sorguhr clock** with a wood and brass movement from the Black Forest. It is only 5.5mm (3¼in) wide and 10cm (4in) high.

A **souscription watch** by Breguet. It has one hand and his secret signature. (*Sotheby's*)

but very soon were filled with triangular ornaments of cast brass, called 'spandrels'. The earliest, from about 1660, had cherubs' heads and were finely chiselled. Later they became less well finished. The cherub spandrel persisted for about 100 years, but many other designs, particularly leaf and scroll, were popular. Spandrels made of brass were GILDED; occasionally they were made entirely of silver.

Spanish market clocks English BRACKET CLOCKS, some with musical and AUTOMATON movements made in the 18th c for export to Spain.

Speaking clock See TALKING CLOCK and T.I.M.

Spelter Commercial zinc; also a name sometimes wrongly used for the ELECTROTYPE used to reproduce French ORMOLU clocks in great numbers in the SECOND EMPIRE period.

Spherical watch Probably the earliest form made (see MUSK BALL WATCH). Small spherical or BALL WATCHES for women are still made to be used as a FOB WATCH or on a chain round the neck.

Spiral hairspring A HAIRSPRING of spiral form. The earliest, of untempered steel, had one and a half to two turns; by the mid-18th c there were four to five turns; modern ones have about 12 turns. The inner end is fixed by a COLLET to the STAFF (axle) of the BALANCE WHEEL. The outer end is fixed to a stud on the BALANCE COCK, or may be curved inwards as an OVERCOIL. See REGULATOR and INDEX.

Split chuck One with split sides so that it can be tightened round the workpiece. The number marked on the face of one for a watchmaker's LATHE is the diameter of the hole in tenths of a millimetre, e.g. No. 2 chuck = 0.2mm and No. 12 = 1.2mm.

Split plates Some early striking clocks had FRONT PLATES in two parts so that the striking and GOING TRAINS could be dismantled separately.

Split seconds A TIMER with two CENTRE SECONDS HANDS, one over the other, and an extra push button. The main push button starts, stops and returns both hands to zero. After the hands are started, the second push button will stop the split hand only. When pressed again, it causes this hand to catch up with the other. Useful for timing both first and second places in athletic events, or a first lap.

Spoon fitting A lever with a spoon end just inside at the top of the door of a LONGCASE CLOCK for releasing a lift-up or SLIDE-UP HOOD.

Sports timer A TIMER of pocket watch shape which is calibrated in fifths to hundredths of seconds, for athletics, or in special ways for other sports (See SPLIT SECONDS). For boxing, 3 minute rounds with 1 minute intervals are shown by the minute hand; for football 45 minutes; for hockey, 35 minutes; and ice hockey 20 minutes; for water polo, 7 minutes with an interval of 5 minutes, and for yacht races, the 5 minute interval before the starting gun is indicated. With a ROWING TIMER, ten strokes are timed and the hand then indicates the strokes per minute. See also TACHOMETER, TELEMETER and CHRONOGRAPH.

Sports timing For world events, a massive and complex operation in which a few large horological manufacturers specialise. See CAMERA TIMER, PIGEON CLOCK, SPORTS TIMER.

Spotting Decorative finish for the PLATES of clocks, watches, chronometers, and inside watch cases. Rows or patterns of spots are produced by fine abrasive on the end of a bone or ivory stick or tool that is rotated.

Spring See MAINSPRING, HAIRSPRING.

Spring barrel See BARREL.

Spring click A short spring with one end formed into a CLICK, instead of this being separate.

A **staartklok** of 1813 with part of the village and the pond painted in the arch and a domed gateway on the trunk. (*Sotheby's*)

Spring detent DETENT ESCAPEMENT for MARINE CHRONOMETERS, invented by BERTHOUD, ARNOLD and EARNSHAW. The detent or lever which releases the ESCAPE WHEEL is mounted on a spring instead of a PIVOT, which eliminates variations caused by wear of the pivot and the necessity to oil it.

Spring lugs Removable spring-loaded bars each side of a wrist watch case through which the looped ends of the strap or bracelet pass.

Springer Specialist who fits HAIRSPRINGS to BALANCES.

Spurs Spikes about 5cm (2in) long on the back of an early LANTERN CLOCK to dig into the wall on which it is hung and prevent it from moving. The clock is hung from a hook by a semicircular iron stirrup above the spurs. Later BLACK FOREST makers used small spurs on DIAL CLOCKS.

Square The squared end of an ARBOR over which a key fits to wind it. Also the squared end of a winding stem.

Staartklok DUTCH CLOCK made in some numbers from the latter part of the 18th c and through the 19th in Friesland, Holland. Looks like a large BRACKET CLOCK but is a hanging version of the Amsterdam LONGCASE CLOCK. The long PENDULUM is enclosed in a narrow trunk with a clover-leaf-shaped bottom and the brass-encased weights hang in front of

this. On top are mounted three figures, normally an angel flanked by two trumpeters. Dials are painted decoratively and the arch too, but this may have a MOON DIAL or AUTOMATA.

Stable clock Large estates often had a large clock with a dial outside above the stables. Some very early iron TURRET CLOCK movements have been found in the lofts of old stables.

Stackfreed Device introduced in the 16th c on the earliest German watches to replace the FUSEE and create a thinner watch. The crude MAINSPRING loses power rapidly as it runs down. To make power output more even, the mainspring turns a cam, on the edge of which a roller is pressed by a spring. This causes extra friction, which decreases as the mainspring runs down because the cam reduces the pressure applied by the stackfeed spring. The turns of the mainspring are also limited by STOP WORK for the same reason.

Stadium timer Large TIMER dial, usually operated electrically or electronically, for sports audiences. Calibrated for the sport concerned.

Stake Metal block with different-sized holes in it used with a set of matching punches (staking set) for making holes, riveting etc. A staking tool has a holder to keep the punch vertical.

Staff Watchmaker's name for the axle of a BALANCE.

A **stackfreed** with a long curved spring on a late 16th c table clock. Note the one-arm balance wheel and bristle regulator on the arm with arrowed end.

Staffordshire pottery   Some clock cases were made from this.

Stage-coach watch   See CARRIAGE WATCH.

Stainless steel   Nickel-chromium steel commonly used for entire watch cases and the backs of ROLLED GOLD or GOLD-PLATED cases, as it resists the acids from the skin. Often completely gold plated. The Hamilton Watch Co. in America used stainless steel rims and INVAR crossings (spokes) in their MARINE CHRONOMETER BALANCES.

Standard time   Time applying in a particular TIME ZONE, or country if this overlaps zones. In Britain, G.M.T. is standard time. Canada has five standard zones an hour apart as the country spreads over five zones. They are: Atlantic, Eastern, Central, Mountain and Pacific Times.

Standard Time Co.   See ELECTRIC PUBLIC CLOCKS.

Standardised terms   Because of confusion when ordering watch parts, the Swiss industry issued volumes of standardised names of parts in several languages in 1950 as part of a plan for standardised watch MATERIAL.

Standing barrel   A spring BARREL which remains stationary. After winding, the ARBOR turns in the opposite direction to drive the timepiece. See GOING BARREL.

Star map   Popular name for a PLANISPHERE, occasionally incorporated in later 18th c clocks.

Star transit   The time at which a star crosses the MERIDIAN.

Star watch   Watch in a star-shaped case. A famous one of c1600 was by David Ramsay, first Master of the Worshipful Company of Clockmakers. It was missing for very many years until it was sold for cash at a James Walker jewellers' branch in the 1960s and returned to the Company by the owner of the chain, J.S. Sanders.

Star wheel   Star-shaped wheel used to give positive movements of CALENDAR and other dials of clocks or watches. A V-shaped spring, called a JUMPER, causes the star wheel to jump swiftly from one indication to the next. A fixed star wheel was used in English REPEATER WATCHES and a moving star in Swiss ones until 1860 when the fixed one was introduced by two Swiss makers.

Station-house clock   Carved wooden BLACK FOREST clock of c1850 in the shape of a gable-roofed railway station. Also called a chalet clock and similar to a CUCKOO CLOCK.

Stator   Part in the magnetic field of a SYNCHRONOUS ELECTRIC CLOCK that does not move.

Steady pins   Short metal pins in a PLATE to locate a part such as BALANCE COCK, the pins fitting closely into holes in the cock. A screw holds the part in place.

Steam-engine clock   In the early days of steam, many clocks were made with cases in the shape of stationary engines in many styles, some with moving parts.

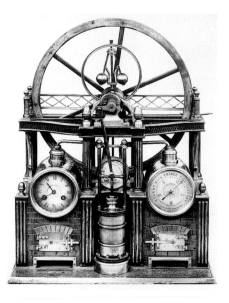

A French **steam-engine clock** that won a prize in the Paris Exhibition of 1899. The piston, large wheel and governor, have a separate mainspring.

The French perhaps introduced them during their Industrial Revolution, but many were made elsewhere. See INDUSTRIAL CLOCKS.

Steel Wrought iron (which contains separate 'free' carbon) was used in time-keepers before steel (an alloy of iron and a very small amount of carbon) was invented in the early 19th c, and gradually introduced for ARBORS, PINIONS, levers, stanchions, and many other parts.

Steep Gothic clock See SHARP GOTHIC CLOCK.

Steeple clock Another name for the American SHARP GOTHIC CLOCK style of wooden SHELF CLOCK.

Stem Winding shaft of a watch with KEYLESS WINDING.

Stem-wind watch Watch with KEYLESS WINDING.

Stepping motor Elementary miniature motor in a QUARTZ WATCH, operated by the FREQUENCY to move the hands, usually in steps in seconds for centre seconds hand watches.

Steuart corrector Arrangement of an electric motor controlled by a MASTER CLOCK pendulum invented by Alexander Steuart to control the public clocks in Edinburgh, the TIME GUN at the Castle and the TIME BALL on Cotton Hill, from the Royal Observatory at Edinburgh. Compare WAITING TRAIN.

Stirrup Iron hoop on the back of a LANTERN CLOCK to hang it from a hook in a wall. Also the wire loop on which the PENDULUM hangs on cheap clocks. Also the part of a pendulum holding the jar of mercury for temperature compensation.

Stockuhr German name for a BRACKET CLOCK.

Stoelklok Means chair clock. A Dutch clock on a stool-shaped wall bracket with a hood, and elaborate painted decoration on both case and bracket decorated, the case having top and side frets of gilded cast lead. There is a short wire PENDULUM rod with usually an oval-shaped BOB, metal pulleys, and brass-encased tapered weights on chains. It has time, strike, and alarm, and rarely a calendar or moon dial. It began to replace the ZAANDAM CLOCK at the beginning of the 18th c. Holland still produces Stoelklokken.

Stone weights Early TURRET CLOCK and some continental iron clocks, e.g. WATCHMAN'S CLOCK, had undressed stones as weights.

Stop finger See FUSEE CAP.

Stop watch A TIMER in pocket-watch form for recording time intervals. See PRODUCTION TIMER, SPORTS TIMER and SPLIT SECONDS.

Stop work Arrangement to prevent a MAINSPRING from being overwound, when the spring coils may bind together and stop the timepiece. Used also on very early watches and clocks and on musical boxes to prevent the mainspring from running *down* too much, thus causing bad timekeeping (or slow music). The most common form on a mechanical watch is the RECOILING CLICK to prevent over-winding.

'Stopper' Watchmaker's name for a watch that stops at infrequent intervals for reasons difficult to trace.

Straight grain Finish used on clock PLATES which leaves straight fine lines close together. Also used on silver dials.

Straight-line lever LEVER ESCAPEMENT with the BALANCE, lever and ESCAPE WHEEL in a straight line, common in Swiss and American watches. The classic English lever has a right-angle escapement.

Strap A leather strap to hold a watch to the wrist, invented by an Englishman, A.E. Pearson, for soldiers who wanted wrist watches during the First World War. It was perhaps invented almost simultaneously in Germany. An early strap had a leather cup to hold the watch. Then loops were soldered to the watch case to take loops in the strap. LUGS are most common today. A spring-loaded bar between a pair of lugs passes through a loop in the strap. Straps are often padded with turned-in edges, being sewn with thread or nylon and/or glued. Leathers, pigskin, crocodile and other skins are used as well as fabric and plastics. The strips of metal that hold the movement in the case of some French clocks are also called straps. See WRIST WATCH.

Strap hinge Iron hinge that looks like a strap, used on the inside of early LONG-CASE CLOCK doors.

Strap work Decoration of interlaced straps used in carving, fretwork and MARQUETRY on some, usually longcase, clocks. It is an arabesque style.

Strasbourg Cathedral clock Elaborate ASTRONOMICAL and AUTOMATON CLOCK in Strasbourg Cathedral, France, first erected in 1354, reconstructed by Isaac and Josias HARBRECHT in 1574 and redesigned and rebuilt by J.R. Schwiligué in 1842. It incorporated a mechanical globe and a mechanical cock that crows three times at noon, now removed and in a museum.

Strike/silent dial Small auxiliary dial with a hand that can be moved to silence the striking.

Striking, Roman See ROMAN STRIK-ING.

Striking clock Clock that sounds the hours on a bell or GONG. Very early clocks did this without indicating the time on a dial. See SALISBURY CATHE-DRAL CLOCK. The striking train is separate from the GOING TRAIN of gears, being released by it at the hours by a system of pins and levers incorporating a LOCKING PLATE or later, a RACK. See CHIMING CLOCK. The rate of striking is controlled by a fast rotating FLY, a form of air brake.

Striking jack Full name of the JACK or figure that strikes a clock bell.

Striking rack See RACK STRIKING.

Stringing Narrow strips of inlay often used near the edges of cases of wood, particularly REGENCY and BALLOON CASES and the doors of LONGCASE CLOCKS. Wider inlays are called 'banding'.

Strut clock A portable TRAVELLING CLOCK with a hinged strut at the back like a photograph frame. Invented c1845 by Thomas Cole, brother of James Ferguson COLE (the 'English Breguet'). The metal case is thin and elaborately decorated, and often had a Swiss watch MOVEMENT. Other makers adopted the style in various shapes, some with pierced frames. Forerunner of the CALOTTE.

Stud Fixed post on which a lever pivots or wheel turns. Also the pin to which the outer end of a HAIRSPRING is fixed.

Stutzuhr A clock not intended to stand on its own, but to be mounted in, say, a piece of furniture.

Style Another name for a GNOMON.

Su Sung's clock MONUMENTAL CLOCK made in 1088 by a Chinese, Su Sung. It had one of the first known ESCAPEMENTS, a water wheel controlled by two steelyards or weigh bridges. The clock was 9–12m (30–40ft) high. On top was a huge power-driven ARMILLARY SPHERE of bronze and inside a room with an automatic CELES-TIAL GLOBE. A five-storey pagoda on the front had doors through which JACKS appeared every quarter hour ringing bells and holding tablets to indicate the hours. The clock consumed ½ ton of water in nine hours, and also contained the earliest ENDLESS CHAIN, oblique gearing, long transmission shafts, cup bearings, and telescopic drive.

Submarine clock INDUSTRIAL CLOCK of the 20th c in this shape with a clock on the side. Some were torpedo-shaped.

Subscription watch See SOUSCRIP-TION WATCH.

Subsidiary dial Extra dial on or near the main one. Some give extra information, e.g. ASTRONOMICAL CLOCK dial, CALENDAR DIAL, EQUATION DIAL, MOON DIAL, PLANISPHERE, seconds dial, UP-AND-DOWN DIAL, TIDAL DIAL, WORLD TIME DIAL. Others are controls, e.g. CHIME/CHIME SILENT, CHIME SELECTOR, STRIKE/ SILENT DIAL, TUNE SELECTOR, and one on some clocks regulates the PENDULUM (See BELL TOP for picture).

Sugar-tongs compensation Two bi-metallic strips fixed at one end and with CURB PINS on the other ends to regulate timekeeping in varying temperatures.

Sully, Henry (1690–1728) Clever but unlucky maker who travelled on the Continent after his apprenticeship and became friendly with Julien LE ROY. He took 60 English watchmakers and their families to Versailles and later St Germain to improve French standards of craftsmanship, but had financial and health problems. Invented the OIL SINK and a marine timekeeper. French revolutionaries removed most of the inscription on his memorial in St Sulpice Church, Paris, which gave him credit for helping the French industry.

Summer Time STANDARD TIME which has been advanced by one hour in the U.K. See DAYLIGHT SAVING.

Sun-and-moon watch Watch with an unusual dial, which appeared about 1700. The minute hand is normal. Hours are shown by an image of the sun travelling round a semicircular slot marked from 6 a.m. to 6 p.m. An image of the moon follows, showing the hours from 6 p.m. to 6 a.m.

Sun-and-planet wheel Epicyclic gear where a toothed wheel runs around another which is fixed. Used in ASTRONOMICAL CLOCKS, ORRERIES and later ASTROLABES to achieve high gear ratios. There is a practical limit to the number of teeth on normal gears. Also used in EQUATION, SIDEREAL TIME and UP-AND-DOWN DIALS. Joseph WILLIAMSON (d.1725) was probably first to use such gearing in clocks.

A **sun-and-moon dial** on a watch by Jack Holman of Lewes, dated 1804. (*Sotheby's*)

Sunburst clock WALL CLOCK with a case imitating sun rays around the BEZEL usually in gilded metal or wood. Also called 'sunray'.

Sunburst hands Clock or watch hands with small 'suns' near the ends, often the hour hand only. Popular in the French Directoire period (1795–1799). Revived on Normandy LONGCASE CLOCKS in the 19th c. The Swiss also used them on watches at this time.

Sundial Method of showing time by shadows cast by the sun according to its direction (COMPASS SUNDIAL), or height in the sky (ALTITUDE SUNDIAL). The earliest were probably Egyptian and spread to the Roman (about 290BC) and Greek Empires. A popular early type was the HEMICYCLIUM. England's earliest sundials are Saxon, and on Bewcastle Cross, Cumberland (c670), and Kirkdale Church, Yorkshire (1060). PORTABLE SUNDIALS were also made from early times. Early sundials showed TEMPORAL HOURS. From the mid-14th c they began to show EQUAL HOURS after an Arab mathematician, Abu'l Hassan, calculated that the GNOMON should be parallel to the Earth's axis. After mechanical clocks were introduced, the sundial remained in use as a master by which to set them. During the 17th and 18th c the best clocks were supplied with portable sundials. In 1980 *Vox Latina* reported the find in the middle of Rome by archaeologists of a 60m (65ft) diameter sundial of the 2nd c AD with a Greek inscription. See ANALEMMA, NOON MARK, SCRATCH DIAL.

Sunk seconds Small recessed seconds dial in a main watch dial to give clearance to the hour hand and enable the watch to be made thinner. If the hour hand circle is sunk too, the dial is DOUBLE-SUNK.

Sunray clock See SUNBURST CLOCK.

Sunrise-and-sunset dial One indicating these changing times at a certain latitude.

Sunrise and sunset dial (the bottom round ones) on a clock by Boxall, Brighton. The dials above them give day and date. Note the Brocot escapement.

Supplementary arc After an ESCAPE WHEEL IMPULSES a PENDULUM in one direction, it escapes and begins to impulse it in the other. The pendulum does not stop dead, however; it continues for a little under its own momentum in a supplementary arc until the swing is reversed.

Surprise piece Safety device in a REPEATING WATCH, such as that in a minute repeater to make sure no minutes are repeated at the quarters.

Suspension Flexible or pivoted mounting of a PENDULUM, usually by a SUSPENSION SPRING. Early VERGE clocks had KNIFE-EDGE SUSPENSION (like a weighing machine). SILK SUSPENSION is another form.

Suspension block or bracket A usually massive PLATE or BAR from which a PENDULUM is hung, especially when fixed to the back of the case, as in a REGULATOR, and not to the MOVEMENT. The pendulum is usually hung from the BACK COCK in a domestic clock.

Suspension spring Short length of clock spring on which a PENDULUM hangs. Possibly invented by William CLEMENT, 1671. French clocks usually had SILK SUSPENSION until c1880.

Swag Decoration such as a festoon of drapery or wreath of flowers or leaves which looks as if it might swing. Often carved, applied or inlaid. Typical of the Adam period.

Swan's neck cresting S-shaped form common on the tops of LONGCASE CLOCKS and occasionally BRACKET CLOCKS from near the end of the 18th c until recent times. Also common on American SHELF CLOCKS. Another name is 'horned cresting'. See GRANDMOTHER CLOCK for picture.

Swatch On 1 March 1983, the Swiss makers E.T.A. announced a quartz watch with the parts reduced from 91 to just 51. Called the Swatch, it was produced to compete with the Japanese, who had taken most of the cheaper end of the market. Many special designs have been produced subsequently, including mechanical MOVEMENTS, a SELF-WINDING watch in 1992, and later one with an integrated radio receiver. Yearly sales reached 20 million by 1993 and there is a Swatch Collectors' Club with 75,000 members world-wide.

Sweep seconds Centre seconds hand sweeping the whole dial.

Swing clock Late 18th c French novelty clock in which the PENDULUM is a model of a child or cupid on a swing, moving to and fro instead of from side to side. Farcot made a number from 1858 to 1862, some with GARNIER escapements. Also called 'swinging doll clock'.

Swinging clock Novelty MYSTERY CLOCK in which the spring-driven clock movement is the top BOB of a COMPOUND PENDULUM and a second normal bob is the lower part. It has KNIFE-EDGE SUSPENSION or is suspended on two steel points above the centre. The pins rest in small cups. In the back of the movement is a small pendulum only a few centimetres long with an ANCHOR ESCAPEMENT. This keeps the whole swinging and controlling time by action and reaction. Made in the 19th and early 20th c in Germany and America. One version is an elephant with extended trunk holding the clock-cum-pendulum. The ANSONIA company made at least seven versions of classical Greek draped female figures and two of men holding the pendulum with the dial on top in a raised arm. In other versions, the compound pendulum is held by a mahogany pillar, or swings in front of a mirror.

Swinging doll clock See SWING CLOCK.

Swiss horological industry Geneva goldsmiths of the 16th c were the first Swiss watchmakers and in the next centuries they specialised in ENAMELLED watches. When the Huguenots were driven from France in 1685, many watchmakers went over the mountains

An American **swinging clock** named the 'Huntress' by the Ansonia company.

into Switzerland. The chief workers were the *cabinotiers*, who turned their own homes into workshops. The Swiss soon adopted the GOING BARREL instead of the FUSEE, and auto raced mechanisation (see INGOLD), particularly in the Neuchâtel area, which started them towards becoming the world's biggest and finest watchmakers. The advent of the ELECTRONIC WATCH left the Swiss unprepared and allowed the Japanese and Americans to take the lead. However, by buying in and then rapidly developing an electronic capacity, followed by reor-

The **Swiss horological industry** once depended on *cabinotiers* working at home in their *ateliers*. This is a life-sized reproduction of a typical home workshop.

ganisation of the industry itself, the Swiss were able to take the lead again alongside Japan. They were effectively saved by the strong brand names they had established, which allowed them breathing space while under attack. The industry is almost entirely in the Valley of the Loire and the Jura mountains.

Swiss lever STRAIGHT-LINE LEVER escapement with CLUB-FOOT ESCAPE WHEEL teeth to divide the LIFT between the PALLET and the TOOTH. BREGUET introduced it in 1793.

Swiss wrist watches, collecting 20th c From the 1980s, as a backlash against cheap and impersonal QUARTZ wrist watches, even the expensive ones, there was an increasing demand for high quality Swiss mechanical watches of the 1920s and 1930s, causing their prices to leap. The demand spread to watches manufactured as late as the 1950s. Top auction houses devoted sales entirely to such watches. A PATEK PHILIPPE calendar watch with moon phase in a platinum case, which cost about £75 when made in 1935, fetched £308,000 at Sotheby's as long ago as February 1990. Such prices are much more than what was being offered for watches and clocks of great antiquarian value. Excellent as such watches are as examples of the art of the watchmaker, their current second-hand prices reflect nostalgia and fashion rather than antiquarian interest. Unrealistic 'investment' values were put on many 20th c fashion and novelty items, including perhaps watches. Other makes in demand include AUDEMARS PIGUET, BREGUET (later as well as the famous earlier ones), CARTIER, JAEGER LE COULTRE, OMEGA, ROLEX, ULYSSE NARDIN, and VACHERON AND CONSTANTIN.

Sympathetic clock See PENDULE SYMPATHIQUE.

Synchronome clock See HOPE-JONES.

Synchronous electric clock Electric clock dial operated from the main supply frequency (50 Hz in the U.K. and 60 Hz in the U.S.A.). Invented by the American H.E. Warren in 1918. Technically it is a SLAVE CLOCK which keeps in step with the generators at the power station. It gained a poor reputation for timekeeping during the Second World War when frequencies often dropped, making clocks slow. Some early ones such as those by Ferranti, Garrard, Goblin, Metamec, SMITHS and Horstmann (time switches) and American ones by Hammond, Ingraham, the Morse Chain Co. (the

Poole), and the Barr Manufacturing Co. are now collected.

Synchronous motor   A mains-driven electric motor constructed so that its speed depends on the mains frequency. See SYNCHRONOUS ELECTRIC CLOCK.

T

T.A.I. International Atomic Time. See ATOMIC TIME.

T-end Some MAINSPRINGS have a T-shaped end pivoting in the BARREL ends.

T.I.M. Original TALKING CLOCK of the British Post Office which spoke the exact time when 'T.I.M.' (now 123) was dialled on the telephone. Inaugurated in 1936, it was accurate to 0.1 seconds and the first voice was Ethel Cain's. In 1984, Brian Cobby's voice took over. The original apparatus was controlled by a FREE PENDULUM and the voice announcements were built up from a series of recordings on glass discs. Paris was the first city to have a speaking clock in 1933.

T-rest T-shaped piece attached to TURNS or a LATHE on which to support a cutting tool.

Tabernacle clock Miniature TOWER CLOCK 15–23cms (6–9in) high, made in the 16th and 17th c. The MOVEMENT was similar to that of a LANTERN CLOCK, but driven by a MAINSPRING and FUSEE instead of a weight.

Table clock Most common form of early clock of the late 16th and 17th c, being drum-shaped, or later square or hexagonal, with feet. Separate ALARM mechanisms were common on early ones. Hexagonal table clocks, in particular, were made in Germany well into the 18th c.

A spring-driven alarm **tabernacle clock** of 1611 with concentric hour chapters I to XII and 13 to 24, with quarter-hour divisions. (*Sotheby's*)

A Dutch **table clock** of c1650 by Egbert Jansen. The outer hand indicates the time and the inner one sets the alarm.

Tablet dial   See DIPTYCH DIAL.

Tachometer   Scale, sometimes combined with a wrist CHRONOGRAPH, to show speed over a given distance. Records the speed in m.p.h. or k.p.h.

Tact watch   Montre-à-tact made by BREGUET for blind people. The watch cover has fixed studs to mark the hours, and a movable pointer which, when turned clockwise by the wearer, is stopped at the correct time and can be felt in relation to the knobs. It was a cheaper alternative to a REPEATER.

A **tact watch** for a blind owner devised by Breguet.

Taille douce   Engraving in very fine lines.

Talking clock   Domestic clock that 'speaks' the time. The earliest were made about 1914, comprising a clock MOVE-MENT, a speech record on a band, an acoustic head, a gramophone needle and horn. Now electronic. See T.I.M.

Talking watch   A watch giving the time to a second, the date and an alarm, by a synthesised voice was launched early in the 1980s by National Electronics and

Watch Co. Hong Kong, mainly for the blind.

Tall clock   Original American name for a GRANDFATHER CLOCK. See LONG-CASE CLOCK.

Tambour (or **tambourine watch**) Another name for a DRUM WATCH or canister watch, the case being like a round tin with the MOVEMENT hinged to it and a perforated lid.

Tammeter   TIME RECORDER used to provide 'Tam ratings' of television audiences. Invented by Bedford Attwood, it records on magnetic tape the times a television receiver is switched on and off.

Tandem-drive barrel   A single spring BARREL that provides two drives, one for the GOING TRAIN (i.e. for timekeeping) and the other for striking or alarm work.

Tangent screw   Worm gear with small indicator dial used to SET UP the MAINSPRING in a FUSEE timepiece which began to replace the RATCHET and CLICK from the second quarter of the 17th c. First mounted on the TOP PLATE, then c1675 between the plates.

Tape chronograph   Early instrument for comparing the RATES of clocks, CHRONOMETERS, and STAR TRAN-SITS. In the simplest instrument, a timekeeping mechanism moves a paper tape under two pens which draw straight lines on the paper. Each pen can be given a jerk by an electromagnet connected to a clock or TRANSIT INSTRUMENT. Therefore humps in the lines compare the rates.

Taper pin   Early method of holding the front plate of a clock or BOTTOM PLATE of a watch to its PILLARS. Iron or steel (occasionally brass) round tapered pins are tapped into holes across projecting ends of the pillars. Also used for FALSE PLATES and dials. Flat, tapered strip wedges (wedge pins) were the earliest fastening in the 14th c, particularly for TURRET CLOCKS. Taper pins were in use until this century, when they were gradually replaced by studs and screwed nuts.

Tardy of Paris Publisher of books on French clocks.

Tavern clock Original name for a COACHING CLOCK or ACT OF PARLIAMENT CLOCK which were in use well before the TAX ON TIMEKEEPERS.

Tax on timekeepers In 1797, William Pitt introduced a tax of 5 shillings (25p) a year on every clock, 10 shillings (50p) each on gold watches, and 2s 6d (12.5p) on silver watches. Clock- and watchmakers had to take out licences. This increased the popularity of the tavern clock, which became known as the ACT OF PARLIAMENT CLOCK. At the same time there was a 'plate tax' existing on gold and silver watch cases. Both Acts were repealed the following year.

Tea-maker alarm Unit comprising a rocking platform with a fixed electric kettle at one end and a teapot at the other. Water in the kettle under a sealed lid keeps that end down. A tube from near the bottom of the kettle exits at the top and over the teapot. There is an alarm clock and a lamp at one side. Before the alarm sounds, the kettle is switched on, and when it boils, hot water is poured by steam pressure into the teapot, which rocks the platform to that end. The kettle is turned off, the light on, and the alarm sounds. There are simpler versions.

Telemeter Scale sometimes combined with a wrist CHRONOGRAPH to record the distance of an event seen and heard, such as a thunderstorm. The recording hand is released when lightning is seen and stopped when the thunder is heard, the hand then indicating the distance away of the storm.

Teflon Trade name of polytetrafluoroethylene (P.T.F.E.), a very low-friction plastic used to coat some parts, e.g, MAINSPRINGS.

Telephone timer A special ELAPSED TIME INDICATOR for use with telephones. Some give the cost of the call.

Telleruhr Literally a 'plate clock'. Made in the 16th and 17th c in Germany (particularly in AUGSBURG) and Austria. Usually hung on the wall but occasionally stood on a pedestal. The flat metal DIAL is in an approximately pear-shaped metal FRAME with elaborately shaped edges, REPOUSSÉ decoration, and sometimes a silver or pewter CHAPTER RING. In some, the short PENDULUM hangs over the front of the dial. The hands are usually elaborately pierced. See TROPHY CLOCK.

A German **telleruhr** in a repoussé case with a silver dial and front pendulum. (*Christie's*)

Tell-tale clock Alternative name for a WATCHMAN'S CLOCK.

Tellurium (or tellurion) Mechanism showing the rotation of the Earth, its orbit round the sun and the effect of its tilted axis, sometimes mounted on a clock. Compare ORRERY.

Temperature coefficient of frequency The change of rate in a QUARTZ CRYSTAL as used in a quartz timepiece with a change in temperature. A typical one is 10 parts in a million a year over a range from 10° to 40°C.

Temperature compensation Method of avoiding TEMPERATURE ERROR, i.e. timekeeping variations at different temperatures, which affect PENDULUMS, BALANCES and springs, QUARTZ CRYSTALS, and most other time standards. COMPENSATION PENDULUMS are designed to keep the lengths invariable. A balance and a HAIRSPRING are affected separately and differently by temperature changes, which is a complication. HARRISON first applied compensation to hairsprings by employing an arrangement like his GRIDIRON PENDULUM to vary the tension of cylindrical hairsprings; then by developing a COMPENSATION CURB for spiral springs. Many developments have been made in COMPENSATION BALANCES for use with hairsprings of differing metals and alloys.

Temperature error Timekeeping error caused by variations in temperature. With a standard one-second pendulum of nearly 100cm (39.14in) long, a 2°C change in temperature causes a change of +/-1 sec/day. A COMPENSATION PENDULUM can eliminate this error. The effect is more complicated with a BALANCE and spring. For watches with brass BALANCE WHEELS and carbon steel BALANCE SPRINGS, the error can be 60 times as great, but it depends on the size of the components and the vibrations per hour. See COMPENSATION BALANCE.

Temporal hours The Egyptians split natural daylight into a number of hours (12) and night time into the same number, and this was adopted by other countries. A daylight hour was therefore different from a night hour and both varied at different times of the year. They were only equal at the EQUINOXES. A temporal daylight hour varies from 50 to 70 minutes in northern Egypt. In London the variation is from 39 to 83 minutes. Early SUNDIALS showed temporal hours. EQUAL HOURS came into general use in European towns between 1350 and 1400 and sundials were scaled accordingly. See MEAN TIME and JAPANESE CLOCKS. Before the 14th c, however, astronomers were dividing a day-and-night period into 24 hours.

Tension spring Term sometimes used incorrectly for FRICTION SPRING.

Terminal curve Curve given to the outer end of a spiral HAIRSPRING to improve ISOCHRONISM.

Terrestrial globe Globe of the Earth driven by a clock. See CELESTIAL GLOBE.

Terry, Eli (1772–1853) American pioneer, the first to mass produce clock MOVEMENTS successfully anywhere. These had wooden PLATES and WHEELS. In partnership with SETH THOMAS, then Simon Hoadley. See PILLAR-AND-SCROLL CLOCK and WOODEN MOVEMENT for pictures.

Testing See RATING CERTIFICATE, TIMEKEEPING TRIALS, KEW A CERTIFICATE and QUALITY STANDARDS.

Testing standards The criteria used for the timekeeping of mechanical watches are ISOCHRONOUS error (see ISOCHRONISMS), POSITIONAL ERROR, TEMPERATURE ERROR and DAILY RATE. There are other standards for the WATER-RESISTANCE of cases.

Tête-de-poupée clock (see overleaf) Type of 17th c French clock reminiscent of a doll's head.

Thermal dial Used on a TIME SWITCH to make or break electric contacts at a given time at a preset temperature.

Thin longcase clock Longcase clock 1.8m (6ft) or more high with a trunk only about 20cm (8in) wide. Some are 18th c, but these cases were also made from about 1840 to take the MOVEMENTS of LANTERN CLOCKS, usually with BOB PENDULUM and ALARM. Such lantern clocks originally had ARCHED DIALS and spiked feet.

Thinnest watch Thin watches are elegant and fashionable. They were made as early as the start of the 18th c by Daniel QUARE. The thinnest mechanical wrist watch movement in quantity production was 1.18mm (0.046in) thick. A SELF-

French **tête-de-poupée** clock in a Boulle case with brass and red tortoiseshell inlays in a pewter ground. It is by Gabriel du Val, Paris, and strikes a single blow at the half-hour. (*Christie's*)

WINDING WATCH only 2.5mm (1/10in) thick and a minute repeater only 3.2mm (1/8in) thick were also made in Switzerland. Extra thin movements are sometimes made into COIN WATCHES. The thickness of quartz MOVEMENT is controlled by the cell size but has approached that of mechanical watches. See SMALLEST WATCH.

Third wheel   Third wheel of a movement counting the BARREL as first and CENTRE WHEEL as second. When there is no centre wheel, that driven by the barrel is still called the 'third wheel'. See THREE-WHEEL TRAIN.

Thirty-hour clock   Clock which runs about 30 hours at one winding and is intended to be wound daily. A few early LANTERN CLOCKS ran for only 12 hours or so. Later clocks went for eight days or more, and cheaper ones 30 hours.

Thomas, Seth (1744–1859)   American clockmaking pioneer who joined TERRY and Hoadley after being apprenticed as a carpenter and joiner. Later he made a fortune on his own with factories producing clocks, brass and wire. He introduced rolled (instead of cast) brass plates. His longcase clock factory powered by water was perhaps the first mass-producing factory. The movements were of wood. Perfected the SHELF CLOCK.

Thoth   Egyptian moon god who was also divider and reckoner of time and had the head of a bird, the ibis.

Thousand-day clock   The Buhl and KUNDO clocks of the 1920s were called by this name and then it was applied to small, battery-operated pendulum clocks of the mid-20th c with TRANSISTOR switching which would run for 1,000 days on one cell.

Threaded pivot   PIVOT that is threaded and works in a threaded hole. Used for small parts such as a CLICK or power that oscillates occasionally, particularly in low-priced American timepieces because of the simplicity of construction.

Three-legged   gravity   escapement   Accurate GRAVITY ESCAPEMENT for TURRET CLOCKS. Two long gravity arms, pivoted at the top, impulse the pendulum one way and then the other. Each arm has a stop on it to hold up one leg of the three-legged escapement wheel. When the pendulum swings to the right, the escape wheel is released to lift and lock the right gravity arm. This arm is then released to give the pendulum an opposite impulse. The original form was the double three legged invented by Lord GRIMTHORPE and used in BIG BEN.

Three-month clock   Some LONGCASE CLOCKS made in the 18th c ran for this period.

Three-quarter plate Watch MOVE-MENT of the 19th c having the TOP PLATE with about a quarter cut away, to enable separate mounting of the BALANCE and spring under a BALANCE COCK for easier removal.

The **three-quarter plate** movement of a fine leyless lever watch by John Kellie, Liverpool. (*Dr Vaudrey Mercer Coll.*)

Three-train clock One with three TRAINS of gears, the middle one for time of day, with striking on the left and chiming on the right.

Three-wheel train Weight-driven clocks running for 30 hours have in the TRAIN a MAIN WHEEL turned by the weight, a THIRD WHEEL, and an ESCAPE WHEEL only. An hour wheel driven from the main wheel pinion turns the hour hand.

Three-year clock A SKELETON CLOCK which needed to be wound only every third year was exhibited by John Pace of Bury St Edmunds, Suffolk, at the Universal Exhibition of 1851. It had six MAINSPRINGS and, when wound up, the main BARREL turned once in 210 days. Others have been made over the years.

Throw A simple hand-turned LATHE used by watch and clockmakers. Work is held between dead centres (i.e. not rotating) and turned in one direction, unlike that in a bow-operated TURNS. A large wheel with a handle drives, by cord, a small loose pulley on the turns which is clamped to the work (by a 'dog') to turn it. Old makers had separate, permanently fixed bench wheels near a vice into which the throw was clamped when needed. It was in considerable use in the 18th and 19th c for many parts and is still used by some restorers.

Thumb screws Screws usually of brass, with large heads, in the base of a clock case, for levelling, turned by the thumb.

Thuret, Isaac (d. 1706) *Horologer du Roi* to Louis XIV (1643–1715), he made the first model of the spiral HAIRSPRING invented by HUYGENS. Others made claims that he was the inventor, so he wrote to Huygens to apologise.

Thuya wood Soft close-grained wood from Africa that is brown with mottled and curled figuring like amboyna wood. Used for veneering and inlay.

Thwaites and Reed Generations of Thwaites from 1735 eventually became Thwaites and Reed of CLERKENWELL in 1808, making clock MOVEMENTS through the 19th c for many other clockmakers, including more famous ones than themselves such as Dwerrihouse, EARNSHAW, ELLICOTT and VULLIAMY. Also makers of TURRET CLOCKS until well after the mid-20th century. The first of the family was Ainsworth, who marked his movements 'A. Thwaites'; then from 1795 Ainsworth and John Thwaites (marked A & I); John Thwaites (marked I. Thwaites); and finally from 1808 to 1940, Thwaites and Reed (marked T & R). The name still survives, the firm eventually having been purchased by F.W. Elliott, Croydon clockmakers. T & R records are in the Worshipful Company of Clockmakers' collection in the Guildhall Library, London. See SIGNATURES. See PAINTED DIAL for picture.

Tic-tac escapement Small ANCHOR ESCAPEMENT which extends over only two teeth of the ESCAPE WHEEL. Used on French and some early English clocks with BOB PENDULUMS. Also called a 'drum escapement'.

Tick Sound made by the release and arrest of a TRAIN of gears by the ESCAPEMENT, made by as many as 40 different sounds in a watch. Ticks vary from 'tocks' because alternate PALLETS arrest the ESCAPE WHEEL and different parts of the MOVEMENT resonate. The sound of a watch tick lasts about 15 MILLISECONDS.

Tick amplifier The sound of a watch tick can indicate many different faults. Watch repairers sometimes use amplifiers to diagnose them.

Ticka pocket watch Not a watch, but a camera made from c1902 to 1907 to look like a watch, for spying or candid camera shots. The 'winding button' was the lens, enabling 25 postage stamp sized pictures to be taken.

Ticket clock Rather like a cylindrical CARRIAGE CLOCK, but shows the time in figures on celluloid tickets, of which there are two sets, one above the other, for hours and minutes. The tickets are like leaves of a book which flip over at the minutes and hours. Invented in 1903. Also called a 'flick leaf clock' or 'Plato clock'.

Tidal dial Indication on some 18th c LONGCASE CLOCKS of times of high and low tides, often shown on the MOON DIAL. The Moon causes tides, so the same mechanism can show tides. Another version was a rising and falling plate representing the sea, operated by a cam, invented by James FERGUSON. They were useful in times when rivers and coastal waters were the principal means of transport. Tidal dials on modern TIME SWITCHES control the flow of sewage or factory effluent into the sea by opening a valve when the tide goes out.

Tide The Saxons divided a day into eight tides, shown by their SUNDIALS. We still use 'noontide' and 'eventide'. The tides were: Morgan 4.30a.m.–7.30a.m.; Daeg-mael 7.30a.m.–10.30a.m.; Mid-dag 10.30a.m.–1.30p.m.; Avenverth dagr 1.30p.m.–4.30p.m.; Mid-aften 4.30p.m.–7.30p.m.; Ondverth nott 7.30p.m.–

10.30p.m.; Mid-niht 10.30p.m.–1.30a.m.; and Ofanverth nott 1.30a.m.–4.30a.m.

Tiffany clock Ornate 2.4m (8ft) LONGCASE CLOCK with 25 dials made in 1893 and now in the Time Museum, Rockford, Illinois, U.S.A. Shows EQUATION OF TIME, GOLDEN NUMBER, EPACT, DOMINICAL LETTER, WORLD TIME, sun cycle, etc.

Tight-rope walker An AUTOMATON clock topped by a glass case showing a tight-rope walker dancing on a rope.

Timby solar timepiece American style TERRESTRIAL GLOBE clock made from 1863 to 1870.

Time No one has succeeded in defining time satisfactorily. It is a concept of mind, representing a change from order to disorder (entropy). It is not absolute. According to the theory of relativity the RATE of a clock depends on the situation of the observer, e.g. a clock in an artificial satellite approaching the speed of light goes at a slower rate measured from the Earth than measured from the satellite. Passage of time is measured by referring to a recurring phenomenon, such as the rotation of the Earth, oscillation of a heavenly body, the vibration of a PENDULUM, BALANCE, QUARTZ CRYSTAL, molecule or atom. Two kinds of time are in ordinary use: time of day and duration of time interval. Living things have built-in BIOLOGICAL CLOCKS.

Time ball World's first accurate TIME SIGNAL, which was installed at the ROYAL OBSERVATORY, Greenwich, in 1833 by John Pond for shipping in the Pool of London. The ball was a wooden frame 1.5m (5ft) in diameter, covered with leather. Originally it was dropped at noon. Then, because noon was occupied with observations of the sun, it was wound halfway up to the top of a mast on the north-east turret at 12.58, and dropped down the 4.5m (15ft) mast at exactly 1p.m. by a trigger release. After 1852, the ball was released automatically by an electric signal from an OBSERVATORY CLOCK. In 1853, one was provided at Deal for ships in the Downs, and others followed at Devonport, Plymouth, Portland, etc. One was erected in the Strand, London, for chronometer makers. The present Greenwich ball is of aluminium on a 9m (30ft) mast and is still operated, but by the National Maritime Museum.

Time determination   Determining exact points in time as accurately as possible for TIME DISTRIBUTION. The fundamental unit of time is the period the Earth takes to rotate on its axis, which is a day. It was once measured by timing the sun from noon on one day to noon on the next, as with a SUNDIAL, but days were found to vary in length (see SOLAR TIME). Then astronomers began observing a CLOCK STAR instead, to obtain SIDEREAL TIME by taking an observation with a TRANSIT INSTRUMENT and comparing the going of the Earth with the going of the OBSERVATORY CLOCKS by means of a TAPE CHRONOGRAPH. Clocks proved to be more accurate timekeepers than the Earth, showing up irregularities in its rotation (see NUTATION and PRECESSION OF THE EQUINOXES), and its slowing down (See LEAP SECOND). Mean sidereal time is sidereal time corrected for these irregularities and can be converted to mean solar time for general use. Time is even more accurately determined from observation of the Earth's orbit, which provides EPHEMERIS TIME and is converted to mean solar time for public consumption. A SATELLITE LASER RANGER is now employed to measure the Earth's rotation using a composite time scale derived from a co-ordinated network of ATOMIC CLOCKS in different parts of the world.

Time distribution   After TIME DETERMINATION, it has to be distributed. The TIME BALL was the first attempt, then the TIME GUN. Electrical distribution began after the Shepherd clock was installed at Greenwich, the public dial at the Observatory gate being the first SLAVE DIAL. It sent signals to a similar clock at the nearby Naval College, to a dial at London Bridge railway station, and to the Electric Telegraph Co. to

release a time ball in the Strand. The Self-Winding Clock Co. of New York, and Normallzeit Gesellschaft, of Berlin, set up electric wires to railway stations, CHRONOMETER makers, and elsewhere. A synchronising signal at a certain time forcibly corrected the hands on the hour. In 1925, Greenwich Observatory installed a SHORTT FREE PENDULUM clock and began broadcasting TIME SIGNALS twice daily from the Post Office transmitter at Rugby. Currently in Europe, continuous time signals are broadcast from M.S.F. Rugby, operated by British Telecom, using time from the ATOMIC CLOCK at the National Physical Laboratory, Teddington, until recently. There are also signals from Mainflingen, near Frankfurt, Germany. Such signals can be picket up audibly by longwave receivers, but are mainly used to monitor radio-controlled clocks, which not only set themselves to time if they deviate, but can also interpret other coded signals to indicate date, month and change over to Daylight Saving, etc. The first commercial models were exhibited by Junghans at the Basle Fair in 1985 and were available in the U.K. from August 1988. Other radio-controlled German and Japanese clocks and watches followed. The U.S.A. has a similar system but the great distance from east to west makes control uncertain. See RADIO TIME SIGNAL and T.I.M., TIME SIGNAL.

Time division   It is believed that division of the hour and degree into 60 parts originated with Babylonian astronomers some 20,000 years ago, who used the sexagesimal system for counting, and perhaps because 60 is divided evenly by 2, 3, 4, 5, 6, 10, 12, 20 and 30.

Time globe   American style TERRESTRIAL GLOBE clock made from c1867–86.

Time gun   Gun fired as a TIME SIGNAL, such as that on Edinburgh Castle. Not as accurate as a TIME BALL because of the sound delay. The earliest guns were fired by the sun's rays to give a SOLAR TIME signal. The time guns at Newcastle and Shields were fired by batteries connected to the CHRONOG-RAPHER at the Post Office.

Time lock Special safe or strong-room lock that enables the door to be opened only after a certain time. Invented by James Sargeant in the U.S.A. in 1872. Early time locks are wound with a clock key when the door is open and set for a certain period of time. When the door is shut and the bolts thrown, the time lock blocks the bolt mechanism until the time has elapsed. Usually two or more clock mechanisms are used in case one should stop.

Time recorder Clock which gives a permanent record of certain events. The first was Whitehurst's WATCHMAN'S CLOCK. In 1885 an American, Bundy, invented a clock that printed the time when keys were inserted, to 'clock in' employees. The modern factory version is controlled by a MASTER CLOCK and automatically stamps cards with the time at which they are inserted, being used for job costing as well as employee control. Another version, compulsory on certain transport vehicles, records the periods of time that they are in motion. See TACHOMETER.

Time service See TIME DISTRIBU-TION.

Time signal Indication of a specific time, usually by a visual or aural signal. Those who wanted private time signals such as the CLERKENWELL CHRONOMETER makers, rented galvanometers from the Post Office at the turn of the 20th century. An electric signal known as the 'time current' deflected the needle twice a day at an exact hour. See CHRONOGRAPHER, RADIO TIME SIGNAL, T.I.M., TIME BALL and TIME GUN.

Time stamp Rubber date stamp which also prints a dial and hand showing the time of stamping. It incorporates a time-piece. Some have DIGITAL DISPLAY. Can be self-contained or be controlled by a MASTER CLOCK. The Warwick Time Stamp Co. was the earliest maker.

Time   switch A   clock-controlled mechanical, electric or electronic switch

for turning processes on and off at prede-termined times. Some have SOLAR DIALS to adjust to times of daylight in the year. First were hand-wound mechan-ical clocks, then electrically rewound clocks, synchronous clocks and QUARTZ CLOCKS. Later versions can control very sophisticated programmes. See ELEC-TRIC   TIME   SWITCH,   GAS CONTROLLER, SOLAR TIME SWITCH.

Time zone If countries employed LOCAL TIMES, then time of day would change with the smallest journey east or west. So in 1884 the world was split into 24 time zones of 15° each. The principal one is 7.5° each side of the Greenwich Meridian. Each zone successively west became an hour earlier and each zone east an hour later. The centre of the zone on the side of the world opposite Greenwich is the DATE LINE. Countries which fall in two zones declare for one or the other, and big countries have several STANDARD TIMES. There are also other local variations including DAYLIGHT SAVING See GREENWICH MEAN TIME, U.T.C., WORLD TIME DIAL.

Timer Pocket watch or clock for measuring short time intervals. The earli-est, in the 18th c, had an arm which pressed against a WHEEL in the mecha-nism to stop it. The first watch in which the hand returned to zero was shown by Nicole and Capt at the London Exhibition of 1862. The push button of a pocket timer is pressed once to start the hands, again to stop them, and a third time to return them to zero. The accuracy depends on the BEAT of the BALANCE. One beating one-fifth of a second is accu-rate approximately to that. For greater accuracy, balances beating up to one-hundredth of a second, and occasionally more, were used. Today the quartz timer gives high accuracy at low cost. See SPORTS   TIMER,   PULSE   METER, TACHOMETER, TELEMETER, SPLIT SECONDS,   DECIMAL   TIMER, PRODUCTION TIMER and CHRONO-GRAPH. A clock timer can also have hands that return to zero. See PROCESS TIMER, INTERVAL TIMER, ELAPSED TIME INDICATOR and TIME SWITCH. For sportsmen, skin divers, airline pilots and others needing to judge time intervals, there are watches showing elapsed time from when they are set.

Timekeeper Any person responsible for timekeeping for any purpose such as recording times in sports events or at a factory. See SPORTS TIMING. Used loosely for TIMEPIECE.

Timekeeping trials Special competitions for the performance of timepieces under strict conditions, including tests in differing positions, ovens and refrigerators. In the 18th and 19th c the most important ones were run by the ROYAL OBSERVATORY for MARINE CHRONOMETERS. The most important trials for mechanical watches were controlled by the Geneva and Neuchâtel Observatories, and the prizes were monopolised by Swiss makers and ADJUSTERS. The QUARTZ WATCH has largely eliminated this form of competition.

Timepiece Strictly, a clock or watch showing time of day only and not having striking or chiming.

Timex quartz watch The earliest QUARTZ WATCHES had DIGITAL DISPLAY for novelty and because the power was insufficient for hands. The first Timex quartz ANALOGUE watch of 1975 was a reliable low-priced alternative, now collectable. Instead of a PIN-PALLET ESCAPEMENT pulsing the BALANCE WHEEL, a 49,152Hz QUARTZ CRYSTAL does so. The BALANCE then operates as a STEPPING MOTOR so that its pin pallets actually drive the hands.

Timing a balance and spring To time a BALANCE and spring before fitting it, hold it by tweezers on the dial of an accurate watch and count its BEAT to the seconds dial.

Timing machine Another name for a RATE RECORDER.

Timing screws Screws around the rim of a CUT BALANCE. Also called 'mean time screws'. There are four to adjust the

RATE, since the balance swings more slowly when they are screwed outwards. They are placed at 90° to each other (and also called 'quarter screws') starting from the ends of the arm of the balance. Other screws in the rim are adjusted for TEMPERATURE COMPENSATION and POISING.

Timing washers Tiny washers placed under the screws in the rim of a BALANCE to adjust the RATE at which it swings and also to correct POISE errors.

Timing weights Sliding weights on a CUT BALANCE to adjust TEMPERATURE COMPENSATION.

Tinder-lighter clock See MATCHLOCK CLOCK.

Ting tang Most ancient form of chime on two bells, sometimes struck by two QUARTER BOYS giving one blow on each at quarter past, two at half past, three at a quarter to, and four before the hour. The first bell has a higher note. The HAMPTON COURT CLOCK is ting tang. The system is also used in REPEATER WATCHES.

Tipsy key Winding key for chronometers and watches with a RATCHET so that it could not be turned backwards. Also called a 'BREGUET key'. See BREGUET for picture.

Tip relief Removal of some of the tips of wheel teeth to lessen the chance of jamming.

Tôle clock French version of the SEDAN CLOCK of the early 19th c about 38cm (15in) in diameter with a lacquered or enamelled case.

Tompion, Thomas (1639–1713) Usually regarded as the most famous of all English clock- and watchmakers. Born at Ickwell Green, Northill, Bedfordshire, and trained as a blacksmith, but went to London and became a clockmaker, setting up at 'The Dial and Three Crowns', Water Lane, Fleet Street. Collaborated with Dr HOOKE. Made the first clocks for the ROYAL OBSERVATORY at Greenwich in

1675, the first EQUATION CLOCK, now in the ROYAL COLLECTION, and a YEAR CLOCK as well as the RECORD TOMPION for King William III. Invented a forerunner of the CYLINDER ESCAPEMENT for watches with BARLOW and William Houghton. Became famous in his own time, particularly for watches, of which he produced about 5,500. He made about 650 clocks and also barometers and other instruments. Buried in Westminster Abbey. Succeeded by George GRAHAM. A previously unknown clock by Tompion was found in Canada and sold by Christie's for £880,000 in 1989. It was a NIGHT CLOCK (c1678–80) in a boxwood and ebony PARQUETRY 1.8m (6ft) tall case. Sold at the same auction was probably the first of his four VERGE BRACKET CLOCKS (c1678) with RISE-AND-FALL regulation. See BATH TOMPION, and GRANDE SONNERIE for picture.

Tompion Medal Gold medal awarded for outstanding achievement in horology made from time to time, on the proposal of Gilbert Dennison, by the British Horological Institute. The early awards were to W.H. SHORTT in 1954 (see FREE PENDULUM), Dr Warren Marrison in 1955 (see QUARTZ CLOCK), and Dr Louis Essen in 1957 (see ATOMIC CLOCK).

Tonneau Rectangular wrist-watch case with curved sides and BEZEL, but straight ends, named after the horse carriage shape.

Tools and materials, traditional Old clock- and watchmakers had to forge and shape iron and cast brass from raw copper and zinc. They relied on a forge and anvil, hammers, chisels, punches, files, gravers, burnishers, hacksaws, scrapers, gravers, drills, screw plates and taps, draw plates (for producing wire), a vice, rolls (for rolling sheet), a soldering iron, calipers, rules, compasses, steel points (for marking out) a sand box (for casting plates), wooden and lead patterns of wheels etc., for casting, templates etc, as well as some of the special tools listed below. In earlier times they made their own tools. See ABRASIVE, ADJUSTING ROD, ARKANSAS STONE, BALANCE LATHE, BALANCE WHEEL ENGINE, BARREL ENGINE, BENCH KEY, BLUESTONE, BONE ASH, BOXWOOD, BRASS, BREGUET KEY, BUSHING TOOL, CHALK, CHENIER, DEMAGNETISER, DEPTHING TOOL, DIAL PRINTER, DIVIDING PLATE, DOG SCREW, DOUZIÈME GAUGE, FOUNTAIN OILER, FUSEE ENGINE, GALLOWS TOOL, GLASS BRUSH, GRAVER, HEEL BALL, HOLE-CLOSING PUNCH, HORSE, INDIA OILSTONE, INGOLD FRAISE, JACOB'S CHUCK, JACOT TOOL, LATHE, MAINSPRING GAUGE, MAINSPRING WINDER, MANDREL, MARTIN SCREW PLATE, MONTGOMERIE STONE, OIL POT, OILER, OILSTONE, OILSTONE DUST, PEGWOOD, PITH, PIVOT POLISHING TOOL, PIVOTING TOOL, PLIERS, POISING (DYNAMIC), POISING TOOL, POLE LATHE, RATE RECORDER, REBUSH, RESTORATION, ROTTON STONE, ROUGE, RUNNER, SCREW PLATE, SECTOR, SHEARS, SPRINGER, STAKE, STRAIGHT GRAIN, THROW, TICK AMPLIFIER, TOOTH-TOPPING TOOL, TURNING FRAME, TURNS, TWEEZERS, ULTRASONIC CLEANER, UNDERHAND POLISHING, UNIVERSAL KEY, UPRIGHTING TOOL, VIBRATING TOOL, VICE (BENCH), WATCH TIMER, WATCHMAKER'S LATHE, WATER-OF-AYR STONE, WHEEL-CUTTING ENGINE, WINDER (BENCH).

Tooth-topping tool After WHEEL teeth had been cut in a WHEEL-CUTTING ENGINE, the tops of adjacent teeth were rounded up (or topped) using a special file with opposite concave surfaces, held in a slide to guide it.

Toothless ratchet wheel WHEEL without teeth that cannot be reversed because of a wedging action against a small roller or similar device.

Top plate Traditional name for the PLATE in a watch farthest from the dial, which is on top when the dial is down. In other words, the BOTTOM PLATE is the one under the dial!

Top weight American name for the small weight used to regulate a precision clock PENDULUM. See REGULATION.

Torpedo clock French INDUSTRIAL CLOCK in the shape of a torpedo.

Torque Power produced by a coiled spring or twisted rod.

Torsion pendulum PENDULUM that twists on its SUSPENSION SPRING instead of swinging to and fro. It uses the TORQUE of the spring instead of gravity for its restoring force. Has a slow BEAT, therefore consuming very little power, so that it is used for FOUR-HUNDRED-DAY CLOCKS. Invented by Robert Leslie in 1793. Also used in the ATMOS CLOCK and the Tiffany Neverwind. See LIGHT-HOUSE CLOCK for picture.

A Tiffany 'Never-Wind' battery clock with a **torsion pendulum**. (*J.E. Coleman, U.S.A.*)

Tortoise clock Bowl of water, with hours marked round the rim, in which a metal 'tortoise' floats, to indicate the time. The tortoise is moved round the edge by a magnet turned by clockwork in the base. Invented by Servière. Should be 'turtle

clock'! A more recent version has a duck in a tiny pond. Also called a 'magnetic clock'. One of the MYSTERY CLOCKS.

A **Tortoise clock** signed Gübelin, Lucerne. The floating tortoise indicates the time. (*Christie's*)

Tortoiseshell Thin slices used occasionally to veneer English BRACKET CLOCK cases from c1700 and also on French Buhl cases.

Touch knobs Touch pins or feeling knobs were provided at hours' positions

Touch knobs round the dial of a night clock of the first half of the 15th c from Nuremberg. The dial has 16 'hour' divisions. (*Germanisches Nationalmuseum, Nuremberg*)

on clocks from the early 16th c for telling the time at night. See BLIND MAN'S WATCH.

Tourbillon A watch ESCAPEMENT has POSITIONAL ERRORS. To even out those in vertical positions and improve the RATE, BREGUET invented in 1801 an arrangement for pocket watches in which the entire escapement was mounted on a platform which revolved, usually once a minute, round the fourth wheel. He called it a 'tourbillon'. George DANIELS still makes them in the U.K. See KARRUSEL.

Toutin, Jean (1578–1644) A worker in ENAMEL in Châteaudun, France, who devised a method of painting with enamels which was an improvement on the earlier LIMOGES methods. Used for watch cases, which were first enamelled white, next painted in colours, fired again, then fired once more with transparent glaze.

Tower clock Another name for a TURRET CLOCK.

Tower of Babel clock Famous ROLLING-BALL CLOCK representing the famous tower, made by Hans Schlottheim for Emperor Rudolf II between 1595 and 1604. A crystal ball ran round a spiral track in a minute to unlock the ESCAPEMENT and was restored to the top by a spring-operated conveyor belt.

Tower of the Winds Octagonal tower at Athens, each side representing a wind and having an inclined sundial. Originally housed a clepsydra or WATER CLOCK. Built c100BC.

Trade signs Early clockmakers, like all tradesmen of the time, indicated their business by signs or symbols to advise customers who could not read. Only public houses do so now. TOMPION'S was 'The Dial and Three Crowns', Graham went to 'The Dial and one Crown' in Fleet Street, and was followed there by Mudge. Pinchbeck has a more literal sign in Fleet Street: 'The Astronomico-Musical Clock'.

Train Series of engaging WHEELS and PINIONS as used in a timepiece; thus the GOING or timekeeping train, striking train and chiming train. The gear ratio is very high, being stepped up in mechanical clocks and stepped down in SYNCHRONOUS ELECTRIC ones. The train of an eight-day clock with going train comprises the MAINWHEEL, the CENTRE WHEEL and PINION, the THIRD WHEEL and pinion, and the ESCAPE WHEEL and pinion (plus the MOTION WORK). The striking train and the chiming train are separate from the timekeeping train. A watch train follows the same pattern as a clock with the addition of a fourth wheel (from which a small off-set seconds hand is sometimes driven before the escape

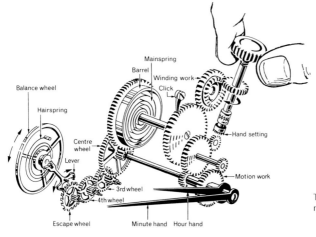

The typical **train** of a mid-20th c mechanical wrist watch.

wheel). A centre seconds hand is driven by the fourth wheel which is concentric with the centre wheel. A month clock has an intermediate wheel and pinion between the main wheel and centre wheel with a step-up ratio of 4:1 so that instead of eight days it runs for 32 days. Also it is wound in the opposite direction. A watchmaker identifies a train by the number of ticks per hour (the BEAT), most watches usually having an 18,000 train, also referred to as 'a count of 18,000'. See FAST TRAIN. To provide the power needed to drive a BALANCE without a spring, very early timepieces had a THREE-WHEEL time train, the CONTRATE WHEEL being driven by a five-leafed pinion.

Transistor   Transistor switching was the first step from electric to electronic time-pieces. The French LIP ELECTRIC WATCH of 1956 was the first watch in which it was employed.

Transistorised pendulum   The first application of electronics to a clock was when the French firm A.T.O. changed the electric contact on the pendulum of a BATTERY CLOCK for a transistor in 1956.

Transit   Apparent movement of a star when the Earth rotates.

Transit instrument   Special telescope rigidly fixed in an east–west direction, but capable of being swung north–south. It is adjusted to point to a CLOCK STAR each time the Earth rotates. Hence intervals between seeing the same star are 24 hours of SIDEREAL TIME. The astronomer turns a hand-wheel to move a 'wire' (actually made from spider's web) across the eyepiece in time with the apparent star movement. This operates electric contacts which make blips on the moving paper tape of a TAPE CHRONO-GRAPH, which also records seconds from the OBSERVATORY CLOCK for comparison. Very accurate observations can be taken of some clock stars by the photo zenith tube, which is connected to the observatory's SIDEREAL CLOCK and photographs star transits and clock records.

Transparent clock   During the Directoire and EMPIRE periods (1790–1830), French makers sometimes used glass for clock PLATES and WHEELS, particularly for SKELETON CLOCKS.

Transporting a clock   Moving a spring-driven clock with PLATFORM ESCAPEMENT within a house presents no problems, except for the need to wedge the BALANCE with a piece of folded tissue paper to stop the clock, which should be cushioned for longer journeys. The same applies to a MARINE CHRONOMETER but two opposing tissue-paper wedges would be better. Lock the gymbal system; there is a lever to do this. A weight-driven PENDULUM clock must be transported with the pendulum and weights removed, otherwise severe damage will be done to it. If it is a LONGCASE, first remove the hood and put it on the floor with the glass towards to the wall to avoid kicking it. This will be moved separately. If necessary, fasten the door firmly with sticky tape. Remove the pendulum carefully using both hands round the MOVE-MENT to lift the spring out of the PENDULUM COCK. Make sure the spring does not catch on the CRUTCH. Fasten the pendulum to a strong strip of wood of the same length with sticky tape for separate transport. Wind the clock almost fully to retain the lines on their barrels. Remove the weights and label the left one 'strike' and the right one 'going'. If there is a middle one, the three weights must be labelled 'strike', 'going', and 'chime' from left to right as they may be of different weights. If the SEATBOARD is firmly fixed and the MOVEMENT safely fastened to it, they can be moved with the clock. If the seatboard is not fastened, move it carefully forwards to remove it and the movement for separate transport. Follow the relevant parts of the same procedure for a spring-driven clock with pendulum such as a French ORMOLU clock or MARBLE CLOCK. Open the back and unhook the pendulum; then wedge the CRUTCH with a piece of folded tissue paper to stop the spring from working overtime. Remember that marble clocks can be very heavy. See SETTING UP A CLOCK.

Travelling case Soon after the PORTABLE CLOCK was invented, cases were made in which to carry them safely. Some for DRUM CLOCKS, made of tooled leather with locks c1550, still exist. The practice continued for all shapes and sizes of clocks into the CARRIAGE CLOCK era in the 19th c. Wooden boxes were often leather covered, except those for MARINE CHRONOMETERS.

Travelling clock Spring-driven non-pendulum clock for travelling. Formerly a CARRIAGE CLOCK which fitted into a special case, or a SEDAN CLOCK. Now a CALOTTE and usually an ALARM. Today usually electronic. See PENDULE D'OFFICIER.

Travelling watch Large 17th–19th c watch for carriage use. See CARRIAGE WATCH.

Treatments and finishes See BANDING, BARLEYCORN, BASSE TAILLE, BLACK POLISH, BLOIS ENAMEL, BLUING, BOULLE MARQUETRY, CHAMPLEVE ENAMEL, CLOISONNÉ ENAMEL, DAMASCENE, EBONISE, ENAMEL, ENGINE TURNING, ENGRAVING, FRENCH PLATE, FRENCH SILVERING, FROSTING, GADROONING, GARTER BACK, GILDING, GOLD DIPPING, GOLD FILLED, GOLD LEAF, GOLD PLATING, GRAINING, GREY, GRISAILLE ENAMEL, GUILLOCHÉ, GUNMETAL, HARD ENAMEL, HARD GOLD PLATING, HIGH BRASS, JAPANNING, LACQUER, LACQUER GILDING, LIMOGES ENAMEL, MARQUETRY, MERCURIAL GILDING, NACRE, NIELLO, ORANGE SHELLAC, ORMOLU, PAPER DIAL, PARQUETRY, PIQUÉ, PLANISHING, POLISHING, PRINKED, RELIEF ENAMEL, REPOUSSÉ, ROCOCO, ROLLED GOLD, ROSETTE, SEAWEED MARQUETRY, SILVERING, SNAILING, STRAIGHT GRAIN, STRAP WORK, TORTOISESHELL, TUDOR ROSE, TULIP DECORATION, VELVET DIAL, VENEER, VERNIS MARTIN, WATER GILDING.

Trial number Number used to express the performance of chronometers and watches in Observatory trials.

Trickle escapement One used to slow down striking or some other action instead of a FLY or speed governor. Often like a TIC-TAC ESCAPEMENT without a PENDULUM.

Trimmer A tiny capacitor used to adjust a QUARTZ CRYSTAL watch to more accurate timekeeping frequency. A crystal cannot be produced absolutely accurate and the trimmer will alter the resonant frequency of the circuit just enough to 'trim' it.

Triple-cased Watches for the TURKISH MARKET often had an extra outer case over the PAIR CASE.

Triple complication CHRONOGRAPH, REPEATING WORK and PERPETUAL CALENDAR with a MOON DIAL in one watch.

Tripping If a mechanical watch is badly adjusted or is given a sharp twist, a tooth may trip so that the BALANCE is given two IMPULSES instead of one. The swing increases and teeth keep tripping so that the watch gains rapidly. Also the term used for the rapid motion of a clock CRUTCH when the PENDULUM is removed.

Trophy clock Another name for a plate clock or TELLERUHR, as these had name plates on each side of the dial surround for engraving when used as prizes in Germany. The same clocks were often wedding presents.

Trottoise Direct-drive seconds hand, usually a centre seconds hand.

Troubadour case French style in the EMPIRE period (1800–30) and after, influenced by the flamboyant Gothic churches. Also called 'Cathedral style'.

Trumpeter clock Of similar origin to the Black Forest CUCKOO CLOCK but the bellows blow trumpets instead of cuckoo notes. Some also operate drums at the hours.

Trunk-dial clock A development of the ENGLISH DIAL which, when the

PENDULUM was incorporated, became the DROP-DIAL CLOCK. The LONG PENDULUM improved the timekeeping and it became the trunk dial clock, but still a hanging WALL CLOCK.

Trunnion The short rod through the end of a SUSPENSION SPRING to hold a pendulum on its BACK COCK.

Tubular chime Chime on lengths of tube in a LONGCASE CLOCK. A late development, from the end of the 19th c.

Tudor rose Decoration used in some early English clocks before c1675, a rose being engraved in the centre of the dial.

Tulip decoration Decoration, such as FINIALS and ENGRAVING on English clock MOVEMENTS and cases in the 17th and 18th c, often included tulips because of the Dutch influence.

Tulip hand Very early style with an end of tulip shape.

'Tulip' Tompion Famous GRANDE SONNERIE bracket clock made by Thomas TOMPION about 1680 and so called because the FINIALS on top of the case are like tulips.

Tumbling pallet verge Attempt by some makers such as LE ROY in Paris and Larcum Kendall (1721–95) in London, to reduce the considerable RECOIL of the VERGE by using IMPULSE faces 180° apart. Known as the 'Flamenville escapement' in France. Another attempt to solve the problem was the CROSS-BEAT ESCAPEMENT. See also DEBAUFRE ESCAPEMENT and GRASSHOPPER ESCAPEMENT.

Tumbling tourbillon Revolving ESC-APEMENT (such as the TOURBILLON or KARRUSEL) that also turns at right angles to its other rotation to eliminate even more POSITIONAL ERRORS. First demonstrated at a lecture in October 1979 by its maker Richard Good, of Seaford, East Sussex, who subsequently designed a triple tourbillon movement, with the escapement rotating in all three planes. The same result was independently

Tubular chimes in a longcase clock of the 1950s.

achieved by Anthony G. Randall, of Eastbourne, East Sussex. Examples by both makers are exhibited at the Time Museum, Rockford, Illinois, U.S.A.

Tune selector Auxiliary dial on a MUSICAL CLOCK with tune names and a moveable hand to select the tune to be played at the next hour.

Tuning-fork watch First practical electronic watch, introduced by the Bulova Watch Co., U.S.A., in 1960, but invented by a Swiss, Max Hetzel. Timekeeping was guaranteed to a minute a month. A tuning fork, about 2.5cm (1in) long, is kept vibrating at 360 cycles a second by coils of 16,000 turns of wire and a miniature battery all within a normal-sized watch. A tiny pawl on the tuning fork drives a wheel of less than 2.5mm (1/10in) diameter with 300 teeth, which turns the hands without apparent jerks. There is no tick, but a high-pitched hum, and only 12 moving parts against 19 in an ordinary and 25 in a SELF-WINDING wrist watch. The power consumed is eight-millionths of a watt. Used for TIME SWITCHES in early artificial satellites. There are still small, but fixed, POSITIONAL ERRORS in two positions of up to +/-5 sec/day.

Tuning-fork clock A tuning fork kept oscillating by electric pulses was devised in London in 1923–4 to measure short intervals of time accurately. It was called a phonic chronometer. The most successful version was the MAGNETIC ESCAPEMENT version devised by C.F. Clifford of Horstmann, Bath, U.K. Japanese makers employed it and also SMITHS in the U.K., who called their clock the Accutyne.

Turkish market Turkey began buying English clocks from before 1700 and several London makers were concentrating on it in the mid-18th c. LACQUER and TORTOISESHELL cases were popular as were MUSICAL CLOCKS playing on bells or pipes. Turkish numerals were used. Makers included Christopher Gould, Markwick and Markham, and George Prior. Edward Prior made many watches for the Turkish market.

Turning angel The clock of old St Paul's Cathedral turned the figure of an angel to point to the sun (whether obscured or not) to indicate the time.

Many clocks for the **Turkish market** such as this were made by Marwick and Markham, London working between c1725 and c1805. (*Sotheby's*)

Turning frame Frame with fixed centres to hold work while rotating it by a bow in one hand and cutting it with a graver in the other. Watchmakers call this arrangement TURNS. If driven by an endless cord using a hand-wheel or treadle, it becomes part of a THROW.

Turnip watch Popular name for the thick silver watches made by the English in the 19th c, usually with VERGE ESCAPEMENT and a deeply convex glass. Austrian examples were called VIENNA PIES. See OIGNON.

Türler cosmic clock Very complicated astronomical clock completed in 1995 for the Zürich watch dealers, Türing, in the Lucern workshops of Jörg Spöring to the design of Dr Ludwig Oechslin, who designs ULYSSE NARDIN astronomical watches. It stands 2m (6ft 6in) high and the four dials show: (1) the sun and moon rising and setting, SOLAR TIME on a 24-hour CHAPTER RING and eclipses of the

Sun and Moon; (2) a TELLURION showing the Earth in its ECLYPTIC (engraved
with the zodiac and the months) circling
the sun in SIDEREAL TIME and itself
being orbited by the moon every 27 days 7
hours and 43 minutes; (3) the PLANETAR-
IUM, which is a version of the ORRERY,
the nine planets orbiting the sun in correct
eccentric orbits (except for Pluto's extreme
one, indicated by a hand) – the times of the
various orbits are correct, Pluto's being
nearly 248 years; (4) mean time by one-
second pendulum, giving hours, minutes,
seconds, year, decade, century and mille-
nium. The perpetual calendar works on a
400-year GREGORIAN cycle. On top is an
ARMILLARY SPHERE with the Earth as
the centre of the universe and the planets
in concentric revolving spheres, the outer
one completing a revolution in 25,794
tropical years representing the PRECES-
SION OF THE EQUINOXES. The gear
ratio between this and a half-beat of the
pendulum is 10^9.

Turns Elementary form of LATHE used
by watch- and clockmakers for centuries.
It comprises two fixed points, the
'centres' between which the work is fixed.
A bow of cane turns the work backwards
and forward, the gut 'string' being given
a turn round it. The watchmaker holds
his cutting tool with one hand and 'bows'
with the other. It is very accurate but was
almost entirely displaced by the THROW,
and then the watchmaker's lathe, except
in non-industrial countries.

Turntable clock Heavy clock on a
turntable base, so that it can be easily
rotated to adjust the PENDULUM from
the back. Edward EAST, Thomas
TOMPION, Joseph KNIBB and Daniel
QUARE all made such clocks with
PILLARS on all four corners and the back
of similar design to the front.

Turret clock General name for a large
public clock, although many early ones
were in the bodies of churches, not in
the tower or turret. Originally called
'great clock'. First made in the 13th c
(see   SALISBURY   CATHEDRAL
CLOCK). The FRAMES were then heavy
wrought-iron cages which degenerated
to   BEDPOST   and   other   POSTED
FRAMES. A particularly English type of
clock had a VERTICAL FRAME. The
flat-bed form, invented in France, is
now universal. See FLAT-BED MOVE-
MENT for picture. After GRIMTHORPE,
more and more had GRAVITY ESCAPE-
MENTS (see for picture), LONG
PENDULUMS and, in this century,
AUTOMATIC WINDING, which avoids
a long chute for the weights and the
need for a CLOCK WINDER. Some are
electric, operated from a MASTER
CLOCK; others are SYNCHRONOUS
ELECTRIC although this is not ideal for
public clocks because such clocks stop
during power cuts. Also called a 'tower
clock'. See PIN-WHEEL ESCAPEMENT
(picture).

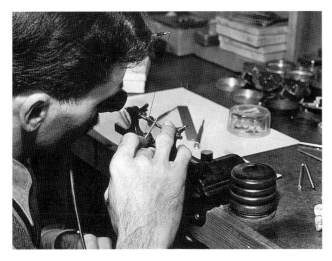

A watchmaker using a **turns** at
Thomas   Mercer's   marine
chronometer factory at St Albans
in the 1950s.

Tweezers   A large variety of tweezers is available for watch and clock work, from very fine ones with pointed ends for HAIRSPRINGS to curved, angled and square-ended ones.

Two-day chronometer   See MARINE CHRONOMETER. Two-day clocks were made occasionally.

Two-hand clock   Came into popular use c 1660 after the invention of the PENDU-LUM. Only very rare previously. See ONE-HAND CLOCK.

Two-pallet escapement   The great majority of ESCAPEMENTS have two PALLETS which are joined, but this term was originally used when the PALLETS were not physically joined as in the 'tumbling pallet' of A. Thiout (1692–1767), the CROSS-BEAT, the GRASSHOPPER and the GRAVITY ESCAPEMENTS.

Two-plane lever   Watch ESCAPEMENT

of 1803–4 by John Grant where the PALLETS move *across* the ESCAPE-WHEEL teeth, somewhat like the PIN-WHEEL ESCAPEMENT for clocks.

Two-seconds pendulum   A pendulum BEATING two seconds, which is about 4m (13ft 4in) long. It is more accurate with longer duration of going for the same weight fall than a shorter one. Thomas TOMPION used them in his clocks for the ROYAL OBSERVATORY in Greenwich. B.L. VULLIAMY made a number of clocks with them from about 1816 including those at Horse Guards Parade, HAMPTON COURT, the Cremille (Victualling Yard), Plymouth, Christ Church, Oxford and Basingstoke Parish Church and Town Hall. Clocks by other makers with two-seconds pendulums are those at Westminster Palace (BIG BEN), ST PAUL'S CATHEDRAL, Birmingham University, Lisburn Cathedral, Co. Down and over a dozen more over the country. See LONG PENDULUM.

U

U.T.C. International name for Co-ordi-nated Universal Time used to measure the Earth's rotation and provide time of day. Based on the atomic year adopted by ten countries, including the U.K. and the U.S.A. at 0hr 0min 0sec on 1 January 1958. More accurate measurement of irregular-ities in the Earth's rotation, caused GREENWICH MEAN TIME to be replaced by U.T.C. on 1 January 1972. Leap seconds were introduced to be used when needed (the first being in October 1972) because the Earth is also slowing down. See GREENWICH TIME SIGNAL, T.I.A., TIME ZONE.

Ulm Early German watchmaking centre. The main ones were NUREM-BERG and AUGSBURG.

Ultrasonic cleaner Machine for clean-ing watch and clock parts by agitating their cleaning liquid at very high frequency such as 20,000 cycles a second. A transducer is used to energise the fluid in a small tank.

Ulysse Nardin Name of a man of 24 who, after a short apprenticeship with a well-known chronometer maker, set up his own business in 1846 high in the Jura mountains north-west of Neuchâtel to make alarm watches and MARINE CHRONOMETERS which over the years won 4,800 awards and prizes for the family. They were used by around 60 shipping companies. However, the economic crisis of the 1970s and the advance of QUARTZ CRYSTAL technol-ogy caused financial failure and Rolf Schnyder, with a group of investors, took over the company in 1983 and produced a remarkable complicated astronomical watch for the 1985 Basle Fair. It has five hands turning at different rates on the same axis, and appeared on the title page of the *Guinness Book of Records*. This was followed in 1988 by the Planetarium Copernicus, which showed the solar system with five moving planets. Both were designed by Dr Ludwig Oechstin, who later designed the GMT + World Timer, on which the hours, but not the minutes, can be changed by an ingenious mechanism.

Unadjusted Watches imported into America attracted a lower tariff if regu-lated but not fully adjusted and were stamped 'unadjusted' on the plate.

Unbreakable glass A watch 'glass' made of Perspex, Plexiglass, or other plastics material. See GLASS.

Unbreakable watch spring One made of an alloy tougher than carbon steel, usually containing such alloying metals as nickel, chromium, cobalt, manganese, molybdenum and beryllium.

Uncut balance A BALANCE WHEEL with a complete uncut rim. See OVALIS-ING BALANCE.

Under-compensated State of a watch that gains in low temperatures and loses in high ones.

Under-dial work Mechanism such as MOTION WORK mounted between the DIAL PLATE and the dial itself. Also called 'cadrature'.

Undercut BALANCE STAFFS and PINIONS were often cut back (grooved) at sharp corners, originally to retain oil (although later this was discovered not to work), and later for artistry, as seen in CHRONOMETERS and fine watches.

Underhand polishing Method of obtaining a flat polished surface by rubbing part, cemented to a flat tool if small, on a flat polishing lap.

Underslung chimes Chiming rod gongs mounted underneath a movement.

Undersprung Where a HAIRSPRING is mounted underneath the BALANCE WHEEL instead of above it, as is common with FULL PLATE movements.

Unequal hours See TEMPORAL HOURS.

Uniform time Time that has been corrected for all known irregularities. See UNIVERSAL TIME, EPHEMERIS TIME and TIME DETERMINATION.

Universal clock WORLD CLOCK or world time clock.

Universal Genève Formed as wholesalers in 1894 under a different name, the firm started manufacturing watches named Universal from bought-in parts in 1934. Twenty years later, they moved to Geneva and added that to the company name. From 1952 to 1957 they registered five important patents, the most remarkable of which was a small winding ROTOR that could be incorporated in the MOVEMENT, enabling them to make what was then the thinnest automatic wrist watch in the world. See SELF-WINDING WATCH. Their Janus watch has dials on each side to show time in two different time zones. The front one is orthodox. The back one has JUMPING HOURS in an aperture. Subsidiary dials indicate whether it is day or night.

Universal joint A joint in a shaft that allows the shaft to be bent but still able to be rotated. Its main application in horology is in LEADING-OFF WORK. An early TRAVELLING CLOCK was hung from a universal joint to allow for the swaying of the coach.

Universal key Winding key able to fit different sizes of winding squares.

Universal ring dial Two flattened rings, pivotted diametrically at right angles to each other. The outer one represents the

MERIDIAN and the inner one the equator. The outer one carries a pivoted bridge with a moveable cursor and when the dial is correctly aligned, a spot of sunlight will shine on the inner surface of the inner ring to indicate LOCAL SOLAR TIME.

Universal sundial Most sundials are designed to work in only one latitude. See GNOMON. A universal one can be adjusted to any latitude. See UNIVERSAL RING DIAL.

Universal Time Correctly, Co-ordinated Universal Time. See U.T.C.

Universal time dial Alternative name for WORLD TIME DIAL.

Unlocking Part of the action of a LEVER ESCAPEMENT, when the BALANCE WHEEL is freed to be given an IMPULSE.

Up-and-down dial Dial indicating the state of the winding. The first MARINE

A striking carriage clock of c1900 with two **up-and-down dials** by A. Nicole Nielsen, London. (*Christie's*)

CHRONOMETER that MUDGE made in 1774 had one. By about 1820, a marine chronometer without one was very rare. BREGUET used them occasionally on watches, and in the 1950s, one Swiss manufacturer introduced them for SELF-WINDING WATCHES. Easy to fit to a FUSEE movement, but a GOING BARREL needs DIFFERENTIAL GEAR-ING. See MARINE CHRONOMETER for picture.

Uprighting tool A 19th c tool comprising a platform to which work is clamped. It has upright guides to hold a drill, centre punch, etc., exactly square to the work. Similar earlier tools had hollow runners with drilling spindles.

Urn clock One shaped like a vase, first popular in France in the Louis XVI period and right through the Directoire and EMPIRE periods to about 1830. There is often a REVOLVING BAND marked with hours under the rim. A figure, animal or pointer indicates the time. Some had fixed hours and minutes and moving hands.

Urn finial FINIAL shaped like an urn or vase and used as decoration on the tops of some English BRACKET CLOCKS.

U.S.A. horological industry See AMERICAN HOROLOGICAL INDUSTRY.

Usher collection Well-known watch collection in Lincoln, England.

Usher and Cole One of the last English MARINE CHRONOMETER makers, with Frodsham and MERCER (the very last).

Ut tensio, sic vis Law of the spring, discovered and thus stated by Robert HOOKE, meaning 'as the tension is, so is the force', or the force produced is directly related to the tension.

An **urn clock** of the Louis XVI period. The blue urn is on a white marble base. (*Sotheby's*)

V

Vacheron and Constantin One of the few remaining Swiss makers who produce all their own parts and MOVEMENTS, assembling them in their own factory. Founded in Geneva by 24-year-old Jean-Marc Vacheron in 1755, the company claims to be the oldest watch manufacturer in the world with uninterrupted production. It began producing the newly developed wrist watches in the 1900s, receiving orders for the American forces. Although making some complicated watches and producing the thinnest watch in the world at the time 2.45 mm (1/10in) to celebrate their 200th anniversary, they have continued to concentrate on more orthodox watches of high quality.

Vacuum case Sealed clock or watch case from which air has been largely evacuated. Used mainly for high-precision pendulum clocks. (See RIEFLER and SHORTT) to reduce BAROMETRIC ERROR. Also reduces the IMPULSE needed to keep the PENDULUM in motion by about 80 per cent. The Glycine Co. of Switzerland sold vacuum-cased wrist watches in the 1950 and 1960s to reduce wear and improve timekeeping. QUARTZ CRYSTAL oscillators are also affected by air pressure and are enclosed in high-vacuum hermetic capsules.

Vallet suspension Version of a BROCOT SUSPENSION common in French MARBLE CLOCKS.

Vane The fan acting as an air brake on a FLY to slow striking etc.

Variation Difference in the RATES of a timepiece in various conditions of e.g. temperature or position.

Vase clock See URN CLOCK.

Velvet dial Early Dutch clock style of a metal (sometimes silver) CHAPTER RING on a velvet background. Employed on the first PENDULUM clock, invented by HUYGENS.

Veneer Very thin slices of wood used to finish clock cases. The earliest were saw-cut, often with multiple saws fixed in a frame. These veneers occur until the early 19th c and are much thicker than later ones. The next method was to shave the trunk in a large LATHE, like sharpening a pencil, so that grain patterns repeated themselves. Most woods were used, including ebony, then walnut, olive etc., and mahogany generally from c1750. The veneers were glued to carcases of cheaper wood such as pine. See MARQUETRY, PARQUETRY.

Verge alarm Alarm bell with a hammer operated by a VERGE ESCAPEMENT, used mainly on LANTERN CLOCKS, but on many other types until the early 19th c.

Verge escapement Earliest mechanical clock ESCAPEMENT, comprising a WHEEL shaped like a king's crown (and called the CROWN WHEEL), the teeth of which are released by two PALLETS on an ARBOR (axle) which carries a FOLIOT. The foliot swinging slowly to and fro controls the RATE. Probably invented in the 13th c. Used in BRACKET CLOCKS until the 19th c, in watches with a balance and spring as late as 1885 in CLERKENWELL, London, and in JAPANESE CLOCKS even later.

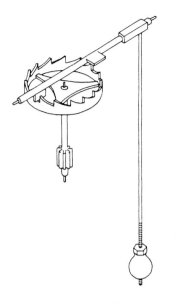

A **verge escapement**, one controlling a balance wheel and one controlling a pendulum. The earliest controlled a foliot.

Vernal equinox First day of Spring when the periods of night and day are equal.

Vernis Martin French method of imitating oriental lacquer invented by the Martin brothers c1730 and widely used on French clock cases in colour.

Vertical escapement VERGE ESCAPEMENT. See HORIZONTAL ESCAPEMENT.

Vertical frame One of the earliest forms of construction of large church or tower clocks in England until the late 18th c. It was made of 15cm (6in) oak beams like an empty door frame but with a third vertical member off-centre. It is believed that the wooden ones were made in the West Country and later ones of iron came from the Midlands. The WHEELS and pin wheels were arranged in a vertical line and all originally had VERGE and FOLIOT ESCAPEMENTS and were striking, always slowed by a vertical FLY or flail. Most were converted to PENDULUM and the only one in original condition is in the National Trust's Cothele House, Calstock, Cornwall.

There are wooden frame clocks at Leintwardine in Shropshire and at Sharnbrook in Bedfordshire. Iron frame clocks are found at Marston Magna, Somerset, Sydling St Nicholas, Dorset, EXETER CATHEDRAL and Castle Combe, Wiltshire.

The **vertical frame** of wood and the underslung foliot of an indigenous English clock in Cothele House, Calstock, Cornwall.

Vertical positions Edge up positions of a watch under timekeeping tests for POSITIONAL ERRORS.

Vibrating Term used by watchmakers for trying different HAIRSPRINGS with a BALANCE while holding one end of the spring with tweezers or a clamp with the lower balance PIVOT on the glass top of a VIBRATING TOOL.

Vibrating tool Adjusted BALANCE and spring in a glass-topped box used as a standard for counting the VIBRATIONS of a balance and spring under test.

Vibration Half an oscillation, e.g. the time of the swing of a PENDULUM or BALANCE in one direction only.

Vice, bench Various types of bench vice were used by clockmakers. Small ones usually had hinged jaws and larger ones sliding jaws, useful for clamping other tools such as TURNS or BARREL and FUSEE ENGINES. When parts were to be hammered as with large clocks, a post (or leg) vice, which had a long leg resting on the floor, would be used.

Vice, hand Small vice used by clock- and watchmakers. Some have a hinge held apart by a spring and closed by a wing nut. Smaller types can be held or placed in a hole in the bench and some-times have part of the jaws made as a bow spring. There is often a vertical groove across the middle of the jaws to hold a piece of wire vertically.

Victoria and Albert Museum collection The development of decora-tion is shown by clocks and watches made from 1500 to the mid-19th c in the Department of Metalwork. They include the earliest dated English BRACKET CLOCK signed 'Francoy Nowe, 1588', and a very large collection of watches. A collection of clocks in the Department of Woodwork illustrates their history as domestic furniture.

Victorian clock REGENCY designs remained popular in Great Britain at the beginning of the Victorian period from 1837 to 1901 but they developed into elab-orate ornamentation. Black wooden BRACKET CLOCK styles were reintro-duced with the glitter of extra brass ornament and Gothic styles became more earnest. The SKELETON CLOCK under a glass dome was very popular and so was the heavy black French MARBLE CLOCK.

Vienna pie Popular name for a fat Austrian watch like a TURNIP WATCH or OIGNON.

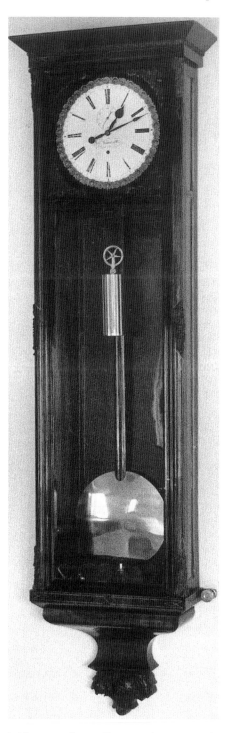

A **Vienna regulator** with a month movement by Rommel of Vienna.

Vienna regulator Type of wall time-piece produced in Vienna in the first half of the 19th c. It has a slender and elegant, but strong, wooden (usually mahogany) case with full-length glass panels in the front and sides. The earliest were hand-made and of high quality, some going for a month at a winding, with weight drive, and a seconds PENDULUM with a black wooden rod, large polished brass lenticular bob and BEAT ADJUSTER. The gut weight line is normally red in colour. From after 1850, cheaper clocks, similar but with shorter cases, were produced by factory processes and, misleadingly, still called by the same name. Most do not strike and have three-quarter second pendulums. Those made for export usually have 'seconds' dials with 15, 30, 45, 60 subdivisions, although the seconds hand turns once in 45 seconds! Some even smaller versions were well made, with spring-driven strike or chime and weight-driven pendulum. BLACK FOREST makers copied the basic design and produced large numbers of cheap clocks, including those with the 'fast' seconds hands. They were also made in other countries.

Virgule escapement Watch escapement invented c1750, with similar layout to the CYLINDER ESCAPEMENT, but not so popular. Its PALLETS are comma-shaped and do not retain oil for long.

Visible escapement Used sometimes to describe a French MANTEL CLOCK with BROCOT ESCAPEMENT on the front of the dial.

Volute balance spring Another name for a flat balance spring.

Volvelle Disc or spiral calculator for conversion of, say, solar to lunar time.

Vulliamy, Benjamin Lewis (1780–1854) Maker of fine clocks and ROYAL CLOCK-MAKER. Many clocks by him are in the ROYAL COLLECTION. Tendered for the making of 'BIG BEN'. Claimed to have invented the BEAT PLATE. Converted many earlier clocks to LEVER ESCAPE-MENT and replaced some old MOVE-MENTS with his own, which upsets anti-quarians. The Vulliamys favoured pierced 'spade-shaped' (heart-shaped) hands.

This 19th c mantel clock by Le Roy et Fils, Paris, has a visible escapement, a calendar and moon dial, with thermometers reading Fahrenheit, Centigrade and Reamur. (*Christie's*)

W

Wag on the wall Popular name for a cheap hanging WALL CLOCK with an exposed PENDULUM below it, popular during the 18th c. Manufacture in the BLACK FOREST continued until recent times. Alternative name for COW'S TAIL or Dutch wag.

Waggon-spring clock American SHELF CLOCK which, to drive it, has a heavy leaf spring, like the half-elliptic road spring of a veteran motor car, instead of a clock spring. The spring is fixed across the bottom of the case, one end driving

An American **waggon-spring clock**. The spring is across the bottom of the case.

the GOING TRAIN and the other the striking. Invented by Joseph Ives, about 1818, and only made in the U.S.A.

Waiting train System invented in 1907 by Gents of Leicester for synchronising the dials of tower and other clocks with a MASTER CLOCK. A very heavy PENDULUM, swinging in a wide ARC, acts as the 'motor' which drives the time train. This pendulum is given a large gaining rate, but is prevented from driving the train too fast because a separate master clock allows it to proceed at 30-second intervals. The pendulum 'motor' is impelled by a HIPP TOGGLE, independently of the master clock. The energy stored in this pendulum allows it to drive the hands of very large public clocks where a mechanical or synchronous movement might fail.

Walker and Finnemore See SIGNATURES.

Wall clock Most popular of all styles in the past, when most clocks were weight-driven. Some were directly fixed to the wall, but many LANTERN CLOCKS stood on brackets fixed to the wall. Surprisingly, very few of the spring-driven so-called BRACKET CLOCKS were actually mounted on wall brackets, the large majority being TABLE CLOCKS. Spring-driven clocks for wall mounting included the CARTEL CLOCK by the French, the DIAL CLOCK by the English and Germans, and many others.

Wallace collection Famous art collection in Hertford House, Manchester Square, London, which includes some fine French clocks.

Walnut case Walnut-veneered wooden

290

clock cases were made from the late 17th c to c1760.

Waltham Watch Co. The American Watch Co. was incorporated in 1859 out of a merger of watch importers Appleton, Tracy and Co. with the Waltham Improvement Co., which had been set up six years earlier to promote the building of a factory in Waltham for the Boston Watch Co. In 1885, the American Watch Co. became the American Waltham Watch Co., and in 1925 the Waltham Watch Co. Gold Waltham watches were status symbols in the U.K before the Second World War.

Wandering hour dial   17th c watch dial without hands. There is a semicircular slot marked 0-I-II-III-IV along the bottom edge for quarter-hours, and 0–60 along the top edge for minutes. An appropriate numeral indicating the hour moves around this slot. Similar to a NIGHT CLOCK dial. The idea was repeated in later centuries.

A **wandering hour dial** on a late 17th c watch by Reynier Tempesaar. (*Christie's*)

Warning, the   The short interval before a clock strikes, when the striking train is

released, then held up until the precise moment. It can be heard, and the object is accuracy.

Warren motor   The first self-starting SYNCHRONOUS ELECTRIC CLOCK motor, invented in the U.S.A. in 1918 by Henry Warren.

Warship clock   One set in a model warship, a number of which were made during the French Industrial Revolution.

Watch   Originally the name meant time-keeping or GOING TRAIN, as opposed to clock or striking train. It became attached to the portable timepiece when the MAINSPRING was invented to replace the weight. The earliest were probably Flemish or Burgundian, but the only survivors are German of about 1540 and French of 1551. These were ball-shaped (wrongly called NUREMBERG EGGS), but were soon displaced by drum-shaped or oval ones of about 5cm (2in) diameter. They had VERGE ESCAPEMENTS with a DUMBBELL BALANCE or BALANCE WHEEL. Iron or steel was used for construction before about 1560 and brass afterwards. Early German watches had STACKFREEDS; English and French ones had FUSEES. These were worn on a cord round the neck. After the long waistcoat was popularised c1675, watches went into waistcoat pockets. The BALANCE SPRING was incorporated in most watches after 1680 making them more accurate and encouraging minute hands. The CYLINDER ESCAPEMENT replaced the VERGE for about 150 years and encouraged seconds hands. LEVER ESCAPEMENTS came into general use after about 1825. Almost all watches had them until the ELECTRIC and the QUARTZ WATCH were introduced from the 1950s. The rate of manufacture was stepped up by the LEPINE CALIBRE and that of cheap watches by the methods of JAPY, ROSKOPF and WATERBURY, until today watches are produced by auto-matic processes in many tens of millions a year. The WRIST WATCH is compara-tively recent, having become popular only in the last 60–70 years. An average mechanical wrist watch has about 130 parts which require about 1,400 machining operations in manufacture. About half production today is mechanical and half quartz. See TRAIN.

Watch case The first cases were round, globe-, or pomander- (ball)-shaped, then drum-, canister- or tambour-shaped. In the late 16th c, the sides became rounded. In the first part of the 17th c, many were oval. FORM WATCHES were also popular then, as were enamelled cases, which continued into the 19th c. The pocket watch came with the inventions of the BALANCE SPRING and waistcoat c1675, but they were still large. Cases became less decorative in the late 18th c. BREGUET introduced the slimmer pocket watch. WRIST WATCH cases c1914 were at first adapted small pocket watches. Gold, silver, nickel silver, GUNMETAL, and in this century stainless steel, were the most used materials.

Watch paper Printed or otherwise decorated paper or cambric placed in the back of the PAIR CASE of a watch to prevent chafing. Nearly all watchmakers had their own designs, which included pictures of beauties of the time, EQUATION OF TIME tables, advertisements, mottos, etc.

Watch sizes See SIZES.

Watch stand Stand made of wood with a hook for holding a pocket watch overnight because it performed better than when lying down. Some had thermometers and other indications.

Watch strap See STRAP.

Watch timer Either an instrument, the RATE RECORDER, or a skilled man, the watch ADJUSTER.

Watchmaker Originally a craftsman who made watches and clocks. The timekeeping part of a clock was then also called the 'watch'. Now almost invariably a repairer or retailer. See WATCH.

Watchmaker's lathe Special small precision LATHE, bench-mounted and electrically powered. Many special fitments are available for wheel-cutting, screw-cutting, slitting, screw-polishing, filing, taper-turning, milling, grinding etc. See THROW and TURNS.

Watchman's clock Clock to indicate the time at which a night watchman makes his rounds. Invented by Whitehurst of Derby in 1750, whose version had a large rotating disc with pegs round its edge. The watchman struck a lever which pushed in a peg at the time of his visit. In the modern version the watchman carries a small TIME RECORDER. Keys are chained in the places he must visit. On his rounds he inserts each key and turns it, which gives a time indication and the key number on a paper tape sealed in the recorder.

Water clock The earliest were Egyptian c1400BC, being pottery bowls with straight, sloping sides and a leak hole near the bottom. After filling, the decreasing

An early **watchman's clock** to indicate the time when he made his visit. (*Mauthe Museum, Germany*)

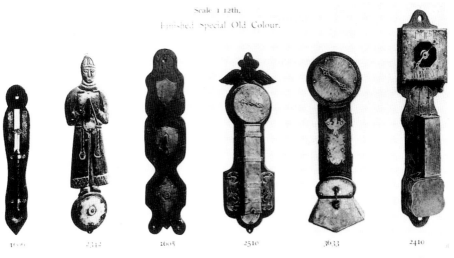

Scale 1 12th.

Finished Special Old Colour.

1000   2312   1605   2510   3633   2410

Some **water clocks** that are fakes offered in a 1960s catalogue of items made for antique dealers to sell.

water level inside shows the passing
hours. Different scales show the different
TEMPORAL HOURS of different months.
Introduced into Rome and Greece BC and
gradually made more and more elaborate
in the early centuries AD, with floats that,
by a cord, moved a hand round a dial,
figures that pointed to scales, and mechanisms for striking bells. Reached its
culmination in the elaborate clock of SU
SUNG in China. See SINKING BOWL.
Water clocks of various designs in brass
and wood with floats and dials which
appear old can be found in antique shops
today. Some are even marked with a 17th
c date. They were made in the 20th c, most
of them by the Pearson-Page Co. of
Birmingham which showed several in its
catalogues until the 1920s.They are not
even reproductions.

Water gilding Term wrongly used for
MERCURIAL GILDING or fire gilding.
Actually a process used by picture
framers and some clock case makers to
gild wood or gesso (plaster of Paris and
size on wood) employing powdered gold
dissolved in aqua regia (mixed nitric and
sulphuric acids). The mixture was soaked
in a rag, the rag burned, and the ash
rubbed on the surface to gild it.

Water-of-Ayr stone Dense but soft grey
stone used to shape soft metals, particu-

larly brass or silver, or polish out file
marks. Found in Stair, Scotland.

Water-wheel   clock INDUSTRIAL
CLOCK of the 1800s in which a water
wheel rotates.

Waterbury   long-wind   watch See
WATERBURY ROTARY WATCH.

Waterbury rotary watch Benedict and
Burnham of Waterbury, Connecticut,
U.S.A., were offered a rotary watch by an
entrepreneur, E.A. Lock, but turned it
down. It became the AUBURNDALE
ROTARY WATCH. Later Lock persuaded
D.A. Buck to design one. This was
accepted by the Waterbury firm. It had a
DUPLEX ESCAPEMENT, 58 parts, and a
2.15m (9ft) long MAINSPRING using the
case as the BARREL. The movement
rotated once an hour in the case on the
TOURBILLON principle. There were two
models, one with full plates for $4 and
one with open-work plates and dial,
allowing some parts to be seen, for $4.50.
Prices were about half those of Swiss
imports and less then the Auburndale
rotary. The first cases were of celluloid
but later of nickel. In 1880, production
was taken over by a subsidiary, the
Waterbury Watch Co., which by 1891 had
produced 1.5 million of them. Winding
took 150 half turns of the stem.

Production of the rotary model (Series E) ended in 1891, but Waterbury continued to make a three-quarter-plate short-wind movement until 1898. The company was then bought by the New England Watch Co., but this failed in 1912. Then in 1914 it was purchased by Ingersoll.

Waterbury tourbillon watch See WATERBURY ROTARY WATCH.

Waterproof Term for watches now disallowed by many countries. See WATER-RESISTANT.

Water-resistant An unsealed watch case 'breathes', drawing in air when cold and expelling it when warm. It may draw in perspiration from the wrist or moisture from the air, which is deposited on steel parts and rusts them. A water-sealed case prevents this and also stops hairs and dust (which can be harder than steel) being drawn in and forming a grinding paste with the oil. The first water-resistant pocket watch was the EXPLORER'S WATCH and the first water-resistant wrist watch was made by Rolex. Special cases are made for skin diving and tested to the equivalent of 300m (980ft) and more. Waterproofing can deteriorate through wear and the non-replacement of sealing washers. Even a water resistant watch may show a milky moisture deposit on the glass in cold weather from air sealed in it. The main sealing places are at the back of the case, the glass and the button. A standard test is for the case to resist admission of water at atmospheric pressure and at 2.45kg/cm² (35lb/in²) for five minutes.

Wear Clocks and watches wear at the PIVOTS and holes, sometimes oval at holes because of side pressure. However, the traditional combination of steel pivot and brass hole will run for centuries. The harder metal normally wears first because quartz dust in the air becomes embedded in the softer brass and grinds the steel. Steel running in corundum (ruby and sapphire jewels) also has a low rate of wear. An unloaded toothed wheel, e.g. a JOCKEY WHEEL, wears before one in a gear TRAIN. See BEARING.

Webster collection Fine collection of clocks and watches including many FORM WATCHES, broken up and sold on the death of Percy Webster, their owner, in 1954.

Wedding anniversaries In the American Jewelry Industry Council list, gifts for the first anniversary are clocks and for the fifteenth, watches.

Wedge-of-pie stackfreed A STACKFREED with extra steep angles.

A **wedge-of-pie stackfreed** in an old watch. (*Elsworth H. Goldsmith Coll., U.S.A.*)

Wedge pin See TAPER PIN.

Wedging Using PITH, cork or folded tissue paper under a balance wheel to prevent its moving during transport.

Week Unit of time without relationship to any astronomical period, being based on the Bible's Old Testament account of the Creation. Unlike astronomical periods it has a fixed number of days which is convenient for commerce etc., but not calendar calculations. See GREGORIAN and JULIAN CALENDARS. Some Buddhist countries have lunar months only and no weeks.

Weekdays On some early Teutonic calendar clocks, days were symbolised by engravings: Sun for Sunday; Moon for Monday; Tiw (god of law) for Tuesday; the god Woden for Wednesday; Thor (god of war) for Thursday; Fria (goddess of love) for Friday; and Saturn (the Roman god of agriculture) for Saturday.

Weight drive Every mechanical clock before about 1450 was driven by a weight hanging from a rope wound round a drum or BARREL. Weights have continued in use to the present time because they provide constant force, unlike springs. Early weights were of stone. Later, cast iron and lead (enclosed in brass until the end of the 18th c for the best clocks) were used. Early LANTERN CLOCKS were roughly adjusted by adding lead shot to a cap on the top of the weight. Blocks of stone, sometimes dressed to a shape, were not uncommon for TURRET CLOCKS. Later SHIFTERS were often used.

Welch rotary clock See ROTARY CLOCK.

Wells Cathedral clock Large iron clock made before 1392 and now in the SCIENCE MUSEUM COLLECTION, London, which strikes (being controlled by one of the earliest LOCKING PLATES) and chimes. Converted to ANCHOR ESCAPEMENT and PENDULUM in the 17th c. The Wells clock and SALISBURY CATHEDRAL CLOCK, which are very similar, may have been made under the instruction of Bishop Erghum from Bruges, who was at Salisbury from 1375 to 1385 (see LIGHTFOOT). The clock once operated Jack Blandifer (see JACK) and the other AUTOMATA in the cathedral but was removed in 1835 in favour of a new movement.

Westminster chime Familiar chime of the WESTMINSTER PALACE CLOCK (BIG BEN), set going in 1859, which was taken from the fifth bar of Handel's *Messiah*, 'I know that my Redeemer liveth', and modified by Mr Crotch and Dr Jowett originally for St Mary's Church, Cambridge, in 1793–4. Copenhagen City Hall clock has a modified version.

Westminster Palace clock Clock popularly known as BIG BEN, in a tower of the Palace of Westminster, the official name for the Houses of Parliament. The first clock there was in a tower built about 1365. It struck a great bell every hour. This was followed by another in a new tower after the Commonwealth, striking on GREAT TOM. After the Houses of Parliament were burnt down in 1834, Sir Charles Barry was commissioned to build a new Palace of Westminster and when the tower of the present Westminster Palace was nearly finished in 1844, he wrote to B.L. VULLIAMY for plans of a clock. Another prominent maker, E.J. DENT, objected and asked also to be allowed to tender. It was then decided to ask the Astronomer Royal, G.B. AIRY, to draw up a specification, and submit it to Vulliamy, Dent and Whitehurst of Derby for tender. Most clockmakers though thought that Airy's condition, that the first blow of each hour should be accurate to a second, was impossible for so huge a clock. These included Vulliamy, who withdrew. Dent won the contract and Airy asked Lord GRIMTHORPE to supervise the making of the clock. Grimthorpe, a ruthless and sharp-tongued lawyer, was also a brilliant amateur clockmaker. During the 15 years of design and construction, Dent died and his stepson Frederick Dent was appointed after a legal battle. Grimthorpe had battles with the architect, the Astronomer Royal (who resigned from the committee), the bell founders, the authorities, and other clockmakers; there were intrigues, and litigation. He received no payment and had been far-sighted enough to have a contract at the beginning giving him real power, with the result, he said, '. . . every possible attempt was made to get rid of both it and me. No official who joined in those attempts cared three half-pence how the clock was made. Luckily I did care. . . .' The final cost of the clock (including recasting Big Ben, the bell) was under £6,000. The cost of the iron frame provided by the architect was about £6,600! The clock was set working in 1859 and proved the most accurate large clock ever made. It has Grimthorpe's GRAVITY ESCAPEMENT, and a TWO-SECONDS PENDULUM weighing about 315kg

(700lb). The three weights for timekeeping, striking and chiming, weigh 76kg (1.5cwt) 1524kg (1.5tons), and 1524kg (1.5tons) respectively. The MOVEMENT looks like an elderly printing press and is about 5m (16ft) long by 1.5m (5ft 6in) wide. Since 1913 it has been wound electrically. Winding by hand used to take over 30 hours a week. At one stage, Grimthorpe considered AUTOMATIC WINDING, operated by the weight of people walking over Westminster Bridge. It reported its timekeeping to the Royal Observatory at Greenwich by telegraph daily from 1863 until 1940, when the line was destroyed in an air raid. In that period, the error never exceeded four seconds and was usually within one second. The movement was never at any time controlled by the Observatory. The dials are nearly 7m (62.5ft) in diameter, the centres being 55m (180ft) from the ground. The minute hands are 4.3m (14ft) long and weigh 102kg (2cwt) each. The minute spaces are 30cm (1ft) square. Until 1900 the dials were lit by gas burners; then lighting was by fluorescent cold cathode tubes and now by cold cathode lamps. On 5 August 1976, as the clock was striking 3.45a.m., it exploded, breaking the main FRAME and throwing parts all over the clock room, some through the ceiling. The cause was the failure of a FLY, which acts as a SHOCK ABSORBER. When the chiming mechanism was reconstructed a safety brake was fitted and the clock set going in November 1977.

Wetherfield collection   Most famous collection of English clocks, containing the RECORD TOMPION, amassed by David Wetherfield, a coal merchant, over 30 years, and offered for auction in 1928 after his death, but sold privately to Francis Mallet and Percy Webster for £30,000. See WEBSTER COLLECTION. The book 'A Guide to Dating English Antique Clocks' based on the Wetherfield Collection (N.A.G. Press), is an examination of the clocks by the present author.

Wheatstone, Sir Charles   (1802–75) Distinguished scientist who also invented an electric clock in 1840 in which electromagnets forced the PENDULUM to swing and eliminated mechanical switches. The principle was applied successfully in Switzerland in the MAGNETA system. See BAIN CLOCK.

Wheel   One of the larger gears in a watch or clock. Usually made of brass and pierced to give it four spokes, called 'crossings'. The teeth of small gears are of CYCLOIDAL form because the common involute gear is unsuccessful on a small scale. See PINION.

Wheel barometer   Mercury barometer in which a small weight on a cord over a WHEEL rested on the surface of the mercury and turned a hand over a dial. Early clockmakers also made barometers.

Wheel-cutting engine   Machine for cutting wheel teeth, invented c1650 and based on the DIVIDING PLATE. One type is used for clocks and another for watches. The cutting wheel was formerly turned by hand. The earliest engines were of brass, the best being from Lancashire, and France in the 18th and 19th c. Later made from iron and driven by cords from a treadle. Early factories drove them by steam and cut wheel blanks in batches using a milling cutter. In the 20th c cheap wheels were cut by hobbing, the wheel being turned while cutting teeth in it.

White-dial clock   Name commonly given to a LONGCASE CLOCK with a painted dial, which followed the traditional brass dial from about the 1770s, and was made in large numbers in the U.K. and U.S.A. Already by the 1780s, brass dials were the exception and soon all but disappeared. The first white dials had SPANDRELS painted in the corners and a MOON DIAL or the maker's name in the arch, if there was an arch. From the early 1800s, coloured scenes began appearing in the arches and coloured flowers or other features in the corners and as the years went by these often became very elaborate. See FALSE PLATE, PAINTED DIAL.

Whittington chime   Also called the 'Bow chime'. Eleven-bell chime based on an old six-bell version of 1905 used in Bow church. A different American version has the same name.

Whizzing work Striking of some BLACK FOREST CLOCKS is not controlled by a COUNT WHEEL but by a *Surrerwerk* (whizzing work) where the hammer tail is moved so that the correct number of pins on a barrel causes it to strike the appropriate hour. The name comes from the fact that the striking train runs long enough to strike 12, despite the actual number of blows struck.

Whole-clock Ancient name for 1–24 hour counting, also called 'big-clock' hours or ITALIAN HOURS. The 1–12 system now common was called 'half-clock', 'small-clock', or 'German' hours.

Whole-plate Used for a watch with two full-sized plates, as opposed to half-plates and quarter-plates, where the TOP or BACK PLATE is approximately one of these sizes.

Wig-wag tool One for polishing a PIVOT or PINION leaves by moving backwards and forwards. In some the work is given the reciprocating movement.

Wig-wag watch One in which the wearer's movements caused the watch movement to bounce in a frame in the case to wind the MAINSPRING. Made for a time from 1931 by Louis Miller of Bienne. See AUTOWRIST, ROLLS WATCH and SELF-WINDING WATCH.

Willard brothers Four noted American clockmakers, Benjamin (b.1743), Simon (b.1748), Ephraim (b.1750), and Aaron (b.1752). Simon designed the BANJO CLOCK. Their WALL, SHELF and LONGCASE CLOCKS are valued as antiques.

Willard H. Wheeler collection American private watch collection sold at Sotheby's, London, for a total of $27,760 in 1961.

Williamson, Joseph (c1669–1725) Eminent maker who claimed to have made all English EQUATION CLOCKS up to 1719, including equation work for QUARE'S clocks; however, TOMPION produced his own. Probably the first to use differential gearing for opposite dials.

Wilsdorf collection Collection of enamelled watches made by H. Wilsdorf, founder of the firm of Rolex, Geneva, in London.

Winchester chime Six-bell chime used and named by 20th c clockmakers but not in fact in the city of Winchester.

Winder, bench To avoid time wasted by hand-winding watches, even with a BENCH KEY, a spring-driven winder was used from the early 19th c. Later, electric ones were introduced.

Winder, spring See MAINSPRING WINDER.

Winding button Button or 'crown' of a watch used for winding, hand- and date-setting a mechanical watch through the KEYLESS work. Those on QUARTZ WATCHES do not have the winding function.

Winding clocks PENDULUM clocks are wound from the front to avoid disturbing the pendulum by turning them. LEVER ESCAPEMENT clocks are wound from the back. MONTH CLOCKS are wound anti-clockwise.

Winding holes A clock with a high winding hole in the dial probably has a FUSEE. Two holes mean a striking clock and three chiming as well. Holes with rings of grooves round them were common from c1690 to c1710. Dial holes with WINDING SQUARES out of centre usually indicate a replacement dial or a MARRIAGE.

Winding indicator See UP-AND-DOWN DIAL.

Winding square Square end of a clock or watch ARBOR on which a winding key fits. Also a bench tool for winding MOVEMENTS.

Winding stop See FUSEE STOP.

Windmill clock INDUSTRIAL CLOCK like a windmill with rotating vanes, made in the 1800s.

Wine-press clock French Industrial Revolution clock in this shape. An INDUSTRIAL CLOCK.

Winged lantern clock LANTERN CLOCK with banana-shaped PENDULUM BOB which swings through slots each side of the case and is protected by triangular wings. Used from the late 17th to the early 18th c.

A **winged lantern clock**. Note the fish pendulum indicator.

Wire gong Another name for a ROD GONG and a more accurate description of the spiral gong in American clocks.

Wire lines Woven metal cable used to suspend clock weights instead of gut lines.

Wire-loop suspension Wire loop on the back of a movement to which the PENDULUM rod is hooked. Used in cheap BLACK FOREST (including cuckoo) and American wooden clocks. Also called 'roller suspension' because the pendulum is loose to swing on its suspension instead of being restrained by it.

Wire spring CLICK spring made from wire and used in cheap clocks and watches instead of ribbon spring.

Wisdom clock In the 15th c, for some reason, the large mechanical clock became associated with the wisdom of Solomon and particular ones were called 'Wisdom clocks'. In the Bibliotheque Nationale, Paris, is a book by Jehan de Souhande entitled 'Le Livre d'Horloge de Sapience.'

Wolf's teeth Very robust tooth form, the teeth being angled in one direction as on a ratchet wheel. Used for one of the first INDEPENDENT SECONDS watch hands with DEAD BEAT action and in some old watches for TRAIN wheels also. Found especially in KEYLESS WINDING wheels.

Wooden movement Clock with main parts of wood, including the PLATES, WHEELS and DIAL. The earliest were probably BLACK FOREST CLOCKS from about 1680. The wheels (except for the brass ESCAPE WHEEL) continued to be

The **wooden movement** of a tall clock by the American maker, Eli Terry. (*Yale University Art Gallery, U.S.A.*)

The very unusual **wooden movement** of a watch.

made of wood until 1791 when Hofmaier of Neustadt introduced cheap cast brass wheels. Wooden ARBORS and LANTERN PINIONS were retained and the arbors often painted silver or gold to imitate metal. The first PRECISION CLOCK made by James or John HARRISON, in Yorkshire, was wooden and was claimed to keep time to one second a month for ten years! Mass-production of cheap wooden clocks was started in the U.S.A. in 1809 with LONGCASE movements by Eli TERRY, followed by Seth THOMAS and Silas Hoadley. These were often sold without cases, which were added by local cabinet makers. Terry even made wooden TOWER CLOCKS, one being in the Congregational Church at Terryville, Connecticut. There is a Russian wooden watch in the Zwinger Museum, Dresden.

Woodpecker escapement Form of PINWHEEL ESCAPEMENT in some early 19th c Austrian clocks to provide DEADBEAT seconds with a half-seconds PENDULUM. One of two impulse PALLETS is hinged to prevent IMPULSE in one direction. Also called COUP PERDU.

Woods for cases Earliest BRACKET and LONGCASE CLOCKS had cases of ebony or ebony veneer, or were stained black. (The fashion appeared again during Queen Victoria's mourning, when many old clocks were stained.) PARQUETRY appeared c1670 to 1680, MARQUETRY from c1675 to 1725, walnut c1670 to 1730, solid oak at most times outside London,

carved oak in the provinces c1760 to 1790, Japanese lacquer c1695 to 1715 and at intervals to c1775, mahogany mainly from 1750 whence it became common everywhere, and solid pine from c1750 to the machine age.

Works Popular name for MOVEMENT or MODULE.

World clock Clock with a WORLD TIME DIAL. Often included in ASTRONOMICAL CLOCKS. There is a clock in the Zwinger Museum, Dresden, made in 1690 by Andreas Gartner, which shows the time in all latitudes on 360 supplementary dials.

World time dial Shows the time in any part of the world. As the Earth revolves once in 24 hours, an hour hand turning once in 24 hours is needed. One method is to mark the main countries or towns of the world round the BEZEL. Another is to provide an extra dial that can be rotated; if the timepiece is in London, the bezel is turned until the point on it marked 'London' is opposite the hour hand. The hour in another place can be read opposite its name on the 24-hour dial. As TIME

The **world time dial** of a mid-20th c Kienzle clock. Lines from cities on the map indicate the hour of night or day on the moving dial in the sector. The hand indicates minutes.

ZONES vary by whole hours, an ordinary minute hand will give minutes for all zones, i.e. if it is 16.20 G.M.T. in London, it is 11.20 in New York, 17.20 in Paris and 19.20 in Leningrad. Adjustment must be made for the few countries, including India and central Australia, that vary by half an hour from the standard time, as well as for local variations such as British SUMMER TIME. Another method is to have a model of the globe, or a drum or band carrying a Mercator projection map, revolving once in 24 hours. This has the advantage that a darkened screen can cover the map during the dark hours. Other versions are a stationary map of the world with a moving band indicating the hours, and a stationary map with actual times shown in numerals on the main countries. Clocks, and later watches, were made with them.

Worm escapement   In 1887, the New York Standard Watch Co. made 12,000 watches with WORM GEARING driving the ESCAPE WHEELS. They were unsuccessful. Leonardo da Vinci drew a clock TRAIN with a worm gear c1500!

Worm gearing   Small gear like a screw thread which drives a toothed wheel. The two shafts are at right angles to each other. It provides a big reduction in speed ratio.

Worshipful Company of Blacksmiths Many early clockmakers, most of whom were blacksmiths, joined the blacksmiths' guild. When they tried to split to form their own company, the blacksmiths refused and it was not until some years later, in 1631, that they succeeded.

Worshipful Company of Clockmakers See CLOCKMAKERS' COMPANY.

Worshipful Company of Goldsmiths   One of the earliest City livery companies, incorporated in 1327, which controls the Assay Office which by law has to test precious metals and HALLMARK them if they are up to standard and destroy them if they are not.

Wrist chronometer   A wrist watch that

has obtained a RATING CERTIFICATE according to the Swiss definition.

Wrist watch   Regarded as impractical novelties for many years, wrist watches were at first inaccurate compared with pocket watches because of POSITIONAL ERRORS. One of the earliest known, for the Bavarian daughter-in-law of the Empress Josephine, was made in 1806 and showed the time of day on one side and the date on the other, the bracelet being set with pearls and emeralds. It is in the Auguste Seiler collection, Vevey, Switzerland, as is another EMPIRE-period watch with AUTOMATA and a velvet band. MINIATURE POCKET WATCHES of the 1850s were sometimes fitted to precious metal bracelets and later into holders on leather wrist straps. In 1890 the Berlin government ordered wrist watches for naval officers from C. Girard Perregaux, La Chaux-de-Fonds, Switzerland. They were in gold cases and may not have been for service duties. Gallet and Co. of Switzerland tried to introduce silver wrist watches to America, but the New York agents returned them. H. Wilsdorf of Hatton Garden, London, interested some customers before 1910 and so did J.W. Benson, but it was in Paris that they succeeded, even if only as a passing fashion. During the First World War, artillery officers found them more practical than pocket watches. See STRAP. After the war, wrist-watch manufacture expanded and by the 1930s it had relegated pocket watches to second place. After the Second World War, the pocket watch was reduced to special functions and fashion. Curiously, the RING WATCH is very much earlier than the bracelet or wrist watch.

Wrist-watch guard   Metal grille to protect the fragile glass of a wrist watch used during the First World War. The grille has lugs through which the strap passed. It continued in use after the war.

Wycherley, John   (1817–91) Pioneer watchmaker who set up an EBAUCHE factory in England with T.P. Hewitt at PRESCOT in Lancashire using steam power.

X

Xylophone clock Cheap version of a CARILLON CLOCK by BLACK FOREST makers in which the hammers struck the tuned pieces of wood of a *Holzernes G'lachter* or folk xylophone.

Y

Yachting timer Used for racing. A short hand indicates the five-minute warning preparatory and start times on a 15-minute dial and a long hand shows 60 seconds in one revolution.

Yankee clock Name given by the English to the early imported rolled brass Connecticut clocks c1845.

Year clock Clock that runs for a year at one winding. The most famous is a spring-driven striking and chiming Mostyn Tompion clock made for King William III by TOMPION, which has had only four owners. The present owner, The British Museum, paid a record price for it at the time. A record has been kept of all who wound it. Analysed by R.A. Fell in 1950, its mechanical efficiency was found still to be much higher than modern clocks. Some SKELETON CLOCKS were made to run for a year using ganged MAINSPRINGS. In 1881, the Harder Year Co. in America produced about 400 FOUR-HUNDRED-DAY (year) clocks, although such a clock is not usually called a 'year clock'. Battery and quartz clocks commonly run longer. A SIDEREAL year clock by Matthew BOULTON was accepted by the British Treasury in lieu of taxes in 1987.

Yoke Small ROCKING BAR or frame that is moved by pulling the winding button (or depressing a small PUSH PIECE on the first KEYLESS pocket watches) to change the drive from winding to setting.

Yorkshire clock Yorkshire makers had the largest output of clocks, particularly LONGCASE, from the late 18th to the mid-19th c. The typical style was PAINTED DIAL and mahogany case with a small door and wide trunk with free-standing hood PILLARS and SWAN'S NECK CRESTING. They, and many other provincial clocks, are still fine pieces of furniture and good timekeepers today.

Z

Z-balance Standard balance used by John ARNOLD and Son from c1791 to 1818. Looks like a Z in shape and used initially with a gold HAIRSPRING.

Zaandam clock Dutch clock made in Zaandam at the end of the 17th c. The MOVEMENT stands on a wooden platform and the PENDULUM is attached well above the movement to a backboard. The vertical VERGE ARBOR has a horizontal CRUTCH which engages a slot in the pendulum rod.

Zappler Style of 18th c clock from southern Germany and Austria with a rapidly wagging PENDULUM in front of the DIAL, and usually two feet and a support for standing on a table or elsewhere.

A tiny **zappler clock**. Note the circular pendulum 'rod' at the front of the clock.

Austria specialised in miniature ones, 2.5–5cm (1–2in) high, often with porcelain or Wedgwood dials. *Zappeln* means 'quick dancing'.

Zebra Tiny strip of plastic material with a succession of flexible segments that are alternately conducting and insulating. Used in digital electronic watches to connect the display unit to the printed circuit by a single unit.

Zenith Georges Favre-Jacot started making complete pocket watches in Le Locle, Vallée de Joux, Switzerland, in 1865 by machinery and tools he designed and made himself. The quality was so good that he won a Grand Prix at the Universal Exhibition in Paris in 1900, the first of over 1,500 such awards. He then began producing NEUCHÂTEL CLOCKS and was quickly into the new wristwatch production. Zenith not only continued to make all parts of the watch but supplied other manufacturers. They made the first SELF-WINDING WATCH with 36,000 FAST BEAT. In the late 1960s and early 1970s, the Zenith Radio Corporation of Chicago gained control, introduced the QUARTZ WATCH and, believing that the mechanical watch was finished, got rid of all the machinery. The take-over failed and a Swiss group acquired Zenith and began mechanical watch production again. In 1995, their new automatic movement won the Best Mechanical Movement of the Year award.

Zeppelin clock Model of a zeppelin airship with a clock in the middle. Two 'clouds' form PILLARS and the gondola hangs between them. French, last quarter of the 19th c.

Zeroise To return the hands to zero by a

push on a timer or chronometer. See FLY BACK.

Zinc compensation Where a PENDULUM rod comprises a steel rod and a zinc tube which expand in opposite directions so that the rod remains effectively the same length at different temperatures.

Zodiac Band of sky through which the sun, moon, and planets appear to move. It is divided into twelve angles of 30 per cent known by their 'signs' and sometimes shown on ASTRONOMICAL CLOCKS.

Zone On many clocks of the late 17th to early 19th c, the dial comprised a brass plate with a circular brass band showing the hours, etc. (the CHAPTER RING), attached to it. The area inside the ring is the zone. At first it was plain and polished with a Tudor rose engraved in the centre, but soon almost invariably became a MATTED DIAL.

Zones, time See TIME ZONES.

Zulu time Airline jargon for GREENWICH MEAN TIME, which was used for navigation.